English Poetry of the Eighteenth Century 1700–1789

David Fairer

Longman

An imprint of **Pearson Education**

London · New York · Toronto · Sydney · Tokyo · Singapore · Hong Kong · Cape Town
Madrid · Paris · Amsterdam · Munich · Milan

Pearson Education Limited

Head Office:
Edinburgh Gate
Harlow CM20 2JE
Tel: +44 (0)1279 623623
Fax: +44 (0)1279 431059

London Office:
128 Long Acre
London WC2E 9AN
Tel: +44 (0)20 7447 2000
Fax: +44 (0)20 7447 2170
Website: www.pearsoneduc.com/literature

First edition published in Great Britain in 2003

© Pearson Education Limited 2003

The right of David Fairer to be identified as Author of
this Work has been asserted by him in accordance with
the Copyright, Designs and Patents Act 1988.

ISBN 0 582 22777 1

British Library Cataloguing in Publication Data
A CIP catalogue record for this book can be obtained from the British Library

Library of Congress Cataloging in Publication Data
A CIP catalog record for this book can be obtained from the Library of Congress

10 9 8 7 6 5 4 3 2 1

Set in 10/12pt Sabon by Graphicraft Limited, Hong Kong
Printed in Malaysia

The Publishers' policy is to use paper manufactured from sustainable forests.

English Poetry of the Eighteenth Century

Longman Literature in English Series

General Editors:
David Carroll, formerly University of Lancaster
Chris Walsh, Chester College of Higher Education
Michael Wheeler, University of Southampton

For a complete list of titles, see back of book

Contents

For Nick & Jane – and in time Matthew

Editors' Preface

The multi-volume Longman Literature in English Series provides students of literature with a critical introduction to the major genres in their historical and cultural context. Each volume gives a coherent account of a clearly defined area, and the series, when complete, will offer a practical and comprehensive guide to literature written in English from Anglo-Saxon times to the present. The aim of the series as a whole is to show that the most valuable and stimulating approach to the study of literature is that based upon awareness of the relations between literary forms and their historical contexts. Thus the areas covered by most of the separate volumes are defined by period and genre. Each volume offers new and informed ways of reading literary works, and provides guidance for further reading in an extensive reference section.

In recent years, the nature of English studies has been questioned in a number of increasingly radical ways. The very terms employed to define a series of this kind – period, genre, history, context, canon – have become the focus of extensive critical debate, which has necessarily influenced in varying degrees the successive volumes published since 1985. But however fierce the debate, it rages around the traditional terms and concepts.

As well as studies on all periods of English and American literature, the series includes books on criticism and literary theory and on the intellectual and cultural context. A comprehensive series of this kind must of course include other literatures written in English, and therefore a group of volumes deals with Irish and Scottish literature, and the literatures of India, Africa, the Caribbean, Australia and Canada. The forty-seven volumes of the series cover the following areas: Pre-Renaissance English Literature, English Poetry, English Drama, English Fiction, English Prose, Criticism and Literary Theory, Intellectual and Cultural Context, American Literature, Other Literatures in English.

David Carroll
Chris Walsh
Michael Wheeler

Acknowledgements

We are grateful to the following for permission to reproduce copyright material:

Liverpool University Press for extracts from *Thomas Gray: Contemporary Essays* by William B. Hutchings and William Ruddick (eds.), 1993; Blackwell Publishers for extracts from *A Companion to Literature from Milton to Blake* by David Womersley (ed.), 2000; to Cambridge University Press for extracts from *The Cambridge Companion to Eighteenth-Century Poetry* by John Sitter (ed.), 2001; to Edinburgh University Press for extracts from 'Organising Verse: Burke's *Reflections* and English Poetry', *Romanticism*, Vol 3: 1 by David Fairer, 1997; The Coleridge Bulletin for extracts from the article 'Eighteenth-Century Poetic Landscapes' by David Fairer (CB New Series B, Spring 1999, pp. 1–18); and to AUP for extracts from *Collected Poems of Thomas Parnell* by Claude Rawson and F.P. Lock (eds.), 1989.

Author's Preface

During the 1990s eighteenth-century poetry became a particularly exciting field to work in. After Roger Lonsdale's pioneering anthologies of 1984 and 1989, the subject opened out in several directions and new voices began to be heard. Many women poets, labouring-class poets, and provincial poets emerged from obscurity. Editions, anthologies, microfilms and databases made accessible an extensive corpus of verse, and with relative suddenness the eighteenth-century scene became a busier and more various one. At distance it may have appeared to some like a vision from Pope's *Dunciad*, where a swarming mob threatens the cultural *status quo* with its cat-calls and waved papers. Seen close at hand, however, dozens of unfamiliar poets became recognisable as individuals with distinctive features and interesting things to say, and the noise was revealed as conversation in new accents. It became clear that the best way to understand all this was to move around and take a better look from different angles. No longer was the generalised survey enough, with its standard vocabulary, its tidy categories, its prominent landmarks, and appropriate value judgments.

This dynamic and mixed scene forms the subject of this book. Throughout its writing I have been conscious of breaches of decorum. While attempting to stand back so as to judge objectively and see things in their due proportion, I have been repeatedly aware of being pulled forwards, of being drawn into odd conversations, picking up phrases and noticing surprising details; but with the uncanny feeling that big issues and larger patterns were forming at the same time. Out of a critical study was growing a literary history, but not the one recognisable from traditional 'survey' courses on the subject. A less familiar story of eighteenth-century poetry offered itself, in which venerable concepts like 'Augustanism' and 'poetic diction' no longer seemed precise enough to be useful; it became evident that distinctive 'romantic' and 'sublime' modes were available from the very beginning of the century, and were later developed in various ways, while also being questioned – not least in the 1780s and 90s; and the familiar trajectory of the century's poetry from satire to sensibility, and from the classic towards the 'pre-romantic', appeared false. Mid-century poets like Akenside, Collins, Gray, and the Wartons, were striving for a purer Greek classicism to replace a French-influenced neo-classical style, in a campaign to recover more primal forms that sat happily with their native Spenser-Milton tradition. The classic/romantic divide did not fit the facts, and both terms asked to be realigned. As a corollary to this, fissures opened up within notions of 'wit' and 'politeness', so that they became less descriptive than argumentative, while 'imagination' seemed to gain in critical and creative importance from 1700 onwards.

Women's voices in particular challenged the old model, to the extent that a 'Finch to Barbauld' course would need to offer a different trajectory from the more traditional 'Pope to Wordsworth' one. Finding how to integrate women poets into eighteenth-century literary history (rather than leave them in a separate category with their own styles and interests) was a particular challenge, and meant rethinking the shape of the larger narrative. In the verse letter, in the romantic mode of the early decades, in sensibility and satire, in the sublime lyric, and in topographical and ethical poetry, women not only spoke strongly, but found new things to say, and seeking to do justice to their work has sometimes involved generic reassessment. In this study the term 'genre' itself, with its suggestion of defined categories, has often given way to 'mode', a concept that allows for a greater mobility and responsiveness in the poetic voice. As well as deliberately mingling well-known and less familiar voices, this book consciously sets men and women into dialogue. Pope, for example, encounters Finch, Montagu, Egerton, and Jones; and later in the century Smith and Bowles help to characterise each other, and Barbauld introduces Cowper. Others like Collier, Dixon, Leapor, Yearsley and Wilson challenge the conventions they exploit, and in different ways question decorums of poetic behaviour.

The work of Alexander Pope was unrivalled during the century for its range and richness. But rather than view him as a 'central' figure (implying that everyone else moves round him) or as the occupant of a lofty eminence, I have aimed to keep him moving amongst the throng. We repeatedly encounter him in different chapters and in varied company, and view his work from many angles without letting it dictate a set of values to everyone else. Other poets too, even individual poems, reappear in slightly different guises. What might be thought overlaps are, I hope, rather a recognition that texts can be illuminated from several perspectives.

Eighteenth-century poems were not isolated artefacts: they often spoke to each other, sometimes overtly as answers, imitations, or parodies, but also in subtler ways. In a society that valued good conversation, a single voice is usually waiting to become part of a dialogue; and during this period some publishers played their part through miscellanies or pirated collections where texts could be provocatively mixed together. The eighteenth century was a miscellaneous age, when ideas of mixture entered cultural and constitutional debate; and in the opening chapter I have chosen to emphasise (in a publishing rather than political context) how high and low, public and private, legitimate and proscribed, the formal and the spontaneous, could work together. This will I hope set the keynote for a study that stresses the conversational nature of ideas and of texts.

Texts can also be contexts, and the role of 'background' in a book of this scope has to be carefully controlled. Fortunately, James Sambrook's invaluable volume in this Longman series offers a range and depth of period context that no specific study like mine could attempt. The poetry I discuss, however, often engages so directly with the life of its age that politics, economics, religion and philosophy become an integral part of the subject. My conviction that eighteenth-century poetry is characterised by dynamic ideas and lively debate involves interweaving contextual material at many points – but I hope never without a sense of how the poets contributed to the pressures and arguments of their time. Gone for ever, I trust, are the days when the eighteenth century was thought to be an age of certainty, stasis, consensus, and restraint, when objective general truths outlawed the particular or quirky, and reason and sense lorded it unquestioned over passion and subjectivity. Within this scenario the poets of mid-century in particular were forced to play the role of hesitant or neurotic personalities trapped in an uncertain half-light between a confident Augustanism and an equally confident Romanticism; their aspirations were seen as frustrated, their language compromised, their strength etiolated, their minds disturbed, and they were shunned by Johnsonians on the one side and patronised by Wordsworthians on the other. If this book does nothing else, I hope it will recover the 1740s and 1760s as decades of youthful confidence and experiment in poetry. I want in the pages that follow to offer a more 'organic' reading of poetic developments during the ninety years of my title – not in terms of a unifying system, but in the eighteenth-century sense of 'organisation' as 'living in all its diverse and varied parts'. The patterns and features of this living organisation are far richer than any single volume can convey.

My debts are many. The most longstanding is to Roger Lonsdale for being over the years a model of impeccable and self-effacing scholarship. More recently, collaborating with Christine Gerrard on *Eighteenth-Century Poetry: An Annotated Anthology*, under the guidance of Andrew McNeillie of Blackwells, was both a delight and invaluable groundwork for writing this book – the research for both has inevitably overlapped. A debt that can never be adequately acknowledged is to the many critics and editors of eighteenth-century poetry whose work has become part of the fabric of the subject. Anyone writing today on this topic will, like me, be especially grateful for the work of John Barrell, Margaret Anne Doody, William Dowling, Howard Erskine-Hill, David Foxon, Dustin Griffin, Donna Landry, Claude Rawson, Pat Rogers, James Sambrook, John Sitter, and Howard Weinbrot. I am aware that through restrictions of space and considerations of accessibility that guide this series I have often not been able to take explicit account of the multifarious critical debates over the poets, texts and genres treated here. To do this would have required a different and much more extensive kind of book. In specific areas, John Goodridge's work on Dyer and labouring-class poetry has been valuable, and Nick Groom's research on manuscript and oral traditions has helped me, as has Chris Mounsey's knowledge of Smart, Bill Christmas's of Duck and Collier, Juan Pellicer's of John Philips, and Tim Burke's of Yearsley; Bridget Keegan introduced me to the delights of Anne Wilson.

Several passages in this volume have appeared, in different form, as follows: some of the material on Gray appeared in *Thomas Gray: Contemporary Essays*, ed. W.B. Hutchings and William Ruddick (Liverpool, 1993); on Henry James Pye in *Romanticism*, 3 (1997); on Pomfret and landscape in *The Coleridge Bulletin*, 13 (Spring 1999); on Thomson and Akenside in the

Blackwell *Companion to Literature from Milton to Blake*, ed. David Womersley (Oxford, 2000); and on the Spenser-Milton tradition in *The Cambridge Companion to Eighteenth-Century Poetry*, ed. John Sitter (Cambridge, 2001).

Turning nearer to home, I am grateful to my colleagues Shirley Chew, Robert Jones, and Alistair Stead for reading drafts of individual chapters; to Vivien Jones and Wolfram Schmidgen for many valuable conversations; and to John Whale who as always saw the direction of my argument more clearly than I did, and helped me keep it in view. I also owe a great deal to some of my recent Ph.D. students, and want to thank Gurion Taussig for his thoughts on 1790s friendship, Colin Winborn for our discussions about Crabbe, and Mel Kersey for his Ossianic enthusiasm, and his help with the appendices. Thanks also to the Special Collections staff of the Brotherton Library for making research such a pleasure. I am grateful to the School of English and the University of Leeds for research leave, and to the AHRB for an award under their 'matching leave' scheme, which enabled me to finish the book. As current General Editor of the series, Chris Walsh has given invaluable support and encouragement, and Derek Alsop was an exceptionally helpful reader. My biggest debt of all is marked by the dedication. Nicholas Roe's work on the Romantic poets has been an inspiration over many years, and has helped me see the eighteenth century in a wider perspective; and Jane Stabler has been the finest and most generous intellectual guide at every stage of the project.

DF
Leeds
June 2002

Chapter 1

Between Manuscript and Print

The manuscript looks like a printed book. Its nineteen leaves are written with meticulous care in a small italic hand that mimics type. The lines are neatly spaced just as on a printed page, including even the 'catchwords' (the first word of the next page set in each right-hand corner). There are running head-lines, and in the titles of the four poems each large individual capital letter is elegantly shaped. It seems newly delivered from the printing house.

The text is Alexander Pope's handwritten manuscript of his own 'Pastorals', done in 1704 at the age of sixteen.[1] He would not see them in print for another five years, but already he was thinking of what they should look like. This superfine copy was made so that his first work could be read by possible patrons and men of influence, and the teenager succeeded brilliantly. On the opening page, just opposite his introductory 'Essay on Pastoral', Pope proudly writes: 'This Copy is that wch past thro the hands of Mr Walsh, Mr Congreve, Mr Mainwaring, Dr Garth, Mr Granville, Mr Southern, Sr H. Sheers, Sr W. Trumbull, Ld Halifax, Ld Wharton, Marq. of Dorchestr. D. of Bucks. &c.' – a sparkling list of practising poets and literary connoisseurs from the aristo-cracy, the professions, and the world of public affairs. As the manuscript cir-culated amongst them, corrections or re-wordings were suggested, and Pope accepted some of them as he continued to revise his work. However, one figure missing from Pope's roll-call of literary gentlemen is the manuscript's most important reader of all – the publisher Jacob Tonson.[2] Tonson, the foremost printer-bookseller of the age, could claim the copyright for Shake-speare, Milton and Dryden, and in Pope he spotted another star in the mak-ing. It was he who launched the young man's poetic career by publishing the *Pastorals* in his 1709 *Miscellany*.

We are between two worlds here. On one side is a cultural elite, circulating, judging and correcting Pope's manuscript, and on the other is a shrewd busi-nessman eager to add him to his publisher's list. Throughout the rest of his writing career (1709–1744) Pope would bestride these worlds. He formed for himself a network of influential and cultured friends whose tastes and interests he shared (and helped to shape), but at the same time he was the writer who, more than any other, manipulated the world of print to his own advantage. Out of the first he achieved a virtually unassailable cultural authority, and out of the second he made his fortune.

Pope was only the most successful exploiter of a period in poetry's develop-ment when the cultures of manuscript and print overlapped and engaged with each other as never before, and it is this concept of a fruitful interplay between the two modes (collaborative as much as antagonistic) that will guide this chapter. Rather than see an 'old' world being replaced by a 'new' one (a democratised print culture displacing a courtly manuscript culture; or innovatory 'Moderns' battling with traditional 'Ancients'[3]), I want to explore some of the ways in which the two modes worked with, and even mimicked, each other, and see how poets relished their entanglements. At the same time, the aim is to use the poetic texts to bring into focus some of the preoccupations of recent cultural historians – politeness, print capitalism, and the public sphere – while being conscious of the tensions and contradictions that make it dangerous to generalise about the period. The London of Tonson and Pope was in many ways an impolite world that talked much about politeness, an emerging capitalist market that exploited networks of patronage, a world that published the private, and cheated as much as it debated. The literary scene in the period 1700–44 cannot truthfully be called a single 'culture', and even that term (as we now use it) risks oversimplifying diversity. There were growing pressures, and therefore new possibilities. Many writers were aware of becoming 'authors' in a confused marketplace where the status of any text might suddenly be transformed from private to public, where its readership might alter overnight, its origins and ownership be disputed, or its meanings twisted. In offering an angle of entry into the poetry of the period through this confusion, I find it useful to think in terms of the cultural implications of a creative interplay between manuscript and print.

During the earlier 'Restoration' period (the reign of Charles the Second, 1660–85) much poetry circulated in manuscript, and both gentlemen and ladies had their private commonplace books into which they could transcribe copies of others' verses as well as their own. A poetical taste and ready wit were the expected accomplishments of any 'man of affairs', and upper-class women could cultivate the former while knowing when to conceal the latter. An aristocrat or busy politician might also employ a professional scribe to compile a poetical miscellany for him. Many of these handwritten books still survive, and the practice continued until 1750 and beyond.[4] But by the first decade of the new century the market for printed poetry was greatly increasing. The new polite literary journals, *The Tatler* (1709–11), *Spectator* (1711–12, 14), and *Guardian* (1713) stimulated a taste for verse. Cheap reprints began to be widely available, and poetry miscellanies of all kinds enjoyed a surge in popularity. Arthur Case's bibliography records 57 different printed miscellanies for the period 1651–75; 63 for 1676–1700; 113 for 1701–25; and 136 for 1726–50 (the increase in sales was even sharper, given that after 1700 items tended to run into many more editions).[5] The old network of poetic patronage did not break down, but found new ways of exerting its influence in the print market.[6] The Whig grandees who had been the cultural establishment since the time of Charles the Second became the nucleus of the celebrated Kit-Kat Club. Their patronage system, presided over by Lords Somers and Halifax, developed a 'publishing arm' in Richard Steele and Joseph Addison, authors of *The Spectator*, and they in turn nurtured new poetic talent and helped channel it into print. At Button's Coffee-House, where Addison presided over the poetry scene, aspiring writers for *The*

Guardian could post their contributions into a letter-box shaped like a lion's head.[7]

By 1725 there was an extensive nationwide network of printers and book-sellers,[8] but the London trade was dominant, especially in its close working relationship with the literary culture of the metropolis, where poetical clubs and côteries of 'wits' formed, dissolved, and re-formed as political alliances shifted. Individual coffee-houses developed a distinct literary or political character. They took in journals and pamphlets, and a poem or letter headed 'Will's Coffee-House' could be in print the next day.[9] More than ever before there was an easy and tempting access to publication, and some booksellers had a network of writers to supply copy, edit material, or pass on manuscript poems that came their way. They distributed their sale catalogues among coffee-houses with a literary clientele, and might hold book auctions there, as Edmund Curll did at the Temple Coffee-House near his shop. It has been calculated that by 1739 London had 551 coffee-houses and two thousand clubs.[10] The sheer concentration of cultural forces inside the six square miles of the capital meant that the circulation of ideas was rapid and diverse, and generated considerable energy. 'By visiting four or five coffeehouses one might meet most of the leading scientists, theologians, and writers of the day – and hear talk about the others'.[11] To this list we could add financiers, printers, journalists and politicians. The seething metropolitan world stamped its character on much of the poetry of the 1700–44 period. Now extending beyond the restricted ambit of the court, this busy, sociable, literate and eloquent society formed an arena for the kind of cultural debate that could no longer be seen as 'elite' and was much more attuned to our modern concept of 'public opinion'.

In a theory that has been extremely influential on recent eighteenth-century cultural studies, Jürgen Habermas saw this world of the coffee-house and of Addison and Steele's *Spectator* as inaugurating, and virtually defining, what he called 'the public sphere'.[12] His far-reaching term (*Öffentlichkeit* in German – roughly the equivalent of the Russian *glasnost*, 'openness') is a conceptual space (i.e. a cultural atmosphere) liberated from the Court and State on the one side (i.e. public authority and state power), and on the other from the 'private realm' constrained by the family within the system of civil society. In Habermas's 'public sphere' people come together not as private selves or instruments of the state, but as disinterested individuals meeting for 'rational critical debate', free of party- or self-interest. Habermas is easier to summarise than to quote, and the fine tunings and larger-scale revisions of his theory that have proliferated in recent years are usually clearer and more carefully historicised than the original. His theory has been criticised for largely excluding the role of women, and I think this is linked to a more deep-seated problem with his categories: Habermas's stress on disinterested rational discussion simply won't fit the literary playground explored in this opening chapter, which like any playground has its cheats, sneaks, and bullies. The 'public sphere' pictured here is not separated out from state power or the private realm – on the contrary, its poetry exploits both systems by entangling courtly and bourgeois codes (Pope's *Epistle to Dr Arbuthnot* is an example). Something was clearly happening to the old establishment in the difficult move from a court politics to a more national politics in the wake of the 1707 Act of Union between England and Scotland (which saw the creation of 'Great Britain' under a single parliament). But the debate at all levels of society, from the court to the political clubs, was never free of faction and self-interest, and the poetry of the period is everywhere marked by such divisions.

In a literary culture becoming obsessed with 'publication', the notion of an emergent 'public sphere' of debate is a useful one, but it was much more contested and impolite than Habermas allows, and in the figures of Robert Harley, Lord Hervey and Lady Mary Wortley Montagu we have three representatives of Court and State who played an active part in it. Habermas stresses Addison's project for encouraging polite debate through the influence of *The Spectator*; but another significant person, Edmund Curll, the publishing pirate, also thrived in the new market-place. This chapter argues that, just as the London print market was acutely conscious of exploiting the manuscript, so the poets who supplied them could make tactical use of publication and manipulate the printed medium as part of the meaning of their work. Print capitalism and cultural capital fed each other.[13]

Between the foundation of the Bank of England in 1694 and the financial crash known as the 'South Sea Bubble' (1720), poetry began engaging with the new economic model being established in the metropolis. Concepts of value, integrity and permanence were having to defend themselves in a society where the old 'wealth' of land and property was transforming into a dynamic concept of 'money'. Success came to those who mastered the new fluid economy of production-circulation-consumption. These were the decades when our modern notion of an 'economy' began, and the distinction between manuscript and print reflects this – but not in quite the way we might expect. It is true that printed material circulated far more swiftly and unpredictably, and was responsive to variables like supply and demand, profit and loss. At the same time, however, a manuscript (such as a letter) has a fluidity and intimacy that printing lacks. A handwritten poem or note can be spontaneous, immediate, private and personalised, while a printed text is fixed, authorised, published, marketed, and finally criticised by a 'public'. But just as Pope's manuscript mimicked the licensed dignity of print, so printed works could play with elements of the casual, unlicensed and surreptitious. There is no simple equation here, and generalisations are dangerous. What can be said, I think, is that poets were alert to these factors and creatively exploited the tensions between them. Such contradictions sharpened their wits and helped give them an awareness of duality (between public and private, laboured and spontaneous, fixed and fluid). Some of the power of early eighteenth-century satire, for example, comes from its resourcefulness in exploiting the interplay between authoritative broadcast statement and a more elusive personalised suggestiveness. Poets of the period are acutely conscious of the medium through which their thoughts are being conveyed, and the uncertainties of reception by a reading public make them sensitive about how they are projecting and directing their voices.

This was an especially complex issue for women poets, who had to negotiate the problem of speaking in public at a time when such a thing was repeatedly cautioned against, even in normal conversation. *The Ladies Library* (1714) warned that 'a young Lady should never speak, but for Necessity, and even then with Diffidence and Deference' (e.g. ask politely for the butter). She should have the prudence 'to know when to talk and when to be silent'.[14] A caricature of the 'female philosopher' or 'petticoat-author' was a favourite turn on the comic stage (Lady Knowell, Mrs Lovewit, or Phoebe Clinket), and the woman writer was caught between being an unsexed scholarly pedant or an over-amorous poetess who had crossed the line of respectability. The frontispiece to volume one of *The Ladies Library* shows a woman sitting in a library poring over a huge printed volume, her head propped on her hand as she concentrates hard, while beneath her are two naked cupids sitting amongst discarded love letters. Between print and manuscript, she is compromised either way – hardening into a philosopher, or sinking to a coquette.

In the case of Anne Finch, Countess of Winchilsea, this problem was negotiated in an interesting way. In the 'Preface' to her volume of poems she is careful to point out that during her career at court she had resisted circulating her poems in manuscript, as she regarded it as too public a gesture:

> it is still a great satisfaction to me, that I was not so far abandon'd by my prudence, as out of a mistaken vanity, to let any attempts of mine in Poetry, shew themselves whilst I liv'd in such a publick place as the Court, where every one wou'd have made their remarks upon a Versifying Maid of Honour; and far the greatest number with prejudice, if not contempt.

In 'such a publick place as the Court' it would have been for her, not private circulation, but a kind of publication. Finch had allowed one or two things out, but regretted it ('I have writ, and expos'd my uncorrect Rimes, and immediately repented; and yet have writ again, and again suffer'd them to be seen'). But she has finally been prevailed upon by her friends, she says, to put this collection together. The 'Volume' in question, however, is not a printed book, but the handsome folio manuscript of her poems which is now in the Folger Library, Washington, transcribed by her devoted husband.[15] She introduces it with a formal 'Preface' just as if it is being published: 'the following Poems . . . tho' never meriting more than to be once read, and then carelessly scatter'd or consum'd, are grown by the partiality of some of my friends, to the formidable appearance of a Volume; tho' but in Manuscript, and have been solicited to a more daring manifestation, which I shall ever resist . . .'[16] This kind of half-way 'publication' allowed her poems to be handed round in an authorised and monitored way among her intimates, without the more haphazard circulating of individual papers. Thereafter a handful of pieces filtered into print (including her best known poem, 'The Spleen'), but her resistance to the 'more daring manifestation' was not finally overcome until 1713, with *Miscellany Poems, on Several Occasions. Written by a Lady.* The book is anonymous and there is no preface other than a note by the bookseller to say that 'Permission is at last obtained for the Printing'.

A printed text most obviously represents an expansion of readership: a poem circulating in manuscript among friends or fellow-courtiers could be read in its printed form by a thousand people in a day, a fact which increased a writer's awareness of the divide between privacy and publicity. A poem's *notional* reader and *actual* reader might therefore be very different, so that the writer had to be more alert to matters of taste and tone, and perhaps work harder to create a responsive readership. As we shall see in Chapter 4, this had particular relevance for the verse letter, a form that flourished by acknowledging the meeting of manuscript and print. What could be taken for granted among a group of known friends and patrons might have to be argued out for the purchasing public, and this in itself has stylistic implications. I am not suggesting that in this period printed verse was different in style from manuscript verse (that would be a risky generalisation – and quite untrue), but that poets became increasingly aware of how their voice was being projected, and questions of manner, tone, persona, etc. featured more consciously in the writing of poetry.

A printed book (as any graduate student contemplating their freshly bound thesis will know) somehow claims more authority for itself than mere manuscript, and at the same time imposes a new responsibility on its author. In the eighteenth century this dual recognition was sanctioned by the law. On one side was the Licensing Act of 1662, reinforced by the Stamp Act of 1712, as a result of which every printed item had to carry the name of a printer or bookseller, and all works under about 100 pages had to be registered at the Stamp Office and a duty of two shillings a sheet paid. This was obviously useful in cases of sedition or libel, when the printer of an anonymous work could face imprisonment, the stocks, or mutilation. On the other side was the new Licensing Act (known as the first 'Copyright' Act), effectual from April 1710, which for the first time gave authors ownership of their printed work. The printers had been hoping for a confirmation of their perpetual copyright, but the Act instead established the principle that all rights originated in the 'inventor' (the author) and remained theirs, to hold or contract away, for up to 28 years.[17] Far from settling matters, however, the law was infringed, challenged, and manipulated. There continued to be disputes over rights to literary property, and questions were repeatedly raised about a text's origins, authorship and integrity. It was fertile ground for the lawyers – but also for the satirists, who thrived on any engagement between instability and authority, and who could exploit the various competing forces in a literary culture that was creatively caught between manuscript and print.

It is this duality which characterises Pope's satire, *The Dunciad* (1728), a poem that exploits the power of the printed book to become a permanent monument to its culture, while still threatening (like a piece of paper thrust hurriedly into the pocket) to record fleeting incidents and personal embarrassments. It is a classical epic ready to incorporate the smutty epigram. Structured as a heroic fable presided over by the goddess Dulness, the poem superimposes the frantic profusion of London's popular culture upon a structural framework drawn from Homer's *Iliad* and Virgil's *Aeneid*. Beneath the passing show are unsettling reminders of other more permanent cultural values. At its surface the poem offers vivid sketches of the printers and booksellers, hack journalists, versifiers, pamphleteers, pornographers, and impresarios, all competing to supply and distribute the new street 'culture' in the marketplace. Pope used his young friend Richard Savage (the man with papers in his pocket) to supply him with embarrassing news and gossip from 'Grub Street' – the generic name for that part of the City to the East of Temple Bar contained by the symbolic locations of Smithfield Market, 'Bedlam' lunatic hospital, Newgate prison, and St Paul's. Amongst the narrow lanes the many printing shops were conveniently jumbled with the garrets of the hack writers who supplied them. Marking out this urban topography[18] where manuscript turned into print, two significant channels intersected. *Fleet Street*, leading westward out to fashionable St James's and Westminster, crossed over the murky *Fleet Ditch* running south to empty its stinking refuse into the Thames. Pope hardly needed to invent a metaphor for cultural collision.

When published, *The Dunciad* was not just a poem, but a dynamic cultural phenomenon, and Pope was both its poet and stage-manager. The anonymous volume entered the world on 18 May 1728 as a modest duodecimo of under sixty pages, and the London literati were roused into a panic: 'a Crowd of Authors besieg'd the Shop; Entreaties, Advices, Threats of Law, and Battery, nay Cries of Treason were all employ'd to hinder the coming out of the *Dunciad*. On the other Side, the Booksellers and Hawkers made as great Efforts to procure it'.[19] *The Dunciad. An Heroic Poem. In Three Books* carried on its title-page a false Dublin imprint that suggested it had originally appeared in Ireland (where British copyright did not apply), and to hint that it was the product of some Irish wit – possibly his friend Jonathan Swift. The bookseller was named as Anne Dodd, a London pamphlet-distributor who later made a sworn affadavit that her name had been used without her knowledge. Inside, the 'Publisher' offered the poem as a response (by a friendly admirer) to the recent barrage of 'Pamphlets, Advertisements, Letters, and weekly Essays, not only against the Wit and Writings, but against the Character and Person, of Mr Pope'. As for the manuscript of the poem, 'How I became possest of it, is of no concern to the Reader'. Thus did the anonymous Pope cover his tracks, and as if to symbolise the elusive nature of his text, the frontispiece shows a monumental altar built from closed, leatherbound volumes (of Cibber, Dennis, Blackmore and others) on the top of which perches an inscrutable owl holding in its beak a manuscript scroll of *The Dunciad* which has unfurled in the wind. It is a figure of Wisdom, but one that might easily fly from our grasp.

With the text of the poem itself Pope played a similar game. Aware of legal dangers, he substituted tantalising dashes for individual names, and this encouraged opportunists (including Pope's enemy Edmund Curll) to print various 'keys' to the poem's characters. One bookseller kept a manuscript 'key' in his shop for customers to consult. All this worked so well that the following year Pope was able to issue his grand 180-page 'Variorum' edition (a term applied to texts of the classics printed with a learned commentary and manuscript variants). In this version he named names, and the lines of poetry were grotesquely padded out with mock-learned notes, and with layer upon layer of prefatory material and appendices. Pope's great joke was that within twelve months of its first sly appearance, the little book had swelled into a monumental classic fit to be hide-bound and stacked on a library shelf. In keeping with its new status (and to protect it from prosecution) the 'Variorum' was distributed privately by Pope's three most aristocratic friends – the Lords Burlington, Oxford, and Bathurst – and the booksellers had to order copies through them. The final baffling accolade was the book's formal presentation to King George the Second by the Prime Minister, Sir Robert Walpole. Patronised by the cultured nobility and hawked by the pamphlet-sellers, Pope's was a protean satiric object in its marketing alone, a meeting-point of Court and street.

Such a poem could not stay still, and Pope accumulated more material for his work, the result of which was *The New Dunciad: As it was Found in the Year 1741. With the Illustrations of Scriblerus, and Notes Variorum* (1742). The prophecies of the original poem are shown to be fulfilled: the mighty goddess now holds the nation in thrall, and all aspects of its cultural life are infected. A preface notes that this new manuscript 'was found merely by Accident . . . but in so blotted a condition, and in so many detached pieces, as plainly shewed it to be not only incorrect but unfinished', and the editors ask 'If any person be possessed of a more perfect Copy of this Work, or of any other Fragments of it', they should 'communicate them to the Publisher'. The literary world was therefore to expect more. After this brilliant 'trailer' Pope's game continued the following year when he integrated this vision of universal nemesis as the fourth book of a re-written and extended *Dunciad in Four Books* (1743). The hero was changed from Lewis Theobald, pantomime-writer turned Shakespeare editor, to a more national figure in the Poet Laureate Colley Cibber, a larger-than-life comedy actor and self-publicist through whom Pope could link the popular theatre to the Court. By now, however, the true (anti-)hero was the malign master-spirit Dulness herself.

I have stressed *The Dunciad* as an unstable phenomenon at the meeting-point of manuscript and print, and this duality runs through the poem. Underneath the regular lines of verse the fussy editorial footnotes play a teasing game, hinting at the existence of a whole archive of manuscript *Dunciads* waiting to be explored, and offering their intriguing variants – 'In a manuscript Dunciad (where are some marginal corrections of some gentlemen some time deceas'd) I have found another reading of these lines . . .', reads one such note (to II. 183) offering an alternative couplet to that printed above. The fact that it is a description of the publisher Edmund Curll winning the pissing competition increases the joke. Not only do we have the 'official' printed couplet ('Thro' half the heav'ns he pours th'exalted urn; / His rapid waters in their passage burn'), but beneath it we are given the manuscript variant ('And lifts his urn thro' half the heav'ns to flow; / His rapid waters in their passage glow'). The editor's discerning comment only prolongs Curll's discomfort: 'This [variant] I cannot but think the right: For . . . tho' the difference between *burn* and *glow* may seem not very material to others, to me I confess the latter has an elegance, a *Jenesçay quoy*, which is much easier to be conceiv'd than explain'd'.

Hitting on the 'right' word is the driving force of Pope's satire. The artistry of his couplets repeatedly shapes the untidiness and chaotic energy of the 'dunces' into memorable forms. Creating his 'classic' text, Pope works his lines free of the process that must have made them. By an act of satiric displacement, the untidiness, the rejected drafts, the scribbled notes, the torn scraps of paper, the sheer labour of the manuscript, become the medium in which the poem's new poet-hero, Cibber, is immersed:

> Swearing and supperless the Hero sate,
> Blasphem'd his Gods, the Dice, and damn'd his Fate.
> Then gnaw'd his pen, then dash'd it on the ground,
> Sinking from thought to thought, a vast profound!
> Plung'd for his sense, but found no bottom there,
> Yet wrote and flounder'd on, in mere despair.
> Round him much Embryo, much Abortion lay,
> Much future Ode, and abdicated Play;
> Nonsense precipitate, like running Lead,
> That slip'd thro' Cracks and Zig-zags of the Head (I, 115–124)

Deep in the abyss of writer's block, Cibber becomes an emblem of art as incomplete process. He is surrounded by abandoned manuscripts, scraps of writing that have failed to come alive by finding their true form. Everything is in a fluid state of possibility, nothing is achieved and 'right'. Pope, like most of us, understands the agonies of moving from *thoughts* to *language*, the difficulties of reaching out word by word into the emptiness of the blank page as we grope for clear meaning or a well shaped idea. He understands that poetry comes to life between the draft manuscript and the printed text. It is the finished artefact that is the permanently living thing – all the confused energies of its making can be allowed to drop away. The life is now in the 'made' thing (the *poesis*). Cibber, however, is in the business of patching up, putting things together as best he can: a scrap might furnish part of an ode, and bits of his unfinished play can be stitched onto some of Molière or Fletcher. It will all be packaged and marketed somehow. In this way the hero of *The Dunciad* inverts the proper relationship between working manuscript and finished print, and his book collection reflects this. On his library shelves instead of the great classics, are ranks of volumes whose pompous bindings enclose what is little more than scrap paper. In this culture of expensive packaging the contents have managed to 'scape the martyrdom of jakes and fire'. Out of reach on the top shelves of Cibber's 'Gothic Library' slumber the black-letter books of the Middle Ages ('There Caxton slept, with Wynkyn at his side, / One clasp'd in wood, and one in strong cow-hide', I, 149–50). For Pope they offer the conclusive image of books as dead matter – not till the 1750s would these be reopened and (as we shall see) come back to life in English poetry.

However, as I argued earlier, the relationship between process and product is not clear-cut. Pope does not want the printed work entirely to shed the life and intimacy of manuscript. Much of the power of *The Dunciad* comes from the way it preserves a sense of spontaneous life within the finished structure. Pope learned from Dryden here, but even more than his early mentor, he is able to catch the quirks of personality and the tactile qualities of the different media they represent. Many of his satiric portraits preserve qualities of the sketch rather than the solid finished book, and this distinction can be seen by contrasting the delicate gestures of the Italian opera-singer ('a Harlot form soft sliding by, / With mincing step, small voice, and languid eye', IV, 45–6) with the pounding repetitions of the pedantic schoolmaster who is obviously waving a book at us ('Since Man from beast by Words is known, / Words are Man's province, Words we teach alone', IV, 149–50). Of these two quotations, one gives us instant details, the other rigid concepts, and together they catch the dual nature of Dulness: the first figure is fanciful and whimsical, the second solid and mechanical. Dunce-art is either one or the other. What it lacks is an ability to infuse the finished portrait with the spontaneity of the sketch. We are back in Cibber's study – scattered papers around him and heavy volumes above him. As Dulness's special embodiment, he cannot bring together the life of the one and the finish of the other.

The art of Pope's *Dunciad* does just that, embracing the varied throng of dunces with a wider epic action that allows us to place and judge them (in Chapter 3 we shall revisit the poem from that vantage-point). But inside the poem's wider argument is a wealth of living detail, so living that it is easy to catch modern echoes – the self-consciousness of the nervous chat-show guest (''Twas chatt'ring, grinning, mouthing, jabb'ring all,' II, 237), the awesome charisma of the TV chef ('a Priest succinct in amice white / Attends; all flesh is nothing in his sight! / Beeves, at his touch, at once to jelly turn', IV, 549–51), the media mogul who expects flattery to order ('He chinks his purse, and takes his seat of state: / With ready quills the Dedicators wait', II, 197–8), and the latest literary sensation pursued by all the publishers, with the goddess Dulness as his agent:

> She form'd this image of well-body'd air;
> With pert flat eyes she window'd well its head;
> A brain of feathers, and a heart of lead;
> And empty words she gave, and sounding strain,
> But senseless, lifeless! idol void and vain! (II, 42–6)

With the brilliant verb *window'd* Pope catches at once the transparency of the medium that seals the idol off from life. This poet doesn't reach out and engage with real experience, just gazes blankly with a whimsical mind and an unresponsive heart: one flies away (*feathers*), the other sinks down (*lead*). No wonder when the winning publisher claims his prize, there is nothing of substance there – it has just been a temporary phenomenon.

But publishers made money from the temporary and illusory. If Edmund Curll is finally cheated of his prize ('A shapeless shade, it melted from his sight', II, 111) it is an appropriate punishment for the London bookseller-publisher who seemed to have the power to transform a regulated print market into a profitable free-for-all. Pope turns Curll's magic against him when all the manuscripts he has deviously procured float back to their rightful owners:

> To seize his papers, Curl, was next thy care;
> His papers light, fly diverse, tost in air;
> Songs, sonnets, epigrams the winds uplift,
> And whisk 'em back to Evans, Young, and Swift. (II, 113–6)

At this time a lot of manuscript poetry was being 'handed about' London. Will's coffee-house was the favourite literary haunt of 'Isaac Bickerstaffe' (Richard Steele's man-about-town persona in *The Tatler*), and here he could be sure of picking up the latest piece. He writes on 16 April 1709: 'After the Play, we naturally stroll to this Coffee-house, in hopes of meeting some new Poem, or other Entertainment, among the Men of Wit and Pleasure'. Papers would be passed round the tables, and a hawker would call in with the latest printed poem or single-sheet broadside. Three days earlier in the second issue of *The Tatler* Isaac had written from Will's: 'There has lain all this Evening, on the Table, the following Poem . . . I thought it deserv'd to be consider'd, and made more Publick', and the poem itself (by Steele's protégé William Harrison) then follows. Some aspiring poets must have hoped their paper would be picked up like this and find its way to a printer; but others might be less happy. The Tatler, in his role as talent-spotter, plays with this idea. Printing some 'perfectly new' lines by 'an ingenious Kinsman of mine, Mr. Humphrey Wagstaff', Steele confesses: 'I stole out of his Manuscript the following Lines: They are a Description of the Morning . . . All that I apprehend is, that Dear *Numps* will be angry I have publish'd [them]'. Under this elaborate disguise, Jonathan Swift's popular 'Description of the Morning' appeared in print for the first time.[20] Given that Swift was actively assisting Steele with the paper in these early months, the fiction of the poem as a furtively copied extract is an interesting one. Consisting of just nine couplets, the 'Description' is itself a kind of illicit sketch of a London street in the early morning. There is no *action* as such, just a series of *activities*. We are given a glimpse of the invisible scene-shifters who work behind the drama of life – the apprentice scraping dirt from outside his master's door, and a servant preparing to scrub the stairs with her mop. The actors are offstage, and as we watch the scene being prepared we are caught between the events of the previous night and the events of the day to come. Hackney coaches are bringing men home from their liaisons; Betty is rumpling her bed before her mistress sees it has not been slept in; and the bailiffs are gathering round doorways ready to make an arrest for debt. Although the poem is not a fragment, it is presented to the reader as being part of some more significant whole that we are never given – just like the human figures it describes. Steele's story of copying it from a longer manuscript poem therefore becomes an integral part of the joke.

If Steele and Swift could exploit the idea of an unsanctioned copy of verses (it helped give *The Tatler* a streetwise quality), a publisher like Edmund Curll depended for his livelihood on the ready availability of literary manuscripts procured by fair means or foul. He often purchased papers that had been circulating round the town, 'and considered himself at full liberty to make what use he chose of property thus legally acquired'.[21] Curll has been considered the lowest form of book-trade life, especially by bibliographers and Pope scholars. Certainly he had a carefree attitude to literary property, used inventive title-pages as a marketing tactic, exploited reputations, spread scandals, published private letters, dabbled in erotica and sensationalism – but in so doing he gave the public what it wanted. The irony is that Curll and others like him were creating the very conditions that the poets exploited. He used them, as they used him. All of them had an investment in keeping the market humming, raising its curiosity, and meeting its demands. Steele, Swift and Pope, no less than Curll, played games with printed texts and 'private' papers. They all understood the reading public's fascination with how print could open up secret worlds, and they knew the *frisson* when the printing-press and private papers met (and the more embarrassingly the better).

Curll's network for procuring manuscripts was second to none. When in January 1707 a rumour circulated that he had got hold of a collection of poems by Matthew Prior, the poet's previous publisher moved very quickly and announced in the *Daily Courant* that 'all the Genuine Copys of what Mr. Prior has hitherto written, do of right belong, and are now in the hands of Jacob Tonson, who intends very speedily to publish a correct Edition of them'. But Tonson's spoiling tactic failed to prevent Curll's volume appearing within the week – while his own 'genuine' and 'correct' edition was not published for nearly two years. Tonson claims a double sanction here: in *his* edition Prior's verses will be both 'genuine' (from manuscripts in his own hand – not some third-hand copy, he implies) and 'correct' (accurately printed). But all the poems had in fact been printed before, and in one sense Curll's edition was far too genuine for Prior's liking because it reprinted two politically embarrassing satires that had appeared anonymously in the 1690s. Prior indignantly denied authorship and they were omitted from Tonson's official edition; but modern scholarship confirms them as his.[22] Who was the deceiver here?

Manuscript material by some authors was highly sought after. Anything associated with, or written by, Pope was marketable (and the one could always be turned into the other), as were verses by his friends Swift and Gay. A poem by 'a Lady of Quality' could also command a premium, since for an aristocrat any involvement with the book trade was still considered impolite and socially demeaning. When in 1716, therefore, Curll procured copies of three social satires by Lady Mary Wortley Montagu, written in rumoured collaboration with Pope and Gay, the result was predictably sensational. Knowing the taste of the market, Curll published them as *Court Poems*, and on the title-page he played with the idea that these were private jottings not meant for the public gaze: 'Publish'd faithfully, as they were found in a Pocket-Book taken up in *Westminster-Hall*, the Last Day of the Lord *Winton*'s Tryal'. This clearly represented an invasion of aristocratic space, and the intriguing titles of the poems seemed to confirm this: 'The Basset-Table', 'The Drawing-Room', and 'The Toilet'. What might the verses reveal about their courtly owner, who it seems had been attending the trial of one of the Jacobite 'traitors' involved in the 1715 rebellion? In the Advertisement Curll stirred up the question of authorship by 'reporting' on his tour of the coffee-houses where he had publicly read from the notebook: 'Upon Reading them over at *St. James's Coffee-House*, they were attributed by the General Voice to be the Productions of a LADY of *Quality*. When I produc'd them at *Button*'s, the *Poetical Jury* there brought in a different Verdict; and the Foreman strenuously insisted upon it, that Mr. GAY was the *Man*'. But then 'a Gentleman of distinguish'd Merit' reported to him: 'Sir, Depend upon it, these Lines could come from no other Hand, than the Judicious Translator of HOMER' (i.e. Pope). Thus did Curll arouse the public's curiosity in his enigmatic text, and manage to have the best of all three worlds – 'every Body is at Liberty to bestow the Laurel as they please', he announced.

Reading Lady Mary Wortley Montagu's poems in this 'pirated' edition sharpens their erotic charge. As we turn the crisp pages (they still are) of Curll's small pamphlet (rather than print them in handsome folio he produced something closer to the supposed pocket-book original) we seem to have broken into a world of court intrigue and female intimacy. Mimicking the songs of innocent Arcadian shepherdesses, these aristocratic beauties speak couplets that palpitate with frustrated passion: a displaced favourite of the Princess of Wales regrets her years of respectable abstinence ('For Thee, Ah! what for Thee did I resign; / My Passions, Pleasures, all that e'er was mine'); an ageing mistress is jealous of her younger rival (''Tis true her Face may boast the Peach's Bloom; / But does her nearer whisp'ring Breath perfume?'); and a woman finds sexual excitement over the card-table ('With eager Beats his *Mechlin* Cravat moves: / *He Loves*, – I whisper to my self, *He Loves*'). Such whispers, like the whispering lace of her lover's cravat, tell us we are overhearing a coterie-language, which only increases the charged atmosphere of these select interiors: 'There, careless lies the Rich *Brocade*, unroll'd; / Here, shines a Cabinet of Burnish'd Gold'. The exotic material unfolds while the cabinet holds its secrets. Society gossip from this world of winks and nods gains a voyeuristic dimension with its public readership; but at the same time the satiric element is also increased. The direct intimacies of the privately circulated paper become, on publication, part of an ironic interplay of public and private, and the whole value-system of this claustrophobic world is brought into question. Suddenly Roxana's disillusionment finds its way out to a public audience:

> I know the *Court*, with all its Treach'rous Wiles,
> The *False Carresses*, and *Undoing Smiles*.
> Ah PRINCESS! learn'd in all the Courtly Arts,
> To *cheat* our Hopes, and yet to *gain* our Hearts.
>
> ('The Drawing-Room', 49–52)

Pope was furious at Curll's publication of these poems that had grown out of his own intimate friendship with Lady Mary, and he felt protective towards them (his elegant transcription of 'The Basset-Table' is now in New York Public Library). The poet's revenge was memorable, and appropriately both a private and a published one. Taking direct physical action, Pope tricked Curll into drinking an emetic. He then immediately sent to the press 'A Full and True Account' of the terrible aftermath of his joke, in which he describes the violently vomiting bookseller confessing his misdeeds to the world. We have already seen how Pope used Curll's urinary pyrotechnics in *The Dunciad* as an image of cultural pollution, and in the same poem Curll almost loses the race with Tonson by slipping in a dirty deposit outside his own shop ('Obscene with filth the miscreant lies bewray'd, / Fal'n in the plash his wickedness had laid', II, 75–6). Curll therefore becomes for Pope the man who turns a private act into a public performance. He was an unsavoury character who picked up things he shouldn't.

Pope, a professional author advancing with his magisterial translation of Homer, and with a respectable list of subscribers to satisfy, wanted to regulate his own appearances in print. He was preparing for the publication of his *Works*, sumptuously issued in June 1717, which would set him before the public as a 'classic' (and not yet thirty years of age!). He was also moving in aristocratic courtly circles as never before, a close friend and neighbour of the cultivated Earl of Burlington, and an intimate of the Princess of Wales's three maids of honour. Mixing in the very world of Lady Mary's *Court Poems* the young poet enjoyed playing the gallant, and some of Pope's witty verses were circulating in manuscript around this group. They showed how he had perfected the smutty, suggestive, 'trifling' mode of the Restoration court-rake, whose aim was to make the ladies blush, giggle, then sigh. His 'A version of the First Psalm. For the Use of a Young Lady' is in this mode, parodying the language of the metrical psalm by applying it to the marriage-bed:

> *She* shall bring forth most Pleasant Fruit,
>   *He* Flourish still and Stand,
> Ev'n so all Things shall prosper well,
>   That this Maid takes in Hand.[23]

Also being passed round were some of his court epigrams, some verses on prudery, and a 'Court Ballad' ('To one fair Lady out of Court, / And two fair Ladies in . . / . . Come these soft lines with nothing stiff in / To Bellenden Lepell and Griffin'). It was quite a distance from the aristocratic pastoral of Hampton Court to Curll's shop in Fleet Street, but that is where the manuscripts soon found themselves. To his delight the publisher was able to issue them, along with some crude things not by Pope, as *Pope's Miscellany* (1717), announcing to his clients that 'all [Pope's] Writings for the Future, except Homer, will be Printed for *E. Curll*'. The poet and the publisher, in their satiric embrace, seemed to become more mutually involved as the dispute went on. If a self-fashioning author could use his publishers – as Pope did Tonson and Lintot – to present himself formally before the public in a controlled way, then there was always a Curll to make the picture a more untidy and unauthorised one. But the ability of print to spread confusion and play games was something the poets themselves could use when it suited them. For a satirist especially (as we have seen with *The Dunciad*) the anarchic potential of 'Grub Street' as a medium for scandal, deceit, controversy, mimickry, and all kinds of creative deception, proved invaluable.

This was the world in which the 'Scriblerians' thrived. They were a small group of friends (Pope, Swift, John Gay, Thomas Parnell, and Dr John Arbuthnot) who in 1713 constituted themselves as the Scriblerus Club, distancing themselves from Addison's polite Whig circle at Button's, of which Pope and Gay had earlier been members. They began meeting together to compile 'The Works of the Unlearned', a spoof monthly review that would ironically celebrate the very worst of current writing. Their collective persona, 'Martinus Scriblerus', was the embodiment of 'Grub Street' pretentiousness, and through his voice they would parody all the follies in the literature and learning of the age. Their regular meetings, usually at Arbuthnot's apartment in St James's Palace (he was one of the Queen's physicians), were convivial, witty, and by the end of the evening probably hilarious. In addition to the five, the club had one 'honorary' member, who gave their enterprise another courtly dimension. This was Robert Harley, Earl of Oxford, the head of the current Tory government, 1710–14, who joined in their gatherings with enthusiasm and enjoyed forgetting the pressures of the day in their company. Pope recalled that Harley 'used to send trifling verses from court to the Scriblerus Club almost every day',[24] and some of the notes between them, carried by servants along the corridors of St James's, were later printed, and a few of them still survive. In one room of the palace the fate of the government might be at stake, while beyond the back stairs the Scriblerians were writing their hero's memoirs: 'One day it will be no disgrace / In *Scribler* to have had a place', wrote Swift and Parnell, 'Come then, my lord, and take your part in / The important history of *Martin*'. Harley's verse reply is headed 'April 14, 1714. Back Stairs, past Eight'. One manuscript invitation asking him to join them consists of five couplets, each in the handwriting of its author. Parnell's couplet is the most shapely and well styled ('For Frolick Mirth give ore affairs of State, / To night be happy, be to morrow great'); in his couplet Swift, alluding to the Duke of Buckingham, is more brisk and direct ('In other Words, You with the Staff, / Leave John of Bucks, come here and laugh'), and Gay, whose *Shepherd's Week* was hot off the presses that month, adopts a tone of rustic simplicity ('Leave Courts, and hye to simple Swains, / Who feed *no* Flock upon *no* Plains'). In the variety of tone and manner, this comes close to poetry as conversation. Spontaneous manuscript verses such as these, the staple of coffee-house and dinner-table, remind us of the public milieu in which much poetry of the period was conceived, and if such writing appears formal and artificial to us, it is because we have lost a sense of verse as sociable communication. We should also be aware of how easily the public and private could intersect. Walking down the corridor, Harley was clearly moving from one sphere of activity to the other, but which was the more 'private'? The world of the nation's affairs where politically he might keep his thoughts to himself? Or the group of friends who encouraged sociable communication? In this period the word 'society' could refer to the intimacies between two people, and there is no doubt that it was in 'private' that the Prime Minister became more open.

John Gay, one of the most playful of satirists, was the secretary of the club; but their delight in compiling materials outran the ordering and revising, and soon the targets for their humour widened to include versifiers, party hacks, editors, critics, theatrical producers, exhibitionists, even theologians and scholars. The papers in the Scriblerian archive accumulated. They set out first to write the biography of their anti-hero, under whose name they could publish their satiric material, and they also planned to claim as Scriblerus's any work they thought deserved the attribution. In doing so they were anticipating Curll, who would himself go on to invent a 'J. Addison' and 'J. Gay' for the title-pages of his books (only these were '*John* Addison' and '*Joseph* Gay'). Thus did the satirists, just like the rogue publisher, blur the line between authentic and spurious.

After a few months of intense activity in 1714, the group momentum was lost when Swift returned to Ireland. But Martinus Scriblerus remained a shared joke and a satiric inspiration for them, and sporadic informal 'meetings' took place till 1718, and again when Swift visited England in 1726. The 'club' proved in the end to be, not a formal publishing project, but a gleeful accumulation of manuscripts by a collaborative authorship who entrusted individual ideas and jokes to their public spokesman, Scriblerus. His material became a kind of common fund from which all of them could draw, and over the years the voice of Martinus Scriblerus seeped out into print in various forms. In 1726 his ideas and spirit infused themselves into *Gulliver's Travels*; in 1728 he gave the world his anti-poetics, *The Art of Sinking in Poetry*; in 1729 he wrote footnotes for Pope's *Dunciad Variorum*; and in 1741 his *Memoirs* finally reached print.

The various ingenuities of Edmund Curll and the Scriblerus Club dramatise, almost in caricature, some of the complexities of the 'literary scene' of this period. The persisting manuscript culture of the court was encountering the emerging book trade, but this was not a case of a polite world being superseded by a vulgar one. The meeting was more symbiotic. With their sexual innuendo, coded references, or intimate pen-pictures, court verses made good copy, especially when a 'key' could be provided, and a scandal hinted at. It was almost as though print had become the ideal medium for drawing out their suggestiveness and salacious potential. Publication only served to emphasise private meanings. Nor should we assume that all court versifiers, or their subjects, wanted to avoid being seen in print.

Pope's *Rape of the Lock* (1714) treads along this knife-edge between privacy and publicity. Its court world is one of private languages and social codes, and its plot hinges on how a small secret manuscript (the love letter) might lead to public humiliation. Through this society of beaux and belles meaning circulates by whisper and gesture, by the rapping of a snuff-box or the precise language of the fan (which had developed its own set of coded messages depending on how it was held or moved). Beneath what seems a trivial verbal surface, wars are being fought and scores settled:

> In various talk th'instructive hours they past,
> Who gave the ball, or paid the visit last:
> One speaks the glory of the *British* Queen,
> And one describes a charming *Indian* screen;
> A third interprets motions, looks, and eyes;
> At ev'ry word a reputation dies.
> Snuff, or the fan, supply each pause of chat,
> With singing, laughing, ogling, and all that. (III, 11–18)

The passage ends in a silent wink – we don't need to be told what *that* is. The atmosphere of the whole poem is caught here. It is a world in which anything might become significant, and where every detail asks to be interpreted – but by whom, and to what end? Who is controlling interpretation? The endless interplay between tangible and intangible, with its hints and suggestions, creates a kind of erotics of meaning. Looks can kill; a curl of hair can draw a man to destruction; a card game be a sexual trap; coffee arouse daring thoughts and give x-ray vision; powder and perfume assume electric potency. In the middle of this dangerous world is Belinda, a girl caught in two minds about publicity. In the poem's playful allegory, she is torn between the sylphs (her airy spirits) who delight in showing her beauty off in public places, and Umbriel the gnome (her dark internal spirit) who in his journey to her spleen stirs the fears and suspicions deep inside her. In the social world there is an equivalent duality: Clarissa, with a knowing worldliness, wants Belinda to exploit her charms, make a good marriage, and take her place in society; but the prudish Thalestris can see only her public shame:

> Methinks already I your tears survey,
> Already hear the horrid things they say,
> Already see you a degraded toast,
> And all your honour in a whisper lost!
> How shall I, then, your helpless fame defend?
> 'Twill then be infamy to seem your friend! (IV, 107–112)

The distant court beauty will become cheapened once the gossip about her 'fall' begins to circulate, and her health is drunk in the coffee-houses.

The writer of Thalestris's lines was someone who knew how easily a private, inner world could be opened out to the public gaze. We have seen how Curll and his network exploited the market for embarrassing material. The title of one of his miscellanies (printed in 1718) is eloquent: *Letters, Poems, and Tales: Amorous, Satyrical, and Gallant. Which passed between Several Persons of Distinction. Now first Published from their respective Originals, found in the Cabinet of that Celebrated Toast Mrs. Anne Long, since her Decease.* Anne Long had been 'honoured' by the Kit-Cat Club in having a toasting-glass dedicated to her, inscribed with verses celebrating 'bright *Longy*'s Health ... With eternal Beauty blest, / Ever blooming, still the best; / Drink your Glass, and think the rest' (p. 2). This *degraded toast*, whose cabinet has been opened, had been Swift's close friend, and some papers of his were among those printed. This embarrassment caused another woman friend to advise

Swift that any similar material of his own should be 'committed instantly to the flames, for you being stigmatisd with the name of a Wit, Mr Curl will rake to the Dunghill for your Correspondance'.[25] Pope's *Rape of the Lock* understands the implications of such worries, and expresses an underlying anxiety about the nature of the social world itself, and on what basis it functions. Is a neurotic aristocratic côterie really a 'society' at all? The poem confronts the problem of finding a place for the private realm (what we would term a 'self') within a public context. It is the difference between Thalestris's precarious 'honour' and Clarissa's 'virtue':

> How vain are all these glories, all our pains,
> Unless good sense preserve what beauty gains:
> That men may say, when we the front-box grace,
> Behold the first in virtue, as in face! (V, 15–18)

Both passages imagine what men will 'say' about Belinda; but their tone and manner are quite different. Thalestris offers an unsettling picture of a crying girl (we hear Belinda sobbing at 'the *horrid* things they say') who becomes isolated from her social group ('Twill then be infamy to seem your friend'), while her name circulates round the clubs – perhaps in a witty 'toast'. As she withdraws prudishly and guiltily into her self, her detachable 'honour' (like the papers in Anne Long's cabinet) is made free of by others. There is a gap between her 'self' and her social being. For Clarissa, on the other hand, the public world is spacious and welcoming, and Belinda can physically take her place in the forefront of it. Here the talk isn't sly and secretive, but open, easy and sympathetic (this is the key to eighteenth-century 'politeness'). The self is her public person, not something she hides at home; and what circulates through society is the real and mature Belinda – at least Clarissa would like to think so. The exclamation 'Behold!' (line 18) suggests that her inner quality would be as much on display as her beauty. Freed from sylphs and gnomes, a fully socialised Belinda would no longer be split between her visual surface and her hidden interior.

Belinda refuses Clarissa's advice, and her little society fragments into an angry mêlée, an uncivil war of beaux and belles. The lock of hair itself also disintegrates, but as he draws to an end, Pope identifies it with his own *Lock* (his poem), and imagines its fate. Will it circle aimlessly in the moon's wake, trailing behind other meaningless manuscripts that once had a value for somebody (like old love letters – 'There broken vows, and death-bed alms are found, / And lovers' hearts with ends of riband bound', V, 117–8)? Or, as he confidently announces, will its publication preserve it in a higher sphere for future ages ('This Lock, the Muse shall consecrate to fame, / And 'midst the stars inscribe *Belinda*'s name!', V, 149–50)? Such stellar publicity for the *Lock* would transcend its private origins. As Pope remarks in his prefatory letter to Arabella Fermor (Belinda's original): 'this Piece . . . was intended only to divert a few young Ladies . . . But as it was communicated with the Air of a Secret, it soon found its Way into the World. An imperfect Copy having been offer'd to a Bookseller, You had the Good-Nature for my Sake to consent to the Publication of one more correct'.[26] Such is the way with secret commun-ications. But Pope is here creating a fiction. The supposed 'imperfect' copy that 'found its Way' to a publisher was in fact an authorised early version which Pope himself gave to be printed in Lintot's *Miscellany* (1712), and he then expanded it from two cantos to five. His prefatory letter is intended to give readers the *frisson* of decoding a text with a secret at its heart – one meant to circulate surreptitiously round 'a few young Ladies' at court. Beyond this, all his poem now needed was a 'key', and this Pope himself provided in a pamphlet under the pseudonym 'Esdras Barnivelt', *A Key to the Lock, Or a Treatise proving, beyond all Contradiction, the dangerous Tendency of a late Poem entituled The Rape of the Lock, to Government and Religion* (1715). Through such presentational devices, the poet created the sense of a myster-ious manuscript behind the published poem. It allowed him a further satiric dimension, one linking private gossip to public sedition.

Within the general notion of an 'overlap' between a manuscript culture and a print culture are many specific instances like this, in which 'publication' kept its sense of 'making public', of putting into the public domain something that already existed in the private sphere. A printer might use the idea to attract purchasers; but poets too could exploit an ambivalence between the public and the intimate, and enhance their work's meaning by reminding the reader of the textual immediacy behind the mediation of print. As Anne Finch wrote about her 1713 volume of poems: '[we] only to the Press repair / To fix our scatter'd Papers there'.[27] I have tried to suggest that this aspect of the literary world in the early eighteenth century provides a dynamic context for reading some of its poetry. When we encounter texts in books, it is helpful to be reminded of the degree to which they were once living words – and can live again.

Notes

1. For a facsimile and transcription, see *The Last and Greatest Art: Some Unpublished Poetical Manuscripts of Alexander Pope*, ed. Maynard Mack (Newark, London and Toronto, 1984), pp. 19–71.

2. See Tonson's letter to Pope, 20 April 1706 (*Correspondence*, ed. Sherburn, I, 17), and *The Last and Greatest Art*, p. 21, note 10.

3. See Alvin Kernan, *Samuel Johnson and the Impact of Print* (Princeton, 1987), and Joseph M. Levine, *The Battle of the Books: History and Literature in the Augustan Age* (Ithaca and London, 1991).

4. The Brotherton Collection, University of Leeds, includes forty-five manuscript miscel-lanies and commonplace books from the period 1660–1750.

5. Arthur E. Case, *A Bibliography of English Poetical Miscellanies, 1521–1750* (Oxford, 1935).

6. See Dustin Griffin, *Literary Patronage in England, 1650–1800* (Cambridge, 1996).

7. *The Guardian* 98 (3 July 1713) and 124 (3 August 1713).

8. See Henry R. Plomer, *A Dictionary of the Printers and Booksellers who were at work in England, Scotland and Ireland from 1668 to 1725*, ed. Arundell Esdaile (London, 1922).

9. Poetical contributions and amorous letters to *The Tatler* tended to be headed 'Will's Coffee-House' by the editor, Sir Richard Steele.

10. Roy Porter, *Enlightenment* (London, 2000), pp. 35–7. See also R.J. Allen, *The Clubs of Augustan London* (Cambridge, Mass., 1933).

11. *Memoirs . . . of Martinus Scriblerus*, ed. Charles Kerby-Miller (New York and Oxford, 1988), p. 35.

12. *The Structural Transformation of the Public Sphere* (1962), trans. Thomas Burger (Cambridge, Mass., 1989).

13. Two important discussions of these related concepts are: Jonathan Brody Kramnick, *Making the English Canon: Print-Capitalism and the Cultural Past, 1700–1770* (Cambridge, 1998), and John Guillory, *Cultural Capital: the Problem of Literary Canon Formation* (Chicago, 1993).

14. *The Ladies Library*, 3 vols (London, 1714), I, 56.

15. Heneage Finch began to compile the manuscript c. 1694–5. See Barbara McGovern, *Anne Finch and Her Poetry. A Critical Biography* (Athens and London, 1992), pp. 69–70.

16. *The Poems of Anne Countess of Winchilsea*, ed. Myra Reynolds (Chicago, 1903), pp. 7–8.

17. See Harry Ransom, *The First Copyright Statute* (Austin, 1956). For a discussion of Pope's astute dealings with publishers, see the Appendix, 'Pope and Copyright', in David Foxon, *Pope and the Early Eighteenth-Century Book Trade*, rev. and ed. James McLaverty (Oxford, 1991), pp. 237–51.

18. The classic study is Pat Rogers, *Grub Street: Studies in a Subculture* (London, 1972).

19. Richard Savage, *A Collection of Pieces in Verse and Prose, which have been publish'd on the Occasion of the Dunciad* (London, 1732), p. vi. Maynard Mack notes that the description was possibly written by Pope (*Alexander Pope: A Life* [New Haven and London, 1985], p. 457 and note).

20. *Tatler* 9 (30 April 1709).

21. Ralph Straus, *The Unspeakable Curll* (London, 1927), p. 12.

22. See *The Literary Works of Matthew Prior*, ed. H. Bunker Wright and Monroe K. Spears, 2 vols (Oxford, 1971), II, 822–3 and 827.

23. The Psalm's ostensible publisher, Mrs Burleigh (a front for Curll), 'advertised . . . her willingness to show the *Version* in Mr Pope's own handwriting to anybody who cared to come to her shop' (Straus, p. 64).

24. Joseph Spence, *Observations, Anecdotes, and Characters of Books and Men*, ed. James M. Osborn, 2 vols (Oxford, 1966), p. 95.

25. Lady Elizabeth Germain – Swift, 27 May 1735 (*The Correspondence of Jonathan Swift*, ed. Harold Williams, 5 vols [Oxford, 1963–5], IV, 342).

26. See *The Poems of Alexander Pope*, ed. John Butt (London, 1963), p. 217.

27. 'Mercury and the Elephant. A Prefatory Fable', 47–8 (Reynolds, p. 4).

Chapter 2

Debating Politeness

Some of the finest poetry of the 1700–1750 period is fascinated by 'polite' modes, while at the same time working with ideas of impurity, impoliteness and indecorum. Perhaps satire thrives at a time when a system of values is under threat and new forces are challenging an old cultural hegemony (whether it be 1381, 1598, 1820, or 1963)? Certainly in the early eighteenth century, satire's characteristic witty inversions and juxtapositions have special power in an age that is trying to reconcile the energies of the new cultural market-place with a need for polite social cohesion and civic responsibility. In a world striving for 'politeness', the crude and indecent can have a powerful satiric effect.

The term 'polite' has become inextricably associated with the eighteenth century, to the extent that it can appear to characterise the culture of the age as a whole. In summarising what he calls its 'master metaphor' of refined sociability, Lawrence Klein consciously paints a picture of politeness that verges on parody: 'an idealised vision of human intercourse, peopled by gentlemen and ladies, sited in the drawing room or coffeehouse, engaged in intelligent and stylish conversation about urbane things, presided over by the spirit of good taste'.[1] All we need to add is the image of powdered wigs, and the scene is complete. For many, this still remains the site of much eighteenth-century poetry, and it was a conscious decision to substitute another picture at the opening of this book. Nevertheless, politeness was an aspiration to many, and for young poets seeking patronage and hoping to make their way in the world, the various polite codes (in language, tone, etc.) were useful to learn.

Politeness was also contentious, and had a political colouring; and beyond its devotees, some were suspicious of its motives and its principles, and others (like Clarissa in *The Rape of the Lock*) urged a polite mode that did not sacrifice the inner life to social engagement. As we have already glimpsed in Chapter 1, in the early decades of the century poetry had an uneasy relationship with polite discourse. In this chapter, therefore, I want to complicate the idealised picture by suggesting that there were competing notions of politeness during the 1700–1750 period. Distinctions are always useful, and it is possible to recognise, beyond the polished social performance, a more subtle mode of politeness which involved opening out the private realm into a social context.

The underlying principle of politeness in this period is well expressed by the Earl of Shaftesbury in his *Essay on the Freedom of Wit and Humour* published in 1709 – the year *The Tatler* began:

All Politeness is owing to Liberty. We polish one another, and rub off our Corners and rough Sides by a sort of *amicable Collision*. To restrain this, is inevitably to bring a Rust upon Mens Understandings. 'Tis a destroying of Civility, Good Breeding, and even Charity it-self, under pretence of maintaining it.[2]

Shaftesbury is referring to the derivation of the word 'polite' from the Latin *politus* ('polished'). The concept relies on the kind of sociable 'give and take' that tends to smooth out differences. Politeness therefore depends on assisting, and to a degree regulating, the dynamics of social and mental interaction. It sets itself against anything awkward, stubborn, selfish, mean, insensitive, shocking, loud, oppressive, angry, or egotistical. Ideally, as free human beings in a liberal society (encouraged to learn, choose and judge), we grow in understanding by interacting with others – Shaftesbury's *amicable Collision*. At the heart of eighteenth-century politeness, therefore, is an active sociable education, a dynamic concept that would prevent the *Rust* of self-satisfaction from coating the mind, and open it up to new ideas and wider sympathies.

Shaftesbury's belief that a cultured mind needed to have continual refreshment was the underlying premise of *The Spectator*. As a polite publishing project, it set its face against everything that the scurrilous Curll and his like stood for. Addison had been responsible for changing the character of its predecessor, *The Tatler*, from a 'tattling' coffee-house news-sheet into a regular essay,[3] and the new daily journal aimed to continue in that mode, observing the varied social world, laughing at its follies, but also encouraging the public discussion of ideas and literature. It would be 'amicable Collision' not aggressive invasion. 'Mr Spectator' himself was a carefully balanced persona, a man at ease in many surroundings (the coffee-house, the theatre, or the financial Exchange), not as a participant, however, but as a detached onlooker: 'In short, where-ever I see a Cluster of People I always mix with them, tho' I never open my Lips but in my own Club ... Thus I live in the World, rather as a Spectator of Mankind, than as one of the Species'.[4] Unlike Steele's tattler, this man differentiates between the sociable and the intimate, silently guarding his privacy while joining the London scene. Once again, an uneasiness about intimate interaction is evident, and Addison's answer is to maintain a level of disengagement (perhaps better expressed as 'fascinated disinterestedness'). *The Spectator*'s project involved making the paper itself a kind of social and intellectual currency within the polite economy, a mode of exchange between its readers that substituted for a more personal converse. Mr Spectator gave people things to talk about.

The Spectator wanted people to be polite, but it was surrounded by evidence to the contrary – as Steele wrote in no. 38 (13 April 1711): 'The wild Havock Affectation makes in that Part of the World which shou'd be most polite, is visible wherever we turn our Eyes'. If Mr Spectator felt hemmed in, he nevertheless had to create a polite readership for himself out of those very people. The paper's tone of urbane and genial conversation was therefore crucial in developing a *rapport* with the public and engaging their attention. Things loud, scandalous and abrasive could always tempt the passing purchaser (Curll had relied on that); but in order to establish a settled readership for their journal, Addison and Steele knew that politeness could bring ends and means together. They were careful not to raise their voices, and to sub-sume the corrective element within a genial social commentary that used good-humoured raillery and gentle caricature. Readers, on seeing their affectations and 'little follies' mirrored in its pages, might be persuaded to brush up their behaviour as well as their coats.

Their minds were not to be neglected either. Addison stressed this point in setting out his aims in the tenth issue (12 March 1711): 'The Mind that lies fallow but a single Day, sprouts up in Follies that are only to be killed by a constant and assiduous Culture'. Unlike our modern media-driven term 'cul-ture' (a value-free concept describing the framework of thought and style within which it is assumed everyone in a society lives), Addison's is a valuable resource that has to be actively worked for and assiduously cultivated (Latin *cultus*), or else it will be lost. It is not something you find yourself in, or which happens to you, but something you achieve through knowledge and experi-ence. Addison's next sentence is a famous one: 'I shall be ambitious to have it said of me, that I have brought Philosophy out of Closets and Libraries, Schools and Colleges, to dwell in Clubs and Assemblies, at Tea-Tables, and in Coffee-Houses'. By 'Philosophy', Addison is not thinking of abstruse topics, but of Socrates' practical emphasis on *how to live* (he has just likened himself to that philosopher). This sounds idealistic; but it is also a way of creating a readership. Addison is projecting (correctly, as it happens) how *The Spectator* will help bring about a polite culture by spreading through sociable spaces, not as private reading, but as matter for civilised conversation. It seems impolite not to be grateful. But his often-quoted sentence is also deceptive, and we need to re-work the polished prose in order to understand some of the complexities behind his project, and their implications for eighteenth-century poetry.

Returning to his list of venues, we might notice how it smooths over the social and political tensions of the period. Many 'Clubs' (still unregulated at this time)[5] were private, factional, male-oriented, controversial, and with a specific agenda – very different from the formal 'Assembly' of mixed com-pany, defined by Ephraim Chambers as 'a general meeting of the polite per-sons of both sexes for the sake of conversation, gallantry, news, and play'.[6] The gulf between the decorum of the tea-table (over which the woman pre-sided) and the busy freedoms of the coffee-house was no less great. The fact that a 'polite' man would often circulate round all four venues in a single day makes us realise that eighteenth-century sociability was not a simple thing, and that politeness also needed adaptability, and a sense of what might be appropriate in different settings. The poems of this period, as we shall see, demand a similar alertness from the reader. However polished and polite the surface, we should be aware of the tensions beneath. Addison's phrase can be read merely as a list; but if we try and imagine it as a verse couplet, the juxtapositions become more suggestive and uneasy:

> We note distinctive smells, and various noises:
> Assemblies, Clubs, Tea-tables, Coffee-Houses.

(an eighteenth-century poet would have rhymed better). Putting Addison's elegant prose into couplets sharpens our sense of distinction. The balance of the lines helps us weigh the individual words. This is no longer an innocent list, but a set of juxtapositions that play off each other. The polish of the heroic couplet does not therefore smooth out difference, but challenges us to embrace variety.

There seem to be two aspects of politeness here. One emphasises smoothing away difficulties and finding a public ease of expression – the tendency (in Shaftesbury's words) to 'rub off our Corners and rough Sides'. The other is still polite, but seeks to accommodate, rather than suppress, difference (the word *Collision* needs to be emphasised here), and in doing so the hitherto private realm is opened to more varied sociable experience. In using the word 'Shaftesburian' for the former I don't want to suggest that Shaftesbury's own concept is limited to social polish. Politeness for him is part of a wider system of reason and virtue. Indeed, in thinking about the poetry of this period it helps to be aware of the term's full range. As with those other problematic concepts 'decorum' and 'correctness', it is too easy to see politeness as erasing the complex, awkward and resistant. The best verse is subtly responsive to these elements. A good example is Clarissa's speech at the beginning of the last canto of *The Rape of the Lock*, where she is urging Belinda not to withdraw from the social world (they continue her words quoted in Chapter 1):

> Oh! if to dance all night, and dress all day,
> Charm'd the small-pox, or chas'd old age away;
> Who would not scorn what huswife's cares produce,
> Or who would learn one earthly thing of use?
> To patch, nay ogle, might become a Saint,
> Nor could it sure be such a sin to paint. (V, 19–24)

These lines are interesting for their rather sharp corners: the sudden bump into the fearful *small-pox*; the risk Clarissa takes with *huswife's cares* (when she is persuading Belinda into marriage); the healing and visionary aspects of a *Saint* transposed into patching and ogling respectively. Her opening *Oh!* could be elegiac or exasperated. The edgy complexity of Clarissa's tone, her refusal to smooth over the difficult choice that faces the young lady, challenges Shaftesburian politeness, and the unease continues as she turns fully to the elegiac mode, while at the same time prising its constituent elements apart:

> But since, alas! frail beauty must decay,
> Curl'd or uncurl'd, since Locks will turn to grey,
> Since painted, or not painted, all shall fade,
> And she who scorns a man, must die a maid;
> What then remains, but well our pow'r to use,
> And keep good humour still whate'er we lose?
> And trust me, dear! good humour can prevail,
> When airs, and flights, and screams, and scolding fail. (V, 25–32)

The lyrical sadness of elegy meets the brisk inevitability of epitaph (*beauty must decay*, it reads, *all shall fade*). Clarissa's words are not cosmetic ones

(*Curl'd or uncurl'd, painted, or not painted* – such things no longer matter), and the chill wind still blows round them. But out of this bleak picture comes a sudden warming of the tone, the reassuring move from *she* to *we*, and the direct personal appeal (*trust me, dear!*). Good humour can help you through it. The lines are beautifully polished, and they have the polite aim of socialising Belinda by extricating her from Umbriel's selfish prudery; but they work by accommodating, rather than repressing, the awkward truths of adult life, and they invite Belinda to open herself to them. Clarissa avoids the smooth and compromising, and insists on making fine distinctions. Her combination of judgment and sympathy prevents the telling-off (line 32) from itself being just a *scolding*.

Pope's poetic subtlety is in part a function of his distance from the Shaftesburian aspect of politeness.[7] He doesn't work to its optimistic agenda, and as he matured as an artist, the mere smoothness of correct verse (which he had mastered so early in the *Pastorals*) became too easy. He needed that awkward rhythm of Clarissa's 'Charm'd the small-pox' (V, 20) to convey an uncomfortable idea. Social and metrical accommodations are important, but a mere easiness often oversimplifies. Comparisons can be unfair, but in this next passage we encounter a poet who is describing in verse the principles of Shaftesburian politeness. As he runs through the social, political, and moral agenda, his polished lines make it seem just a little too easy. The ease with which he handles the balanced couplets conveys a jaunty impression that becoming polite will solve all the world's problems. It is Samuel Boyse addressing James Forrester, a disciple of Shaftesbury and author of *The Polite Philosopher* (1731). He is paying tribute to Forrester's 'philosophic Mind',

> Which, like the Statues wrought by *Phidian* Art,
> Is one fair whole, complete in every Part;
> May cure the lighter Follies of the Age,
> Cool Bigot Zeal, and banish Party Rage;
> Expose Ill-nature, Pedantry o'ercome,
> Strike Affectation dead, and Scandal dumb;
> Restore fair Converse to its native Light,
> And teach Mankind with Ease to grow polite! (43–50)[8]

This is an extreme example, admittedly, but it tells us much about what some devotees of the polite took from Lord Shaftesbury's benevolist philosophy. For Shaftesbury and his followers (notably Francis Hutcheson), polite human interaction was part of a wider framework in which moral virtue is beautiful. That is because it is attuned to the harmonious System of Nature (we shall encounter this notion again in Chapter 7). In Boyse's poem the moral beauty of the philosophic mind is signified by Pheidias' classical Greek sculpture (*one fair whole*), in which all the elements are smoothly harmonised. By contrast, vice is ugly and jarring. The reader of Forrester's guide will therefore see how polite conversation can be beautiful (*fair Converse*) and can defeat all the selfish passions. Here we are in a different world from that of Pope's Clarissa, who warned Belinda against the destructive passions of the self, not by recommending moral beauty, but by urging her to face life's practical realities. In the above passage, Boyse's *Ill-nature* and *Affectation* are easily dispatched (like figures in an allegorical painting); Pope, however, knows that they lurk within everyone, and so in his poem they are the twin 'handmaids' inside Belinda's spleen (*Rape of the Lock*, IV, 25–38). Such forces are part of our humanity, Pope implies, and have to be accommodated, not dismissed from the picture.

Shaftesburian politeness is an optimistic mode, based on an assumption that human beings are by nature sociable, educable, and capable of self-restraint. The emphasis tends to be on public presentation. James Miller, in his *Of Politeness. An Epistle* (1741), defines it in those terms:

> Ask you, *What's True Politeness*, you'd reply,
> ''Tis nothing but *well-dress'd Humanity*:
> 'That fairest Offspring of the Social Mind,
> 'Nurs'd by Good-nature, by Good sense refin'd.' (11–14)

Miller's polite *Offspring* is triply fortunate – in its parent, its nurse, and its tutor. But it is they who take the moral initiative: the central figure remains an abstraction. This kind of politeness is worn with the social ease of someone who knows they are perfectly turned out. There is a static quality being invoked here, rather than a dynamic sociability that is adaptable to different companies (we might say it is the difference between the decorum of being *well-dress'd* for a special occasion and being *appropriately dressed* for any occasion). Human curiosity or adventurousness appear to be frowned on in a world where '*true Politeness* holds the *golden Mean*' (326). After satirising vice and folly as extremes of behaviour, Miller returns to politeness as the regulator that pulls things to the centre. The reader is warned

> Never from Virtue's *Middle-path* to swerve,
> But one *just Mean* thro' Life's whole Course preserve.
> With this *due Caution* constantly behave,
> And ne'er appear too *giddy* or too *grave*. (329–32)

In Miller's competent hands, the polished couplets swing between alliterative opposites ('ne'er appear too *giddy* or too *grave*', and, two lines later, 'never speak too *little* or too *long*'), while the moral centre remains an unanimated blank. There is something mean-spirited about this *Mean*, which is alien to poets like Pope, Swift, Gay, and Johnson, who value the energies of life, while being aware of the dangers they can lead us into. Miller's untroubled final lines call to mind Swift's Houyhnhnms, the race of horses whose unfallen Nature allows them to live in accordance with Shaftesbury's ideal of Reason and Virtue:

> Thus *Nature*'s, *Reason*'s, *Virtue*'s Laws obey,
> And safely go where Hertford leads the Way,
> Thus plough your Course, thus steer between the Shelves,
> *Polite* to Heav'n, your Neighbour, and Yourselves. (360–3)

Everything in the poem leads smoothly to that conclusive *Thus*. It is a polished, harmonious performance; and with a graceful gesture Miller turns an elegant compliment to Lady Hertford, one of the age's most generous patrons of poets.[9] It is the final polite ingredient of a text that perfectly embodies the quality it celebrates. Both the success and the limitation of the eighteenth-century 'polite' poem are evident. We have only to hear Pope addressing his friend, Lord Cobham, to know that there is a complex, exciting world beneath the surface of Miller's kind of politeness:

> Our depths who fathoms, or our shallows finds,
> Quick whirls, and shifting eddies, of our minds?
> Life's stream for Observation will not stay,
> It hurries all too fast to mark their way.
> In vain sedate reflections we would make,
> When half our knowledge we must snatch, not take.
> On human actions reason tho' you can,
> It may be reason, but it is not man . . . (*Epistle to Cobham* [1734], 29–36)

Confronted by the treacherous waters of the human mind, a poet's *sedate reflections* are sure to be frustrated – and how subtly Pope picks up the visual irony in *reflections*. He takes the traditional image of the poetic moralist contemplating by a gentle stream, and turns it into a scene of puzzlement and frustration. Something smooth and polished might reflect easily, but a perfect surface will only conceal the complexity of human nature.

Poets of the period recognised that politeness could be a sham performance, a concern for the veneer of manners rather than the substance of virtue;[10] but they were happy to ridicule it in one context, and exploit it in another. Poets addressing a patron had an investment in being polite, thereby showing at once both their skill in writing smooth verses, and their awareness of social decorums (this would make them an appropriate house-guest). Edward Young, who began as an aspiring protégé of Addison's, was a master of the polite mode, and the opening lines of his poem, *On the Late Queen's Death, and His Majesty's Accession to the Throne, Inscribed to Joseph Addison, Esq., Secretary to Their Excellences the Lords Justices* (1714), are a fine example of flattery by reflection. Young offers his patron the essence of Shaftesburian politeness:

> Sir, I have long, and with impatience, sought
> To ease the fulness of my grateful thought,
> My fame at once and duty to pursue,
> And please the public by respect to you.

No sharp corners here. Everyone is pleased: the poet is pleased in being able at last to relieve himself of the gratitude that has been swelling inside him; Addison himself will be pleased at the compliment; and the public will be pleased to see a man they so respect honoured in this way. Besides being able to give all this pleasure, Young has the added satisfaction of restoring his own physical equilibrium, while simultaneously performing his *duty* and increasing his own *fame*. In just four lines he has masterfully created a polite economy in which everyone gains, and no voice is dissonant. The art of pleasing is seen here in its perfection.

Fortunately Young was also skilled at the satirical mode, and in his sixth satire, 'On Women', a polite performance is wittily exposed by someone who knows its language all too well:

> Lavinia is polite, but not profane;
> To church as constant as to Drury-Lane.
> She decently, in form, pays Heaven its due,
> And makes a civil visit to her pew.
> Her lifted fan, to give a solemn air,
> Conceals her face, which passes for a prayer:
> Curtsies to curtsies, then, with grace succeed;
> Not one the fair omits, but at the Creed. (21–8)

Young brings two rituals together so that they amusingly overlap. Attending church becomes just another polished social performance, and the vocabulary of politeness shows the emptiness of her religion. In paying her weekly *civil visit*, Lavinia accords Heaven all the respect she would a Duke at an elegant assembly. Her one concession to solemnity is conveyed through her fan; and she has mastered the etiquette of curtseying, without knowing when to kneel at the creed. It is clear she has the airs and graces, without the substance.

A polite smoothing over of difficulties is also, of course, the politician's art. In his poem on politeness Samuel Boyse announced its potential to 'banish Party Rage', and this was one of the hopes of *The Spectator*, which professed to be above the political warfare of the time by declaring in the first issue 'an exact Neutrality between the Whigs and Tories'.[11] But a polite neutrality could also be a subtle political manoeuvre. As a Whig himself, Addison had been a strong supporter of Britain's active role in the European War, which was finally brought to an end by the Tory Peace of Utrecht in 1713. Towards the end of Anne's reign the conduct of the war was the big political divide. The Whigs celebrated the glorious feats of the Duke of Marlborough, while the Tories attacked the European campaign as wasteful and the Duke as corrupt. After Marlborough's victory at Blenheim (1704) Addison's own patron, the Whig Earl of Halifax, commissioned a celebratory poem from him, and in the wake of its success Addison became in 1706 an under-secretary of state in the Whig government. The poem was *The Campaign* (1705), and it is no surprise to find the tactics, imagery and vocabulary of politeness being used to convey an unproblematic reading of Marlborough's success. The following passage is a fascinating example of how a polite mode can make a political point by exploiting ease, smoothness, and harmony:

> Our god-like leader, ere the stream he past,
> The mighty scheme of all his labours cast,
> Forming the wond'rous year within his thought;
> His bosom glow'd with battles yet unfought.
> The long laborious march he first surveys,
> And joins the distant *Danube* to the *Maese* . . . (63–8)

Inside Marlborough's godlike mind a single grand conception slides effortlessly into place, eliding time and space, thought and action. The whole campaign takes shape within him (a few lines later he is 'Big with the fate of Europe'). Words like *battles*, *labours*, and *laborious* are easily subordinated to his all-embracing *scheme*. The army is absent; the difficult crossing of the Moselle is merely the passing of a *stream*; the rivers Danube and Maese are made to transcend geography. Everything in the passage is commanded into harmony and ease by Marlborough's shaping vision – which turns out to be God's also, because this polite war is part of the divine plan: '[He], pleas'd th'Almighty's orders to perform, / Rides in the whirl-wind, and directs the storm' (249–50). This is typical of the poem as a whole, which suppresses the doubts and difficulties, the diplomatic setbacks, and much of the terrible untidy suffering, in order to deliver a polished text. The battlefield becomes another polite economy with no rough edges or nasty corners. This account of the war doesn't encourage awkward questions. Well might Addison conclude in his final reassuring paragraph that there has been nothing in his poem to offend or startle us: 'Thus wou'd I fain *Britannia*'s wars rehearse, / In the smooth records of a faithful verse'. How easily the phrase 'faithful records' can be implied while being diplomatically hidden.

The Shaftesburian polite mode had an inherent tendency to move from sociable ease to smoothing away political or ethical difficulties. With a benign and harmonious Nature co-operating, its confident expansiveness also made it the appropriate mode for celebrating free trade and benevolent empire. The polite negotiations of the drawing-room could transpose themselves without difficulty into a wider world economy, in which Britain's ships mastered the oceans and helped make the world polite:

> The Time shall come, when free as Seas or Wind
> Unbounded *Thames* shall flow for all Mankind,
> Whole Nations enter with each swelling Tyde,
> And Oceans join whom they did first divide;
> Earth's distant Ends our Glory shall behold,
> And the new World launch forth to seek the Old. (395–400)

Everyone gains from the smooth flow of commerce. This is Pope, in *Windsor-Forest* (1713), using the language of Shaftesburian politeness to celebrate the Treaty of Utrecht. It is a useful optimistic mode for a pro-government spokes-man, and Pope would never be able to play that part again (by 1714 the Whigs were back in power, and were to remain so for nearly fifty years). But as well as being a polite gesture towards reconciliation, the passage may also have a hint of irony. If in his poem celebrating war, the Whig Addison had shown Marlborough commanding the elements of water and air, Pope can now harness them to welcome the benefits of a Tory peace (*free as Seas or Wind*).

By 1729 this kind of language was still in government hands, but now it was that of the pro-Walpole Whigs defending the Prime Minister's policy of avoiding a war with Spain. Edward Young was again ready to make his voice heard, and in his extended ode, *Imperium Pelagi. A Naval Lyric*, he offered the vision of how a British-led commerce, spreading through the ocean's arteries, was helping to socialise even the most disparate nations by drawing them into a polite international exchange:

> Trade between lands can polish fair,
> Make earth well worth the wise man's care;
> Call forth her forests, charm them into fleets;
> Can make one house of human race;
> Can bid the distant poles embrace;
> Hers every sun, and India India meets. (IV, 73–8)

In this development of an untrammelled polite economy, *polish* and *charm* can do a great deal. Young's optimistic vision, in which world trade has become an internationalised version of the Shaftesburian System of Nature, shows how far the language of harmonious ease could be stretched. Out of this discourse will grow the imagery of Britain's cultural hegemony as she reaches her arms gracefully around the globe and brings all people within her familial *embrace.*

We need to return to Addison at this point in order to recall that other subtler and more problematic kind of politeness in which differences are not erased, but instead challenge a polite writer to accommodate them. He is writing seven years after *The Campaign*, and his earlier poetic ease has now become the more complex social comedy of the essayist. In this passage Mr Spectator is reporting on the internationalism of London's financial centre, the Royal Exchange:

> It gives me a secret Satisfaction, and, in some measure, gratifies my Vanity, as I am an *Englishman*, to see so rich an Assembly of Country-men and Foreigners consulting together upon the private Business of Mankind, and making this Metropolis a kind of *Emporium* for the whole Earth ... I have often been pleased to hear Disputes adjusted between an Inhabitant of *Japan* and an Alderman of *London*, or to see a Subject of the *Great Mogul* entering into a League with one of the *Czar* of *Muscovy*.[12]

The richness of difference is preserved in the *Assembly* (the term reminds us that it is a polite concourse of individuals). Addison wittily implies that in this miniature world-forum all *Disputes* might be amicably resolved and *Leagues* formed through a sociable politics. But rather than elide contrasts into harmonious ease, Addison deliberately stresses the bumps and jostlings of human business, in the midst of which the self becomes more dynamic and expansive, intrigued by the variety with which it is mixing:

> I am infinitely delighted in mixing with these several Ministers of Commerce, as they are distinguished by their different Walks and different Languages: Sometimes I am justled among a Body of *Armenians*: Sometimes I am lost in a Crowd of *Jews*, and sometimes make one in a Groupe of *Dutch-men*. I am a *Dane*, *Swede*, or *French-Man* at different times ...

Mr Spectator delights in the distinctness and variety of the human *Commerce* and in his own chameleon-like shifts of identity. The phrasing catches the degrees of *mixing*: he is *justled*, then *lost*, then *one in a Groupe*, before becoming each nationality in turn. Addison's power as a prose stylist lies not in ease, but in his subtle registering of individual nuances.

I have dwelt on this passage from *Spectator* 69 because it exemplifies that other polite economy of difference and variety. For every specimen of ease and elision, eighteenth-century poetry offers an equivalent example of the resistant, varied and distinct. Addison's Exchange works by assembling contrasting individuals and allowing the opposed forces of supply and demand to find common ground. The poetry of the period offers many examples of this kind of 'Order in Variety'.[13] Whether the items are the trinkets on a dressing-table, pictures on a fan, or people in the street, the poet enjoys moving amongst them, catching their essence, and differentiating their materials, scents, colours, sounds or smells. Rather like an affable guest at an assembly, the reader is invited to enjoy a series of varied encounters, to appreciate contrasts or odd juxtapositions, and savour particular qualities, while recognising through them the full spectrum of human nature. The effect remains polite because it is a sociable mixing, and the individual ingredients work together, each contributing to the whole picture. It is in this sense that the following picture of the London street-markets is polite:

> Shall the large Mutton smoak upon your Boards?
> Such, *Newgate*'s copious Market best affords;
> Would'st thou with mighty Beef augment thy Meal?
> Seek *Leaden-hall*; Saint *James*'s sends thee Veal.
> *Thames-street* gives Cheeses; *Covent-garden* Fruits;
> *Moor-fields* old Books; and *Monmouth-street* old Suits.
> Hence may'st thou well supply the Wants of Life,
> Support thy Family, and cloath thy Wife.[14]

In this passage from John Gay's *Trivia: Or, the Art of Walking the Streets of London* (1716) the polite is pushed to a satiric limit, and is tested without being broken. As with so much in *Trivia*, the material of the London street does not appear polished, graceful or harmonious, and Shaftesburian politeness would not be at home here. But like Addison at the Royal Exchange, we readers are drawn into a series of sociable encounters. We are conscious throughout the poem of a thoughtful and friendly guide in our walk, who supplies a companionable voice that is varied and intriguing, but never over-insistent. We notice how Gay's phrasing is nicely modulated, with the opening pair of questions being posed in slightly different terms; and the diction is likewise varied (*affords*, *sends*, *gives*). In this kind of sociable politeness anything vague, predictable, fawning or bland will not do. Like a good host, the poet has to entertain and interest us, varying the tone and the topic as in good conversation. Gay's poetic voice has a strongly imprinted character, one that combines an endearing element (*Books* are one of the staple *Wants of Life*) with a teasing edge (would a wife want to be clothed from the second-hand stalls in Monmouth Street?). The reader enjoys the company. As he talks, Gay's tactic is to remain polite while steering us through the full range of London's public street-life.

Unlike his friend Gay, Jonathan Swift makes an uneasy partner. He typically relishes outraging polite expectations. The power of his satire partly lies in the way it refuses to embrace variety, and instead pushes difference into blatant incongruity. Rather than being an amused partner, Swift's reader is often manoeuvred into uncomfortable complicity (a very different thing). In 'The Lady's Dressing-Room', as Strephon explores each of the contents of Celia's boudoir, both he and we are made uneasy by the juxtapositions, as we move in a single line from the contents of her chamber-pot to the smell of mutton cutlets. Swift makes us register the offensiveness, and unlike Addison or Gay's sociable encounters, his scenario is a voyeuristic one: we feel we are spying on a very personal embarrassment. The difference can be seen in a passage paralleling the one from Gay's *Trivia* quoted above. At the end of his 'Description of a City Shower' (1710) Swift similarly collects together the specialities of London's local markets, but the result is very different:

> Now from all Parts the swelling Kennels flow,
> And bear their Trophies with them as they go:
> Filth of all Hues and Odors seem to tell
> What Street they sail'd from, by the Sight and Smell.
> They, as each Torrent drives, with rapid Force
> From *Smithfield* or St. *Pulchre*'s shape their Course,
> And in huge Confluent join'd at *Snow-Hill* Ridge,
> Fall from the *Conduit* prone to *Holborn-Bridge*.
> Sweepings from Butchers Stalls, Dung, Guts and Blood,
> Drown'd Puppies, stinking Sprats, all drench'd in Mud,
> Dead Cats and Turnep-Tops come tumbling down the Flood. (53–63)

These are not the ingredients for a meal, but the city's waste-products. The mercantile supply-lines of Gay's polite urban economy have become the sewers of hell. Throughout Swift's poem, the sudden city-shower has functioned as satire itself, de-forming, discomforting, and exposing everything in its path. As we reach the torrential ending, we realise that questions are being raised about the nature of the satirist and his role in society. Is he cleansing the urban scene or is he forcing nastiness into the open when it had better have stayed hidden? It was a problem Swift kept returning to (and which still causes debate among his critics). My own view is that he felt strongly the necessary impoliteness of satire, and wanted it to expose and sweep away, not accommodate. For him, it was the fate of the useful broomstick to become worn and dirty itself: '[he] rakes into every slut's corner of Nature, bringing hidden corruptions to the light, and raises a mighty dust where there was none before; sharing deeply all the while in the very same pollutions he pretends to sweep away.'[15] This is not just a rueful prediction of his own later career, but a characterisation of the satiric tradition of Juvenal and Rabelais, within which Swift makes a home. (Unlike Pope, Swift did not find that Horace's urbane, polite and witty voice suited him.) Swift's *Nature* is certainly not Shaftesbury's. Lurking in that dusty *slut's corner* is Hobbesian man in his state of nature, like a Yahoo in its dirt. It will always be there polluting the rest of the room.

Pope also understood the satiric role of the 'impolite', and in *The Dunciad*, his most Swiftian work, we see a series of parody assemblies in which the constituent elements are madly self-driven as they merge into an undistinguished mass. It is the inverse of a polite economy in which sociable individuals preserve their separate characters to form a varied and satisfying whole. In the poem's dunce-world 'individuality' is just quirkiness and obsession, and 'sociability' is the gang or the crowd. For the demagogue Dulness there is only the market and the masses (blatantly so), but no such thing as society.

As for Shaftesbury's harmonious System of Nature, Book Three gives us a glorious parody of it by taking us inside a theatre where a pantomime is in progress. In this fantasy world all the machinery is working smoothly, and what amounts to an alternative universe shows what will happen when refined human mechanisms fulfil their ultimate ambition:

> Thence a new world to Nature's laws unknown,
> Breaks out refulgent, with a heav'n its own:
> Another Cynthia [the moon] her new journey runs,
> And other planets circle other suns (III, 241–4)

This system, in which physical constraints are transcended, time and space brought to order, and all desires satisfied, bears the imprint of a single consciousness. Unfortunately it is that of Colley Cibber ('Son!', he is told, 'what thou seek'st is in thee! Look, and find / Each Monster meets his likeness in thy mind', III, 251–2). Rather than challenging the self, the world becomes just a reflection of it. In this benevolent system where desire elides smoothly into fulfilment (as it does for Swift's Houyhnhnms), Nature and the self embrace. We are at once reassured, however, that there is also a divine mechanic behind the spacious firmament, one '[whose] nod these worlds controuls (III, 255)'. This is the great impresario and theatre-manager, John Rich. He is the divine commander of all these forces, thinking them into action:

> Yon stars, yon suns, he rears at pleasure higher,
> Illumes their light, and sets their flames on fire.
> Immortal Rich! how calm he sits at ease
> 'Mid snows of paper, and fierce hail of pease;
> And proud his Mistress' orders to perform,
> Rides in the whirlwind, and directs the storm. (III, 259–64)

And with that last line, which is lifted whole from Addison's *The Campaign*, we are invited to recall Marlborough doing Queen Anne's bidding on the battlefields of Europe.

Pope understood the dangers of ease, and though he always admired Addison, there was something about his polite manner of mastering social forms, his ability to manipulate by pleasing, or control by easing, that Pope's rough sides found uncomfortable. The satirist in Pope perhaps thought his widely admired fellow-writer had gained power by practising too much polite system-building of his own. In his unforgettable portrait of Addison, later incorporated into *An Epistle to Dr Arbuthnot* (1735), he pictures 'Atticus' as the master of a kind of politeness that has become both too easy and too calculated – he is one 'born to write, converse, and live with ease' (196). Pope's charge is one of timid evasion. How readily could James Miller's Shaftesburian politeness ('one *just Mean* thro' Life's whole Course preserve') turn into cowardice? How sad if Addison fitted this devastating picture of a compromised politeness that is merely self-enhancing:

> Damn with faint praise, assent with civil leer,
> And without sneering, teach the rest to sneer;
> Willing to wound, and yet afraid to strike,
> Just hint a fault, and hesitate dislike;
> Alike reserv'd to blame, or to commend,
> A tim'rous foe, and a suspicious friend;
> Dreading ev'n fools, by Flatterers besieg'd,
> And so obliging, that he ne'er oblig'd;
> Like *Cato*, give his little Senate laws,
> And sit attentive to his own applause . . . (201–210)

Pope's sketch is itself, of course, a brilliant exercise in the polite. It is decorous to an extreme, being tentatively placed in the conditional subjunctive throughout ('were there One . . . ?' 'Shou'd such a man . . . ?', and the final couplet, 'Who but must laugh, if such a man there be? / Who would not weep, if *Atticus* were he!', 213–4). As Pope steers his way between the alternatives, more of Miller's phrases come to mind ('With this *due Caution* constantly behave . . .', 'Never from Virtue's *Middle-path* to swerve'). Such a path now seems weakness rather than strength. Instead of opening out the private realm into a social context, 'Atticus' has been reserved, hesitant, and suspicious, hiding his selfish motives behind a public façade. Set against him is the ampler figure of *Cato*, someone who ought to embody the Roman virtue of bringing public and private ideals courageously together, but who has been compromised here by the superimposed image of Addison holding court to his own *little Senate* at Button's coffee-house. In one brilliant stroke, Pope not only makes this point, but confronts Addison with the hero of his own tragedy, incidentally reminding him of the fact that he, Pope, had written the prologue to it. In fact, Addison's *Cato*, and some of the poems connected with it, can offer us in miniature a case study of how politeness in this period was not a single uncontested quality, but matter for debate.

In his tragic verse drama, which was the hit of the 1713 theatre season, Addison attempted to represent the ideal relationship between an individual and society. The author had designed it to be above party politics, and his hero to represent the principle of personal honour in the service of civic liberty. In the opening words of his prologue, Pope combines a Roman dignity with a sense of literature's moral power:

> To wake the soul by tender strokes of art,
> To raise the genius, and to mend the heart;
> To make mankind, in conscious virtue bold,
> Live o'er each scene, and be what they behold . . .

The lines have strength and grace, like a fine classical sculpture; the balanced phrases elegantly intersect (just varied enough to avoid monotony). The soul is tender, the virtue bold, the genius lofty, the heart whole. Difference is drawn into harmony, and humanity comes to life through the *strokes of art*. The play of wit is shaped and directed by a polite sense of a mixed human wholeness.

Addison's audience, however, were split down the middle, but not in the way we might expect. At performances of the play, Whigs and Tories tried to outdo each other in applauding the noblest speeches so as to claim the sentiments for their own party. Each wanted the lofty Cato for its spokesman. What might have been a polite occasion became divisive and a little raucous. When the play was published it was prefaced by several celebratory verses. The faithful Ambrose Philips did his best, but his opening ('The mind to virtue is by verse subdued') is one of those lines that doesn't improve with acquaintance. More ambitious and successful was Laurence Eusden, Fellow of Trinity College, Cambridge (and soon to be Poet Laureate), who painted a flattering picture of party difference and critical prejudice being subsumed into universal pleasure:

> Yet crowds the sentiments of every line
> Impartial clapped, and owned the work divine.
> Ev'n the sour critics, who malicious came,
> Eager to censure, and resolved to blame . . .
> Sullen approved, too obstinate to melt,
> And sickened with the pleasures which they felt.
> Not so the fair: their passions secret kept,
> Silent they heard, but as they heard they wept . . . (9–18)

Eusden is trying to represent the occasion as a polite one. *Cato* has drawn its whole audience together; even the *sullen* and *obstinate* are won over; sourness, malice, and censure fail; the critics are forced to conform. But while he says this, Eusden doesn't quite manage to harmonise his scene. Beyond the applauding *crowds* of the opening line both the critics and the ladies (*the fair*) are resistant to sociability: their private inner worlds create an awkward tension. The word *sickened* rather sours the *pleasures*, and the silent weeping of the ladies makes the clapping crowds seem a little hollow. This uncomfortable polite scene, offered as a tribute to Addison's lofty aims, seems to be waiting for someone to prise its various cracks apart and develop the satiric implications. Pope was only too willing to oblige. These are his verses 'On a Lady who P—st at the Tragedy of Cato':

> While maudlin Whigs deplor'd their *Cato's* Fate,
> Still with dry Eyes the Tory *Celia* sate,
> But while her Pride forbids her Tears to flow,
> The gushing Waters find a Vent below:
> Tho' secret, yet with copious Grief she mourns,
> Like twenty River-Gods with all their Urns.
> Let others screw their Hypocritick Face,
> She shews her Grief in a sincerer Place;
> There Nature reigns, and Passion void of Art,
> For that Road leads directly to the Heart.

The resistant elements of the audience described by Eusden, who were deeply moved in spite of themselves, find an emblem in Celia. Like them, she keeps her responses *secret*. In a parody of the mechanisms of sensibility, Celia's body registers the sincerity of her emotions; and the pathways of *Nature* allow her to give *Vent* to feeling that is expressed directly, without the need for *Art*. Celia's system harmonises mind and body, incorporates openness, spontaneity and ease, and is presided over by a benign *Nature*. What finer picture could be drawn of Addison's polite enterprise? He had hoped to embrace political difference and draw his competing audiences into one under the banner of a new national integrity; but for the next thirty years political, religious and cultural divisions grew, if anything, wider.

Cato was a huge critical success; but perhaps fortunately for poetry, Pope, Gay and Swift resisted Addison's charm. If the poets of the Whig cultural establishment who circled round him seemed to have an investment in polite consensus, a disenchanted breakaway group like the Tory Scriblerians relished the possibilities for guerilla warfare in the cultural undergrowth. 'Consensus' could be seen as preserving the *status quo* at the expense of political principle. By the late 1730s a new opposition poetry developed that reinfused a moral dimension into the polite, and announced its own national consensus under the banners of patriotism and virtue. Although sympathetic to the cause, Pope remained uneasy about surrendering his satiric weapons in order to write idealistic verses about the nation's destiny.[16] At the same time, another poet who resisted conformity was forwarding the 'patriot' agenda in a satire that refused to be optimistic about the future and resolutely disclaimed the language of politeness.

Consensus was never the speciality of Samuel Johnson. His resistance to the Shaftesburian art of smoothing away difficulties is everywhere seen in his friend Boswell's sparkling biography, with its many incidents of confrontation and 'talking for victory'.[17] 'He appeared to have a pleasure in contradiction', says Boswell, 'especially when any opinion whatever was delivered with an air of confidence'.[18] Yet Johnson also wrote an essay on 'The Necessity of Cultivating Politeness', in which he stressed the importance of 'complaisance'; and on one notable occasion he 'insisted that politeness was of great consequence in society', and quoted Addison's *Cato* to make his point.[19] Few men could make politeness so disconcerting. This ability to disrupt others' opinions of himself, to discompose neatly arranged systems, and to work against the grain of anything easy, smooth, flowing, and confident, was in Johnson virtually a moral requirement. It was also a particular strength of his poetry.

London: A Poem (1738), Johnson's free imitation of Juvenal's Third Satire, indicts Britain's capital as a sink of political and moral corruption, and one symptom is its invasion by the subtle conventions of politeness. Everywhere the poet looks he finds people 'lost in thoughtless Ease, and empty Show' (103), becoming tainted with French manners ('Studious to please, and ready to submit, / The supple *Gaul* was born a Parasite', 123–4). His speaker rejoices that in comparison the stout British are not polite by nature, and Johnson knows how to give his verse exactly the impetus it needs to convey the shift from French to British manners:

> In ev'ry Face a Thousand Graces shine,
> From ev'ry Tongue flows Harmony divine.
> These Arts in vain our rugged Natives try,
> Strain out with fault'ring Diffidence a Lye,
> And get a Kick for awkward Flattery. (127–31)

After a politely predictable couplet that is bland and balanced (all Grace and Harmony, shine and flow, polish and ease), the language becomes suddenly uncomfortable. Johnson's mimicry cannot resist packing the last two lines with as much thoughtful matter as possible. Two whole embarrassing scenes, from *King Lear*, say, or *Timon of Athens*, are concentrated into those ten-syllable units. The easy flow is halted; we are made to concentrate our minds and forget the music. Johnson is full of matter, when it matters. We notice, too, how the *fault'ring* and *awkward* are morally redeemed by the resistance they set up. Not to please is often truer.

In *London*, and in other of his poems, Johnson is aware of how insidiously things *flow*. Anything that does so encourages predictability, and with it, lack of active thought and moral preparedness. His poetry tends not to ingratiate itself through fluency, because he wants to keep us unsettled, ready for surprises. Johnson's world has corners that keep you alert for what might be waiting (the word 'ambush' occurs in both his major poems). Smoothness can easily inveigle itself into your confidence, then let you down:

> For Arts like these preferr'd, admir'd, carest,
> They first invade your Table, then your Breast;
> Explore your Secrets with insidious Art,
> Watch the weak Hour, and ransack all the Heart . . . (152–5)

The *Arts* of pleasing fall naturally into their ingratiating rhythm, and after the first line we are waiting for the dangerous corner. These are people who use practised flattery to move easily from public graces to personal intimacies, get the key to your heart, and then violate your personal feelings. 'How,' says Johnson, 'when Competitors like these contend, / Can surly Virtue hope to fix a Friend?' (144–5). *Virtue* in this context is *surly*: it resists the flow, refuses the soft word; but it regards true friendship as a permanent fixture, not part of a fluid sentimental economy. Johnson therefore sees a link between the *insidious Art* of pleasing and the text of sensibility – both find the private space and disturb it:

> Others with softer Smiles, and subtler Art,
> Can sap the Principles, or taint the Heart;
> With more Address a Lover's Note convey,
> Or bribe a Virgin's Innocence away.
> Well may they rise . . . (75–9)

The sentimental scenario of the love letter brings together literary and social trickery. Its fluent phrases and the lover's sexy look combine to catch the girl's fancy. In both cases it is a triumph of *Address* – of 'manner' over substance. It is 'style' that seduces her impressionable mind. Reality would simply get in the way. It follows that in the second line Johnson gives a negative turn to images of organic subjectivity: natural inner growth (*sap*) is weakness, and emotional colour is a *taint* (the girl's rising passion and her blush are signs of her gullibility). For Johnson, the language of sensibility, by becoming invasive, turns bad. The whole love scene is a *bribe* of the private feelings.

Against this responsive weakness Johnson presents the strength of fixed *Principles*, which in all his writings occupy and defend their chosen ground. They resist the blandishments of poetic fiction by 'taking a stand' on 'real' experience; not 'swayed' by imagination, but 'grounded' in judgment. These are 'the standing principles of action, and the test by which every thing proposed to the judgment is rejected or approved',[20] and they form the solid core of Johnsonian thinking about life and art (the latter always subordinate to the former). At the heart of the Johnsonian critical enterprise is therefore a judicious discrimination, a sorting of the genuine from the sham, the significant from the trivial, the lasting from the temporary. The Johnsonian critic entrusted with this task works by evoking values that are accepted as permanently valid and important, rejecting the temporary, faddish, fanciful, subjective, and whimsical. This bulwark of principle was firmly in place throughout Johnson's mature career, at a period when poetry and the novel were increasingly engaging with the subjective mechanisms of sensibility. What used to be called the 'Age of Johnson' was more truly the age of Johnsonian resistance to the tastes of his time.

To understand just what Johnson was resisting we can glance briefly at a text that shows sensibility in full performance. The beautiful Bellaria is seated at the spinet (a small harpsichord) and everything that Johnsonian 'principle' fought against, and his own poetry challenged, is about to come into play:

> See! with what blushful bend the doubting fair
> Props the rais'd *lid*—then *sits* with sparkling air,
> Tries the touch'd notes—and, hast'ning light along,
> Calls out a short complaint that speaks their wrong.
> Now back'ning,[21] aweful, nerv'd, erect, serene,
> Asserted *musick* swells her heighten'd *mien*.
> Fearless, with face oblique, her formal hand
> Flies o'er the ivory plain with stretch'd command;
> Plunges, with bold neglect, amidst the keys,
> And sweeps the sounding range with magic ease . . .
> Oh! far-felt influence of the speaking string!
> Prompt at thy call, the mounting soul takes wing;
> Waves in the gale, fore-runs th'harmonious breeze,
> And sinks, and rises, to the changeful keys.[22]

The keynote is emotional responsiveness, which is given a physical form. Bellaria and her expressive *musick* become one (the sounds seem to shift their mood according to her posture, *back'ning*, *aweful*, *nerv'd*, *erect*, *serene*). She runs the whole gamut of feeling. Both her body and the hearer's are taken over by other forces. The mechanisms of the keyboard and the mechanisms of human emotion intertwine. The notes themselves seem to be endowed with life, uttering a *complaint that speaks their wrong.* As each is pressed, the *speaking string* reaches to the hearer's soul, irresistibly mediated by the beauty of Bellaria herself ('To *see*, but kills us—and to *hear*, we die', 22). With her *stretch'd command* she controls the whole performance like Marlborough on the field of Blenheim. Metaphor is no longer subservient to 'reality', but becomes part of our perception of the scene. Here, the momentary, the suggestive, and the subjective take over; expression, look, fluency, ease, show, Grace, with lots of *Address* and *insidious Art*, are everything. What a swirl of feeling this is – a chain of touch-and-response links all together (fingers, keys, strings, notes, soul) and overrides distinctions between the tangible and intangible. Aaron Hill's poem delights in these affective conflations of body and spirit. His heart is ransacked. For him it is what being alive to experience means. This is the text of eighteenth-century sensibility.

For Johnson, such experiences need to be set against the permanent facts of human experience. The physical avenues of sensibility are, after all, only temporary, and eventually 'Time . . . shuts up all the Passages of Joy' (259–60). In *The Vanity of Human Wishes* (1749) Johnson views the enchantments of music from the perspective of old age with its deterioration of the faculties, when

> No Sounds alas would touch th'impervious Ear,
> Though dancing Mountains witness'd *Orpheus* near;
> Nor Lute nor Lyre his feeble Pow'rs attend,
> Nor sweeter Musick of a virtuous Friend . . . (269–72)

With grim humour, Johnson offers the *dancing Mountains* as an ironic back-drop to bodily decay. What is more, it is virtuous friendship that makes a *sweeter Musick* than anything instruments can create. Music, like everything else, has to come to terms with human truths.

The Vanity of Human Wishes, Johnson's reworking of Juvenal's Tenth Satire, repeatedly stops the flow of experience in its tracks. It is as if language itself must be reined in and made to concentrate on the matter in hand: 'With fatal Sweetness Elocution flows, / Impeachment stops the Speaker's pow'rful Breath' (18–19). The most persuasive orator will be silenced, and the *flow* of the first line once again becomes awkwardly blocked in the second. A spontaneous metrical elegance seems to give way when Johnson concentrates his (and our) thoughts. The poem's opening couplet, for example ('Let Observation with extensive View, / Survey Mankind from *China* to *Peru*'), betrays a breezy confidence that, as experience closes in, will soon have to look more solemnly at how 'Still drops some Joy from with'ring Life away' (306). The poem's histories of fallen greatness[23] swing from easy confidence to awkward fall; grand sweeping gestures turn the corner into uncomfortable realisations. The tide turns, and the flow is reversed. Cardinal Wolsey rides his good fortune by controlling the direction of patronage and favour. He seems immune from the current that swirls everyone else: 'Turn'd by his Nod the Stream of Honour flows, / His Smile alone Security bestows' (103–4). Without physical exertion, the mere facial gestures of politeness exert complete command. Even the warlike Charles XII is a master of the polite arts, and his conquests are expressed as emotional victories that win compliance from all around him ('O'er Love, o'er Fear, extends his wide Domain, / Unconquer'd Lord of Pleasure and of Pain', 195–6). He rules unopposed over the sensibilities of others. It is all too easy, and will come to nothing. In their inevitable fall, both men are shown the cheat; they become vulnerable to the same polite negotiations they had once controlled. Wolsey's career changes direction at a glance ('At length his Sov'reign frowns . . .', 109). Johnson cuts through the complexities of religion and politics to focus on a single facial detail. He knows how precarious politeness is, and how it depends on the subtlest of hints. Now it is Wolsey who is looking to catch the eye of others ('Where-e'er he turns he meets a Stranger's Eye', 111). With a similar twist Johnson turns the fate of the 'vanquish'd Hero' Charles XII into a polite comedy of manners ('Condemn'd a needy Supplicant to wait, / While Ladies interpose, and Slaves debate', 213–4).

As the poem moves to its last unavoidable question, the uncertain eddies of politeness give way to a current so all-commanding as to put the social game into perspective: 'Must helpless Man, in Ignorance sedate, / Roll darkling down the Torrent of his Fate?', 346–7). The turn from *sedate* to *Roll* is sudden and complete. No arts can resist death, and it is left to genuine prayer to do what it can:

> Pour forth thy Fervours for a healthful Mind,
> Obedient Passions, and a Will resign'd;
> For Love, which scarce collective Man can fill;
> For Patience sov'reign o'er transmuted Ill;
> For Faith, that panting for a happier Seat,
> Counts Death kind Nature's Signal of Retreat . . . (359–64)

Juvenal's great peroration recommends asking for 'a sound mind in a sound body' (*mens sana in corpore sano*), and such soundness is also a Johnsonian ideal. But Johnson moves the prayer towards the Christian triad of Faith, Hope, and Love,[24] but with a difference. In place of Hope, whose fanciful optimism made Johnson memorably suspicious,[25] is the more grounded and disciplined Patience, a resistant quality that for him is never far from Endurance. This can rule over *transmuted Ill*, a phrase that expresses Evil's insidious shiftiness. Surrounded by the fluid motions of politeness and sensibility, Johnson clung to things that didn't move – 'self dependent power can time defy, / As rocks resist the billows and the sky'.[26]

It is difficult to assimilate Johnson into any discussion that doesn't centre on himself. Like St Peter jangling his keys in Milton's *Lycidas*, he is a sobering presence, and he leaves reverberations after his visit. Reminding Lord Chesterfield (that embodiment of eighteenth-century politeness) of the times when 'I waited in your outward rooms, or was repulsed from your door', Johnson looked back at how 'I was overpowered, like the rest of mankind, by the enchantment of your address', only to find himself 'long wakened from that dream of hope'.[27] Impoverished writers struggled to make their way in

London's literary marketplace, and for years Johnson like many others was forced to produce 'hack' journalism to order, confronted by the alternatives of 'Toil, Envy, Want, the Garret, and the Jail' (*VHW*, 160. *Garret*, in a hit at Chesterfield, was later changed to *Patron*). To penetrate beyond the *outward rooms* of an influential or wealthy patron could change your life. But Johnson had to make his own way, and for him the polite arts became inextricably associated with those humiliating occasions of waiting on the Great.

The literary scene sketched out in these first two chapters was an intensely stimulating one; but it could also be claustrophobic. The kinds of politeness Shaftesbury and Addison promoted were indeed possible in the limited social world of early eighteenth-century London; but vicious enmities and grudges were equally likely. Johnson exposed the manoeuvrings and power-play, and these could embroil those who cultivated aloofness like Pope and Montagu. At every turn we seem to be confronted with contradictions. A print culture that was in part an anarchic playground in which pirates and hacks flourished also produced Pope's handsome *Works* (with its polite preface) and the polite *Spectator* (in its handsome folio sheets). It was a culture that Pope, Swift and Johnson thrived in, and both Curll and Addison turned to their advantage. Indeed this last paradox is symbolised by a book of poems printed in 1719. As Addison lay on his death-bed (a polite scenario in which he staged a dignified farewell to his friends), an attractive octavo volume was published in which his Latin poems were elegantly translated by a specially commissioned team of writers. The book's publisher was Edmund Curll – and, very impolitely, he had not asked Addison's permission.

Notes

1. Lawrence E. Klein, *Shaftesbury and the Culture of Politeness: Moral Discourse and Cultural Politics in Early Eighteenth-Century England* (Cambridge, 1994), p. 8.

2. Shaftesbury, *Sensus Communis: An Essay on the Freedom of Wit and Humour* (1709), I, ii.

3. See *The Tatler*, ed. Donald F. Bond, 3 vols (Oxford, 1987), I, xvi–xvii.

4. *Spectator* 1 (1 March 1711). *The Spectator*, ed. Donald F. Bond, 5 vols (Oxford, 1965), I, 4.

5. Many of the political clubs were Whig, ranging from the Hanoverian Club (which elected Lady Mary Wortley Montagu as its 'toast' in 1713) and the Patriot Club, to the notoriously republican Calves-Head Club, and various 'Mug-House' clubs which occasioned several riots and were suppressed by the Riot Act of 1715. The best known Tory clubs were the factional October Club (which turned on Harley and caused a split in the Tory party), the Saturday Club, and the Brothers. Swift was a member of the latter two before the smaller Scriblerus Club began. See Robert J. Allen, *The Clubs of Augustan London* (Cambridge, Mass., 1933).

6. Ephraim Chambers, *Cyclopaedia* (1751).

7. See Stephen Copley and David Fairer, 'An Essay on Man and the Polite Reader', in *Pope: New Contexts*, ed. David Fairer (New York etc, 1990), pp. 205–24.

8. Samuel Boyse, 'To the *Author* of the *Polite Philosopher*', printed in his *Translations and Poems*, 2nd ed., 1738. The full title of Forrester's work is *The Polite Philosopher; or, an Essay on that Art which makes a Man Happy in Himself, and Agreeable to Others* (Edinburgh, 1734).

9. The Countess of Hertford (1699–1754) included James Thomson and Richard Savage among her protégés.

10. Dr Johnson memorably remarked of Lord Chesterfield's ultra-polite *Letters to his Son* that 'they teach the morals of a whore, and the manners of a dancing-master' (*Boswell's Life of Johnson, Together with Boswell's Journal of a Tour to the Hebrides and Johnson's Diary of a Journey into North Wales*, ed. George Birkbeck Hill, rev. by L.F. Powell, 6 vols [Oxford, 1934–64], I, 266).

11. *Spectator* 1 (1 March 1711). Bond, I, 5.

12. *Spectator* 69 (19 May 1711). Bond, I, 292–3.

13. Pope, *Windsor-Forest*, 15.

14. Gay, *Trivia*, II, 543–50.

15. Swift, 'A Meditation upon a Broomstick' (1701).

16. See Christine Gerrard, *The Patriot Opposition to Walpole: Politics, Poetry, and National Myth* (Oxford, 1994), pp. 68–95.

17. *Life*, IV, 111 (May 1781).

18. *Life*, III, 24 (5 April 1776). Boswell himself was often the victim of Johnson's roughness (see III, 337–8 [2 May 1778]).

19. 'The Necessity of Cultivating Politeness', *Rambler* 98 (23 February 1751); *Life*, V, 82 (21 August 1773). 'I think myself a very polite man', he told Boswell on 30 April 1778 (*Life*, III, 337).

20. *Rambler* 7 (10 April 1750).

21. *Back'ning* means 'drawing back'.

22. Aaron Hill, 'Bellaria, at her Spinnet', in *The Works of the Late Aaron Hill, Esq.*, 4 vols. (London: Printed for the Benefit of the Family, 1753), pp. 141–5.

23. Johnson updates the Roman poet's examples. Juvenal's Sejanus becomes Sir Thomas Wolsey, and Hannibal becomes Charles XII of Sweden.

24. 1 *Corinthians*, 13:13.

25. *Rasselas* (1759) was addressed to 'Ye who listen with credulity to the whispers of fancy, and pursue with eagerness the phantoms of hope . . .' (Ch. 1).

26. Johnson's ending to Goldsmith's *The Deserted Village*, 431–2.

27. Johnson – Earl of Chesterfield, February 1755. *Life*, I, 261–3.

Chapter 3

Wit, Imagination, and Mock-Heroic

By the beginning of the eighteenth century the concept of wit seemed to be approaching its 'sell-by' date. Its mixture of mental agility and verbal dexterity, its creative playfulness with images, ingenious turns, and unexpected combinations of ideas, had long been part of any writer's equipment, and poets especially were keen to point out its links to the notion of genius – the 'spark' and 'quickness' of creative inspiration. But one age's wit is not another's, and a younger generation is eager to claim its own. Just as Shakespeare mocked (in *Love's Labour's Lost*, for example) the laboured 'scholastick' wit of the older generation and was praised for the youthful, sweet Ovidian wit of his poems, he in turn would pass from fashion. By 1647 one writer in Puritan England was disparaging the 'old fashion'd wit' of Shakespeare's clowns, which 'our nice times would obsceneness call'; and after the Restoration of Charles the Second in 1660 a new theatre audience found 'that which the World call'd Wit in *Shakespeare*'s age' to be as unfashionable as 'Doublet, Hose, and Cloak'.[1] At court it was mastery of the new 'frenchified' rapier-like verbal wit that won esteem, and a practised performer could range through stinging epigrams, shafts of satirical humour, cynical *jeux d'esprit*, or flirtatious sexual paradoxes.

After forty years the tide was turning yet again, and in the character of Mirabell in William Congreve's *The Way of the World* (1700) we find a new man who is rejecting his former rakish life and becoming attuned to the finer feelings of his partner Millamant. The pair are drawn together by valuing sincerity. Underneath their verbal teasing, true feelings and sympathies are beginning to stir. The alert interplay of wit is still there, but it now has a human truth grounding it. Congreve contrasts this with the flippancy of Mirabell's former cronies, Fainall, Petulant, and Witwoud, whose style is growing dated. Congreve wanted his audience to feel the superficiality of Witwoud's response when it is suggested that his friend Petulant is '*unsincere*' – '[W]hat if he be?' (he replies) ''Tis no matter for that, his Wit will excuse that: A Wit shou'd no more be sincere, than a Woman constant; one argues a decay of Parts, as t'other of Beauty'.[2] This kind of cynical cleverness, the wit of Rochester and Etherege, was ceasing to be acceptable, and writers were attacking the modish scepticism that went with it: 'Dissoluteness and Irreligion are made the Livery of Wit', one complained also in 1700, and in the same year another noted that nobody could be 'that self-admir'd thing, a Wit' without having 'the prevailing Humour of Scepticisim'.[3] Wit was becoming associated with free-thinking and the licentious behaviour of the Restoration court. In 1709 Lord Shaftesbury commented:

We have seen in our own time the Decline and Ruin of a false sort of Wit, which so much delighted our Ancestors . . . All humour had something of *the Quibble*. The very Language of the Court was *Punning*. But 'tis now banish'd the Town [i.e. the respectable parts of London], and all good Company . . .[4]

In face of what amounted to a crisis over the function of wit, the concept diversified. Definitions of 'true wit' and 'false wit' abounded; for some it needed regulating, for others it was itself the regulator. The philosopher Thomas Hobbes (1651) had made 'natural wit' a vital intellectual power in which judgment was brought to bear on the anarchic imagination.[5] John Dryden seems to have been torn between theory and practice, and in both he was influential. Although he defined 'wit' as 'a propriety of thoughts and words; or, in other terms, thoughts and words elegantly adapted to the subject,'[6] as a satirist in *Absalom and Achitophel* (1681) he presented it as potentially un-stable and bordering on intellectual anarchy ('Great Wits are sure to Madness near ally'd', 163). The tendency to make wit its own overseer was opposed by Addison, who in *Spectator* 62 (11 May 1711) took issue with Dryden's theory as being 'not so properly a Definition of Wit, as of good Writing in general'. Addison wanted to recognise wit's anarchic tendencies and ensure that it re-mained responsible to a separate judgment. He therefore argued on behalf of John Locke's distinction between wit as the *linking* of images ('wit lying most in the Assemblage of Ideas, and putting them together with Quickness and Variety') and judgment as *distinguishing* between them ('judgment . . . lies quite on the other Side, in separating [ideas] carefully one from another').[7] Addison remarked: 'This is, I think, the best and most philosophical Account that I have ever met with of Wit'. Shaftesbury provoked further debate by awarding wit a much freer licence as a kind of truth-test in which witty raillery could expose vice and hypocrisy by subjecting any idea to satiric mockery.[8]

All this certainly makes for a confusing mixture of functions; but mod-ern readers can take comfort in the fact that poets and critics of the early eighteenth century also found wit an enigmatic quality, whose definitions and counter-definitions tended to keep it elusive. It seemed clear to most of them that wit was an important ingredient in poetry, with one aspect being the creat-ive 'spark' of imagination (this was stressed by John Dennis, as we shall see in Chapter 7), and that a degree of directing and shaping was also required, with preferably some connection to human experience, or 'nature'. Much depended on which element was emphasised. For Matthew Prior, wit's primal imaginat-ive creativity could engender falsehood, when 'airy Seeds of casual Wit / Do some fantastic Birth beget / . . . / The happy Whimsey You pursue; / 'Till You at length believe it true,'[9] whereas for Lady Mary Wortley Montagu, the danger lay in wit's being trivial and superficial: in her view it had been rescued by Addison's ability to '[s]hew that True Wit disdains all little Art / And can at once engage, and mend the Heart'.[10] These seem to describe two extremes, yet both writers would probably have agreed that, for good or ill, wit was poetry's vital (i.e. 'living') ingredient.

Pope certainly thought so, and in his youthful *Essay on Criticism* (1711) he brought wit to centre-stage.[11] This forceful and brilliantly worked poem is in the tradition of the verse 'art of poetry' established by Horace's *Ars Poetica*, of which notable modern examples had been Boileau's *L'Art poétique* (1677), John Sheffield, Duke of Buckingham's *Essay upon Poetry* (1682), and the Earl of Roscommon's *Essay on Translated Verse* (1684). Pope drew from all of them, but instead of producing an amalgam of commonplaces, he shaped a human drama out of the material. Moving between the roles of poet and critic (which for him should go together), Pope interweaves artistic creativity with the constraints of judgment, and it is the play between them that makes the poetry so dynamic. In *An Essay on Criticism* the literary work is the focal point for all kinds of tensions in human life – its releases and frustrations; the hope, confidence and pride; the difficulties, compromises and follies; the sudden inspiration and the laborious technical detail; the problems of individual taste or prejudice, and the role of sympathy; tradition and innovation; learning, self-knowledge, and discretion; the checks and balances that even genius must face; luck, licence and daring; proportion, modesty, and self-criticism; generosity, spirit and boldness; caprice, oddness, and glitter; the perils of passing fashion and linguistic change; the constraints of patronage; the judgment of history and the demands of the market; experience and wisdom; friendship, sincerity, and honesty. It is a remarkable and only partial list, reflecting many kinds of human contradiction. For Pope, the poetic enterprise is not something technical or theoretical, but a human responsibility.

In the poem, wit is placed in this paradoxical context. It is allowed to move around and make a range of points, taking colour from different surroundings. At the opening of the poem it seems to represent creativity: '*Authors* are partial to their *Wit*, 'tis true, / But are not *Criticks* to their *Judgment* too?' (17–18); but a few lines later Pope is drawing both faculties into a human relationship:

> Some, to whom Heav'n in Wit has been profuse,
> Want as much more, to turn it to its use;
> For *Wit* and *Judgment* often are at strife,
> Tho' meant each other's Aid, like *Man* and *Wife*. (80–83)

Ideally, wit should preside over this marriage of poet and critic. Creative wit ought to be more than a spark of genius, and include artistic discretion. Two apparently opposed processes need to be combined. As in the continuing commitment of a loving marriage, he implies, wit should be sustained long enough to be responsible for its energies. Rather than flirting with incidental attractions, it is committed to the whole experience:

> In Wit, as Nature, what affects our Hearts
> Is not th'Exactness of peculiar Parts;
> 'Tis not a *Lip*, or *Eye*, we Beauty call,
> But the joint Force and full *Result* of all. (243–6)

Pope draws wit away from the momentary, and gives it more scope. In doing so he is turning away from the wit of the Restoration rake, for whom the instantaneous is exciting and the detail erotic. In the Earl of Rochester's song

'My dear Mistress' (c. 1685), for example, the poet's witty play on her '*Lip*, or *Eye*' is part of the seduction, a sign of his responsiveness to her intimate promptings:

> Melting joys about her move,
>   Killing pleasures, wounding blisses.
> She can dress her eyes in love,
>   And her lips can arm with kisses. (9–12)

In Rochester's world, wit shares the excitements of erotic initiation, but like the poet's feelings it has nowhere to go once the lyrical moment is over ('If I, by miracle, can be / This livelong minute true to thee, / 'Tis all that heaven allows').[12] Pope's concern for 'the full Result of *all*' prefers the longer commitment of a Mirabell and a Millamant.

In arguing against the rakish wit of Charles the Second's court, when '*Jilts* rul'd the State' (538) and '*Love* was all an easie Monarch's Care' (536), Pope is welcoming a new style, but he is also pleading for a more civil society, in which poetry can appeal to an expanding readership and have wider social aims. He attacks cliquish wit as a throw-back to a society where 'Parties in *Wit* attend on those of *State*, / And publick Faction doubles private Hate' (456–7). What Pope has in mind here is the kind of male, political clubbability still being celebrated by Sir Richard Blackmore in his poem, *The Kit-Cats* (1718). For Blackmore (soon to be one of Pope's 'dunces') the spectacle of 'Contending Wits' is the very thing to be celebrated:

> Their Conversation fed their mutual Fame,
> And made the Bards at Flights much higher Aim:
> For Men of Wit, do men of Wit inspire,
> And Emulation strikes out nobler Fire. (108–111)

Allowing for Blackmore's positive spin, there is something self-enclosed about this picture of mutual congratulation among the members of the Whig 'Kit-Cat' Club.

Hence the importance in *An Essay on Criticism* of a concept of nature that is no longer a Hobbesian inner drive, but a wider responsibility – a principle that can guide and humanise the poet by being a standard outside himself, yet something of which he is a part, and which animates him from within: 'In some fair Body thus th'informing Soul / With Spirits feeds, with Vigour fills the whole' (76–7). Even at the age of twenty-one Pope was wise enough to see that an impulse by itself has only a brief effect, and that someone just living in the moment will be doomed to frustration. This turns out to be Atossa's case:

> From loveless youth to unrespected age,
> No passion gratify'd except her Rage.
> So much the Fury still out-ran the Wit,
> The Pleasure miss'd her, and the Scandal hit. (*Epistle to a Lady*, 125–8)

Atossa lacks the wider understanding that true wit ought to bring. The sparks of her brilliant kinetic personality have never lasted; her selfishness has brought self-defeat; and the power of her impulses has become her impotence. In *Epistle to a Lady* (1735) the tragic wit of the mature Pope embraces her with an extended ironic narrative, which by its steadiness and precision supplies the very understanding she has lacked.

During this period wit was growing away from the earlier emphasis on word-play and intellectual ingenuity. The term was extending into the creative and imaginative areas. In the early years of the century, as the theories of Newton and Locke began to be assimilated, there was a surge of interest in how the imagination worked, and how the mind formed its ideas of the world. Just when the minute mechanisms of sense-experience were being revealed, the size of the universe was expanding as never before. Both microscope and telescope challenged the mind by introducing a vast new scale of things, and this explosion of natural phenomena coincided with a realisation that all knowledge existed for us in terms of individual atomic 'ideas' (mental images). The notion that the human mind could in a sense 'contain' the expanding universe was (as we shall see in Chapter 7) a 'sublime' idea, and one especially exciting for the poets. With its linking of intellect and vision, the concept of 'wit' found a new lease of life in this exploratory context.

In the penultimate essay of his *Spectator* series on 'The Pleasures of the Imagination' (1712), Addison celebrated the way these new 'discoveries' stretched the mind to conceive not only the vast galaxies in infinite space, but also the microscopically small 'in respect of an Animal, a hundred times less than a Mite'. He is struck by a witty thought:

> But if, after all this, we take the least Particle of these Animal Spirits, and consider its Capacity of being wrought into a World, that shall contain within those narrow Dimensions a Heaven and Earth, Stars and Planets, and every different Species of living Creature . . . we might yet carry it farther, and discover in the smallest Particle of this little World, a new inexhausted Fund of Matter, capable of being spun out into another Universe.[13]

Atoms as potential universes – the scale is dizzying. Addison acknowledges that the idea 'appears ridiculous to those who have not turned their Thoughts that way', and that for human creatures imagination cannot visualise such infinities and finally has to hand them over to the intellect. By recognising in these ironies of scale a kinship between the sublime and ridiculous, Addison takes us into the world of the eighteenth-century 'mock-heroic', a mode which became popular at exactly this time, and which exploited the confounding of large and small, the mighty and the petty.

Definitions are tricky, since *mock-heroic* was a new term within the established wider concept of *burlesque* (from the Italian *burla* – 'ridicule' or 'mockery'). *Mock-heroic* began to be used c. 1708 for poems in the higher or 'great' burlesque style, as opposed to those of the 'low' burlesque. In 1710 Edmund Smith distinguished these: 'the great burlesque is much to be preferred to the low. It is much easier to make a great thing appear little, than a little one great'.[14] The latter 'great' burlesque used a lofty style to treat little or everyday subjects for comic or satiric effect. Appropriately, what may be the earliest use of the term 'mock-heroic' is in the title of John Ozell's translation of the poem that began the trend for this kind of writing: *Boileau's Lutrin: A Mock-Heroic Poem. In Six Canto's. Render'd into English Verse* (London, 1708). Boileau's *Le Lutrin* (1674–83) created a miniature epic out of undignified materials – a quarrel over the positioning of a lectern (or singing-desk) in a church. In his dedication, Ozell notes: 'Monsieur *Boileau* calls this Poem of his, *Heroi-Comique*, Mock-Heroic; that is, a Ridiculous Action made considerable in Heroic Verse . . . where things of mean Figure and Slight Concern appear in all the Pomp and Bustle of an *Epic* Poem' (sig.*3). Through the six cantos Boileau's silly clergymen scheme and manoeuvre for power by shifting the lectern, and end up throwing books at each other. Helping to motivate the plot (beautifully tailored to fit Aristotle's three unities) is a vivid trio of alle-gorical figures, Sloth, Discord, and Piety, who manipulate the humans for their own ends. The poet himself has the final word:

> Speak *Thou* these Miracles; I've done my Part,
> And Spun out Eighteen Hundred Lines by Art.
> Nor let the Man's Attempt be rashly damn'd,
> Who from a Simple *Desk* a Second *Iliad* fram'd . . .[15]

This 'great' burlesque genre is, however, an old one. Geoffrey Chaucer's *Nun's Priest's Tale* (late 14C) had treated a fox's invasion of a chicken-run in the language of epic; Ben Jonson's *The Famous Voyage* (1616) described a heroic odyssey up the open sewer of Fleet Ditch; and Dryden's *MacFlecknoe* (1682) celebrated with comic solemnity the coronation of London's anti-poet laureate. Life in the modern city offered a tempting subject for mock-heroic treatment. In the world of epic, the hero could confront the gods, arm for battle, fight dragons, found an empire, or (like Satan in Milton's *Paradise Lost*) voyage between worlds; but as a pedestrian in the modern city he needed all his energy and skill to avoid getting his clothes muddied. As Jonathan Swift watches a rainstorm create havoc in the street, he homes in on an expensively dressed young spark not daring to leave his sedan chair:

> Box'd in a Chair the Beau impatient sits,
> While Spouts run clatt'ring o'er the Roof by Fits,
> And ever and anon with frightful Din
> The Leather sounds, he trembles from within.
> ('Description of a City Shower', 43–6)

Swift's parallel is with the Greek soldiers hiding in the wooden horse, who trembled with fear when the Trojan priest Laocoön struck it with his spear. The capture of Troy as told by Virgil is being re-enacted in the London street, and the young fashion-victim cowers from the raindrops beating on the leather roof, as if they were the drumbeats of battle. The beau's whole world seems to have shrunk. In a mock-heroic poem life may be compressed and acted out in miniature, as it is literally in 'The Puppet-Show', one of Addison's youthful Latin pieces translated into English in Curll's 1718 volume. Here the small wooden figures perform the grandest scenes dressed in purple and gold, and an 'Audacious *Hero*' (like Swift's later Lilliputian Emperor) strikes awe into the beholders: 'Within this humble Cell, this narrow Wall, / *Assemblies, Battels, Conquests, Triumphs, All* / That Human Minds can Act, or Pride survey, / On their low Stage, the *Little Nation* play'.[16] The mock-heroic can transform the humblest setting into a scene of elemental drama. In John Philips's *The Splendid Shilling* (1701) a poverty-stricken Oxford student describes his daily routine as if he were living in the world of *Paradise Lost*. The debt-collector kicking at his garret-door sounds like a summons to Hell. The repeated *thrice* is an unmistakeable epic touch:

> Horrible Monster! hated by Gods and Men,
> To my aerial Citadel ascends;
> With Vocal Heel thrice thund'ring at my Gates,
> With hideous Accent thrice he calls; I know
> The Voice ill-boding, and the solemn Sound.
> What shou'd I do? or whither turn? amaz'd,
> Confounded, to the dark Recess I fly
> Of Woodhole . . . (37–44)

The satiric method is rather different here. Where Swift's frightened beau, anxious for his powdered wig, is mocked and judged from a distance in regular heroic couplets, we enter the imaginative world of Philips's frightened man, a victim of sublime terror, and the blank verse draws us into his vision so that the final word delivers an amusing jolt to us as well. Both passages are mock-heroic, but in different ways, and the contrast marks out two traditions in the mode – and two modes of poetry that co-existed throughout the century.

The Boileau tradition was especially fruitful in the early years of the century. The French poet's idea of expanding a petty quarrel into a universal struggle created what seemed a new poetic vein. *Le Lutrin* found its first English imitator in Dr Samuel Garth, who in the six cantos of *The Dispensary* (1699) used Boileau's satiric strategy to attack the opponents of a scheme for dispensing free medicines to the poor. Garth saw how minute things could be given a mock-grandeur; but to this he added a new forensic element appropriate to his subject, revealing that his actors were not just mouthpieces, but mechanisms of sensation and feeling:

> How Matter, by the vary'd shape of Pores,
> Or [= 'Either'] Idiots frames or solemn Senators.
> Hence 'tis we wait the wond'rous Cause to find,
> How Body acts upon impassive Mind . . .
> How Touch and Harmony arise between
> Corporeal Figure, and a Form unseen,
> How quick their Faculties the Limbs fulfil,
> And act at ev'ry Summons of the Will. (I, 54–65)

A person's whole future could depend on the pores of the skin. Garth's interest in new physiological theory leads him to probe the relationship between thought and action, and raise the intractable problem of voluntary motion in the human body. Garth's people, it is suggested, are not just the victims of the poem's universal forces (Sloth, Envy, Fortune, and Discord), but are sophist-icated machines of malice and idealism. In Garth's hands, Boileau's mock-heroic ironies of great and small gain a new inner dimension from English empirical philosophy. Thanks to *The Dispensary* and to the famous poem it influenced, Pope's *The Rape of the Lock* (1712–17), the British tradition of mock-heroic was able to set epic action alongside the microcosm of the mind. It challenged the vast schemes of Fate and Chance with the intricate mechan-isms of recent theories of perception. It is in this spirit that Addison's pup-pets are given their final touches by the wood-turner ('Then adds he active Wheels and Springs unseen, / By which he artful turns the small Machine, / That moves at Pleasure by the secret Wires . . .'). Looked at in a causal way, modern discoveries were mock-heroic in implication – all vegetation depended on microscopic tubes of sap; the minutest nerve-impulses could prompt hu-man actions; and the brain cells of a single mortal had explained the physical laws of the universe. To recognise this scientific dimension of mock-heroic helps us recover its more complex potential.

In the Lockean mind, great and small, heroic and trivial, could co-exist (one idea was there no bigger than another). In light of this, poets were becoming aware of how, by combining or associating ideas, words created an infinite range of mental pictures. In his final 'Pleasures of the Imagination' paper Addison discussed how writers might exploit similes and metaphors: 'a Truth in the Understanding is as it were reflected by the Imagination; we are able to see something like Colour and Shape in a Notion, and to discover a Scheme of Thoughts traced out upon Matter'.[17] This far-reaching statement (which chal-lenged Hobbes's separation of metaphor from truth) shows how an early eighteenth-century poet could see meaning in terms of imaginative colouring and conceive an idea embodied in language. Descriptive and creative elements, in other words, might coincide. With its sportive juxtapositions of image, mock-heroic was brought to the centre of this field of poetic possibility. It achieved its effects by encouraging contrasting ideas to converge, and used its witty combinations to challenge traditional categories and linguistic decorums. In this way it was able to go beyond satirising the trivial, by raising questions about the notion of value itself. It allowed great and small to engage more unpredictably. The result could make an immediate humorous point, but also be more deeply suggestive about our human place in nature's scheme:

> Intent his Ball the eager Gamester eyes,
> His Muscles strains, and various Postures tries,
> Th'impelling Blow to strike with greater Force,
> And shape the motive Orb's projectile Course.
> If with due Strength the weighty Engine fall,
> Discharg'd obliquely, and impinge the Ball,
> It winding mounts aloft, and sings in Air;
> And wond'ring Crowds the Gamester's Skill declare. (137–44)[18]

The laws of physics are played out on the fairway, and just for once (how rare!) theory and practice joyously coincide. At the simplest level, James Arbuckle's witty description of the perfect golf-shot applies the pompous language of scientific certainty to fallible human endeavour (as all golfers know, it is just a matter of the correct relation between the *weighty Engine* and the *motive Orb*). Does this make the passage merely a satire on the pointlessness of golf?

According to much modern criticism, eighteenth-century mock-heroic satire uses the heroic to *critique the trivial*. Richmond P. Bond makes this point concisely in relation to Pope's *Rape of the Lock*, where 'the frailties of Society are treated as heroic material and made to appear more trivial by the contrast'.[19] From this viewpoint, a poet who employs the language of Homer's *Iliad* to describe a quarrel over coffee, or compares a court lady's petticoat to Achilles' shield, is exposing the emptiness of the unheroic daily scene. But this idea by itself limits mock-heroic to confirming a value-system that is already in place. Arbuckle's aim, I would suggest, is not to judge the flight of a golf-ball against the motions of the planets and decide that one of them is trivial. We don't need mock-heroic to confirm such humourless commonplaces. To locate the richer comic meaning in the passage, we can try placing it in the reassuring Newtonian world of 1721, where the heavenly spheres follow their untroubled eternal courses. How the poor human golfer aspires, only, as we soon discover, to fall short ('But when some luckless wayward Stroke descends, / Whose Force the Ball in running quickly spends, / The Foes triumph, the Club is curs'd in vain . . ., 145–7). We might pick up the comic pathos of the sportsman haplessly caught between Law and Chance, tension and freedom, the weight and measure of the physical world and the ecstasy of the spirit, that like a skylark *mounts aloft, and sings in Air*. The golfer's epiphany is all the greater for his body's distortions as it aims for perfection. Mind can master the universal laws, but matter will always lag behind. The witty juxtaposition seems to be doing more than satirising golf as a trivial pursuit.

Arbuckle was interested in the imagination, and was one of the first writers to describe the concept of imaginative sympathy or self-projection (our modern 'empathy'). In 1722 he called it 'this imagining *Faculty*, . . . A Facility of placing our selves in Circumstances different from those we are really in'.[20] The idea is crucial to eighteenth-century aesthetics, and it is useful to know that such a theory was available at this period. The imagination was a dynamic and unstable power that helped you see differently, and it was recognised to have a freedom of association that worked in unlicensed ways. Mock-heroic wit, with its vivid image-combinations, was not therefore the best way for a poet to reinforce existing categories and assert stable values. With its creative delight in finding new angles on experience, it tended to work more unpredictably, and raised questions of value by entangling great and small at the level of the 'idea' (image) in the mind.

The early eighteenth-century mind was a sensorium in which ideas associated in multiple ways, and where 'things' were freed from physical laws to have a wild life of their own, as they do within Belinda's imagination in *The Rape of the Lock* ('Here sighs a Jar, and there a Goose-pye talks; / Men prove with child as pow'rful fancy works, / And maids turn'd bottles, call aloud for corks', IV, 52–4). Here the result is grotesque and disturbing, but Pope was also aware of the positive possibilities when images combined in the mind. Something so trivial as a coffee-break could become a magic ritual:

> For lo! the board with cups and spoons is crown'd,
> The berries crackle, and the mill turns round:
> On shining Altars of *Japan* they raise
> The silver lamp, the fiery spirits blaze:
> From silver spouts the grateful liquors glide,
> And *China*'s earth receives the smoking tyde. (III, 105–10)

The *shining Altars of Japan* are lacquered ('japanned') tables, and the turning mill is the coffee grinder. But beyond this literal explanation the images register richer possibilities of scale and location. The altars and silver lamp combine to suggest a church interior with its incense-burners and exotic rituals; the last line even hints at some distant volcanic eruption. In this moment of uneasy poise just before the poem's catastrophe Pope is creating a miniature drama of fire, water, and earth. But all for the moment is ordered and contained around the coffee-table, where the tension builds before pent-up forces are released and an act of violation brings elemental chaos.

Belinda and the other characters live surrounded by trivial imported goods (tea and coffee, silk fabrics, china, perfumes, ivory combs, snuff), and studies of the poem have usefully explored these as commodities brought to the coffee-table or dressing-table thanks to an exploitative economic system, a trade in luxury items to which society awards a false value.[21] Mock-heroic in this way exposes the materialist fruits of British colonialism. Exotic trivia are certainly an important part of *The Rape of the Lock*, but it is interesting to note the degree to which they are subjectivised and subsumed into human mental experience – evidence of that explosion of phenomena that made matter's relation to mind so intriguing at this period. The materialist aspect is vital; but unless we also recognise the mechanisms that transform objects from thing to idea, we shall miss a whole dimension of Pope's art. On entering Belinda's world these physical data become part of an internal drama, and alongside the critique is a sense of wonder at how they impinge on thought and feeling. Coffee and brocaded silk join together at the vital moment to arouse the Baron's thoughts and prompt him to cut the lock. Caught in Belinda's erotic ambience (the sylphs), the two trivial items convey the imaginative *frisson* of the moment:

> Strait hover round the fair her airy band;
> Some, as she sipp'd, the fuming liquor fann'd,
> Some o'er her lap their careful plumes display'd,
> Trembling, and conscious of the rich brocade.
> Coffee, (which makes the politician wise,
> And see thro' all things with his half-shut eyes)
> Sent up in vapours to the Baron's brain
> New stratagems . . . (III,113–20)

The sylphs register our (and the Baron's) consciousness of the tactile silk, tantalisingly out of reach. The mind-altering drug does the rest.

Several of the supporting objects in *The Rape of the Lock* soon starred in mock-heroic poems of their own, including Gay's *The Fan* (1713), Francis Chute's *The Petticoat* (1716), Arbuckle's *Snuff* (1719), and Francis Hauksbee's *The Patch* (1724), and to these we might add the anonymous *Rape of the Smock* (1717). In these poems the trivial object is raised in importance so that it transcends mere substance and is awarded a fetishised significance in the games of love. The 'spacious Canopy' of the *petticoat* safeguards a woman's reputation and (by hiding any swelling) protects her from scandal. The distraught Chloe, who has discovered a pimple on her face, is rescued when the goddess Juno sends down a *patch* to cover her 'Shame'. In order to save her honour Cælia bargains for the return of her stolen *smock* by offering to sleep with the thief and reclaim the compromising garment ('Yet, tho' 'till now, my Heart was like a Rock, / I'll sooner yield, than you shall keep the *Smock*'). In Gay's *The Fan*, the object whose invention, construction and decoration we witness becomes the vehicle for an expresive rhetoric with which a woman can 'touch the Heart' and 'humour each Expression' more effectively than any orator. As part of the burlesque equation, physical items like these play an active part in the human drama, and are simultaneously both object and idea. An extreme example of this is the way Arbuckle traces on the tobacco-leaf (before its transformation into snuff) an organic fusion of body and soul:

> What curious Lines compos'd of many a Thread,
> From the great Stem in vagrant Branches spread
> The secret Conduits where the fragrant Soul
> Transfus'd, perspires and vegetates the whole,
> Which in their Texture, and their Use contain
> An apt Resemblance of the human Brain . . . (565–70)[22]

With remarkable wit, Arbuckle superimposes the two living organisms (brain and leaf) so that they become a single idea, and traces how the *fragrant Soul* spreads through each. Snuff carries the essence of life to its inevitable end ('at last they must / Be bury'd there, and Dust return to Dust', 571–2). With a final turn, however, the poet imagines himself buried in the tobacco-field, and his body and soul becoming part of the natural cycle:

> There as it moulders, shall it kindly feed,
> And with its Substance cloath the embryo Seed.
> The earthly Parts shall to the Stem adhere,
> The rest exhale in aromatick Air.
> So fragrant shall my Mem'ry be . . . (635–9)

In Arbuckle's skilful hands, the creative juxtapositions of mock-heroic have been pushed to such an extreme that they fuse into a single witty idea. What might be comically incongruous has somehow been naturalised. Indeed, the concept of an organic life-force moves Arbuckle's poem into the world of the georgic (see Chapter 5), a mode that will develop a new register for mock-heroic language and use it to express the interconnectedness of the human and natural worlds.

We have seen how the British tradition of mock-heroic exploited the image or 'idea' with an awareness of its role in mental perception, and how this opened up imaginative possibilities. The association of ideas gave an extra dimension to wit's playful doubleness. In individual poems, often differing widely in effect, two opposing items fruitfully converge. This can range from a localised verbal pun (generally frowned upon as what Addison called 'false wit') to the large-scale ironies achieved when one poetic mode is superimposed on another. It is most obviously at play in techniques of comparison, ranging from explicit simile (x is like y) to concealed metaphor. In the final section of this chapter I want to look at a few examples of this chameleon quality at work, and locate the meeting-point of imaginative force and verbal detail.

In the first example, I would suggest, wit is present in different aspects of the artistry, linking the word-play to the wider theme of doubleness. It is the opening quatrain of a sixteen-line poem (first printed in 1703) by Anne Finch, Countess of Winchilsea, called simply 'A Sigh':

> Gentle Air, thou Breath of Lovers,
>   Vapour from a secret Fire,
> Which by Thee it self discovers,
>   Ere yet daring to Aspire.

There is wit in the idea that a lover's sigh is both a soft movement of air and the exhalation of something burning inside. It is both calmness and passion, air and fire (the refined elements of life itself). The rhyme-words of lines 3 and 4 wittily play on the paradox of the moment: *discovers* also means 'reveals', so that the sigh is both a revealing of the lover's passion, but also perhaps the moment when the lover, at this expressive instant, discovers it for the first time – a revelation to both of them? *Aspire* also has the concealed meaning of the Latin *adspiro* ('breathe upon'), which echoes the opening line, suggesting what unspoken hopes hang upon a single breath. In a poem about secret communication (the idea is an oxymoron) these hidden meanings discover themselves in a way that is locally witty but also with an unforced naturalness, thanks to Finch's artistic intelligence embracing the whole. It is eighteenth-century wit at its most refined. Compared with this, Rochester's baroque extravagance is like a busy Rubens painting ('Melting joys about her move, / Killing pleasures, wounding blisses'). Finch's lines avoid gestures and prefer to contain – and sustain – the moment of love.

In the second passage, wit has a very different effect. Again there is doubleness, but this time the gap is a blatant one, and the ironies therefore bolder. In his 'Elegy, To an Old Beauty' (published posthumously in 1722), Thomas Parnell recommends an older woman to withdraw from the youthful social whirl and become a dignified observer rather than an increasingly desperate participant. In the final lines he makes his point through a satiric parable. A 'wise *Athenian*' is walking through a public fair ('Gimp' is a decorative trimming):

> Unmov'd by Tongues and Sights, he walk'd the place,
> Thro' Tape, Toys, Tinsel, Gimp, Perfume, and Lace;
> Then bends from *Mars*'s Hill his awful Eyes,
> And *What a World I never want?* he cries;
> But cries unheard: For *Folly* will be free.
> So parts the buzzing gaudy Crowd, and He:
> As careless he for them, as they for him;
> He wrapt in *Wisdom*, and they whirl'd by *Whim*. (61–8)

Part of the wit of this passage is the way the two worlds refuse to join together: they converge uncomfortably, but then separate, each a satire on the other. The poem appears to be heading towards a philosophical summing-up from the perspective of the 'wise *Athenian*', and line 62 is spat out like the famous 'puffs, powders, patches' of Pope's *Rape of the Lock*. The figure of Wisdom seems to have both the moral high ground and the commanding male perspective from which to survey the trivial scene ('bends from *Mars*'s Hill his awful Eyes'). But before he can point the moral his speech is stopped in its tracks ('But cries unheard'), and the lines then pivot round, with one alliterative slogan capping the other ('*Folly* will be free'). The 'buzzing gaudy Crowd' go their way, and he his. The chiasmus of line 67 ('he for them, as they for him' – abc-cba) neatly catches their antipathy while drawing them into a single equation, and *Wisdom* is forced to pair up with *Whim* in the outrageous final line. The two of them weigh equally, one in each hand – philosophical self-absorption and the social whirl. The poem's wit is wiser than either. The parable that Parnell offers his Old Beauty turns out not to be very comforting.

In the third passage, wit itself takes revenge. As elsewhere in Jonathan Swift's poetry the wit has a sharp edge to it (bitter, but sometimes part of a refreshing cocktail). In 'The Lady's Dressing Room' (1732) Strephon has been peering into things he shouldn't, exploring with horrified fascination all the contents of Celia's boudoir (from greasy towels to her chamber-pot):

> But Vengeance, Goddess never sleeping
> Soon punish'd *Strephon* for his Peeping;
> His foul Imagination links
> Each Dame he sees with all her Stinks:
> And, if unsav'ry Odours fly,
> Conceives a Lady standing by:
> All Women his Description fits,
> And both Idea's jump like Wits:
> By vicious Fancy coupled fast,
> And still appearing in Contrast. (117–26)

Here, wit's capacity to combine dissimilar things is linked to the workings of imagination (*Fancy*). Swift is playing with Locke's theory of association, by which two ideas (however remote) can become associated in the mind if they are perceived simultaneously. Whether the subject wishes it or not, one image will in future recall the other. In Strephon's consciousness the beauty and the stench will always be *coupled fast*, and in that final rhyme the irony of wit itself is captured – the intimacy of opposites. As we look back along Swift's rhymes, each pair appears to consist of opposed or jarring ideas: *sleeping/ Peeping*, *links/Stinks*, *fly/standing by*, *fits/Wits* (the paradox of wit's appropriateness). Once again, along with wit comes irony, working in the gap between the ideas. It inhabits the space across which wit playfully leaps.

A final example is the powerful ending of Lady Mary Wortley Montagu's 'Epistle to Lord Bathurst' (?1725), addressed to a man who had briefly been her lover. The poem wittily inverts the gender-stereotyping of traditional satires on women by picturing him as a coquettish and whimsical creature forever shifting in his fancies. This comes to a climax when Montagu compares his affections with the desert ('the sands of Afric's burning plains') – empty, arid, formless, and shifting with every wind:

> The lightest leaf can leave its figure there;
> The strongest form is scatter'd by the air.
> So yielding the warm temper of your mind,
> So touch'd by every eye, so tost by wind (61–4)

In the first couplet the paradox is set out. The *lightest* can succeed where the *strongest* fails. We would normally associate a *leaf* with being *scatter'd by the air*, but here it is the *strongest form* that is dispersed, while the leaf has power to leave its mark (with an appropriate echo, *leave* still bears the imprint of *leaf* – the smallest things register here). In these four lines Montagu is wittily offering a moral critique of the Lockean mind (a blank sheet on which the minutest sense impressions register). The empirical Bathurst is sensitive to the slightest impression of his senses, but any mere *form* (honour, truth, integrity, faith) simply does not register. A flickering eyelash will devastate him, but a promise be forgotten.

Montagu then turns to herself, offering her own nature as the opposite of his ('Oh! how unlike has heav'n my soul design'd!', 65), and she ends the poem with this very different symbolic landscape:

> So num'rous herds are driven o'er the rock;
> No print is left of all the passing flock:
> So sings the wind around the solid stone:
> So vainly beat the waves with fruitless moan.
> Tedious the toil, and great the workman's care,
> Who dare attempt to fix impressions there:
> But should some swain more skillfull than the rest,
> Engrave his name upon this marble breast,
> Not rolling ages cou'd deface that name;
> Through all the storms of life 'tis still the same:
> Tho' length of years with moss may shade the ground,
> Deep, tho' unseen, remains the secret wound. (70–81)

Nothing could be further from the Lockean sensorium than this unyielding rocky landscape where no mere *impressions* will take. In place of Bathurst's mock-heroic doubleness and shifting sensibility stands substance and form: the resistant rock of principle in which a single strong feeling is deeply engraved.

With a witty turn, Bathurst and all the others become *the passing flock*, and those hackneyed images of centuries of frustrated love, the *wind* and *waves*, sing and moan in vain. No lyric moment here. With a partly rueful, partly proud boast, she sees herself as a relic of the past, a piece of inscribed marble hidden by moss, like a remnant of a ruined temple. Unlike Bathurst's incongruous leaf settling on the desert sand, her landscape is at least one where things can live and grow, however hidden the life is. Even the carved stone has a *secret wound*.

These four extracts show something of the range of verbal wit in the poetry of the period, from word-play and paradoxes, to more extended ironies. Each of them works in some way between different viewpoints that either clash or play together, whether it is Finch's secret communicativeness of spirit and body, or Parnell's glimpse of the stubbornness of wisdom and folly, Swift's unsettling association of beauty and filth, or Montagu's clash between the fleeting and the enduring. But as we have seen, wit-as-imagination is also present in its wider capacity to complicate any single viewpoint by shifting the angle of vision and playing across that gap we call irony.

Of the four passages, perhaps the term 'wit' comes under some strain in the last. At the end of Montagu's poem, what has begun as a satiric juxtaposition grows into something more expressive. Wit plays between the two landscapes of sand and rock, but the poem becomes interested in exploring and questioning the second landscape, and something like a 'self' begins to emerge. The subtlety of effect can no longer quite be contained by wit's interplay. Meanings unfold and the nuances work more organically. Faced with what we might call Montagu's 'contemplative' quality, the term 'wit' comes to seem restrictive, and we start casting round for other concepts such as imagination or sensibility to describe what is going on in the poem.

There is a sign here of why wit eventually lost the centrality it still had when Pope wrote his *Essay on Criticism*. It was having to stretch too far, and modes were developing for which the word 'wit' seemed inadequate. Literary terms are useful only for as long as they help us understand the mechanisms and effects of writing. By the time Pope died in 1744 the idea of the 'spark' of wit could be seen, even by a fervent admirer of his, as too limited. In *An Essay on Satire: Occasion'd by the Death of Mr Pope* (1745) John Brown argued that Pope's work deserved a more exalted language for the creative act:

> Fantastick wit shoots momentary fires
> And like a meteor, while we gaze, expires . . .
> But genius, fir'd by truth's eternal ray,
> Burns clear and constant, like the source of day:
> Like this, its beam prolifick and refin'd
> Feeds, warms, inspirits, and exalts the mind . . . (473–80)

Brown finds *wit* too limiting a word for Pope's achievement, since for him it can no longer subsume (as it once did) the notion of *genius*. The critic, who needs to distinguish the terms, acknowledges Pope's mastery of wit's pyrotechnics, but now sees this as a secondary quality – 'matchless wit but wins the second praise' (487). It is on a similar basis that Joseph Warton in his *Essay on Pope* (1756) would demote the poet to the second class (of those who 'possessed the true poetical genius, in a more moderate degree'). In Warton's scale, 'men of wit, of elegant taste, and lively fancy' only rank third. Another writer confirms how far wit was slipping out of favour by mid-century, and suggests one more factor in its decline:

> Why must each rhimer be a wit?
> Why mark'd with that loath'd epithet?
> For envy, hatred, scorn, or fear,
> To wit, you know, are often near.
> Good-natur'd wit, polite, refin'd,
> Which seeks to please, not pain the mind,
> How rare to find! (155–61)

This is an anonymous 'Young Lady' writing in 1748.[23] Her complaint centres on the fact that wit has become associated with the aggressive aspects of human nature – the preserve of the satirist. Instead, she wishes to encourage the kind of *polite* poetry based on human *good nature*, on giving pleasure rather than pain. In doing so, she is voicing the emergent sensibility of mid-century, which places itself within the sociable discourse of 'politeness'. It is perhaps no coincidence that this concept appears to have grown in stature as 'wit' slipped from favour.

Notes

1. *The Shakespeare Allusion-Book: A Collection of Allusions to Shakespeare from 1591–1700*, ed. J. Monro, rev. E.K. Chambers (1952), I, 46; I, 511; II, 138. For the shifts in Shakespeare's reputation during the seventeenth century, see *Shakespeare: The Critical Heritage*, ed. Brian Vickers, 6 vols (London, 1974–81), I, 1–18.

2. Congreve, *The Way of the World*, I. i. 371–3.

3. These writers were James Buerdsell and Samuel Parker. They are quoted by Edward Niles Hooker, 'Pope on Wit: The *Essay on Criticism*', in *Eighteenth-Century Literature: Modern Essays in Criticism*, ed. James L. Clifford (London, etc., 1959), pp. 42–61; p. 48.

4. Earl of Shaftesbury, *Sensus Communis: An Essay on the Freedom of Wit and Humour* (1709), I. ii.

5. Thomas Hobbes, *Leviathan*, I. viii.

6. Preface to *The State of Innocence* (1677).

7. John Locke, *An Essay Concerning Human Understanding* (1689), II. xi. 2.

8. Shaftesbury called for '[a] Freedom of Raillery, a Liberty in decent Language to question every thing, and an Allowance of unravelling or refuting any Argument, without offence to the Arguer' (*Sensus Communis*, I. iv).

9. Matthew Prior, *Alma: or, The Progress of the Mind* (3 cantos, 1718), III, 31–6.

10. Lady Mary Wortley Montagu, 'Her Palace placed . . .' (known as 'The Court of Dulness'), *Essays and Poems*, ed. Robert Halsband and Isobel Grundy (Oxford, 1977), p. 248.

11. E.N. Hooker's classic essay (see note 3 above) discusses Pope's poem in the context of the debates on 'wit'. Another significant reading, in terms of a principled but flexible human 'judgment', is David B. Morris, 'Civilized Reading: The Act of Judgment in *An Essay on Criticism*', in *The Art of Alexander Pope*, ed. Howard Erskine-Hill and Anne Smith (London, 1979), pp. 15–39.

12. Rochester, 'Love and Life', 13–15.

13. *Spectator* 420 (2 July 1712). Bond, III, 575–6.

14. Quoted by Johnson, *Lives of the Poets*, ed. George Birkbeck Hill, I, 322–5. In 1712 Addison informed the readers of *The Spectator*: 'Burlesque is therefore of two kinds, the first represents mean Persons in the Accoutrements of Heroes, the other describes great Persons acting and speaking like the basest among the People' (*Spectator* 249 [15 December 1711]. Bond, II, 467).

15. *Boileau's Lutrin: A Mock-Heroic Poem*, tr. John Ozell (1708), p. 120.

16. 'Machinæ Gesticulantes', translated as 'The Puppet-Show', *Poems on Several Occasions. With a Dissertation upon the Roman Poets; by Mr. Addison* (London: E. Curll, 1719 [actually 1718]), p. 69. The English translations of Addison's eight Latin poems were by Thomas Newcomb, George Sewell, and Nicholas Amhurst.

17. *Spectator* 421 (3 July 1712). Bond, III, 577.

18. James Arbuckle, *Glotta. A Poem, humbly ascribed to the Right Honourable the Marquess of Carnarvon* (Glasgow, 1721), p. 11.

19. Richmond P. Bond, *English Burlesque Poetry*. Harvard Studies in English VI (Cambridge, Mass., 1932), p. 14.

20. *Dublin Journal* (1722). See Walter Jackson Bate, 'The Sympathetic Imagination in Eighteenth-Century English Criticism', *ELH* 12 (1945), 144–64.

21. See Laura Brown, *Alexander Pope* (Oxford, 1985), pp. 8–28. Another viewpoint on mercantilism in the poetry of the period is Louis A. Landa, 'Of Silkworms and Farthingales and the Will of God', in *Studies in the Eighteenth Century*, II, ed. R.F. Brissenden (Canberra, 1973), pp. 259–77.

22. James Arbuckle, *Snuff: a Poem* (Edinburgh: James McEuen and Company, 1719), p. 28.

23. 'A Mirror for Detractors. Address'd to a Friend, By a Young Lady', printed in Samuel Bowden's *Poems on Various Subjects* (Bath, 1754), pp. 325–32 (p. 332). The poem is dated '1748'.

Chapter 4

The Verse Letter

The eighteenth-century verse letter brings into play many of the ideas raised in the previous chapters. No poetic form is more obviously 'between manuscript and print' in the ways it entangles private and public, allowing a glimpse of the handwritten letter through the formalities of a printed page. As a sociable communication it is expected to accommodate both wit and politeness – to entertain and surprise without forgetting the presence of an addressee and the decorums that involves. As we shall see, the category of 'verse letter' takes in a wide range of poetry, from formal 'epistles' to other kinds of direct address. In 1762 a popular poetry-guide informed its readers:

> This species of writing, if we are permitted to lay down rules from the examples of our best poets, admits of great latitude . . . It is suitable to every subject; for as the Epistle takes [the] place of discourse, and is intended as a sort of distant conversation, all the affairs of life and researches into nature may be introduced.

The verse letter is not defined by topic, but by how it communicates. The image of *distant conversation* tells us this is not simply one individual addressing another, but people conversing. The speaking voice is part of a social exchange in which the writer *introduces* subjects for discussion. The guide also stressed the element of relaxed informality in this polite form:

> the true character of the Epistle is taste and elegance; nothing therefore should be forced or unnatural, laboured, or affected, but every part of the composition breathe an easy, polite, and unconstrained freedom.[1]

The verse letter negotiates between the constraints of politeness and an idea of *unconstrained freedom*. This seems a contradiction, but it expresses the way the form develops strategies for working under cover – taking liberties politely, and speaking in two directions simultaneously. While in its sentiments the letter might be advocating honesty, sincerity and integrity, the poem could be interesting for the ways in which it performs intimacy, polishes spontaneity, and mediates directness. In this genre the potential for irony is considerable and available for satiric use.

In looking at examples of the verse letter it is helpful to differentiate the 'poet' from the 'voice' or personality the poet projects, and the 'reader' (us) from the 'addressee' (the letter's supposed recipient). The gaps that are possible between each of these create the distance across which conversation can take place. Thinking about the nature of the various relationships (between poet and addressee, say, or between the voice and the reader) can give a critical point of entry into a poem. The following lines from Edward Young to his new and extremely rich patron, George Dodington, set out the relationship of poet and addressee almost in contractual terms:

> And now a poet's gratitude you see;
> Grant him two favours, and he'll ask for three.
> For whose the present glory, or the gain?
> You give protection, I a worthless strain.
> You love and feel the poet's sacred flame,
> And know the basis of a solid fame;
> Though prone to like, yet cautious to commend,
> You read with all the malice of a friend . . . (3–10)[2]

Young is performing the role of a protégé flattering and seeking favour from his patron, and part of his flattery is the way he grants his addressee the intelligence to understand their respective duties. Young's tactic is to create an 'honest' speaking-voice that can distance itself from the mercenary poet – and even defame him (*a poet's gratitude you see* . . .). By line 6 this voice is confiding in Dodington about its shortcomings (*a worthless strain*). But because this voice has the freedom to speak sincerely, the praise when it comes (lines 7–8) is projected as the voice's truth, rather than the poet's flattery. At the end, with the word *friend* the poet is able to reclaim the voice as his, and accept his patron's judgment on his work. In doing so he boosts himself by revealing how Dodington takes an interest in correcting his verses (here *the malice of a friend* is preferable to a distanced politeness). But Young is also directing the passage at his readers, impressing us with his verbal and social skills. We admire the way frankness transcends politeness, praise disowns flattery, and genuine friendship underpins the poet-patron relationship. Young has intelligently played his own variations on a hackneyed and mercenary theme. Under the great Dodington's *protection*, and having established his credentials with us, Young can now proceed to satirise the follies of London society.

The Universal Passion (1725–7), from which the passage comes, was a great success with the literary public and showed that Georgian London could be responsive to the style and satiric tactics of Horace (65–8 BC). It could even be said that the Roman writer contributes to the epistle's conversation by being a model for its civilised and lively intercourse. Most readers of the day would sense Horace's familiar presence. His satires and epistles were thought to embody the essence of genial conversation. The Horatian tone was flexible, sprightly, and engaging; it was a voice that didn't hector or preach, but could alternate the sweet and the spicy; the wit made its point sharply and moved on; the seriousness never became solemn; the manner was easy and informal, while being shrewd and intelligent; above all the Horatian personality was principled, moral and reliable, but also capable of a humorous self-deprecation. And overarching all these dynamic yet balanced ideas, was the notion of balance itself, Horace's *modus in rebus* ('measure in all things' – not compromise, but rather a sense of weighed commitment among extremes). Who would not want such an amiable and enlivening presence in any conversation?

Pope, for one, found Horace a useful ally in the 1730s when he felt the need to take stock of his recent career as a satirist and defend himself from critical attack. In 1733, in the first of what became a series of 'Imitations of Horace', he adapted the Latin poet's *Satire II.1* to his own purposes. Addressed to a lawyer friend (in Pope's case, William Fortescue), the letter here becomes literally a conversation, with the poet using Fortescue (as Horace does his friend Trebatius) to help forward his argument about the role of the satirist in society. As a well-meaning but nervous legal consultant, his worried interruptions about the dangers of libelling the great, and his advice to stick to safe subjects that will not arouse the public's hostility, allow the poet to project several voices in response: disingenuousness, wounded innocence, honest frankness, justified pride, grand idealism, stubborn independence, touchiness, indignation, defiance, peace-loving impartiality – an unstable mixture.

All this might look like inconsistency and opportunism, were it not for the thread of conviviality that runs through Pope's poem. This strand is most obviously represented by the 'best Companions' who share the poet's leisure hours (121–38), and by the presence of the addressee Fortescue; but in the 1730s it was also there in the amicable proximity of Horace's text, printed on the facing page and showing the reader at every page-turn that the poet was being guided and supported by the civilised Augustan voice. A reader can see how ingeniously Pope has used his Latin original to 'hit' his own case, and in particular how he identifies himself not only with Horace's self-portrait, but also with the poem's idealised picture of Lucilius the satirist (Lucilius 'was kind only to virtue and her friends', Horace says). Pope claims this as his own principle:

> Hear this, and tremble! you, who 'scape the Laws.
> Yes, while I live, no rich or noble knave
> Shall walk the World, in credit, to his grave.
> TO VIRTUE ONLY and HER FRIENDS, A FRIEND . . . (118–21)

Placed in capitals, it is the loudest statement in the poem. Such self-assured egotism could make the reader uneasy; but it is lent grace and decorum by appearing alongside Horace's lines about Lucilius. Just at the moment when Pope seems to be shouting, he is most clearly part of a conversation between texts.

In Pope's hands the verse letter tends to be radial in nature, reaching outwards from a set of core values shared by poet and addressee to survey the fools and knaves who are busy upsetting the world and frustrating themselves. Rather than self-contained statements, it prefers to offer 'Wide and more wide, th'o'erflowings of the mind'.[3] In *Epistles to Several Persons* (1731–5) and *An Essay on Man* (1733–4) Pope's strategy is to present the particular addressee as a friend in whom varied or even opposed qualities achieve a satisfying mix. In them, unlike his satiric victims, diverse energies have happily combined to form a person of integrity and humanity (for Pope, integrity is always a compound, never an isolated quality). In *Epistle to a Lady*, after all the self-defeating female excesses, Martha Blount is celebrated as a well mixed cocktail ('Reserve with Frankness, Art with Truth ally'd, / Courage with Softness, Modesty with Pride, / Fix'd Principles, with Fancy ever new; / Shakes all together, and produces—You', 277–80). The poet implies that she is the person who understands him best, and best reflects his art. In Pope's verse letters the results of such mixing are living examples of the 'gen'rous Converse' that was his ideal in literary criticism.[4] The human character at its finest is for him a conversation between the passions, and he usually makes his addressee the person with whom the reader would most happily sit down and discuss the poem. Turning to Lord Bolingbroke near the close of *An Essay on Man* ('Come then, my Friend, my Genius . . . !', IV.373), he presents his friend as embodying the work's ideal mix of principles. He is the person in whom they live and humanly converse:

> Teach me, like thee, in various nature wise,
> To fall with dignity, with temper rise;
> Form'd by thy converse, happily to steer
> From grave to gay, from lively to severe;
> Correct with spirit, eloquent with ease,
> Intent to reason, or polite to please. (IV, 377–82)

Praising Bolingbroke, Pope finds himself defining a successful Horatian verse letter.

If all this sounds very reasonable and good-humoured, we have to remember that it was under the aegis of Horace that Pope produced some of his most scathing satire – and it was *Satire II.1* that led him in this direction. Perhaps he should have seen the danger in identifying himself so blatantly with a classical ideal. It gave ammunition to his enemies, and with *Satire II.1* he made two influential ones. From his Horatian vantage-point he released satiric arrows of his own – at the body and mind of Lady Mary Wortley Montagu ('From furious *Sappho* scarce a milder Fate, / P-x'd by her Love, or libell'd by her Hate', 83–4) and at her friend Lord Hervey as an effeminate rhymester ('The Lines are weak, another's pleas'd to say, / Lord *Fanny* spins a thousand such a Day', 5–6). These were opportunistic shots rather than integrated portraits, and they depended on the poet's classical authority for their full dismissive effect. For Montagu and Hervey, however, to be glanced at gratuitously in a snatch of nasty gossip, as if Horace himself were speaking, was not only an outrage against them, but a belittling of the great Roman writer. In replying to Pope, Montagu (with Hervey's encouragement[5]) was determined to turn his Horatian weapon against him, and twist it in the process. As in her other attacks, she understands him so intimately and is such an intelligent reader of his work that she knows exactly where to strike, and what tactics will wound him artistically and emotionally. *Verses Address'd to the Imitator of Horace. By a Lady* (published anonymously in 1733, three weeks after Pope's poem) was the most coruscating and effective personal attack Pope faced in his lifetime.[6] In its structure and tone it is a verse letter of very different character from his, and one that gives the epistle form a new intense focus.

From the moment the poem begins we know Montagu has her eyes on the physical object. She looks at Pope's parallel text not as a symbol of friendly collaboration with Horace, but as a parody. She is determined to prise the two of them apart and turn the Roman poet into Pope's harshest judge:

> In two large Columns on thy motly Page,
> Where *Roman* Wit is stripe'd with *English* Rage;
> Where Ribaldry to Satire makes pretence;
> And modern Scandal rolls with ancient Sense:
> Whilst on one side we see how *Horace* thought;
> And on the other, how he never wrote . . . (1–6)

The printed page shows contrasting stripes, not communing souls. If Pope's epistles create out of disparate materials an integrated core of values reinforced by friendship and the Horatian spirit, Montagu's verse letter offers a reverse image of mere incongruity: Pope's art is neither polite nor witty, but relies on angry incidental gestures and jokey gossip (*Ribaldry* and *Scandal*), whereas Horace shows how satire can draw *Wit* and *Sense* together (here she is reminding Pope of the ideals of his youthful *Essay on Criticism*). Montagu knows how much Pope has always invested in judging the human being and the work of art together ('For each *Ill Author* is as bad a *Friend*', he had said)[7], and so her tactic is to picture Pope's body and mind as expressing the failures of his art ('Thine is just such an Image of *his* Pen, / As thou thy self art of the Sons of Men: / Where our own Species in Burlesque we trace', 11–13). She also knows that Pope values a sharp focus and an economy of the passions, so she addresses him as someone so caught up in rage and hate that every point is blunted and every detail blurred:

> *Satire* shou'd, like a polish'd Razor keen,
> Wound with a Touch, that's scarcely felt or seen.
> Thine is an Oyster-Knife, that hacks and hews;
> The Rage, but not the Talent to Abuse;
> And is in *Hate*, what *Love* is in the Stews.
> 'Tis the gross *Lust* of Hate, that still annoys,
> Without Distinction, as gross Love enjoys . . . (25–31)

Pope's effects, she suggests, are cheaply bought and thoughtlessly indulged, like sex in a brothel – and the implication is that he lacks the proper tool for the job. Montagu touches on each of Pope's sensitive points with her razor, keeping her hand steady, knowing (as only a former lover could) where the pain lurks. Her task is to discipline her hate and keep her poise, or else the poem will contradict its own principles.

If Pope's Horatian epistles reach out on the conversational model, Montagu's verse-letter achieves its effects from the reverse – an insistant homing-in on the addressee. The spotlight is on him alone, cut off from his accustomed social context of readers and friends. Montagu effectively severs these sympathetic links. For *society* she substitutes a set of amused *spectators* who watch the little porcupine-satirist erect the spines on its back ('Cool the Spectators stand; and all the while, / Upon the angry little Monster smile', 75–6), and Pope's friends and readers are made to shun his company. Using his favourite word *converse*, Montagu excludes Pope from the polite circle ("'Twill make thy Readers few, as are thy Friends; / Those, who thy Nature loath'd, yet lov'd thy Art, / Who lik'd thy Head, and yet abhor'd thy Heart; / Chose thee, to read, but never to converse', 92–5). The things Pope always aimed to bond to-gether, head and heart, art and life, reading and conversing, are coolly sliced apart. By the time the climax comes, Montagu's poem has developed from an accusation into a curse, gradually isolating Pope's body for visual attention, and repeatedly moving in towards it. Now stripped of all his supportive con-text, he is ready to be branded and finally exiled from the poem, 'an Out-cast, and alone' (102) like the first murderer:

> And with the Emblem of thy crooked Mind,
> Mark'd on thy Back, like *Cain*, by God's own Hand;
> Wander like him, accursed through the Land. (110–112)

Montagu has excluded him from the Horatian poem, and in doing so has produced a verse letter of a different character, one that is less an epistle in the classical sense than a grotesque inversion of that more obsessive one-to-one mode, the love letter.

If, as is probable, Pope thought Lord Hervey the instigator of these *Verses*, then we can see his revenge being realised in the 'Sporus' portrait in *Epistle to Dr Arbuthnot* (1735). It is certainly an appropriate response.[8] For the concen-trated forensic cruelty of his enemies' poem Pope creates inversely the picture of a human explosion, a man of parts that are now only gesturing fragments coupling obscenely with each other – like an allegory of Anarchy in an un-written canto of *The Faerie Queene*: 'Half froth, half venom, spits himself abroad, / In puns, or politicks, or tales, or lyes, / Or spite, or smut, or rymes, or blasphemies' (320–2). As Pope's imagination gets to work, Hervey is turned into the anti-matter of the Horatian poem, a disgusting negation not only of the social graces ('So well-bred spaniels civilly delight') but also of pleasant good humour ('Eternal smiles his emptiness betray'), of conversational ex-change ('And, as the prompter breathes, the puppet squeaks'), of friendly intimacy ('at the ear of *Eve*, familiar Toad'), of lively wit ('His wit all see-saw between *that* and *this*'), and of agreeable variety ('Now high, now low, now master up, now miss'). This figure in whom opposites have failed to harmon-ise becomes 'one vile Antithesis'. It is a brilliant satiric creation, and the effect is even greater for the way 'Sporus' is made to draw into himself all the negative aspects of the Horatian virtues. The fact that the Roman poet had become a point of dispute between Pope and Hervey only makes the satire more appropriate.

In the rest of *Epistle to Dr Arbuthnot* Pope pointedly reassembles his own life and ideals in Horatian terms. The epistle is remarkable for being knitted together from various manuscript drafts he had accumulated, and from two already published passages.[9] Pope's most personal poem, on the subject of moral and artistic integrity, is therefore a defiant gesture of reconstruction, offering a sustained narrative portrait of himself as writer, friend, and son.

Addressing the verse letter to John Arbuthnot, a man who for him represented healing and friendship, Pope reclaims Horace as his mentor, and re-occupies a humane social space for himself – but one from which he can shut out the busy, anonymous, and threatening crowd.

With a spontaneous cry of alarm, the poem opens with a defiant closure ('Shut, shut, the door, good John! fatigu'd I said, / Tye up the knocker, say I'm sick, I'm dead . . .', 1–2). The exhausted poet reaches Twickenham, a refuge where he can reassess the barrier separating the public writer and the private man, and where he need be at home only to sympathetic guests. The opening paragraphs are still exclamatory, nervous, indignant, a little loud, spoken less to the reader than to anyone who will listen ('They pierce my thickets, thro' my Grot they glide . . .', 8); but by the end of the letter, having fashioned a self for publication and brought the reader closer, the poet has relieved the tensions between his interior world and the clamour outside. Away from the pressure of the public's 'now' he has reconnected himself to principles of continuity and reconciliation, finding them in the parental roots of his career. What he values as a writer, he says, is an honest independence inherited from his father, a man of integrity who held to his path through life and spoke 'the language of the heart'. The principles of Pope's art are reasserted as domestic ones, and in the final paragraph he leaves us with a picture of himself as his mother's nurse, extending her life as his friend Arbuthnot had prolonged his.

Such personal and domestic aspects were suited to the verse letter as a form, with its ability to incorporate elements of confession and intimacy. Its customary speaking voice was not projected across a stage but focused on a moving quill, and this encouraged a range of dynamics from spontaneous exclamation to *sotto voce* passages. Emotions could break through at any point, with a reminder of the process of writing itself. The anonymous author of a poem entitled 'A Letter to my Love.—All alone, past 12, in the Dumps' (1734) is clearly writing to the moment, and part of her message is the sheer frustration of trying to communicate her thoughts on paper: 'Angry, the scrawling side I turn, / I write and blot, and write and burn'.[10] Subtle shifts of tone could work expressively, as in a regular prose correspondence between friends. Indeed, one of the qualities of a good letter-writer was an ability to colour language with the equivalent of a glance or gesture.[11] A so-called 'familiar' letter was exactly that – individually nuanced in a way the addressee would understand, who could recall a look or vocal inflection, and 'hear' the writer's words in a particular way. Sending a poem to the Blount sisters in 1717, Pope glosses his transcription by saying 'it ended with a deep Sigh, which I will not tell you the meaning of'.[12] Addressing his *Epistle to a Lady. Of the Characters of Women* (1735) to Martha Blount, Pope could rely on her to supply the full range of tonal nuances on which the poem relies. He is conscious that it demands from both writer and reader an awareness of momentary effects:

> Come then, the colours and the ground prepare!
> Dip in the Rainbow, trick her off in Air,
> Chuse a firm Cloud, before it fall, and in it
> Catch, ere she change, the Cynthia of this minute. (17–20)

Perhaps we can hear in the last line-break a *catch* in the voice at the critical moment? Whether writing to, about, or as a woman, Pope associated with women this quality of immediacy and minute responsiveness, and valued its challenge to his art.

Some of the best verse letters of the century are written by women who are alert to this challenge of spontaneity and welcome the liberating possibilities of addressing a friend on paper. They are often conscious of the medium itself and the excitement of communicating experience from a distance. Elizabeth Tollet opens her verse letter 'To my Brother at St John's College in Cambridge' with an exclamation of delight in the alphabet, which allows her to convey such a multitude of thoughts to an absent loved-one: 'Blest be the man, who first the method found / In absence to discourse, and paint a sound!'[13] Thanks to the conversational aspects of the form a letter-writer has power to manipulate tone and assess her materials in the act of presenting them. Commentary and observation are the essence of the epistolary mode, and this means that grand gestures are soon cut down to size, and pretentious rhetoric is likely to encounter the off-hand remark (this is the natural home of the 'aside'). The sympathetic addressee is always there expecting to be entertained, demanding variety and waiting to smile at bits of anecdote and gossip. Impersonation and confession are also part of the mix and exploit the familiar letter's considerable vocal range, from announcing to whispering. The writer has power to imprint her personality on the medium and engage with her own character. In the hands of intelligent poets like Mary Jones and Mary Leapor, the Popean epistle is amenable to all these aspects, and both of them infuse the form with a genial liveliness that takes it in a new direction. Jones's 'Epistle to Lady Bowyer' (c. early 1736) and 'Of Desire: An Epistle to the Hon. Miss Lovelace' (probably from the same period) are steeped in the language of Pope's *Epistle to a Lady* and *Epistle to Dr Arbuthnot* (both 1735), and she had recently read the poet's published correspondence with 'inexpressible Pleasure', commenting: 'I have always admird the Author, but now I love the Man'.[14] Leapor too was devoted to Pope's work: 'the Author she most admired was Mr. *Pope*, whom she chiefly endeavoured to imitate'.[15] Both women liked his disengagement from the worldly scramble and his association of close friendships with artistic integrity. The Popean persona of the 1730s was sympathetic to their sense of themselves as private voices in a busy cultural marketplace. But they were not slavish imitators. In their hands the verse letter's comic potential was developed in interesting ways.

For Jones and Leapor a poem is less a composed work than a compulsion to live on the page, an actualising of mental energy,[16] and as such it is in danger of being compromised by entering the world through performance or publication, and thus being taken out of their hands. The poem is in a sense already a self-performance, whose fate is to be endlessly repeated before an audience. In her 'Epistle to Lady Bowyer' Mary Jones expresses her awareness of the gulf between the living poem and the formal self-publication of her *Works* (which came about in 1750):

> Well, but the joy to see my works in print!
> My self too pictur'd in a Mezzo-Tint!
> The Preface done, the Dedication fram'd,
> With lies enough to make a Lord asham'd!
> Thus I step forth; an Auth'ress in some sort . . . (29–33)

The poems are sidelined by the artificial public *self* of print. The *Auth'ress* who steps forward is authorised not by the quality of her poems but by the necessary formalities, nicely undercut by the way the confident gesture trails off into a mutter (*in some sort . . .*). A similar anticlimax faces her while she hovers in an antechamber waiting for an audience ('With face unmov'd, my poem in my hand', 58). A gossipy maidservant who has 'winked' her from the crowd is interrupted by a summons from the footman:

> Sick at the news, impatient for my lord,
> I'm forc'd to hear, nay smile at ev'ry word.
> *Tom* raps at last,—'His lordship begs to know
> Your name? your bus'ness?—Sir, I'm not a foe.
> I come to charm his lordship's list'ning ears
> With verses, soft as music of the spheres.
> 'Verses!—Alas! his lordship seldom reads:
> Pedants indeed with learning stuff their heads;
> But my good lord, as all the world can tell,
> Reads not ev'n tradesmen's bills, and scorns to spell.
> But trust your lays with me . . . (66–76)

Again Jones is aware of the artifice of facial and verbal expressions. As she mimics the footman, the tone shifts from his routine impersonalities (*Your name?*), to her sharp response (*I'm not a foe*), followed by a playful poeticism (*verses, soft as music of the spheres*) which he predictably fails to hear in full (*Verses!*). Then we are given the footman's attack on *learning* in a speech that modulates into a satire on aristocratic ignorance, revealing how lordly *scorn* can spread from master to servant, and service become tinged with contempt (*not ev'n tradesmen's bills*). A final patronising touch from this eighteenth-century Malvolio (*trust your lays with me*) concludes what has been a vivid encounter between poetry and the world of business.

The antechamber was Mary Jones's public space – waiting to be admitted (and usually welcomed) to where she did not belong. She lived in her brother's Oxford College and stayed at Windsor Castle or with titled friends, though she was neither a member of the college, the court, nor the aristocracy. She was thus in the ideal position to listen to and observe an elite society – in it, but not of it. Her private space was the 'closet' of the letter, where she could talk freely. She tells her friend, the Hon. Martha Lovelace: 'I've spent the afternoon very silently in a great deal of Company; and am now retired to my Closet to talk. Happy, if Miss *L.* would likewise retire from the Croud to hear me'.[17] Jones's verse letter, 'Of Desire', addressed to Martha, is the poem of someone who looks and listens intently. It offers lively sketches of society people pursuing desire, ambition and hope. Clearly influenced by Pope's *Epistle to a Lady*, Jones nonetheless does something interestingly different with her characters. Like his, they are in the grip of self-deluding imagination, and touched with pathos; but where Pope traps his figures in little ironic plots within a wider moral system that he has spun round them, Jones tends to allow them their moments of fragile hope and keep poetic justice suspended. The Doctor of Divinity angling for promotion in the Church may eventually succeed (we don't know), but in the meantime Jones simply watches him:

> Bless me! the Doctor!—what brings him to court? . . .
> Why stands he here then, elbow'd to and fro?
> Has he no care of souls? No work to do?
> Go home, good doctor, preach and pray, and give;
> By far more blessed this, than to receive . . . (103–110)

Rather than proceed to punish him, Jones rescues the man from his worldly jostlings: 'Then let him soar, 'tis on devotion's wing; / Who asks a bishopric, asks no bad thing: / A coach does much an holy life adorn . . .' (115–7). But while indulging him like this the words deliver a silent judgment. We feel how *devotion* is being cheapened, and we know that his soul will hardly take wing in a coach and four. The voice of these poems is forgiving, even patronising, but behind it is a shrewd and self-possessed woman who is used to implying more than she says. The reader becomes one of her friends whom she can trust to get the message.

With another of her characters Jones lets the reader see worldly desire being fulfilled. In a neat reversal of Pope's 'Sporus' portrait, we begin with a picture of the man's self-humiliation ('Will none the wretched crawling thing regard, / Who stoops so very low, and begs so hard?', 97–8); but as we watch in contempt, the thing metamorphoses and takes wing:

> *You* call this meanness, and the wretch despise;
> Alas! he stoops to soar, and sinks to rise:
> Now on the knee, now on the wing is found,
> As insects spring with vigour from the ground. (99–102)

Humility is the chrysalis-stage of career success, and with a verbal twist (*Now on the knee, now on the wing*) Jones shows how life really works – the boot-licker will eventually become the boss, and the laugh will be on us.

As a kitchen-maid, Mary Leapor's space was far more constricted than Jones's, but equally a place where speaking out was a problem. 'Say, *Artemisia*, shall I speak, or no?' is the final question in her 'Epistle to Artemisia. On Fame' (1751), written to her close friend, Bridget Freemantle. This is Leapor's version of *Epistle to Dr Arbuthnot* with its picture of a sensitive author besieged by demanding callers. Like Pope, she confides to her friend the frustration of being used as a diversion for others. She sees her poems, hidden in a little box, as living things whose innocence she is forced to compromise by social performance ('The Babes slept soundly in their tiny Chest. / Not so their Parent . . .', 144–5). Some people have no trouble broadcasting themselves, like Codrus 'Who pour'd thick Sonnets like a troubled Spring' (137); but Leapor feels awkward in her adopted role as 'Mira', the local wonder, holding her regal 'levee' for the curious of the neighbourhood. As she becomes the focus of literary judgment, the act of criticism develops into a social performance tinged with absurdity:

> Once *Delpho* read—Sage *Delpho*, learn'd and wise,
> O'er the scrawl'd Paper cast his judging Eyes,
> Whose lifted Brows confess'd a Critic's Pride,
> While his broad Thumb mov'd nimbly down the Side.
> His Form was like some Oracle profound:
> The list'ning Audience form'd a Circle round:
> But *Mira*, fixing her presuming Eyes
> On the stern Image, thus impatient cries:
> Sir, will they prosper? (73–81)

Who has the truly *judging Eyes* here? There could hardly be a more vivid emblem of how critical judgment sometimes carries itself, and how it can bulk unnecessarily large in the literary experience. Delpho's body interposes between the poet and her audience, working mechanically in a kind of parody of reading focused not on the living words of the poet but on the oracular response of the critic. It is this kind of scenario that the familiar epistle can avoid through its more intimate relationship with addressee and reader, and its relative resistance to formal requirements. Both Jones and Leapor use the verse letter to explore how poetry can challenge over-determined categories and hierarchies, whether in literature or in society. Pope's epistle 'Of the Characters of Women' showed that poetic art could move from imitating life to enacting it, and Jones and Leapor develop this idea. In their work, the life on the page defies the empty forms of social reality. This kind of writing functions on the principle that a verse letter between friends is an honest medium through which the public world can be filtered so as to expose its deceptiveness. Private integrity tests social performance.

This awareness of the verse letter as a means of separating truth from falsehood is taken to an extreme by Sarah Dixon in 'From a Sheet of Gilt Paper. To Cloe' (1740).[18] Here the epistolary voice is that of the paper itself. The sheet speaks to her candidly ('I call myself your Friend', it says) mocking the empty words it must carry from her lover ('That the Sun shines, and CLOE reigns . . .' etc.). Cloe has heard all this vapid nonsense before, and as her eyes wander to the physical paper, it offers her a sincere apology:

> Touch'd with Remorse, tho' guiltless, I
> Approach you with Humility.
> A passive Vehicle I'm made,
> How many Hearts have I betray'd? (25–8)

Falsehood relies on a *passive Vehicle* as go-between. But in this case the paper is determined to become an honest medium; it will reveal the truth, not by being transparent but by asserting an integrity that refuses to be misused. The words of Cloe's lover, the paper declares, represent nothing but 'random Thoughts, which e're the Post / Reach'd his first Stage, were wholly lost' (36–7). A letter's pretence of immediacy (speaking on the page) is revealed as the convenient fiction it is – the writer's sentiments became outdated during transit (we are back with the passionate 'moment' of Rochester). But the spurious 'truth of writing' has been replaced by another kind of immediacy, a 'truth of reading'. One 'now' has taken over from another, and Dixon is clearly thinking about how the meaning of a text can be located. Is it constituted at the moment of writing or the moment of reading? The speaking paper gives no simple answer, but by raising questions about sub-text, reader-response, even deconstruction, it helps Cloe to be a sophisticated modern reader aware that the medium has its own message. A text that is so conflicted and turned against itself must in the end destroy itself. So the paper finally warns Cloe not to be as impressionable as she herself has been:

> White as your *Hand*, I came to *his*;
> Behold the Metamorphosis!
> With Lyes and Nonsense slubber'd o're,
> More vile by far than heretofore,
> Take this kind Hint, despise the 'Squire,
> And gently lay me—on the *Fire*. (42–7)

This self-consuming artefact is at the same time, in human terms, a true and faithful voice. It is determined that the life of the page shall be honest to the end. The gilt-edged paper, it turns out, is not just an active friend, but Cloe's true lover, sacrificing itself for her well-being.

Dixon distrusts the letter-form.[19] She does not allow that its immediacy gives it a licence to evade truth and judgment. In fact, as we have seen, she mediates it through a moral conscience (the paper). What the writer may have thought the truth of his spontaneous feelings is revealed as empty falsehood. The eighteenth-century verse letter often raises questions of this kind, and sees the dramatic potential in setting Licence and Law against each other. The 'now' of experience is made to challenge, or be challenged by, the rules (whether seen as Fate, Law, Morality, or Custom). Writing 'To One who said I must not Love' (1703)[20], Sarah Egerton speaks in desperation about the impossibility of repressing her illicit feelings. Following her friend's advice has proved futile. She has tried playing the field as a coquette, but in vain. She has even tried marriage (*Hymen*), but this last recourse has only imposed an extra legal sanction on her ('I've made the guiltless Torture Criminal', 18). Squeezed between self-restraint and external pressures, she becomes helplessly frozen:

> I'm forc'd to keep the mighty Anguish in;
> Check my too tender Thoughts and rising Sighs,
> As well as eager Arms and longing Eyes.
> My Kindness to his Picture I refrain,
> Nor now imbrace the lifeless lovely Swain.
> To press the charming Shade tho' thro' a Glass,
> Seems a Platonick breach of *Hymen*'s Laws,
> Thus nicely fond, I only stand and gaze,
> View the dear conq'ring Form that forc'd my Fate,
> Till I become as motionless as that. (23–32)

The rhythms have moved away from conversation to a more formalised and balanced pulse. The rhymed couplets (though rhyme is strained to breaking-point in the second half of this passage) give the speaker's language the measure of one who is weighing her experience. The word *Kindness* (26) is stripped of its usual ambiguities in love letters: she cannot be *kind*, even in the sense of 'generous', to him, let alone respond sexually. His image behind the glass membrane puts him further beyond her reach, as if sealed in his own platonic virginity. The spontaneous motions welling up in her are repressed until she becomes a mere picture like him. Her art of self-control has drained her, but Life and Love will only flow and ebb together ('For soon as I have Life I love again, / . . . Departing Love racks like departing Life', 36, 41). It is as though her nature has one law and her conscience another ('Distorted Nature shakes at the Controul', 38). In Egerton's hands the verse letter takes on the character of a soliloquy in a tragic drama.

In this kind of letter the emphasis is on the impossibility of 'converse', the lack of any reaction from the addressee or the lover. Without the sociable dynamics of the Horatian epistle, the text moves towards isolating the speaking voice and making the letter not a means of communication but a receptacle for frustrated emotion. In this, Egerton's poem is closer to the 'heroic epistle' established by Ovid in his *Heroides*, a genre much imitated by Elizabethan and later poets, in which a tragic lover from myth or history (commonly female) writes to her separated loved-one, vents her feelings, and attempts to come to terms with her situation. Egerton seems to be casting herself as such a speaker. Where the Horatian epistle works on a principle of responsiveness, and is always an implied dialogue, if not an actual one, the Ovidian heroic epistle specialises in making the speaking voice repeatedly return to the self. In many cases the addressee will never read it, so all the demands, longings, accusations and pleadings reach out as it were into space. If the Horatian familiar epistle creates presence, the Ovidian epistle is centred on ideas of emptiness and absence, and this contrast creates ironic possibilities. Instead of the reassuring presence of the addressee there is a gap that can only be filled by imagination. The speaker in Pope's heroic epistle, *Eloisa to Abelard* (1717), imagines a reunion with her former lover, and in doing so she seems to be describing the intimacies of familiar correspondence that are now denied her:

> Oh! happy state! when souls each other draw,
> When love is liberty, and nature, law:
> All then is full, possessing, and possest,
> No craving Void left aking in the breast:
> Ev'n thought meets thought e'er from the lips it part,
> And each warm wish springs mutual from the heart. (91–6)

Now nature and law are at odds. Both enclosed in monasteries, he castrated and she vowed to chastity, the lovers are denied this mutuality. The place where warm wishes mixed is now a *craving Void*. In face of the impossibility of communication the voice becomes feverish in its imaginings and increasingly at odds with its calm and unreceptive addressee ('Snatch me, just mounting, from the blest abode, / Assist the Fiends and tear me from my God! / No, fly me, fly me! Far as Pole from Pole', 289–91). Eloisa's reiterated 'Come!' grows perplexed and desperate, and the more demanding her own voice, the more impassive Abelard's image seems:

> For thee the fates, severely kind, ordain
> A cool suspense from pleasure and from pain;
> Thy life a long, dead calm of fix'd repose;
> No pulse that riots, and no blood that glows. (249–52)

Where the Horatian verse letter assumes an alert and responsive addressee who is part of the same society and with whom the speaker can engage, here the addressee is not only out of reach, but is seen as belonging to a different order of nature, like Egerton's lover under glass. Abelard is represented by a calm primal scene that antedates the creation of Adam and Eve ('Still as the sea, e'er winds were taught to blow, / Or moving spirit bade the waters flow', 253–4). He belongs to a world before the language of passion (gales, storms and tides) even existed.

The human reader of Eloisa's letter is left in an uneasy position between judgment and sympathy, conscious of eavesdropping on something intensely private and embarrassing, but also being drawn towards supplying the lack of responsiveness, the missing role of addressee. The intimacy that Eloisa imagines is waiting to be supplied by us. In fact, a slight distancing effect can be felt at the end when Pope brings himself forward as the unknown 'future bard' who will 'join / In sad similitude of griefs to mine' (361–2), identifying himself not just as the poet, but as Eloisa's ideal sympathetic reader. By fulfilling his speaker's final hopes ('Let him our sad, our tender story tell', 366) *Eloisa to Abelard* is, rather oddly, the reply to *Eloisa to Abelard*.

Eloisa's letter is one of the crucial documents in eighteenth-century literature, not merely for the frequency with which it echoes through the poetry of succeeding decades, but because it represents, so early in the century, a kind of test-case of reading. Its first readers encountered it in Pope's *Works* (1717), printed alongside *An Essay on Criticism*, *Windsor-Forest* and *The Rape of the Lock*, and for the volume's purchasers it offered a totally different experience. Rather than being given varied perspectives, the reader of *Eloisa to Abelard* was not only locked into a single consciousness, but one filled with an obsessive idea. The voice of a desperate, pleading woman went unanswered, and there seemed to be no vantage-point from which readers could assess their reactions. Probably most 1717 readers knew the conventions of the Ovidian epistle, but we would be wrong to think that this neutralised the work's immediate effect (its impact on new readers can be powerful even today). What is especially interesting is that historically the poem seems to have been instrumental in creating an appropriate readership for itself. Drawing on the mechanisms of romance-reading, it helped to encourage, and make fashionable, the kind of sensibility that would respond with imaginative sympathy to Eloisa's voice and situation[21] – one that in the next generation would be gripped by Richardson's epistolary novel, *Clarissa* (1747–8).

We can see this happening in several poetic responses to Eloisa's letter. The voice trapped inside Pope's poem waits eternally for an answer, and some of its early readers turned their responses into actual replies. In 'Abelard to Eloisa' (1720) the eighteen-year-old Judith Cowper (later Madan) wrote in the character of an Abelard who was far from impassive. His pulse riots and his blood glows in response to every turn of Eloisa's emotions: 'I hear her Sigh, see the swift-falling Tears, / Weep all her Griefs, and pine with all her Cares' (57–8).[22] The imaginative identification is clear. What is more, this guilt-ridden Abelard declares that Eloisa is the only person who can save his soul by feeling a similar empathy with him:

> A sympathizing Grief alone can cure,
> The hand that heals, must feel what I endure.
> Thou Eloise! alone, canst give me Ease,
> And bid my strugling Soul subside in Peace ... (93–6)

The mechanism of mutual sympathy functions virtually as an erotic union. 'Mine' and 'thine' become entangled (132–40) before both of them 'in blest Concert' find forgiveness and transcendence, united in 'love divine'. It is clear that a teenage reader in 1720 could become completely absorbed in Eloisa's emotions. By 1746, however, an ordained clergyman and Headmaster of Tonbridge School was reacting in remarkably similar fashion, with a sensibility even more attuned to the ebb and flow of feeling. In James Cawthorn's 'Abelard to Eloisa' the speaker is so identified with his addressee that phrases from Pope's poem are repeatedly turned back on her, and she becomes the focus of the same rhetorical climaxes ('Then take me, take me, lock me in thy arms, / Spring to my lips, and give me all thy charms. / No—fly me, fly me ... , 57–9).[23] Cawthorn's Abelard is so frantic and desperate that he is near to death ('stretch me on the racks of vain desire, / Each passion throbbing, and each wish on fire; / Mad to enjoy, unable to be blest, / Fiends in my veins, and hell within my breast', 221–4). Eloisa's *Fiends* have become internalised in Abelard's body, and at several points his letter seems close to spontaneous combustion. This Abelard is eager to outdo his lover in the exquisiteness of his tortures. Imaginative identification has become total absorption. On this principle it is not surprising that these 'sentimental' responses to Pope's verse letter became intimately associated with the original poem, and all three were bound up (literally) into the complete Eloisa-experience. Later in the century *Eloisa to Abelard* was popularly reprinted alongside the replies of Madan and Cawthorn as an appendix to the lovers' original correspondence translated by John Hughes. Many readers therefore encountered them together as part of what was virtually an epistolary novel with illustrations.[24]

A third reader of Pope's verse letter, however, refused to be swept up in all the feeling, and was determined to respond dispassionately on firm ground of his own choosing. In 'Fragment of an Epistle from Abelard to Eloisa' (1721) Charles Beckingham makes his Abelard completely resistant to Eloisa's pleas, and his reply adopts an epistolary style that takes us away from Ovid and back to Horatian common sense. Here the couplets, rather than swinging between emotional extremes, point up Eloisa's inconsistencies and offer her the full force of balanced reasonableness:

> Silence these causeless Griefs, nor let me say
> Thy Soul was *Mine* but for the *happier Day*;
> What! wouldst Thou only *share* the *Hour of Joy*,
> But when the *gath'ring Tempest* threatens, *fly*?
> *Feast* on the *Pleasure*, from the *Care* be *free*,
> And leave the *Bitter Poison* all to me:
> (Alas! how justly could I censure Thee?) (12–18) [25]

Accusing Eloisa of deserting him, this Abelard refuses to let her set the tone. Indeed he turns her rhetoric against her. Where she had used ironically balanced phrases to express her dilemma ('How shall I lose the sin, yet keep the sense, / And love th'offender, yet detest th'offence?', 191–2), Abelard makes them expose her inconstancy ('*Feast* on the *Pleasure*, from the *Care* be *free*'). He reads her unsentimentally, against the grain. He also protests at the way she has exploited his situation to dramatise her own: 'You mourn my *wretched State*, yet make it worse' (35) he says rather petulantly. In answer to her appeal for imaginative engagement, Beckingham's Abelard offers reason and common sense. He even ends by reminding her of her duty as a '*true Loving Wife*' (47).

These three examples of Eloisa's readers writing back offer a sharp contrast between the principles of sympathy and judgment. The first two speakers project themselves imaginatively into her experience; the third stays determinedly outside. The first two Abelards have absorbed Eloisa's subjective consciousness and use her own language; the third selects a different register to get a wider perspective on the situation. The first two pairs of lovers blend romance-like into each other (prefiguring the climax of Keats's *Eve of St Agnes*); the third pair are placed in a social world of ethical choice and obligation ('Yourself the *Sacred Obligation* laid / On ABELARD, and ABELARD obey'd', 5–6). These responses exemplify in polarised form two persistent eighteenth-century literary modes: the sentimental and the satirical. I say 'persistent' because much has been written about a 'shift' around mid-century 'from Satire to Sensibility', as though one mode somehow replaced the other. It is true that during the early decades an interest in the psychological mechanisms of imaginative sympathy and emotional response did make the concept of 'sensibility' or the 'sentimental' increasingly popular; and we shall see it at work in Chapter 6 on the early eighteenth-century 'romantic'. But in tension with this throughout the century was that more objective tendency to adopt ironic judgmental positions on experience and view characters and their actions from a more impersonal viewpoint. This could be an oblique 'satiric' angle that highlighted their features, sometimes grotesquely. Between 1700 and 1800 these modes, with their subjective and objective emphases, existed side by side. It cannot be said that there was a separate 'Age' of satire or sensibility, and Chapter 11 will suggest that a concept of 'sentimental satire' need not be a contradiction. The satiric was never ousted by the sentimental, nor were they mutually exclusive. Some of the most memorable poems, novels and plays (*The Rape of the Lock*, *The Deserted Village*, *A Sentimental Journey*, *The Rivals*) work skilfully between the two. The eighteenth-century reader was perfectly able both to weep in sympathy and laugh at absurdity, and within the same work.

The relationship between sympathetic feeling and objective judgment is the theme of a verse letter that 'writes back' at Pope's *Eloisa to Abelard* in an ingeniously indirect way. It was from the pen of someone who had been invited to interpret Eloisa's situation in the most personal terms. Sending his poem to Lady Mary Wortley Montagu, then in distant Istanbul, Pope alerted her to the significance of one passage, admitting 'I can't tell whether to wish you should understand it, or not'.[26] Montagu, who was receiving 'romantick' letters from him at this time, was clearly meant to see herself as the unattainable beauty alluded to at the poem's close, with Pope as the 'future Bard . . . / Condemn'd whole years in absence to deplore, / And image charms he must behold no more' (361–4). With this gloss in mind, Montagu was being asked to hear behind the frustrated passion of *Eloisa to Abelard* a whispered verse letter *Pope to Lady Mary*. Her immediate response does not survive, but in her *Epistle from Arthur Gray the Footman, after his Condemnation for attempting a Rape* (1721)[27] she also writes about an illicit frustrated passion, in the voice of the opposite sex, and from a cell; but now there is an urgent contemporary scenario.

Montagu gives us the words of a man speaking under the most extreme earthly judgment – sentence of death for having tried to rape the woman he served, and he pleads with her not for release but for sympathy ('My only hope in these last lines I try; / I wou'd be pitied, and I then wou'd die', 5–6). Written around the time of the scandalous court case involving Montagu's friend Griselda Murray (Gray's accuser), the verse letter combines the rhetoric of a frustrated Ovidian lover ('since you will not love, I will not live', he tells her) with a satirical contempt for the foppish suitors who dance attendance on her ('Faint their desire, and in a moment past: / They sigh not from the heart, but from the brain; / Vapours of vanity, and strong champagne', 48–50). In Montagu's poem, Gray's passion does not live in a romantic dream, but breaks through the barriers of class into the material world he shares with Murray. It is not a vision in the mind but a presence in the body ('with labour healthy', he reminds her). Rather than distracting him from his daily duties, Mrs Murray is the focus of them. Defying transcendence, Gray's everyday routine (waiting at table or escorting her from the theatre) becomes erotically charged, and his letter, unlike Eloisa's, shows him lusting after a physical presence:

> I saw the dear disorder of your bed;
> Your cheek all glowing with a tempting red;
> Your night-cloaths tumbled with resistless grace;
> Your flowing hair play'd careless round your face;
> Your night-gown fasten'd with a single pin . . . (76–80)

His eye registers the scene, turning a static *disorder* into living movement. He sees energy and release in everything – except for one stubborn item that refuses to move, or be moved in sympathy. That *single* prohibition is precarious but decisive, the focal point of resistance on which all hangs. In these lines the subjective and the objective are held for a moment in balance, and his life depends on how a reader of his case arbitrates between sympathy and judgment. As an intervention in a contemporary *cause célèbre*, Montagu's verse letter brings a new immediacy to the traditional rhetoric of the Ovidian epistle. Her writer and addressee are living people faced with crucial decisions, and the language gains in sharpness. A detail from Eloisa's dream of Abelard ('the hallow'd taper trembling in thy hand', 328) becomes more palpable when it is focused on the tensed arm of the footman standing by his mistress ('The flambeau trembled in my shaking hand', 37). Behind the erotic charge of Gray's text can be sensed a silent charge of a different kind whose subtext is the fantasised, impotent lover of Pope's imagination.

The verse letter of the early eighteenth century brought together many different voices and ways of reading. It stretched from sociable conversation and Horatian satiric comedy to Ovidian tragic soliloquy; from flattering a patron to pleading for life. But connecting all these varieties was the urge to communicate. In the epistle, even a solitary contemplation (such as Eloisa's) expresses a desperate need to communicate. Whether the speaker and addressee are close friends or tragic lovers, protégé and patron, or rapist and victim, it is the human voice that we hear in all its moods, and as readers we become part of the 'converse', alert to the nuances of speech and aware of other relationships that are being expressed and tested in our company. The eighteenth-century reading public was clearly fascinated by the power of the letter to explore the personal within a public context, and to locate those values that might bring self and society together.

Notes

1. *The Art of Poetry on a New Plan*, 2 vols (London: J. Newbery, 1762), I, 116 (from Chapter XII, 'Of the Epistle').

2. *The Universal Passion. Satire III. To the Right Honourable Mr Dodington* (London, 1725).

3. *Essay on Man*, IV,369.

4. *Essay on Criticism* (1711), 641.

5. Hervey's manuscript corrections to the poem survive, and some passages may be his. Pope believed that 'both sexes had a share in it, but which was uppermost, I know not. I pretend not to determine the exact method of this witty fornication' ('Letter to a Noble Lord, 30 Nov. 1733').

6. See J.V. Guerinot, *Pamphlet Attacks on Alexander Pope, 1711–1744* (1969).

7. *Essay on Criticism*, 519.

8. In the 'Advertisement' Pope remarks that he is responding to attacks by 'some Persons of Rank and Fortune'. A note to the 'Sporus' passage reads: 'It is but justice to own that the Hint of *Eve* and the *Serpent* was taken from the *Verses to the Imitator of Horace*'.

9. See *The Last and Greatest Art: Some Unpublished Poetical Manuscripts of Alexander Pope*, ed. Maynard Mack (Newark, London, and Toronto, 1984), pp. 419–54.

10. *Eighteenth-Century Women Poets*, ed. Roger Lonsdale (1990), p. 147. The author is given as 'The Amorous Lady'.

11. Bruce Redford emphasises a more public aspect of epistolary performance: 'The basic challenge is to find satisfactory equivalents to the resources of an actor: the ironic intonation, the raised eyebrow, the rueful smile, the sudden whisper, the emphatic change of posture, the meaningful glance across the room' (*The Converse of the Pen: Acts of Intimacy in the Eighteenth-Century Familiar Letter* [Chicago and London, 1986], pp. 5–6).

12. Pope – Teresa and Martha Blount, 13 September 1717. *Correspondence*, I, 428–9.

13. *Eighteenth-Century Women Poets*, p. 96.

14. Mary Jones – Martha Lovelace, 7 August 1735 (*Miscellanies in Prose and Verse. By Mary Jones* [Oxford, 1750], p. 313). Jones continued: 'the breast must be a stranger to all tenderness, all the dignities of human Nature, that can read [Pope] without being warm'd with the same Affections' (pp. 313–4).

15. *Poems upon Several Occasions* (1748), sig. A2 ('To the Reader').

16. Both Jones and Leapor evidently wrote fluently and spontaneously. Jones liked to describe her poetry as a feverish effusion: 'I've no longer any feverish Symptoms, my Rage subsides, and Poetry is no more'; 'Yesterday great quantities of my Disorder came away in the following Verses; and I've found my Head much easier ever since' (*Miscellanies*, pp. 213, 292). Bridget Freemantle, who watched Leapor composing, spoke of 'her Thoughts seeming to flow as fast as she could put them upon Paper' (*Poems* [1751], p. xx).

17. Mary Jones – Martha Lovelace, 8 Sept. 1733. *Miscellanies* (1750), p. 293.

18. Printed in Sarah Dixon's *Poems on Several Occasions* (Canterbury: J. Abree, 1740), pp. 128–30.

19. The speaker of Dixon's 'Lines occasion'd by the Burning of some Letters' concludes: ''Twas only Paper dawb'd with Art' (11). See *Poems on Several Occasions*, pp. 179–81. The poem is printed in *Eighteenth-Century Women Poets*, p. 178.

20. Sarah Fyge Egerton, *Poems on Several Occasions* (1703), pp. 42–3.

21. See Walter Jackson Bate, 'The Sympathetic Imagination in Eighteenth-Century English Criticism', *ELH* 12 (1945), 144–64.

22. 'Abelard to Eloisa', printed in *Poems by Eminent Ladies* (1755), pp. 137–43.

23. *The Poetical Calendar* (1746). The poem was included in *Poems, by the Rev. Mr. Cawthorn. Late Master of Tunbridge School* (London, 1771), pp. 56–67.

24. *The Letters of Abelard and Heloise. With a particular account of their lives, amours, and misfortunes: extracted chiefly from Monsieur Bayle, by John Hughes . . . To which are added, four poems by Mr. Pope, and other hands* [with plates], London: T. Lowndes, 1781. There were further editions in 1787 and 1788. (The original letters had already been printed with the poems of Pope and Madan.)

25. Printed in *The Pleasures of Coition; or the Nightly Sports of Venus . . . With some other Love-Pieces*, 2nd ed. (London: E. Curll, 1721), pp. 47–50. It was also issued as part of *The Altar of Love* (1727).

26. Pope – Montagu, June 1717. *Correspondence*, I, 407.

27. First published by Horace Walpole in *Six Town Eclogues. With some other Poems* (1747), and soon after reprinted in Dodsley's popular *Collection of Poems* (1748), III, 298–302.

Chapter 5

Pastoral and Georgic

Thomas Parnell's lines about the pastoral world take us to the heart of an age-old problem. 'Oft have I read', he begins, 'that Innocence retreats / Where cooling streams salute the summer Seats; / Singing at ease she roves the field of flowers / Or safe with shepherds lies among the bowers . . .' Having passed through a country fair, however, he had found 'No Strephon nor Dorinda', but a motley crew of randy, idle, and drunken rustics:

> Are these the Virtues which adorn the plain?
> Ye bards forsake your old Arcadian Vein,
> To sheep, those tender Innocents, resign
> The place where swains and nymphs are said to shine;
> Swains twice as wicked, Nymphs but half as sage.
> Tis sheep alone retrieve the golden age.[1]

Where is pastoral innocence to be found? And how can any modern writer not view Arcadia ironically? By a shift of focus typical of early eighteenth-century satire, the sheep move centre-stage: the incidentals of pastoral become the guardians of its soul. The poet is self-consciously listening to his own bland rhetoric (*the Virtues which adorn the plain*, etc.) before the final rueful comment emerges – conclusive, yet almost in parenthesis, as if he is turning away from the scene. After two thousand years of pastoral poetry Parnell (d. 1718) can find only one unsullied image remaining, and there seems no more to be said.

Yet Parnell died at the end of a decade in which the nature of pastoral had become a topic for debate among the most prominent writers of the time. As a literary mode it was far from exhausted and would soon receive a new lease of life from the next generation of poets. Why did it persist? One reason may be that pastoral had become a kind of punch-bag for hundreds of poets-in-training to test their powers on, in the hope of embarking on the *rota Virgiliana*, that 'canonical progress through the genres'[2] made by Virgil from pastoral (the *Eclogues*), through the 'middle style' (the *Georgics*), to the eventual epic achievement of the *Aeneid*. But long after its ideals had been deflated and its conventions mocked, pastoral survived to be beaten into new shapes. Its malleability, as a mode rather than a genre, offered opportunities for poetic experiment, and the widespread familiarity of its codes allowed for considerable ingenuity and playfulness.

The first decade of the century also saw the establishment of the georgic poem, a more dynamic genre that encouraged poets to engage productively with the contemporary British landscape.[3] After the Act of Union (1707) people seemed to become interested in poetry about the organising and development of the young nation's resources, and georgic's linking of time-hallowed tradition to new skills and opportunities provided a subtle way of confronting wider problems of continuity and innovation. Georgic also gave room for greater variety of tone and topic, and it drew economics and politics more directly into the picture. Work, trade, human ingenuity, social structures, national concerns – all these became features of a poetry that found inspiration in the idea of organic change. But after 1760, as poets looked for new forms of expression, the classical outlines of pastoral and georgic appeared increasingly constraining. The traditional duality of Nature and Art, which in different ways had underpinned each of them, was breaking down or being reconfigured in more subtle ways, and some of their characteristic features were variously absorbed into the wider embrace of topographical poetry and verse of a meditative and didactic character. By bringing pastoral and georgic together, this chapter will stress their differences,[4] and argue that they represent a crucial distinction in eighteenth-century poetry between ironic and organic form. In being a stereotype, pastoral could be inverted, turned round, parodied, and played with; but in order for all this to work it had to remain a stereotype. Georgic, on the other hand, was at home with notions of growth, development, variety, digression, and mixture, and had a natural tendency to absorb the old into the new, and find fresh directions. Pastoral's limitations and georgic's capaciousness were, in other words, equally fruitful; but they marked out different kinds of poetry.

Since the inauguration of the pastoral poem, or 'bucolic', in the third century BC by Theocritus, and its development in the *Eclogues* of Virgil, pastoral writing had been extended during the Renaissance into drama, prose narrative, satire, allegory, and masque. Although its scope had in this sense widened, its conventions and subject-matter remained limited. In the hands of court poets like Sannazaro and Tasso in Italy, or Sidney and Spenser in England, its commitment to the simple lives and language of shepherds and shepherdesses (or in Sannazaro's controversial development, fishermen and fisherwomen) came under strain; but this could give it a *faux-naïf* quality that was useful when engaging with controversial contemporary issues. Spenser's militantly protestant shepherds vigorously attack Romish 'pastors' and complain about being neglected by the great. Shakespeare the dramatist knew that an actual wanderer through English fields and woods would find, not Silvius and Phebe, but William and Audrey. In the uncomfortable 'golden world' of *As You Like It* (1599) a melancholy contemplative turns into a satiric malcontent. During the 1630s, those uneasy years of parliament-free innocence under Charles I, the adequacy of pastoral for dealing with urgent human questions was fully tested by Milton, whose rebellious spirit enjoyed pushing its conventions to breaking-point in his *Ludlow Masque* (1634) and his pastoral elegy, *Lycidas* (1637). In the Eden scenes of *Paradise Lost* (Milton's version of history's original pastoral episode) Adam and Eve are intelligent and dignified, and not yet encumbered with sheep.

The eighteenth century therefore inherited, as Parnell's verses confirm, a pastoral mode that was strained and stretched, and which already had

self-conscious parodic elements embedded in it. The question of its relation-
ship to 'real' life was by then an old one, but it was this very issue that
brought it to the heart of current debate about the nature of poetry. Until the
1650s pastoral had been refreshingly free of rules. It had developed only after
Aristotle's death, and Horace's *Ars Poetica* had ignored it. It was left to two
French critics, Rapin and Fontenelle, to remedy this by constructing a set of
principles within which to contain and judge this form of writing. Rapin's
Dissertatio de Carmine Pastorali (1659) and Fontenelle's *Discours sur la nature
de l'églogue* (1688) were translated into English in 1684 and 1695 respect-
ively,[5] and their contrasting approaches (which reflected the two sides of the
'Ancients v. Moderns' controversy) had considerable influence on pastoral-
writing in Britain. The Aristotelian Rapin declared the *Idylls* of Theocritus
and the *Eclogues* of Virgil to be his absolute models, yet his ideas were filtered
through the *neo*-classical critical tradition, and he repeatedly cited authorities
among the *scholia* and the classical grammarians to support his 'rules' – to the
extent of criticising Theocritus for not following them. Fontenelle, a disciple
of Descartes, placed his faith in reason and experience, and quoted no author-
ities whatsoever. For Rapin, the pastoral was the most ancient form of poetry
and imitated the lives of shepherds in the Golden Age. For Fontenelle it showed
eternal human nature and gave pleasure by picturing a leisured rural life with-
out its toils and coarseness, and with love at its centre. But the neo-classicist
and the rationalist did agree on several points – that pastoral must be simple
and dignified, avoiding courtly wit on one side and rustic clownishness on the
other; and that hard work of any kind was banned.

These critical views raised questions that any aspiring writer of pastorals
was forced to consider: was pastoral, like drama and epic, subject to neo-
classical rules? How directly should a poet engage with contemporary experi-
ence? Should pastoral locate itself in eighteenth-century Britain, or in a timeless
Golden Age? The terms of the British debate were set by French theory.
Dryden's English translation of the *Eclogues* (1697), for example, was pre-
faced by Knightley Chetwood's defence of Virgil, based entirely on Rapin,
'against some of the Reflections of Monsieur Fontenelle'. Dryden's critical
dedication dismissed Fontenelle briskly, but was nevertheless uneasy about
moments when Virgil himself seemed to have lost pastoral 'decorum' and
slipped into the rustic or the pompous.[6]

An early eighteenth-century poet writing pastorals could not help but be
entangled in issues such as these. Ironically, French theory was imposing crit-
ical sophistication on a poetic mode that privileged simplicity. The problem
was to gauge which kind of simplicity was the right one.[7] At his best, Dryden
had shown what could be achieved by combining simple vocabulary and phras-
ing with a dignified manner, as when Moeris in the ninth eclogue sadly con-
fronts his failing memory:

> The rest I have forgot, for Cares and Time
> Change all things, and untune my Soul to Rhyme:
> I cou'd have once sung down a Summer's Sun,
> But now the Chime of Poetry is done. (70–3)

A lofty idea (72) is made to come from the heart rather than the head. The Virgilian *umbra*, that eternal note of sadness, is always convincingly struck by Dryden; but other more lighthearted elements, like the binding of Silenus in Eclogue Six, also come vividly across. Where a masterly translator like Dryden had stylistic choices to make, a poet attempting original pastorals faced many more, and would invite the judgment of any knowledgeable reader. So when the sixth volume of Tonson's *Miscellanies* appeared in 1709 containing two sets of 'Pastorals', by Ambrose Philips and the twenty-one-year-old Pope,[8] the literary world was bound to compare them and assess their critical allegiances. The fact that they seemed to offer a contrast between the principles of Rapin and Fontenelle made this inevitable. Where Philips's poems were firmly located in the English countryside, Pope's (in spite of references to Thames and Windsor) belonged in the timeless landscape of neo-classical pastoral. The result was something of a *cause célèbre*, in which Pope is usually seen to have had the upper hand.

Pope's *Pastorals* were written with critics in mind, and at his shoulder. The four poems circulated round his patrons with an accompanying 'Essay on Pastoral', picking up corrections here and a little burnish there, and were worked at and thoroughly revised to give them simplicity, propriety, and correctness. The teenager, it seems, was determined to please everyone. With assiduous critical diplomacy he followed Rapin and Fontenelle, Chetwood and Dryden, and praised Theocritus, Virgil, Tasso, and Spenser. As regards his first published work Pope was taking no risks. He presents his enterprise as an act of purification, distilling the essence of pastoral by filtering it through the best theories and the best models, and ensuring that 'Nature' is appropriately trimmed and ordered so as not to compromise his Art.

The poetic result is beautifully shaped. Pope uses the heroic couplet elegantly: phrases repeatedly echo each other in pleasing varied patterns, and images are satisfyingly mirrored. The shepherd voices are always conscious of allusion, symmetry and paradox, and a harmonising lyric strain is never absent for long:

> How all things listen, while thy Muse complains!
> Such silence waits on *Philomela*'s Strains,
> In some still Ev'ning, when the whisp'ring Breeze
> Pants on the Leaves, and dies upon the Trees. ('Winter', 77–80)

This is not a song, however, but Lycidas's response to Thyrsis's lament for the dead Daphne. Rather than bring the lyrical moment back to the here and now, as Theocritus and Virgil tend to do, Pope suspends it magically as though the two shepherds are both caught up in something greater. But the nightingale (*Philomela*) is part of a simile, not a presence in the scene. We can gauge the different world of Ambrose Philips by comparing the close of his first pastoral:

> Now, to the waining Moon, the Nightingale
> In doleful Ditties told her piteous Tale.
> The Love-sick Shepherd list'ning found Relief,
> Pleas'd with so sweet a Partner in his Grief:
> 'Till by degrees her Notes and silent Night
> To Slumbers soft his heavy Heart invite. (95–100)

Lobbin has likewise just ended his lament; but the word *Now* brings a real bird into the scene. Her *piteous Tale* alludes to the classical story of Philomela, but without the awkward assumption that the English shepherd knows this (as Pope's does). Lobbin can be comforted just by the music. The idea that nature gives him a *Partner* is a simple but effective one, as is the sympathetic partnering of *soft* and *heavy* in the last line (where his burden is laid down). Philips allows the phrase *doleful Ditties* (96) to add a rustic Spenserian touch that is not out of place. It reminds us that this pastoral is not aspiring to be something else, but feels at home among country people.

It is tempting to see Ambrose Philips as taking risks (not always success-fully) with the homely 'Doric' elements of Theocritus and Spenser, while Pope aims for a more 'Virgilian' smoothness; but this would be to oversimplify both Philips and Virgil. A reader of Virgil's *Eclogues* comes to appreciate how the poet's language is responsive to moments of tension and conflict. He does not smoothe out differences, but allows them to register – though without shifting linguistic gear as Theocritus does. In this respect Philips is sometimes more Virgilian than Pope. Also, the *Eclogues* are partly dramatic, a series of human engagements in which emotions encounter each other, and this is also true of Philips's pastorals. His second pastoral is a dialogue between alienated adoles-cence (the lovesick Colinet) and cheerful old age (the philosophic Thenot), in which natural images register their different thoughts. The scene parallels Virgil's first eclogue, where Meliboeus and old Tityrus meet on the road. The former is heading for exile from his confiscated farm, while the other is return-ing to the home that has been restored to him. Their talk contrasts alienation with joyful expectancy in a passionately evoked local landscape. Virgil's situ-ation is full of irony, yet by the poem's close it is held in suspension, when Tityrus in simple and moving terms offers his friend rest for the night. It is with a sense of its absolute appropriateness that Philips ends his own pastoral with a translation of that final speech, as Thenot makes his young friend Colinet a similar offer:

> This Night thy Cares with me forget; and fold
> Thy Flock with mine, to ward th'injurious Cold.
> Sweet Milk and clouted Cream, soft Cheese and Curd,
> With some remaining Fruit of last Year's Hoard,
> Shall be our Ev'ning Fare: And for the Night,
> Sweet Herbs and Moss, that gentle Sleep invite. (124–9)

With the folding of their flocks (the single detail Philips adds to his source) Colinet's pastoral *Cares* find a homely perspective, and the mental and phys-ical are drawn sympathetically together. Philips has clearly absorbed the Virgilian idea. With such examples in mind it becomes easier to appreciate why he was hailed as Britain's successor to Theocritus, Virgil, and Spenser.[9] Though clearly a 'modern', he could be seen as representing the spirit of the two classical poets (who wrote before pastoral was given neo-classical rules).

The critical acclaim came to a head with a series of five anonymous papers on pastoral poetry in *The Guardian* (1713) written by Thomas Tickell, who like Philips was a member of Addison's literary circle. These favoured the naturalised modern pastoral advocated by Fontenelle, and most of the illustrations were taken from Philips. Pope's more neo-classical poems were completely ignored. Tickell concluded that Philips's pastorals had more 'pretty Rusticity' than Virgil's, and were, with Spenser's, the most successful English writing in that mode.[10] This was just too much for Pope, who wrote a spoof essay of his own and managed to trick the *Guardian*'s editor, Richard Steele, into printing it. *Guardian* 40 pays ironic homage to Philips's 'pretty Rusticity', and choice examples are embarrassingly placed alongside Pope at his most elegant. The effect is like seating a thresher beside a Countess (but who is the more embarrassed?). Pope finds the whole idea of an English 'Doric' hilarious, and as a climax he prints part of a ballad in the Somersetshire Dialect 'which I chanced to find among some old Manuscripts':

> *Rager* go vetch tha *Kee*, or else tha Zun,
> Will quite be go, be vore c'have half a don . . .

Pope's editorial note (parodying E.K.'s glosses to Spenser's *Shepheardes Calender*) explains that *Kee* is 'the *Kine* or *Cows*'. Like the best parody, this is very unfair and very amusing, and has its own energy and logic. Pope shapes Roger the cowherd's instructions into an impeccable heroic couplet whose caesuras are perfectly placed, and in doing so he draws attention to pastoral's uneasy collaboration between nature and art, naivety and sophistication, reality and fiction. At the core of pastoral, this seems to suggest, is a potential gap for ironic play – one that Pope in his *Pastorals* had been determined to close. In the guise of mocking Philips, therefore, Pope's Somersetshire fragment is actually a nightmare inversion of his own *Pastorals*, evoking an all-too-real country world where it is poetic art that is unnatural, and elegance is indecorum.

By being a heavily coded form, the traditional 'Golden Age' pastoral was particularly vulnerable to having its inner logic exposed. What we tend to think of as 'mock-' or 'anti-pastoral' is often more truly the opening out for display of its ironic potential as a mode that is defined by what it excludes. All the things pastoral holds at bay – heroism, politics, money, war, time and death – are there to haunt it from an echo's distance. In *Englands Helicon* (1600) Marlowe's lyric, 'The Passionate Shepherd to his Love', was famously paired with Sir Walter Ralegh's 'The Nymph's Reply to the Shepherd':

> . . . But could youth last, and love still breede,
> Had joyes no date, nor age no neede,
> Then these delights my minde might move,
> To live with thee, and be thy love.

Ralegh intrudes an idea that is always hovering at the edge of pastoral, waiting to invade it. Classical pastoral (as Keats understood in his 'Ode on a Grecian Urn') acknowledges 'realities', but holds itself off from them (Virgil's Tityrus and Meliboeus remain forever seated on the grass, eating their cheese and fruit). Hence the importance in Theocritus and Virgil of notes that echo from elsewhere. This is what gives their pastorals, for all the narrowness of representation, such a richness of implication. In a similar way the poems resist being sub-sumed into either the Golden Age or the world of *negotium* (everyday affairs). Theocritus and Virgil tend to explore moments of suspension between timeless myth and physical reality, when both are there *in potentia*. This is the irony inherent in classical pastoral. Seen in these terms, Ralegh's reply is not strictly 'anti-pastoral', but rather the intrusion of its usually unspoken conscience.

It is helpful to bear these points in mind when dealing with the supposed 'anti-' or 'mock-pastorals' of the eighteenth century. It was Pope's ally, John Gay, who most successfully engaged with pastoral as ironic form. His *Shepherd's Week* (1714) found its stimulus in the dispute between Pope and the Addison circle, and these six rural eclogues (one for each day of the labouring week) are offered to the public in the voice of a Spenserian throwback who seems untouched by modern French elegance ('My Shepherd', Gay writes, 'sleepeth not under Myrtle shades, but under a Hedge').[11] With characters like Cuddy and Lobbin Clout, these pastorals seem at first to be taking Pope's line by ridiculing the Doric rusticity of the Spenser-Philips 'naturalising' school. In Gay's version of the traditional pastoral singing-contest (here a rustic 'squabble') the country ingredients pile up until Gay's lines creak like a market-stall:

> *Leek* to the *Welch*, to *Dutchmen Butter*'s dear,
> Of *Irish* Swains *Potatoe* is the Chear;
> *Oats* for their Feasts the *Scottish* Shepherds grind,
> Sweet *Turnips* are the Food of *Blouzelind*.
> While she loves *Turnips*, *Butter* I'll despise,
> Nor *Leeks* nor *Oatmeal* nor *Potatoe* prize.
>
> ('Monday; or, The Squabble', 83–8)

The ironic 'joke' is that these homely items are assembled in a rhetorical *Collectio* (a gathering of terms at the end) beloved of Renaissance sonneteers. Such effects can be expressively textured, as when in the same singing-contest Cuddy boasts about the soft and frisky Buxoma: 'Clean as young Lambkins or the Goose's Down, / And like the Goldfinch in her *Sunday* Gown' (51–2). In Pope's equivalent pastoral, Strephon's celebration of Delia cannot permit any gap between art and life where irony might gather – and it is the life which is sacrificed. The rhetorical patterning is similar, but here there is no physical reality to compromise it:

> In Spring the Fields, in Autumn Hills I love,
> At Morn the Plains, at Noon the shady Grove;
> But *Delia* always; absent from her Sight,
> Nor Plains at Morn, nor Groves at Noon delight. ('Spring', 77–80)

Suddenly Pope's neatly arranged ingredients (Spring, Autumn, Morn, Noon, Plains, Groves) seem lifeless and predictable. It is Buxoma, pranked out like a goldfinch, whom we remember.

Gay has not accidentally discovered poetry through burlesque, but has creatively tapped into the living sources of classical pastoral, in which shepherds make poetry from the things around them – a currency (linguistic also) that they value and use. The original of both Pope and Gay is the singing-contest in

Theocritus' Idyll Five (imitated in Virgil's third eclogue), in which the two singers refer to goat-skins, olives, locusts, crickets, pine-cones, lamb's wool, honey, milk, heather, baskets of cheese, a wooden pail, and so on. Gay also delights in accumulating such materials ('joking Talk / Of Ashes, Leather, Oatmeal, Bran and Chalk'), and he collects them at the end of his volume in a four-page 'Alphabetical Catalogue of . . . material Things mentioned by this Author'. Gay turns much to laughter, but in doing so he works with the pastoral grain, not against it. The lament of Bumkinet and Grubbinol for the dead Blouzelinda ('Friday') remains moving because it bridges the gap between the conventions of pastoral elegy and the unpromising ingredients of Blouzelinda's life. Gay does not attempt to 'raise' her by suppressing indecorous material. The most famous lines in Pope's *Pastorals* work precisely in the opposite direction, with poetic art creating an amenable subject, not seeking to represent a recalcitrant one. In 'Summer' Pope is exquisitely celebrating the charms of an immaterial presence combining Diana and Flora: 'Where-e'er you walk, cool Gales shall fan the Glade, / Trees, where you sit, shall crowd into a Shade, / Where-e'er you tread, the blushing Flow'rs shall rise, / And all things flourish where you turn your Eyes' ('Summer', 73–6). After this, Gay's lines about Blouzelinda seem to be written with one (winking) eye on Pope:

> Where-e'er I gad, I *Blouzelind* shall view,
> Woods, Dairy, Barn and Mows our Passion knew.
> When I direct my Eyes to yonder Wood,
> Fresh rising Sorrow curdles in my Blood. ('Friday; or, The Dirge', 41–4)

As Bumkinet passes their old haunts, his emotional arousal (*Fresh rising Sorrow*) can only parody his former sexual passion, and the language of the dairy (*curdles*) has its own decorum. At the end of the poem, he and his friend Grubbinol catch sight of 'bonny *Susan*', and their loss begins to be repaired as they carry her off for 'Ale and Kisses'. This ironic turn at the end of a love-complaint is not a sophisticated modern twist, but a characteristic feature of classical pastoral.[12] Whatever was the original stimulus for Gay's *Shepherd's Week*, the result was, as Goldsmith recognised, in 'the true spirit of pastoral poetry. In fact, he more resembles Theocritus than any other English pastoral writer whatsoever'.[13]

Goldsmith's emphasis on the 'spirit' is significant. A key idea behind pastoral is limitation – of place, time, and action. The pastoral space has no unique landmarks, and the history of the form is one of revisitings, repeatings, and superimpositions. The love-complaint, the singing competition, the elegy, and the wooing mark out its generic range, and from the Renaissance onwards these were endlessly reworked. Pastoral transmigrated through different bodies, each a temporary dwelling for its spirit. It is helpful to have such an image in mind when considering some of the many ingenious adaptations of pastoral poetry during the eighteenth century.

Lady Mary Wortley Montagu's *Town Eclogues* (1716) play intriguing variations on the traditional pastoral situations. The shepherd lads and lasses are here the beaux and belles of St James's, but these exotic creatures are trapped in the same endless round of wooing, competing, and complaining. Instead of the glades, streams, and rocks, their limited terrain is marked out by the drawing-room, card-table, and boudoir, and a few select places of aristocratic resort round which they move ('Strait then I'll dress and take my wonted Range, / Through India shops, to Motteux's, or the Change').[14] Flavia, lying on a couch with her looking-glass turned from her, laments her lost beauty ravaged by smallpox; the ageing Lydia rails against the fashionable world she used to command; and two practised 'players', Smilinda and Cardelia, compete in voicing their passion – for men and cards respectively. A lost lover might be foreseen, but a lost queen of clubs is a disaster. Instead of a lamb or a carved cup they pledge a snuff-box and a trinket-case, and their friend Loveit is the judge between them. As the traditional scenario is acted out, their complaints echo one another until the language of love and the language of the card-table chime wittily together – two songs creating a single lament whose terms are interchangeable. Enclosed in their leisured routines, Lady Mary's characters explore the neurotic potential of pastoral romance, in whose rhetoric they are trapped. Mirrors and echoes begin playing tricks, and lines of escape are cut off. These swains and nymphs, she satirically suggests, have turned Arcadia into Hell.

Jonathan Swift also finds the pastoral code fascinating, but rather than explore its spirit, he tends to dwell on the material body that it might wish to discard. In this respect he is a poet of anti-pastoral – ironic play becomes burlesque inversion. He reverses Lady Mary's world of aristocratic minds at leisure, to focus on the labourer's body at work. His miniature 'Description of the Morning' (1709) is filled with busy workers transforming the city street into a parody of a pastoral landscape. Instead of birdsong there are clashing street cries; the delicate breezes and showers are provided courtesy of Moll's whirling mop and the apprentice sprinkling the floor; Phoebus's chariot emerges as a hackney-coach, and the only shepherd in sight is the prison turn-key waiting to pen his 'Flock' after their nocturnal thieving. In the process the pastoral vision is turned inside out to become an early exercise in urban documentary. Swift's later verse satire offers further travesties of pastoral, but imbued with a new element of physical disgust. In his 'Pastoral Dialogue' (1732) the labourers are given a voice in Dermot and Sheelah, two Irish peasants who are weeding a baronet's courtyard while exchanging the most uncourtly of 'endearments'. In Swift's burlesque scene, *Ditch* rhymes with *Bitch*, and *Sluts* with *Guts*, and the lovers' immediate thoughts are on lice, sweat, and bruised bums. But this world too has room for the exotic, represented not by an exquisite snuff-box, but its equally rare equivalent:

> At an old stubborn Root I chanc'd to tug,
> When the Dean threw me this Tobacco-plug:
> A longer half-p'orth never did I see;
> This, dearest *Sheelah*, thou shalt share with me. (25–8)

Swift also delights in the voyeuristic implications of the enclosed world where nymphs and swains act out their pastoral fantasy-games, and he enjoys taking revenge on those who live in its fictions. In 'The Lady's Dressing Room' (1732) Strephon's sexual passion for the absent Celia is brilliantly inverted: although she is gone, he finds so many physical remnants and excreta left behind that her body takes on a horrifying nearness and nastiness, and he becomes trapped in an imaginative world that had once charmed him.

By the time Swift wrote these poems the erotic potential of pastoral had long been recognised. Its intimate encounters free of the constraints of the social world could naturalise sexual feeling by returning it to a prelapsarian innocence. This was the mission of Thomas Purney, for whom the ideal pastoral was a combination of innocence, tenderness, and softness. Aided by his own special theory of poetic 'enervation',[15] Purney produced a set of *Pastorals* (1717) in which pubescent girls and boys indulge their sexual curiosity and play love-games together. There is much soft simpering and fondling of 'paps', and in the first pastoral ('Love and Innocence') the two girls, Soflin and Paplet, watched by Cubbin from a nearby bush, entwine like putti in an erotic fresco:

> So as she said (and who so sweet can sain)
> Her little Leg would in her *Fellow's* twine,
> Then dainty'd droppen Hand in *Soflie* Breast:
> Ah dainty Hand! how *Cubbin* yearn'd to kiss't![16]

Spenserian diction fuses with baby-talk to produce a unique poetic dialect, and in the process pastoral is returned, along with language, nature, and sex, to a primal infantile state. Rather than the innocent Cubbin, it is the modern reader who is made to play the role of voyeur.

Remote in a different way are William Diaper's fascinating *Nereides: or, Sea-Eclogues* (1712), which solve problems of prurience by taking us out into a free aquatic realm in which sea-nymphs and Tritons enact a variety of pastoral episodes modelled closely on Theocritus and Virgil.[17] Diaper's ocean with its varied moods has a range of sensuous possibilities that he fully exploits – 'the vast unseen Mansions of the Deep, / Where secret Groves with liquid Amber weep' (Dedication 'To Mr Congreve, 21–2). In Eclogue XI, the nymph Eune and the Triton Melvin make love near the shore where land and sea meet; but when Eune wakes she finds herself alone on the dry sand, and weeps to see the 'distant Billows rowl' out of her reach. The ensuing climax is both erotic and natural: as she falls back into sleep, the tide begins to turn, and the languorous strength of the water reasserts itself:

> And now returning Waves by slow degrees
> Move on the Beach, and stretch the widen'd Seas.
> *Melvin* approaches with the rising Tide,
> And in his Arms enfolds his sleeping Bride. (52–5)

Diaper celebrates the fluid variety of his medium, to the extent that in 'Eclogue IV' two ocean-dwellers gaze at a distant pastoral landscape and pity its limitations ('But ah! how wretched are those earth-born Slaves, / Compar'd with us, who cut thro' shining Waves!'). The irony is that in their seascape they re-enact all the scenes of classical pastoral.

Diaper reinvigorated the old conventions by finding a new set of imagery. Later poets too, without having recourse to the satiric twists and inversions of Lady Mary and Swift, opened up other expressive possibilities and brought fresh life to the eclogue. Its stereotypical nature allowed for ingenious re-workings and witty substitutions. During the 1740s the mode was resuscitated by the poetic equivalent of blood-transfusion and electric shock. Two young poets towards mid-century used their apprentice-pastorals to announce their originality and ambition – a new language would come from the oldest of forms. In his *Persian Eclogues* (1742) William Collins turned to the Middle East to refresh English verse with what his preface calls the 'rich and figurative' language of Arabian and Persian poetry; but in 'Eclogue the Second' Hassan the camel-driver, fearful and hungry in the empty desert, is forced to recall the familiar 'green delights' that both he and Collins have left behind:

> Here, where no Springs, in Murmurs break away,
> Or Moss-crown'd Fountains mitigate the Day:
> In vain ye hope the green Delights to know,
> Which Plains more blest, or verdant Vales bestow. (23–6)

Once again, here in the desert the pastoral scene is ironically present as an imagined oasis, and the contrast allows Collins's exotic eclogues to be fully savoured. His Oxford friend, the seventeen-year-old Thomas Warton, declared his adventurousness in his title: *Five Pastoral Eclogues, The Scenes of which are Suppos'd to lie among the Shepherds, oppress'd by the War in Germany* (1745). Exploiting the latest news-reports of marauding troops, and interweaving them with evocations of the shepherds' innocent, timeless hiding-places (caves, grottoes, and shady groves), Warton makes the most of atmospheric sound-effects and ruinous descriptions. In his blank-verse dialogues, the lost shepherdess has been abducted by a soldier, and the favourite lamb trampled by a troop of horse.[18]

This reaching out for the exotic and sensational suggests that the formal 'eclogue' with its conversing shepherds was having a final fling. By mid-century it is clear that without such stimuli some readers had become jaded, as William Shenstone wrote:

> So rude and tuneless are thy lays,
>   The weary audience vow,
> Tis not th'Arcadian swain that sings,
>   But 'tis his herds that low.[19]

The singing shepherd was being replaced by the lowing herd. The pastoral setting remained popular and was easily integrated into other poetic forms. Glimpses of Edenic innocence formed part of many descriptive poems, and the moods and imagery of pastoral elegy were infused into contemplative writing. The shepherd in Joseph Warton's *The Enthusiast: Or the Lover of Nature* (1744) is a solitary contemplater of nature, not a conversationalist; and the 'hoary-headed swain' of Thomas Gray's *Elegy Written in a Country Church Yard* (1751) nostalgically recalls a pastoral landscape that is now empty ('One morn I miss'd him on the custom'd hill', 109). New poetic genres offered fresh possibilities. An increasing interest in the lyrical voice re-tuned 'pastoral' in sophisticated ways. As early as 1731, Isaac Thompson was fusing pastoral lament and Ovidian heroic epistle to give his lovelorn shepherd the emotional range of Pope's Eloisa; and Shenstone himself in his 'Pastoral Ballad' transformed the garden into an expression of a neurotic self, registering his emotions in a palpitating lyric rhythm that anticipates Tennyson.[20]

An interest in specific landscapes and the real life of the countryside inevitably had its effect on pastoral. Once Stephen Duck, the Wiltshire thresher, had produced *The Thresher's Labour* (1730) it became increasingly difficult to show pastoral figures 'simply chatting in a rustic row'[21] without rolling up their sleeves and getting to work. Christopher Smart's extraordinary 'Noon-Piece; or, The Mowers at Dinner' (1748) explodes the pastoral scene into assorted fragments: dancing cupids share the picture with English farmworkers; allegorical figures play while Tray the dog guards the workers' lunch; and 'Colin Clout and Yorkshire Will / From the leathern bottle swill' (the Spenserian shepherd sharing a drink with the modern labourer). The implements of work now form an integral part of Smart's scene:

> Their scythes upon the adverse bank
>   Glitter 'mongst th'entangled trees,
> Where the hazles form a rank,
>   And court'sy to the courting breeze.

This is the point where pastoral meets the georgic.

Rapin's view that pastoral represented the earliest of all poetry was widely accepted in the early eighteenth century. Whether or not one agreed with his 'Golden Age' theory, pastoral had become associated with a simplicity of language and manners, and an essential freedom from a specified place and time. Collins and Warton challenged both of these; but in shedding them the pastoral mode somehow lost its centre of gravity, its defining limitation. While this was happening, the georgic poem was becoming popular as a genre that naturally embraced the new and the specific. The paradoxical fact is that georgic was by far the older genre. Its founding text, Hesiod's *Works and Days*, is dateable to the Eighth Century BC,[22] seven hundred years before its defining text, Virgil's *Georgics*. But Virgil's poem was 'defining' in a different sense from his *Eclogues*. As a form that was characterised not by limitation but by its capaciousness, the georgic opened itself to freer reworkings and extension to different topics. Welcoming variety of scenes, details of place and time, and an appropriately specific, even technical, language, georgic flourished by seeking new subjects for attention. If pastoral had found its ironies in repeated scenic superimpositions and revisitings, georgic represented the spirit of 'fresh woods, and pastures new' (Milton's words on leaving pastoral behind).[23] It was therefore an appropriate mode for expressing the energies of trade and colonisation. Georgic's images tend to be dynamic ones that incorporate growth and change and reflect the harnessing of human ingenuity. This said, however, georgic also has one foot in the known and familiar. It remembers the names of things, exploits local knowledge, passes on expertise, recalls histories, recommends the tried and tested. It is interested in reliable tools and techniques. But this doubleness at the heart of georgic should not be seen as a disjunction. What appears at first to be a contradiction between stability and change is really a recognition of the relationship between conserving and extending.

In place of the pastoral's ironic juxtapositions, the georgic poem is keenly aware of mixture and variety. It tends to look for ways of improving existing materials by combining or adding to them. In *The Sugar-Cane: A Poem* (1764) James Grainger goes so far as to make this a general rule for all life on earth: 'In plants, in beasts, in man's imperial race, / An alien mixture meliorates the breed'.[24] New energy comes from drawing varied elements together or recycling what has decayed. There is a link to be made, therefore, between the significance of compost for the georgic tradition, and its celebration of English as a 'mixed' language. In *The Hop-Garden* (1752), on hop-cultivation and beer-making, Christopher Smart praises the loamy soil of Kent in these terms:

> this the hop
> Loves above others, this is rich, is deep,
> Is viscous, and tenacious of the pole.
> Yet maugre all its native worth, it may
> Be meliorated with warm compost.... (I, 83–7)

As if to make his point that the *native* can always be improved, Smart offers us the full mixture of English vocabulary, with its rich absorption of Latin (*viscous*, *tenacious*, *meliorated*) and Norman French (*maugre*). Like other georgic writers he is aware that the fertility of his native English has been increased by a long history of linguistic assimilation. For all its celebration of tradition, the georgic also comes to terms with change.

If pastoral evoked the temperate poise and innocence of the Golden Age, or its Christian equivalent the Garden of Eden, the georgic is located in the fallen world of corruption and death, the changing seasons, and the necessity of human labour. In Genesis 3:23 an angry God insists that mankind has become an integral part of an organic cycle of growth and decay: 'Therefore the Lord God sent him forth from the garden of Eden, to till the ground *from whence he was taken*' (my italics). Providentially, the curse was to become an opportunity. Hesiod had his own version of this fall, and in *Works and Days* (an alternative title might be 'Labour and Time') he announced that his was the Age of Iron, in which mankind 'will never cease from toil and misery by day or night'.[25] Hesiod's Greek poem is the original of the myth that toil is the modern condition in a world where nature no longer offers its plenty freely but demands endless labour from us, at a time when all social cohesion has been lost. The idea lies behind the passage about 'these iron Times' in James Thomson's 'Spring' (from *The Seasons*, 1730), where 'all / Is off the Poise within' (274, 277–8) and nothing is stable or predictable any more. Work in this Hesiodic context offers some way of bringing order and connectedness to what Thomson calls our 'broken World' (318). Throughout *The Seasons* this lack of 'poise', and the need for repeated human effort to accommodate, or even understand, the forces of nature, check the poem's Newtonian optimism so as to create a more complex dynamic. Although finally for Thomson the earth is held in the providential embrace of 'The great eternal Scheme / Involving All, and in a perfect Whole / Uniting' (*Winter*, 1046–8), at the level of human activity those natural forces both forward and frustrate human toil, a double theme that Virgil's *Georgics* had developed.

Critics who detect a complacent and leisured agenda behind the English georgic tend not to mention Hesiod. For Rachel Crawford, for example, the concept of the 'happy swain' is 'central to the georgic vision', which celebrates 'a traditionalist scheme that equates happy labor with the soil'.[26] But the 'Nature' with which the georgic poet works is the same ambiguous power the workers have to confront, a changeable force which nurtures and tortures while it tracks the cycle of the seasons. In *The Thresher's Labour* (1730) Stephen Duck expresses frustration at his repeated annual routine:

> . . . the same Toils we must again repeat:
> To the same Barns again must back return,
> To labour there for room for next Year's Corn.
>   Thus, as the Year's revolving Course goes round,
> No respite from our Labour can be found:
> Like *Sysiphus*, our Work is never done,
> Continually rolls back the restless Stone . . . (275–81)

The undoing of his work, the continual rolling back, seems to owe something to the Hesiodic passage in *Georgic* I, where Virgil's farmer is seen as resisting the depredations of pests and the general tendency in Nature towards degeneration and reversal: 'So it is: for everything by nature's law / Tends to the worse, slips ever backward, backward'.[27]

Set against this principle is the possibility of reconstruction and development – the *en-ergy* that counters the *en-tropy*. Virgil's four-book *Georgics* were being written in momentous years (36–29 BC) when Rome was struggling from a period of civil war to one of peace and unity. After the final defeat of Mark Antony and Cleopatra (31 BC), Octavius Caesar was seen to be uniting the empire, reintroducing the old observances and traditions, founding colonies, and restoring the republican constitution. It was a balance of conservation and innovation, a uniting of the *civis* and the *cultus*, the state and 'culture' in all senses, an ideal time for a poem on the arts of cultivation.[28] Understanding the new project, in 29 BC Virgil read his completed work to Octavius, ending Book I by recalling 'a world in ruins' – 'everywhere / So many wars, so many shapes of crime / Confront us; no due honour attends the plough, / The fields, bereft of tillers, are all unkempt' (I, 505–7); then in the following book on the cultivation of trees and vines he considers how to encourage new growth by sowing and propagating, but also engrafting: 'often we observe how one tree's branches / Can turn, with no harm done, into another's' (II, 32–3). Unless this is carried out, says Virgil, the fruit will deteriorate, 'forgetting its old flavour' (II, 59). There is a natural power in the

Italian soil, but 'every tree needs labour, all must be / Forced into furrows, tamed at any cost' (II, 61–2). Wounds need to be made by slits and wedges, but they will heal and produce a new growth that flourishes as never before.

This georgic narrative was ready made for a period in British history when two nations had recently been engrafted together. In 1707 the Act of Union united the parliaments of England and Scotland and superimposed their national flags. Civil war in the 1640s had been followed by decades of religious upheaval and constitutional uncertainty, and the new 'Great Britain' faced particular problems of continuity and change, both religious and political. This forms the subject of John Philips's two-book poem *Cyder* (1708), which extends the concerns of Virgil to the soil and climate of Britain. For Philips it is a land of mixed soils: some are 'deceitful', 'penurious', 'stubborn' or 'devoid of spirit', others 'kinder'; but each has a 'Force and Genius' that by experience can be made adaptable. What should be avoided is the importation of a 'Rich Foreign Mold' (I,120)—such an 'alien Compost' (there are suggestions of the Hanoverian monarch-in-waiting here)[29] can have only a deceptive and temporary effect. In a long Virgilian passage on engrafting, Philips describes how the orchard-keeper needs to experiment with new relationships,

> and search how far
> Two different Natures may concur to mix
> In close Embraces, and strange Off-spring bear?
> Thou'l't find that Plants will frequent Changes try,
> Undamag'd, and their marriageable Arms
> Conjoin with others. (I, 301–6)

The resulting hybrid will flourish, and 'Ee'r-long their differing Veins / Unite, and kindly Nourishment convey' (I, 282–3). In tune with Virgil's constitutional concerns, Philips's poem seeks to reconcile a continuous tradition of old skills and observances with the cultivation of fresh varieties. Ideally, experience and wisdom should combine with energy and inventiveness, and the new be allowed to develop from the old. The poem's evolutionary politics emerges near the end in a Virgilian picture of the horrors of England's Civil War when pruning-hooks became weapons ('Too oft alas! has mutual Hatred drench'd / Our Swords in Native Blood', II, 486–7). Philips celebrates the fact that 'Cyder-Land' remained loyal to the executed King Charles ('O Best of Kings!'), and that after years of tyranny the nation's liberties had recently been restored by another Stuart monarch, Queen Anne.

In ending his poem with a narrative of British constitutional history, Philips exploits the organic character of the georgic by engrafting it onto its native siblings, the English 'country-house' poem (the tradition of Jonson's *To Penshurst* and Marvell's *Upon Appleton House*) and the prospect poem (Sir John Denham's *Cooper's Hill*), landscape economies that explore geo-historical continuities and disruptions (see Chapter 10). Denham's Royalist survey of Windsor and the River Thames, with its moralised landscape marked by religious conflict, is especially close in mood to Philips, and *Cooper's Hill* remained a potent influence on the naturalised English georgic. Pope's

Windsor-Forest (1713) specifically re-works Denham to celebrate the Tory Peace of Utrecht ('And Peace and Plenty tell, a STUART reigns', 42). In all these poems the small individual landscape tests out at local level the state's capacity to harness into an effective economy those potentially competing forces: freedom and obedience, change and continuity, individual and social good, the arts of war and the arts of peace.[30] In the *Georgics* Virgil had used his native Mantuan scene to signify the keeping of faith, a spot of ground where true values will remain, and where he will dedicate a shrine to Caesar ('where the Mincius, / Embroidering his banks with tender rushes, / In sweeping loops meanders. / In the middle of the shrine, as patron god, / I will have Caesar placed', III, 14–16). In Virgil's imagination the Empire is given a local habitation. Georgic geography in this way opens out a pastoral retreat to patriotic and political themes, reaching from the provincial riverbank to the national picture, and then through time and space to distant lands (on the doors of Virgil's shrine will be carved 'the hordes of Ganges / In battle and our Romulus' victory, / And here great Nile in flood', III, 26–9). Pope's *Windsor-Forest* has a similarly confident centrifugal movement that carries patriotic good faith outwards from his own native stream in the forest (the Loddon) via the national river (the Thames) to colonise the world. The resulting free trade will be of enormous gain to Britain ('Earth's distant Ends our Glory shall behold, / And the new World launch forth to seek the Old', 399–400). The opening up of foreign markets to British shipping was one of the benefits of the Utrecht treaty, and in Pope's poem the 'economy' of forces within a national and global system is here taking on its modern financial sense.

In Walpole's Britain of the 1730s, the georgic had obvious appeal for the mercantile interest. Its language of beneficent growth and exploitation of resources could be used to naturalise the claims of commercial development. The economic writer John Bennet recommended improvements in trading conditions in language that sounds uncannily like a prose summary of a georgic poem:

> . . . the Colonies and Trade of *Great-Britain* may be likened to a most excellent Orchard[31] laid out and planted by Queen *Elizabeth*, suffered to grow by King *James*, unfenced and over-run in the next Reign, supported and taken Care of in the *Interregnum*, put into better Order on the Restoration; and having supplied us plentifully with all Sorts of Fruit ever since, both for our own and foreign Use, at length the Ground wants manuring, the old Walks repairing, the Trees pruning and nailing, and some to be removed, and others new planted; and the Whole, from the Goodness of the Soil, and Benefits of its Situation, capable of receiving prodigious Additions and Improvements. (p. 128)

This extract from Bennet's *The National Merchant: Or, Discourses on Commerce and Colonies; Being an Essay for Regulating and Improving the Trade and Plantations of Great Britain, By Uniting the National and Mercatorial Interests* (1736) shows how naturally the geo-historical economy of the georgic could be made to serve the Whig interest. Its language of manuring, pruning, repairing and planting is less concerned with constitutional theory than with getting the system to function properly. For the Royalist histories of Denham, Philips and Pope, Bennet substitutes a severely practical test of effective state organisation, and a concern with managing the nation's resources. Oliver Cromwell and the two Charleses are assessed on this basis only.

The improving of British industry and trade was one of the purposes of georgic as a patriotic mode. Addressing his 3-canto poem, *Agriculture* (1753), to the future George III (as part of an ambitious project entitled *Public Virtue*), Robert Dodsley aimed 'to delineate such objects of public virtue, as best may deserve the attention of a British Prince'.[32] These included a national oak-planting scheme. Works like John Dyer's *The Fleece* (1757) and Grainger's *Sugar-Cane* can be regarded as up-to-date reports on the state of the nation's cloth industry and its West Indian sugar plantations. Such poems, with their well informed documentation (often supplemented by footnotes) are full of practical advice,[33] and can incorporate quite naturally a specific recommendation (like Dyer's plans for linking the Rivers Trent, Severn, and Thames, III, 604–6) or a hymn to trade (Grainger's 'Mighty commerce, hail!', IV, 322). Both Dyer and Grainger have direct knowledge of what they discuss, and their observations and advice are based on first-hand experience. In his Preface, Dr Grainger notes: 'Medicines of such amazing efficacy, as I have had occasion to make trials of in these islands, deserve to be universally known. And wherever, in the following poem, I recommend any such, I beg leave to be understood as a physician, and not as a poet.' He expects to be judged by practical as well as poetic criteria.

For Virgil the farmer-poet, the ideal of practical organisation is represented by the beehive, which forms the subject of his final book. This analysis of a state-in-miniature brings to a climax the *Georgics*' concern with how civic order should reflect the natural interdependence of all life. The worker-bees are busy and co-operative in maintaining their hive; their energies are focused on the job in hand, and their individual identities are subsumed into communal needs. Shift the perspective slightly and they can be seen to represent the ideal labour-force. Perhaps it takes a British labouring-class poet to understand that somebody is growing very fat on the energies of others – and it is not the workers:

> So the industrious Bees do hourly strive
> To bring their Loads of Honey to the Hive;
> Their sordid Owners always reap the Gains,
> And poorly recompense their Toil and Pains. (243–6)

With these final lines, Mary Collier's *The Woman's Labour* (1739) gives a bitter twist to Virgil's georgic economy. The second couplet is typical of the way she refuses to endorse its thematic patterns. The routines in which she functions are controlled by someone else, and the *Gains* and *Pains* are unequally shared. Unlike Duck's seasonal duties on the farm, Collier's labour is variable piece-work: helping with the harvest, house-cleaning, and washing clothes. Where Duck can at least find satisfaction in the heroic pulse of his threshing ('Down one, one up, so well they keep the Time, / The *Cyclops* Hammers could not truer chime', 40–1) or in the steady routines of his working-day ('Supper and Sleep by Morn new Strength supply, / And out we set again our Works to try', 157–8), Collier's work remains uncomfortable and frustrating. Her couplets tend to be less confident than his, less certain of their progress:

> When to the House we come where we should go,
> How to get in, alas! we do not know:
> The Maid quite tir'd with Work the Day before,
> O'ercome with Sleep; we standing at the Door
> Oppress'd with Cold, and often call in vain,
> E're to our Work we can Admittance gain ... (149–54)

Here the rhythm and rhyme (Duck's *Time* and *chime*) lack energy – no word is giving impetus to others. The monosyllables seem to underline the absence of direction (*we come where we should go*), and what might become a pattern (*tir'd with*, *O'ercome with*, *Oppress'd with*) remains mere repetition. Reading Mary Collier helps us to appreciate that although the georgic acknowledges hard labour, it tends to see work as harnessed to the regular demands of nature. Its larger rhythms are not disrupted by a kitchen-maid oversleeping.

Where Collier's worker-bees toil for little recompense within a harsh human system, Virgil's tiny creatures are granted a glimpse of another dimension entirely. Their labour is potentially visionary, even redemptive – part of a transcendent scheme that mankind can only guess at: 'Some have affirmed that bees possess a share / Of the divine mind and drink ethereal draughts; / For God, they say, pervades the whole creation, / Lands and the sea's expanse and the depths of sky' (IV, 219–22). To see the earth as an animated system came naturally to the English georgic, with its organic modes of thought, and its capacity to engage with the latest scientific discoveries. The mathematics of Newton, Shaftesbury's System of Nature, the worlds of microscope and telescope, combined to give a georgic poem like Thomson's *Seasons* an extra philosophical/theological dimension. Both Hesiod and Virgil had reached from the plough to the stars, but Thomson delights in the new confidence with which an eighteenth-century British poet can contemplate everything from the minute sap vessels in a leaf to the intelligibility of the universe. Thomson's natural world owes much directly to Virgil. He has fully absorbed the *Georgics* both thematically and in detail, and many of its memorable passages have their direct equivalent in his poem: the bees' society, the sexual passion in animals, storm, pestilence, the labours of the agricultural year, exotic excursions to the desert and the frozen steppes, the signs of changing weather – and so on. But Virgil's tentative suggestion of a universal life-force becomes in *The Seasons* the sustaining impetus of all creation. For Thomson, Earth is a living organism whose materials are forever in motion or waiting to have their energies released. In 'Spring' he prays ecstatically to the 'SOURCE OF BEINGS! UNIVERSAL SOUL / Of Heaven and Earth! ESSENTIAL PRESENCE ... !'

(556–7). These are big concepts; but as he goes down on his knees, it is not to pray but to scrutinise the minute mechanisms of plant-life:

> By THEE the various vegetative Tribes,
> Wrapt in a filmy Net, and clad with Leaves,
> Draw the live Ether, and imbibe the Dew.
> By THEE dispos'd into congenial Soils,
> Stands each attractive Plant, and sucks, and swells
> The juicy Tide; a twining Mass of Tubes. (561–6)

The world in miniature with its air (*live Ether*) and ocean (*juicy Tide*) bursts into activity, and the reader's imagination is pulled away from the abstract divine spirit to the rising sap of springtime, the true 'essential' element. The tiny fibres of vegetation become the tangible form of life's organic interconnectedness, its 'soul'. Indeed we have just seen a Virgilian bee 'Cling to the Bud, and, with inserted Tube, / Suck its pure Essence, its ethereal Soul' (511–2).

It is a mark of the adaptability of georgic that it could take as its subject not only the natural world, but the organisation of the human body. For the physician-poet John Armstrong this too was a complex living economy with its equivalent of soil and climate, ripening and decay, energies and diseases. In *The Oeconomy of Love* (1736) the animating principle is the sexual appetite 'from whose quick Impulse Life / Subsists' (286–7), and the human task is to turn this force of nature to best advantage ('we strive not to repress / . . . Her lawful Growth; ours be the Task alone / To check her rude Excrescences, to prune / Her wanton Overgrowth' (278–82). Proper husbandry is therefore vital ('Husband your Vigour well', 544), and variety of cultivation advisable ('Other Pursuits, their equal Share demand / Of Cultivation', 504–5). Armstrong's unembarrassed vocabulary of growth and fruition extends to the topic of puberty ('the parting Breasts / Wanton exuberant and tempt the touch, / Plump'd with rich Moisture from the finish'd Growth', 50–2), and even to a youth's nocturnal emissions ('mid the rage / Of the soft Tumult, every turgid Cell / Spontaneous disembogues its lucid store', 42–4). But this is a fallen georgic world, not a pastoral Eden, and Armstrong is concerned with offering practical advice (and warnings) on everything from aphrodisiacs to impotence.

For him, the body is something to be cultivated with as much care as Virgil's grapes, and just as crops and livestock respond to a routine based on knowledge and experience, so the human body will flourish under a regimen of regular habits. This is the message of Armstrong's best known georgic poem, *The Art of Preserving Health* (1744). Here the necessity of labour becomes a virtue: 'Toil, and be strong', he advises, 'By toil the flaccid nerves / Grow firm, and gain a more compacted tone'. He recommends sustained 'Exercise' – not sudden bursts of energy, but a habitual routine, an awareness of the regular ticking of the body's clock. This placing of human labour within the greater scheme of things, finding a bodily pulse within the broader rhythm of nature, takes us to the heart of the georgic mode:

> ... pliant nature more or less demands,
> As custom forms her; and all sudden change
> She hates of habit, even from bad to good ...
> Slow may the change arrive, and stage by stage;
> Slow as the shadow o'er the dial moves,
> Slow as the stealing progress of the year. (III, 464–71)

Armstrong attunes himself to the organic implications of georgic: the body should be synchronised with nature's measured pace. Time is implacable, and *change* must be accommodated. The less it disrupts, the more surely it will transform.

The georgic was therefore well equipped for engaging with the momentous developments of the Industrial Evolution (as it should perhaps be called), in which the natural energies in soil, rock and water were harnessed to increasingly sophisticated processes. As we have seen, the georgic's variety and adaptability, its interest in how things are organised, its geographical and historical dynamics, and its openness to specialised vocabularies, allowed it to explore economies of many different kinds. It combined a respect for custom and experience with a practical interest in how things work and develop. In Dyer's *The Fleece*, we see the old and new worlds encountering each other, but in a context of continuity. This poem offers a survey of Britain's sheep-farming regions mapped out by the nation's rivers, and a historical account of how the wool trade developed over many centuries. We learn about the various breeds suited to different local conditions; and the individual types of cloth produced.[34] Dyer celebrates practised skills of many kinds, whether it is the efficiency of the Leeds wholesale cloth-market, or the village-woman's deftness at her spinning-wheel. But in the middle of these tributes to traditional techniques appears an alien invader, Lewis Paul's roller spinning-machine (the very latest 1750s technology):

> We next are shown
> A circular machine, of new design,
> In conic shape: it draws and spins a thread
> Without the tedious toil of needless hands.
> A wheel, invisible, beneath the floor,
> To ev'ry member of th'harmonious frame
> Gives necessary motion. One, intent,
> O'erlooks the work: the carded wool, he says,
> Is smoothly lapp'd around those cylinders,
> Which, gently turning, yield it to yon cirque
> Of upright spindles, which, with rapid whirl,
> Spin out, in long extent, an even twine. (III, 291–302)

The *tedious toil* of humanity has been replaced by the spindles' *rapid whirl*. The circles move continuously, their different speeds perfectly synchronised. A solitary worker indicates *yon cirque* as if pointing up to the heavens, and we notice how this new system of *necessary motion* has been naturalised in georgic fashion, unproblematically fitted into James Thomson's vocabulary of Newtonian providence – only here the *harmonious frame* is made of wood and metal. Revolutionary technology is presented as part of a naturally evolving scheme.

When a poet wants to register change as a sudden, disruptive break with the past, the adaptable georgic is no longer suitable. Here the ironies of pastoral come into their own. Pastoral's use of juxtaposition and contrast replaces georgic's concern with intermixture and development. Georgic's growth of experience gives way to pastoral's lost innocence. Part of the power of Oliver Goldsmith's *The Deserted Village* (1770) is its rejection of the georgic mode in favour of a return to pastoral – or rather a frustrated longing to return. The poem moves from the opening description of an Arcadian social circle ('Dear lovely bowers of innocence and ease', 5) to distressing scenes of estrangement and dispersal ('yon widowed, solitary thing', 131), but it refuses to connect up the two visions into an organic whole. Here Time is discontinuous, with the past set against the present; and the only signs of continuity are the lingering bits of vegetation which mark each of the three lost buildings that once gave the village its heart. The 'torn shrubs' (141), 'blossomed furze' (196), and 'yonder thorn' (221) are isolated landmarks that parody a georgic concern with husbandry. In Auburn there is nothing to cultivate. It is part of Goldsmith's indictment of his age that at the centre of his poem is an aching void where georgic might be. The poem finds no space for productive activity, but only its deleterious effects. We are presented not with an economy, but with unreconciled extremes of luxury and want. The poem also has a stylistic gap between its sentimental and satiric modes – circling repetitions for the lost pastoral society ('These round thy bowers their chearful influence shed, / These were thy charms—But all these charms are fled', 33–4) moving to ironic contrasts and inversions for the present scene ('Where wealth accumulates, and men decay'). The text of *The Deserted Village* exemplifies a lost coherence, a lack of common ground and continuous life. In place of this is an isolated pastoral idyll to which the poet cannot return. Instead, he suddenly reaches out to an exotic land of scorpions, tigers and tornadoes, as the place to start a new life – an episode the georgic mode could accommodate, but which here has a suitably disruptive and ironic effect.

If pastoral was able to develop its radical potential for signifying alienation and social division, or for imaging the inauguration of a pristine world (and thus become an appropriate mode of revolutionary discourse in the 1790s),[35] georgic was easily assimilated into the mixed topographical poem discussed in Chapter 10. In *The Task* (1785) William Cowper integrates the art of cucumber-growing, the evil of cruelty to animals, and the history of living-room furniture into a poem concerned with the state of the nation; and his 'Yardley Oak' (1792) celebrates an ancient tree whose organic Burkean constitution has resisted the axe of revolution. Hollow and deformed, it is nonetheless a living system that has experienced the full rigours of the georgic – time, disease, the weather, predators, and decay – yet still manages to renew itself. Remarkably, both pastoral and georgic persisted throughout the eighteenth century, and by transforming and adapting in various ways, were able to offer their contributions to the political debates of the 1790s.

Notes

1. Parnell's untitled poem, from a loose undateable manuscript (here modernised), was first published in Claude Rawson and F.P. Lock (eds.), *Collected Poems of Thomas Parnell* (Newark, etc., 1989), pp. 421–2.

2. John D. Bernard, *Ceremonies of Innocence: Pastoralism in the Poetry of Edmund Spenser* (Cambridge, 1989), p. 6.

3. Anthony Low, in *The Georgic Revolution* (Princeton, 1985), traces a fascinating earlier history of the English georgic mode from the Middle Ages to the seventeenth century.

4. There has been a deliberate tendency in some criticism to conflate the distinct characters of pastoral and georgic. See, for example, Richard Feingold, *Nature and Society: Later Eighteenth-Century Uses of the Pastoral and Georgic* (Hassocks, 1978), p. 16; and Michael McKeon, 'Surveying the Frontier of Culture: Pastoralism in Eighteenth-Century England', *Studies in Eighteenth-Century Culture*, 26 (1998), 7–28. McKeon sees eclogue and georgic as both operating within an 'oppositional structure' (p. 9). See note 26 below.

5. See J.E. Congleton, *Theories of Pastoral in England, 1684–1798* (Gainesville, 1952).

6. Dryden, 'To the Right Honourable Hugh, Lord Clifford', prefixed to the *Pastorals* in his *Works of Virgil, Translated into English Verse* (1697).

7. See Thomas G. Rosenmeyer, *The Green Cabinet: Theocritus and the European Pastoral Lyric* (Berkeley and Los Angeles, 1969), pp. 45–64.

8. *Poetical Miscellanies: The Sixth Part* (London, 1709). Philips's six pastorals (four of which had been printed in 1708) opened the volume, and Pope's four pastorals closed it. See M.G. Segar (ed.), *The Poems of Ambrose Philips* (Oxford, 1937).

9. See George Sherburn, *The Early Career of Alexander Pope* (Oxford, 1934), pp. 117–19.

10. See John Calhoun Stephens (ed.), *The Guardian* (Lexington, 1982), p. 130.

11. 'The Proeme', *The Shepherd's Week* (London, 1714), sig. A4^r.

12. See Theocritus, *Idylls*, VII, 122–7; and Virgil, *Eclogues*, II, 73.

13. From *The Beauties of English Poetry* (1767). *Collected Works of Oliver Goldsmith*, ed. Arthur Friedman, 5 vols. (Oxford, 1966), V, 322.

14. 'Friday', 27–8.

15. 'In order to compose a Pastoral Dialect entirely perfect; the first thing, I think, a Writer has to do, is . . . to enervate it and deprive it of all strength' (Thomas Purney, *A Full Enquiry into the True Nature of Pastoral* [1717]; Augustan Reprint Society, no. 11 [1948], p. 60).

16. H.O. White (ed.), *The Works of Thomas Purney* (Oxford: Basil Blackwell, 1933), p. 16. See Carson Bergstrom, 'Purney, Pastoral, and the Polymorphous Perverse', *British Journal for Eighteenth-Century Studies*, 17 (1994), 149–63.

17. See the details given by Dorothy Broughton (ed.), *William Diaper: The Complete Works* (London, 1952), pp. xxiv–xl.

18. Later 'exotic' reworkings of pastoral include Thomas Chatterton's 'African Eclogues' (1770), Edward Rushton's *West-Indian Eclogues* (Liverpool, 1787), and Robert Southey's 'Botany Bay Eclogues' (1794).

19. 'On certain Pastorals', *The Works in Verse and Prose, of William Shenstone, Esq.*, 2 vols. (London, 1764), I, 210.

20. 'Pastoral VI. The Letter', in Isaac Thompson, *A Collection of Poems Occasionally Writ On Several Subjects* (Newcastle, 1731), pp. 30–34; 'A Pastoral Ballad', *Works of Shenstone*, I, 189–98.

21. Milton, 'On the Morning of Christ's Nativity', 87.

22. M.L. West (ed.), *Hesiod: Works and Days* (Oxford, 1978), p. 31.

23. Milton, *Lycidas*, 193.

24. *Sugar-Cane*, I, 458–9. See John Gilmore, *The Poetics of Empire: A Study of James Grainger's The Sugar-Cane* (London and New Brunswick, 2000), p. 103.

25. *Theogony and Works and Days*, tr. by M.L. West (Oxford, 1988), p. 42. On the pain and discipline of the 'Hesiodic code', see Rosenmeyer, *The Green Cabinet*, pp. 20–3.

26. Rachel Crawford, 'English Georgic and British Nationhood', *ELH*, 65 (1998), 123–58 (p. 135). For Crawford the georgic mode resisted the progressive and commercial, and presented Britain as a 'georgic Eden' (pp. 129, 135–6).

27. *Georgics*, I, 199–200; *The Georgics*, tr. by L.P. Wilkinson (Harmondsworth, 1982), p. 63 (all further quotations are from this translation). In John Barrell's words, the Georgic 'conceives of nature as niggardly, as reluctant to yield its fruits, as always threatening to run wild, as hostile to us, and so needing to be subdued by work' (*Poetry, Language and Politics* [Manchester, 1988], p. 114).

28. On the readership and social context of the *Georgics*, see Gary B. Miles, *Virgil's Georgics: A New Interpretation* (Berkeley, Los Angeles and London, 1980), pp. 1–63 ('The Roman Context').

29. On the politics of the poem, see J.C. Pellicer, 'The Politics of *Cyder*', in John Goodridge and J.C. Pellicer (eds.), *Cyder. A Poem in Two Books* (Cheltenham, 2001), pp. i–xvi.

30. See the classic discussion of *concordia discors* in *Cooper's Hill* and *Windsor-Forest*, in Earl R. Wasserman, *The Subtler Language: Critical Readings of Neoclassic and Romantic Poems* (Baltimore, 1959), pp. 35–168. On Denham, Pope, and the 'paysage moralisé', see John Chalker, *The English Georgic: A Study in the Development of a Form* (London, 1969), pp. 66–89.

31. Bennet's economic allegory compares interestingly with seventeenth-century images of the nation-as-orchard. See the Royalist and Puritan versions discussed by Anthony Low, *Georgic Revolution*, pp. 225–6, 236–7.

32. Robert Dodsley, *Public Virtue. A Poem in Three Books. I. Agriculture. II. Commerce. III. Arts* (1753), dedication. Only Book I was published.

33. In *The Hop-Garden* Smart 'showed himself keen to keep up to date by . . . recommending the use of ventilating fans in hop kilns. Stephen Hales invented these in 1742, the first year of composition' (Chris Mounsey, 'Christopher Smart's *The Hop-Garden* and John Philips's *Cyder*: a Battle of the Georgics? Mid-Eighteenth-Century Poetic Discussions of Authority, Science and Experience', *British Journal for Eighteenth-Century Studies*, 22 [1999], 67–84 [p. 77]).

34. See John Goodridge, *Rural Life in Eighteenth-Century Poetry* (Cambridge, 1995), pp. 91–180.

35. See, for example, the Goldsmithian picture of French peasants celebrating the vintage in Helen Maria Williams, 'Epistle to Dr Moore' (1792), 11–42. In *Rights of Man* (1791–2) Thomas Paine sees natural rights as grounded in the Edenic primal scene. See *Rights of Man*, ed. Henry Collins (Harmondsworth, 1969), pp. 88, 114, 162–3 and 191.

Chapter 6

The Romantic Mode, 1700–1730

To use the term 'romantic' in relation to the poetry of the early eighteenth century might seem anachronistic. The reverse, however, is the case. In the period covered by this chapter the word was widely used; its range of meaning was clear; and poets recognised the romantic mode, and exploited it in their work. The issue unfortunately became confused by the importation of the term towards the end of the nineteenth century to link a heterogeneous selection of poets from the period 1790–1830 as the English 'Romantics' (notably, Blake, Wordsworth, Coleridge, Byron, Shelley, and Keats) by attaching to them retrospectively a label they would have disowned, to form a grouping that would have puzzled them.[1] On the rare occasions those poets use the term, it is in the eighteenth-century sense, and is associated with youthful love, daydreaming, mood-soaked landscapes (especially those inviting meditation or adventure), fabulous fictions, melancholy contemplation, imagined historic or exotic scenes, the trappings of chivalry and enchantment – very much its eighteenth-century frames of reference.[2] In the early 1790s, in fact, this long established 'romantic' was coming under attack from radicals such as Tom Paine, Mary Wollstonecraft, and William Godwin. At this time, supporters of the French Revolution saw the old romantic mode as an *ancien régime* rooted in fictions of historic authority, fanciful prerogatives, time-hallowed titles and traditions, and the mystique of monarchy – all the false enchantments that were defended in Edmund Burke's anti-revolutionary *Reflections on the Revolution in France* (1790).[3] They wanted to strip away such mysteries and create an enlightened social reality, just as the Bastille had been destroyed in 1789 like a tyrant's castle of Gothic romance.[4] In the full glare of day, their new Adam would stride forth to occupy a real world, unencumbered by romantic trappings. The sapling 'Trees of Liberty' that were being ceremonially planted throughout France would replace the gloomy groves and venerable oaks amongst whose gnarled roots the old order reposed and brooded. Light would shine into dark corners, ghosts would be dispelled, and in a pristine setting mankind would awake to its new social responsibilities.

One poet who joyfully encountered the new Adam in July 1790, as he walked across France to the Alps, was William Wordsworth. In a poem based on these experiences, *Descriptive Sketches* (1793), he rouses his soul away from the dreamy gloom of the romantic mode:

> The still vale lengthens underneath the shade;
> While in soft gloom the scattering bowers recede . . .

While pastoral pipes and streams the landscape lull,
As bells of passing mules that tinkle dull,
In solemn shapes before the admiring eye
Dilated hang the misty pines on high,
Huge convent domes with pinnacles and towers,
And antique castles seen through drizzling showers.
  From such romantic dreams my soul awake . . .

(Descriptive Sketches, 270–83)

The whole scene is composing itself for a personal contemplation that never happens. The landscape's dynamics are subjective ones (it is in the poet's mind that the vale *lengthens*, and the bowers *recede*); the poem's consciousness registers a mood through sense-impressions (the *dull* sounds *lull*, and the pine-trees are *dilated* to the eye). Then, as if hanging in the air, *convent domes* and *antique castles* emerge to add their mysterious associations. As the scene's physical reality recedes, it becomes mediated to us through the atmospheric effect of the mist, as the castles are *seen through drizzling showers*. We are conscious less of *what* is being seen than of *how* it is being seen – the poet's perceptions filter the picture for us. But then there is an alarm call, and the soul is jerked out of its *romantic dreams*. Rather than allow the spirit to expatiate in the half-imagined landscape it has shaped for itself, Wordsworth pulls away to a domestic, human scene of a garden and hut, and a 'zig-zag path' leading from it. Castles in the air give way to a humbler dwelling he had not previously noticed, and a path becomes clear.

This passage from Wordsworth is a surviving example of the early eighteenth-century romantic mode. A poem it is close to, Anne Finch's *Nocturnal Rêverie* (a work he much admired), will be one of those discussed in this chapter, where I want to characterise the 'romantic' further, ask how it developed, and explore some of its uses in the poetry of the 1700–30 period in particular. I am not labelling it a 'romantic period' (whatever that means), just attempting to show that alongside the kind of poetry discussed in the opening chapters, concerned with social interaction and the tones of the speaking voice, there was another mode available in which experience was internalised and imagination led thought from the known into the suggestive. Observed reality ceased to be the frame of reference, and a subjective space formed in which ideas in meditation helped articulate a private 'self'. It would not be useful to describe certain poets of this period as 'romantic', just as it would be fruitless to talk of an 'ode poet' or an 'epistolary poet'. A *mode*, like a *genre*, was used for a purpose, and a poet might exploit or extend its potential. Like Pope or James Thomson, a writer could employ the 'romantic' in certain passages to achieve particular effects, without writing a 'romantic poem'. Some worked predictably within the mode, some understood it so well that they were able to develop its possibilities and ironies; others invoked it as part of a wider argument, or engaged with it mockingly for comic effect. However it was handled, the romantic mode was a significant feature in the poetry of the 1700–1730 period, and part of its varied landscape. It deserves to be isolated and its mechanisms understood.

We can approach the site in the company of Isaac Thompson, with the opening lines of a poem published in Newcastle in 1731 (and never reprinted since):

> There is a Rock, whose solitary Brow,
> Is dark with melancholly Shades of Yew;
> Thro' these, the Winds in hollow murmurs blow,
> And beat, with solemn Sounds, the Caves below.
> Fit Place for Contemplation, or for Care,
> To lift the Soul, or pour out sad Despair![5]

This Thompson is giving us not just an appropriate setting, but a scene imbued with thought and emotion. A dialogue is taking place between the external and the internal. The outcrop of rock is a *solitary Brow* garlanded by a funereal wreath, and the poet's consciousness suffuses this feature like the wind playing through and against it. The scene allows entry while offering resistance (the winds *blow through*, but also *beat*). The setting is exposed, but has hidden secrets, a projecting outer *Brow*, but also a deeper interior (*the Caves below*). The poet acknowledges this mental projection of his divided mood, expressing the imagination's paradoxical ability through lofty *Contemplation* to *lift the Soul* up to a higher level of vision, but also to bring inner *Despair*. Release and entrapment; the sublimes of transcendence and of gloom. What is being spoken in these *hollow murmurs* and *solemn Sounds* is not a 'now' of observed experience, but a language of permanent forms that will help him express his sense of betrayal in love.

This is the beginning of a pastoral complaint spoken by the lovesick Colin. This 1731 shepherd of the Northumbrian hills chooses the site to lament the 'faithless Woman' who has left him, and the rest of the poem is written on the stone itself – an emblematic text indeed. As the poem reaches its emotional climax, with his memory of the parting and exchange of vows, there is an interplay between ideas of possession and loss. He cannot lose what he might wish to, and his possessing is fraught with irony:

> ... never shall my Mem'ry lose that Time,
> When clasp'd within your Arms, and you in mine,
> I took the last adieu, and all my Breast,
> Throbs, Thrillings, Pangs, and Agonies possest;
> My Heart destracted 'midst a thousand Fears,
> Swell'd to my Eyes, and melted out in Tears;
> My trembling Limbs could scarce my Weight sustain,
> And Life surpriz'd, stood pausing with the Pain.
> Think then, O False! how in that sad adieu,
> You grasp'd with me, and promis'd to be true!
> Heav'n heard your Vows, as from your Lips they past,
> And Heav'n will certainly be just at last. (63–74)

And there the poem ends. What is finally being betrayed is a system of organic feeling established at the poem's outset, in which *My Heart . . . Swell'd to my Eyes, and melted* out *in Tears*. The prepositions distribute the feeling through the body. And in the phrase *You grasp'd with me*, she is not just grasping him, but is sharing the moment of grasping *with* him. But then the poem stops in its tracks. After all these empathies and interwoven sounds, comes the voice of her vows – as from *your Lips they past*. It is the classical moment of death, the soul departing from the lips, but here it represents a sound (and person) gone dead. It is a bitter conclusion, almost an epitaph, and one which turns the *hollow murmurs* of the poem's opening into sympathetic vibrations.

'Pastoral VI. The Letter', written by a provincial poet about whom very little appears to be known, shows an interesting grouping of features typical of the early eighteenth-century 'romantic' mode, and can help to characterise it. We note that the poem turns away from observed social reality and into subjective experience, which is mediated to the reader through an expressive language. The natural landscape is imbued with the text's controlling consciousness, helping to colour emotion by refracting it into visual symbol. The poem assumes a sympathetic reception from a reader who can imaginatively identify with the feelings being voiced. In particular it is interested in a secret unviolated space that can be entered only on the poet's terms.

This is what the eighteenth century considered 'romantic'. We meet the term when James Thomson, the poet of *The Seasons*, writes to his friend David Mallet in 1729:

> To have always some secret darling Idea, to which one can still have Recourse amidst the Noise and Nonsense of the World, and which never fails to touch us in the most exquisite Manner, is an Art of Happiness that Fortune cannot deprive us of. This may be called romantic, but whatever the Cause is the Effect is really felt.[6]

Thomson's secluded inner space is an imaginative resource, where an *Idea* lodges beyond the remit of reality (*the Noise and Nonsense of the World*), and though it seems intangible, it *touches* him – the *Effect is really felt*. This *romantic* awareness, with its fascination for *exquisite* sensation and the mystery of our response mechanisms, engages with the perceptual problems raised by John Locke's empirical[7] philosophy, particularly the opening up of subjective possibilities in the mind. Here (according to Locke) 'secondary' qualities (sound, smell, colour) register which are not *in* the perceived object but come into being as an 'idea' (image) within the perceiving mind in response to a 'power' in the object itself – one that can easily be seen as a power *over* us, an elusive influence that cannot be objectively located *out there*, yet finds its way *in here*. The response is palpable, the effect *really felt*. It is as though for Thomson, half-apologetically, the intangible *romantic* has become real and true – if his feelings are to be trusted.

The 'romantic' was easily accessed by a mind gripped by strong emotions such as fear, hope, or love, when the imagination was in a heightened state. At the time Thomson spoke of his *secret darling Idea* he was in love, and a 'romantic' landscape often provided an appropriate mental space for a lover's feelings. Typical is the lavish description in William Pattison's 'The Court of Venus' (1728) of the gardens in which 'Love's wild romantick Equipage is laid' (70):

> Here warming Whispers propagate Replies,
> Sweet-melting Murmurs, soft-consenting Sighs;
> With all the Eloquence that Hearts confess,
> With all the Harmony that Eyes express . . .
> When strange Chimeras on a sudden rise,
> Shift the false Scene, and intercept their Eyes;
> Tormenting Jealousies, uneasy Cares,
> Dissembling Hopes, imaginary Fears . . . (75–84)

This paradoxical world of suggestion without substance represents the *romantick Equipage* (trappings) of love. The emphasis is on the intangible: sounds dissolve identities into an all-encompassing mood, in which hearts and eyes commune together. Then the scene darkens to the negative with a ghostly pageant of imaginary beings waiting to enter an allegorical narrative. The passage suggests links between *The Rape of the Lock* (the sylphs as Belinda's *romantick Equipage?* – 'Think what an Equipage thou hast in air', Ariel tells her, I, 45), *Eloisa to Abelard*, Gray's *Eton College Ode*, and the love-allegory in Book Three of Spenser's *Faerie Queene* (1589). Eighteenth-century uses of the word 'romantic' are conscious of its roots in romance, and we shall see in Chapter 8 how a writer like Thomas Warton developed this aspect of the romantic mode at mid-century.

In the decades following Locke's *Essay Concerning Human Understanding* (1690), poets found its implications suggestive – that the mind might be no mere recorder, but a highly sensitised response mechanism to qualities realisable only within itself. It was in 1707, according to the *OED*, that the word *subjective* first broke away from its old meanings of 'submissive and obedient' and 'pertaining to the essence of a thing', and was used to mean 'relating to the thinking subject, having its source in the mind'; and the writer was Locke's friend, Joshua Oldfield.[8] By 1725 the poet Isaac Watts could write that 'Objective certainty, is when the proposition is certainly true in itself; and subjective, when we are certain of the truth of it. The one is in things, the other is in our minds'.[9] The early decades of the eighteenth century, therefore, were a time when the 'subjective' was being redefined as a new kind of truth. This has implications for the 'romantic' in this period, a mode of thought and expression which is particularly interested in the inner space of the subject, and which tends to use Locke's 'secondary' qualities (particularly sound and colour) to register the mind's activity and infuse the outer world with the inner until somehow the self appears to become articulate to itself.

This sounds mysterious, but it is exactly this almost suffocating subjectivity that troubles Pope's Eloisa, a nun trained to make space within herself for the visionary truths of God, but who finds them replaced by her returning memories. We saw in Isaac Thompson's poem that a mental space can be ambivalent (his cave offered possibilities for lofty contemplation but also dark despair). Pope's *Eloisa to Abelard* (1717) inhabits a contradictory internal space of this kind. Social reality has been shut out, and within the convent ('these deep solitudes and awful cells, / Where heav'nly-pensive, contemplation dwells', 1–2) Eloisa is imprisoned and tortured by her newly wakened passions.

Mimicking the procedures of spiritual contemplation, her imagination swings her between heaven and hell in an internalised mental battle (a *psychomachia*). Her cell has turned into the brain's *cellula fantastica*, where (according to Renaissance psychology) the memory's stored images are lodged. She inhabits the kind of space described by Walter Harte in his *Essay on Reason* (1736), where the mind 'romantic Memory detains / In unknown cells . . . / And Fancy emulous of God, creates' (242–5). For Harte, Memory is 'romantic' to the extent that it cherishes images. In the poem, Eloisa's memory projects her inner world back at her. The landscape setting for her enclosed life becomes a sensorium registering her subjective feelings:

> . . . o'er the twilight groves, and dusky caves,
> Long-sounding isles, and intermingled graves,
> Black Melancholy sits, and round her throws
> A death-like silence, and a dread repose:
> Her gloomy presence saddens all the scene,
> Shades ev'ry flow'r, and darkens ev'ry green,
> Deepens the murmur of the falling floods,
> And breathes a browner horror on the woods. (163–70)

It is a deservedly famous passage, an atmospheric scene *par excellence*. But it is no mere mood-picture. We notice that it is a landscape in process, one whose colours are being refracted through a darkening lens that *shades ev'ry flow'r*; her perceptive faculties are half-creating the world they see, so there is no objective relief. Eloisa is in a state close to the subjective 'airy Madness' evoked by Daniel Defoe, which 'makes Men strange Romantick Things propose. / The Head turns round, and all the Fancy's vain, / And makes the World as Giddy as the Brain'.[10] The world becomes a projection of the mind that perceives it. In Eloisa's subjective scene there is no first-person 'I': the melancholy self has become an interposing medium, no longer registering an external scene, but delivering her mood back to her, filtering the sounds (*Deepens the murmur*) and becoming a brooding *presence* that *breathes a browner horror on the woods*. The passage hovers between externalised self and internalised landscape.

If Pope sees Eloisa's subjectivity as imprisoning, Anne Finch, in her 'Nocturnal Rêverie' (1713), offers a twilight landscape that stirs the perceiving self into alert and discriminating activity. In this poem we encounter another aspect of the early eighteenth-century romantic mode, one that moves away from the solipsistic (self-imprisoning) implications of Lockean perception, and uses solitary musing as a release from an oppressive daytime reality where 'All's confus'd' and 'Our Cares, our Toils, our Clamours are renew'd' (this is James Thomson's *Noise and Nonsense of the World*). In her night-piece, the earth having turned to reveal its obverse life, there is granted a 'shortliv'd Jubilee', a kind of empirical democracy in which every detail now has a chance to register itself on the sensorium. All the everyday primary importances and meaningfulnesses are set aside, and the self can wander, picking out the living nuances and details.[11] The scene takes on a dynamic aspect, as substantial things release their 'secondary' qualities – colours, sounds, and smells. These become the vital elements of the scene as objects are mediated or reflected by others:

> In such a *Night*, when passing Clouds give place,
> Or thinly vail the Heav'ns mysterious Face;
> When in some River, overhung with Green,
> The waving Moon and trembling Leaves are seen . . .
> Whilst now a paler Hue the *Foxglove* takes,
> Yet checquers still with Red the dusky brakes . . . (7–16)

In a perceptual sociability where nothing stands alone, the subjective is welcomed into the scene. In this consciousness, what was secondary and insubstantial has become the living essence, and the elements themselves are almost imbued with thought:

> When Odours, which declin'd repelling Day,
> Thro' temp'rate Air uninterrupted stray;
> When darken'd Groves their softest Shadows wear,
> And falling Waters we distinctly hear;
> When thro' the Gloom more venerable shows
> Some ancient Fabrick, awful in Repose . . . (21–6)

The repeated use of *thro'* renders the air a communicating medium, making us alive to the character of things in perception, and aware of how we ourselves are perceiving the scene through the poet's consciousness. In the process, sense impressions become keener. In *Spectator* 411 (published the year before 'A Nocturnal Rêverie'), Addison speaks of the sense of sight as 'a more delicate and diffusive kind of Touch', and Finch's poem everywhere exemplifies such interchanging of the senses, where the mind becomes empirically sharpened:

> When the loos'd *Horse* now, as his Pasture leads,
> Comes slowly grazing thro' th'adjoining Meads,
> Whose stealing Pace, and lengthen'd Shade we fear,
> Till torn up Forage in his Teeth we hear . . . (29–32)

The potential terror subsides once the shape can be heard chewing. It would seem that nothing could be further from the plight of Pope's Eloisa, for whom 'the paths of . . . sense' (69), rather than checking her imagination, pander to it. But Finch's poem has a surprise in store. As her description continues, the senses, having responded so acutely to the scene, relax in contentment, and allow the soul to work its way free:

> But silent Musings urge the Mind to seek
> Something, too high for Syllables to speak;
> Till the free Soul to a compos'dness charm'd,
> Finding the Elements of Rage disarm'd,
> O'er all below a solemn Quiet grown,
> Joys in th'inferiour World, and thinks it like her Own . . . (41–6)

The registering of images has ceased, and now abstract ideas reach for expression. This is not the soul transcending earth, but finding a temporary home in nature. In the course of her meditation, Finch has located a dimension of life that was lost in the daytime bustle. Unlike Milton's platonic Lady in the *Ludlow Masque* (1634), whose 'home-felt' longings fix their gaze beyond the sky,[12] Finch's consciousness finds a space for itself in the created world.

But it is only a parenthesis – literally so. The whole 50-line reverie is sustained through a single unfolding sentence, whose main verb is delayed until line 47, when the poem's opening phrase ('In such a *Night* . . .') is repeated. Everything in between, the whole nocturnal scene, has been a grammatical parenthesis. By a brilliantly expressive syntactical move, the subordinate has taken over, the secondary has moved centre-stage, and a romantic space has emerged in which the subjective life is given play. It is only in line 47, after what seems one long suspended breath, that Finch can use the first-person singular pronoun: 'In such a *Night* let Me abroad remain'. In that way the poem has been not just self-expression, but a kind of self-creation.

Anne Finch understands the nuances of the act of perception, and how the self is implicated. In 'A Nocturnal Rêverie' the poem's consciousness is sharpened and alert, but in her other well known poem, *The Spleen* (1701), she explores the self's darker and more deceptive elements. Once again her art is acutely conscious of the medium in which it is working, and there is a satiric edge to her boast:

> My Hand delights to trace unusual things,
> And deviates from the known and common way
>   Nor will in fading Silks compose,
>   Faintly th'inimitable Rose:
> Fill up an ill-drawn Bird, or paint on Glass
> The Sovereigns blur'd and undistinguish'd Face . . . (83–8)

The melancholy 'spleen', a condition becoming known as 'the English disease', compromises Finch's zeal for clarity. If silk embroidery and the painting of transparencies are not for her, then her splenetic personality will intrude an Eloisa-like dark filter over her perceptions:

> I feel my Verse decay, and my crampt Numbers fail.
>   Through thy black Jaundies I all Objects see,
>   As dark and terrible as thee . . . (76–8)

In the course of the poem, Finch exploits the spleen's capacity for distortion and exaggeration, its 'fond Delusions' and 'fantastick' visions by which the human mind is perplexed. Writing in the irregular Pindaric[13] (a suitably splenetic mode), she works creatively with her temperamental medium, veering between ridicule and sympathy, attempting to find the secret of a 'perplexing Form' that can 'crowd with boding Dreams the melancholy Head' (13) and play havoc with the senses. Like the surgeon she describes, who tried to trace 'through the well-dissected Body . . . / [its] secret and mysterious ways' (139–40) and ended up falling a prey to the spleen himself, the poet is frustrated of any objective vantage-point, since she herself is its victim.

The spleen gave a pathological dimension to the early eighteenth-century romantic mode. It could be conceived as a dilemma in which the self took on a protean[14] quality that destabilised objective judgment. (The poem's opening lines are: 'What art thou, *Spleen*, which every thing dost ape? / Thou *Proteus* to abuse Mankind'.) As we have already seen, the individual imagination (typically viewed at this period as an elusive and contradictory faculty)[15] could create a subjective reality in the mind which might seem delightful, or troublesomely disorienting. Thomas Parnell, in his *Satyr 6: The Spleen* (written in 1702, the year after Anne Finch's ode was published) cannot decide quite how to take his romantic side. He does know, however, that it seems to emerge when he is underneath trees. His poem opens:

> Hail to the sacred silence of this Grove
> Hail to the greens below the greens above
> Oft have I found beneath these shady trees
> A reall in imaginary bliss
> For they my fancy sooth & she's a cheat
> Which can agreably adorn deceit . . .

Parnell has his green thoughts in a green shade, expressing his subjective reality in terms of paradox (*A reall in imaginary bliss*). He knows that there should not be such a thing as imaginative truth, but in this setting he experiences what he goes on to call 'Enchanted reason' (8), and the self seems to undergo a series of magical transformations: 'When I by these am from my self with drawn / I straight become what ere I think upon' (13–14). Parnell seems puzzled and slightly worried by this degree of empathy, and the poem changes tack at this point. His verses remained in manuscript, and were not published till 1989.[16]

On the title-page of Robert Burton's *Anatomy of Melancholy* (1628) one of the illustrations shows the book's presiding genius sitting under a tree, an image that evokes the venerable tradition of philosophic melancholy which can be seen to lie behind the early eighteenth-century romantic mode. The paradoxical intimacy between divine 'philosophic' melancholy and troubled *Black Melancholy* reaches back to Renaissance *melancolia*[17] and its distinction between the base imagination, which pandered to the bodily passions, and the divine imagination, which transcended them. The melancholy figure was capable of both, and could draw delight from gloomy solitude. In his song, 'Hence, all you vaine Delights' (c. 1624) John Fletcher dismissed the busy world and celebrated 'lovely melancholy' in the 'pathlesse Groves, / Places where pale passion loves; / Moonlight walkes, when all the fowles / Are warmly hous'd, save Bats and Owles; / A mid-night Bell, a parting groane, / These are the sounds we feed upon'. Fletcher's song is part of a direct literary line that can be traced from the figure of the melancholy Jaques in Shakespeare's *As You Like It* (1599) philosophising by the root of an ancient oak-tree, to Burton's *Anatomy* and its prefatory poem, 'The Author's Abstract of Melancholy', alternating between the joys and miseries of his condition, through Milton's hugely influential pair of poems, 'L'Allegro' and 'Il Penseroso', composed c. 1631, to Pope's *Eloisa*, on to Thomas Warton's *Pleasures of Melancholy* (1747) with its solitary consciousness celebrating the delights of gloom and terror, and into Gray's *Elegy Written in a Country Church Yard* (1751).[18]

What we have been looking at so far is what happened when the mechanisms of the traditional melancholy, and its more modern version, the spleen, encountered the new insights of Lockean subjectivity. Poets became fascinated by the processes of thought and sensation, and by the hidden internal space of the self, home of James Thomson's *secret darling Idea*, or Parnell's *reall . . . imaginary*, whether seen as a visionary cave, a meditative grove, a nocturnal garden, or Eloisa's *awful cells*. The protean possibilities of this subjectivity (Parnell's *I straight become what ere I think upon*) meant that it could be exploratory and releasing, or constricting and oppressive. The best known inner space of this kind is the one located inside the coquettish Belinda in Pope's *Rape of the Lock* (1714). We enter her 'Cave of Spleen' in Canto Four at the poem's moment of crisis, which will decide whether the cutting of her hair is to be a comic dénouement, or the catastrophe of a five-act tragedy. The vapourish 'grotto, sheltred close from air, / And screen'd in shades from day's detested glare' (IV, 21–2) proves to be an anti-social and neurotic place where desire and fascination turn into fears, and the creative process becomes grotesque distortion.[19] Here everything seems a seminal jumble where all is in process, and the vapours '[o]n various tempers act by various ways' (IV, 61). What is evident is that this subjective realm is not under Belinda's control. Back in the objectively 'real' world, Clarissa urges her to find a new sociable self of 'good sense' and public virtue (V, 9–34), but once Umbriel has emptied the bag which he had filled in the cave, her splenetic inner life bursts out and destroys her little society. Some interior areas, Pope suggests, are best left unexplored.

His friend Jonathan Swift certainly agreed, and in 'The Lady's Dressing-Room' (1732) he prescribed the antidote to romance by taking us on a similar exploration into a disturbing interior. The romantic, this poetic parable implies, is a self-deceiving fancy with no real existence in matter – it can only exist if the material is forgotten. Strephon, the romantic lover who must learn this harsh Swiftian lesson, intrudes into his beloved's private space; but his dream-girl has flown, leaving only *matter* behind. What the curious Strephon finds is the all-too-tangible *process* involved in her making, which remains behind like a dirty discarded chrysalis from which she has flown. As he catalogues the variously extruded substances, the stained towels, her dandruffed combs, the tweezers and snotty handkerchief – all the discarded tools in this workshop of filthy creation – we come to understand upon what Celia's romance has depended. Where Pope had delighted in the insubstantiality of Belinda's charisma, with the airy sylphs evoking those Lockean 'secondary' qualities of colour, sound and scent that helped create her romantic aura, Swift has no time for Sylph-like 'transient colours', 'glitt'ring textures', 'melting music', and perfumed essences. Instead he fixes them into the matrix of substantial reality. By its satiric inversion, his study in the voyeuristic exploration of a private world confirms the existence of an early eighteenth-century 'romantic'. It even flirts with that category itself. In this poem the romantic is not only implied, but assumed. No less than Robert Browning's *Love in a Life* (another text about entering a room after your lover has left), the poem wonders at the alluring mystery of the elusive feminine, who is enchanting others elsewhere – 'She goes out, as I enter'.[20]

The romantic mode I have been identifying has centred on the self as an inner space of subjective experience, and this is what Swift finds distasteful. The romantic mode clearly runs the risk of a Johnsonian critic pointing out that it does not confront 'real life'; that like Strephon it prefers to work with images, not things; that there is an element of self-indulgence haunting these subjective spaces; that the romantic turns life's daytime struggle into a twilight communion celebrating its own fine feelings; that it filters an experience through the self, so that it ceases to be objectively true, just imagined. Fiction is being preferred to fact, and 'where there is fiction, there is no passion'.[21]

The accusations could be multiplied pages further. They represent an ancient charge-sheet. Poetry deceives, fictions aren't true, and images aren't reality. Plato, Calvin, Hobbes, Swift, Johnson, Paine – an odd assortment indeed, but one thing that unites them is a conviction that Truth is not to be sought through mere images. In *Leviathan* (1651) Hobbes had declared that metaphors were openly deceitful (I.8), and that without steadiness and direction a strong imagination was a kind of madness. His materialist premise that 'life is but a motion of Limbs' (Introduction), and that all our sense experience is the physical pressing of objects from without (directly or indirectly), left images with an entirely representational role – or else they were deceptive. Once Locke, however, split apart the qualities of matter (into primary and secondary) so as to give images ('ideas') an evident existence within us, it became possible, as we saw Isaac Watts do, to speak of a 'truth' being 'in our minds' (Locke of course saw the dangers of this[22]). A poet could explore a 'subjective truth' without betraying an objective reality. Practitioners of the early eighteenth-century romantic mode were not pretending that objective and subjective were the same, but were either experiencing an interplay between them (like Pope's Eloisa), or consciously entering a space in which a different order could be communicated (like Anne Finch).

In positing a convergence between the tradition of introspective melancholy inherited from the Renaissance and the issues raised by Lockean perception, I am arguing that poets of this early period were not just indulging themselves by settling into self-pleasing 'landscapes of the mind', but were thinking about the nature of that mind, about the individual 'self' that it implied, and about the notion of 'subjective truth'. Poets of the early eighteenth century found these new subjectivities fascinating, and explored them in different ways. So far I have tended to stress the pathological side, the disturbance and uneasiness that such interiority brought. But this mode could also be used expressively, as a sensibility that channelled more socialised 'natural' feelings such as pity or sorrow. It fed appropriately into elegy, where it could evoke the sincerity of a personal grief. A good example is Thomas Tickell's moving elegy on the death of Addison, prefixed to his edition of the poet's works in 1721.[23] For such a publicly displayed poem, it gives communal mourning an unexpectedly personal dimension, one the reader can imaginatively share. Tickell draws us inside a dark interior stored with memories of a noble past. It is a ceremonial space he shares with others, and the spirit of an old chivalry merges them into a ghostly regiment of dead and living:

> Can I forget the dismal night, that gave
> My soul's best part for-ever to the grave!
> How silent did his old companions tread,
> By mid-night lamps, the mansions of the dead,
> Through breathing statues, then unheeded things,
> Through rowes of warriors, and through walks of kings! (9–14)

The poet releases the Gothic atmosphere of Westminster Abbey at night ('these chambers where the mighty rest') to play its expressive part in the solemnities, and with the words 'Oft let me range the gloomy Iles alone' he then makes a private return to the scene and meditates on the heroic past in terms that would later provide an ironic backdrop to the rustic churchyard in Gray's *Elegy*:

> Oft let me range the gloomy Iles alone,
> (Sad luxury! to vulgar minds unknown)
> Along the walls where speaking marbles show
> What worthies form the hallow'd mold below:
> Proud names, who once the reins of empire held;[24]
> In arms who triumph'd, or in arts excell'd;
> Chiefs, grac'd with scars, and prodigal of blood;
> Stern patriots, who for sacred freedom stood . . . (33–40)

For good or ill, Gray's 'unhonoured dead' had no public stage across which to walk, no proud building to haunt. His 'Village Cato', or rustic Caesar 'guilt-less of his country's blood' (the Roman names are in Gray's Eton manuscript), increase the sense of frustrated potential, a lost history that runs through the *Elegy*. But Tickell's passage too develops its own ironies in its very *luxury*. His crowded gallery of the great, for all their *proud names* on the *speaking marbles*, only *form the hallow'd mold below*. In life they could afford grace and prodigality (39), but with what result? Addison the public patriot, author of *Cato*, and Britain's Secretary of State, is not quite the Addison that is closest to his friend's heart, and even in this private revisiting Tickell is not as alone as he might wish to be.

A further stage is therefore required, in which Addison's ghost begins to haunt the poet 'in nightly visions' when he is alone with thoughts of his friend ('If pensive to the rural shades I rove, / His shape o'ertakes me in the lonely grove', 75–6). But then, in yet another turn, the poet wanders through Addison's own landscapes mourning his absence:

> How sweet were once thy prospects, fresh and fair,
> Thy sloping walks, and unpolluted air!
> How sweet the gloomes beneath thy aged trees,
> Thy noon-tide shadow, and thy evening breeze! (87–90)

By insisting on the freshness and beauty of those *prospects*, on the *gloomes* that were never gloomy, and the *shadow* that was not then the shadow of death, the poet speaks very simply but suggestively, working variations on his friend's bodily absence and spiritual presence. Tickell stages in his poem, then, a succession of romantic scenarios, in which the spirit of the dead Addison, visible or invisible, returns in various guises. His poem engages with a public duty, and also expresses a private need. But with the generosity of a fine elegist, the poet uses the romantic mode not to privatise his grief, but to engage the reader's own sympathetic imagination with it.

A related development of the romantic mode is shown in another antecedent of Gray's elegiac poetry, William Broome's 'Melancholy: An Ode', written on the death of his daughter in 1723. Here the mood of personal grief turns into a bitter survey of human life in all its stages. Its tone shifts to express contempt for the world (in the ancient *contemptu mundi* tradition), and the language of the poem similarly moves from gloomy introspection to become edged with satiric scorn. It begins by creating a familiar atmospheric scene where the speaker's private mood envelops him and the echoes return his own grief ('By Tombs where sullen Spirits stalk, / Familiar with the Dead I walk; / While to my Sighs and Groans by turns, / From Graves the midnight Echo mourns'); but the poem then begins to find a different language as it breaks out of this subjective enclosure to contemplate human fate. We suddenly glimpse the kind of horror that will provide the climax of Gray's 'Eton College' ode, and even catch the language of William Blake's 'Experience':

> With Cries we usher in our Birth,
> With Groans resign our transient Breath:
> While round, stern Ministers of Fate,
> Pain, and Disease, and Sorrow wait. (25–8)[25]

But Broome is not 'anticipating' later writers. He is shaping his own distinctive poem with a series of witty juxtapositions in which words are chosen as uncomfortable neighbours. He relishes the uneasy proximity of *Birth* and *Breath*, and the half-rhyme that forces them together; he stresses the formality (an inviting and a leave-taking) that in lines 25–6 frames the brief second of human life; and the phrase *Ministers of Fate* (from Shakespeare's *Tempest*)[26] chillingly conflates a loving ministering with an implacable supra-human authority that will not be countermanded. After this, he returns to the ghostly image, but now in a context of grotesque physicality ('Man seems already half a Ghost; / Wither'd, and wan, to Earth he bows, / A walking Hospital of Woes', 38–40); and he makes a final dismissal of life's huge emptiness, 'All, to the Coffin from our Birth, / In this vast Toy-shop of the Earth' (51–2). The reader is a little stunned by the way a consoling Nature has been ousted by an incongruous Destiny.

Broome's strong effects are achieved against the grain of romantic melancholy, which is thus crucial to his poem's character. Its opening ('Adieu vain Mirth, and noisy Joys! / Ye gay Desires, deluding Toys!') echoes that of Milton's 'Il Penseroso' ('Hence, vain deluding Joys'), but where Milton moves to a transcendent climax that leaves the material world behind ('Dissolve me into ecstasies, / And bring all heaven before mine eyes', 165–6), Broome continues the logic of Milton's contemptuous opening about life's foolish delusions. Where Milton veers off to embrace the lofty ambitions of 'divinest Melancholy' ('Come pensive nun, devout and pure, / Sober, steadfast, and demure, . . / . . And looks commercing with the skies', 31–2, 39), Broome finally welcomes back his Melancholy, but as a serious-minded, earthbound friend who just walks away from the scene with him:

> Come then, O Friend of virtuous Woe,
> With solemn Pace, demure and slow:
> Lo! sad and serious, I pursue
> Thy steps—adieu, vain World, adieu! (53–6)

Where Anne Finch saw an inevitable return to the everyday world, Broome's speaker, pilgrim-like, leaves it behind in disgust. In his stoical rejection of life's emptiness (the older meaning of 'vanity') he does not find any higher vision.

During the first half of the eighteenth century, however, most poets who drew from 'Il Penseroso'[27] tended to move out from an enclosed space towards the ecstatic possibilities of 'divinest Melancholy.' Bidding the world *adieu* in these poems can often be the start of a new adventure. The young Milton was a student of Renaissance Neoplatonism, a Christianised development of Plato's philosophy, in which earthly life consists of shadowy images that are mere reflections of the true reality in the mind of God; the Truth is beyond the physical world in the ideal platonic 'forms' of all things, and the human imagination can gain some glimpse of these only if bodily things are cast off and the passions of the 'self' transcended. During the 1680s such theories remained influential in Milton's Cambridge in the work of philosopher-theologians Ralph Cudworth and Henry More, and they continued into the eighteenth century through a writer like John Norris (1657–1711), who is an important link between the 'Cambridge Platonists' and eighteenth-century Methodism. Norris's poem, 'To Melancholy' (1692), invokes a mystery that defies the logic of rationalist philosophers by baffling human reason with a deeper *wisdom* (''tis said the brightest mind / Is that which is by thee refin'd. / See here a greater Mystery, / Thou mak'st us wise, yet ruin'st our Philosophy').[28] The neoplatonist Norris was the first to publish a criticism of Locke's *Essay*, arguing that all our ideas and images do not have their source in human sensation (Locke's view), but in God.[29]

Neoplatonic imagery therefore turned the enclosed spaces of the romantic mode into symbols of a bodily confinement from which the soul was preparing to escape. According to this view, there is the possibility of a higher knowledge that is not dependent on our body's perceptions, but to which the soul can respond. Caves and groves were, after all, ancient locations of prophetic or spiritual power (Greek and Roman oracles spoke from them),[30] an idea that is exploited by Sir Richard Blackmore in his poem 'Contemplative Solitude' (1718): 'In silent Groves the Men of old grew wise . . / . . The Soul does there herself compose, / Calmly devout and solemn grows, / Aw'd by the Shade, and Stillness of the Wood' (53, 58–60). The humbler and more constricting the location, the more awesome the escape, and from the humble setting of 'A Closet or a secret Field', says Blackmore, his mind can rise 'to the first Cause, whilst I attend / To Nature's Volume of Divinity' (91–3).[31]

Behind such releases of mind or soul (the two are often equated) are the ideas of *ascent* from material to spiritual, and *expansion* beyond the boundaries of sense experience. Here the divine, rather than redeeming the body, transcends it. The move away from a restricted self-contemplation to an ampler world of spiritual 'forms' was something that Pope's Eloisa found fraught with difficulty. When, however, we read the opening of Mary Chudleigh's 'Solitude' (1703) we seem to be hearing Eloisa the nun before she received Abelard's letter. In this poem, ascending from an enclosed self to 'heav'nly-pensive contemplation' is blissfully easy:

> Happy are they who when alone
>   Can with themselves converse;
> Who to their Thoughts are so familiar grown,
> That with Delight in some obscure Recess,
> They cou'd with silent Joy think all their Hours away,
> And still think on, till the confining Clay
>   Fall off, and nothing's left behind
> Of drossy Earth, nothing to clog the Mind,
> Or hinder its Ascent to those bright Forms above. (1–9)

The kind of internal *converse* Chudleigh has in mind is not an exploration of a 'self' with its feelings and perceptions, but rather a detaching of *Thoughts* from a body that only seems to contain them. Here, ideas are not physically mediated, but exist beyond the range of the senses at an 'ideal' level where the mind can expatiate freely. In contrast, Pope's *Eloisa to Abelard* finds dramatic power and irony in placing spiritual meditation in the modern world of Locke's empirical sense-experience where visionary 'idea' is entangled with the body's stored images. In terms of my characterisation of an early eighteenth-century 'romantic', it is Pope's poem that is working in that mode, rather than Chudleigh's. We can see that her 'Solitude' is opening up another area, one of transcendent vision in which the imagination becomes independent of the 'decaying sense' of human memory.[32] In talking about the poetry of the 1700–1730 period it is helpful to distinguish this 'sublime' mode from the 'romantic'.

If we continue the comparison between Chudleigh's poem and Pope's *Eloisa to Abelard* we should note the difference in verse-form. Where Pope's couplets provide a pulse of physicality – a rhythmic template that Eloisa tests and buffets in her passion – Chudleigh's Pindaric lines expand sympathetically to accommodate the speaker's aspirations. End-stopping can be over-ridden, and through such a flexible form her breath expands as she settles into her meditation without being constantly reminded of a containing metre. Her *bright Forms* are not confined by human measures.

The Pindaric is an appropriate verse for the 'sublime' mode which, as we shall see in the next chapter, is centrifugal in tendency – its energies are directed outwards beyond the self. The early eighteenth-century 'romantic', on the other hand, explores inner spaces, and if there are glimpses of a world beyond, they tend to be glimmerings that have slipped in through the chinks of our mental enclosure. Locke's picture of the human mind is in this sense 'romantic'. In a section entitled '*Dark Room*' (*Essay*, 2.11.17) he argues that 'the understanding is not much unlike a closet wholly shut from light, with only some little opening left, to let in external visible resemblances, or ideas [= images] of things without'. This *camera obscura*[33] is not, says Locke, open to the sun, but is lit by candle-light, 'enough for our purposes' (1.1.5), and inside this space of memory we store our ideas, which are in a state of 'constant decay', their colours fading with time and their outlines becoming less clear (2.10.5). At the heart of Locke's characterising of the human mind, therefore, is an idea of loss (one that Blake's poet-figure, *Los*, will triumphantly challenge). There is something ghost-like about it, as though what was once sharp and descriptive is now becoming fainter. The Lockean mind is haunted by liminal forms – ideas that are neither fully physical nor fully ideal (this was John Norris's charge against Locke's *Essay*), caught in some ambiguous state as resemblances of the real. From these we have to piece together what we 'know', a memorial reconstruction that will always be tinged by the elegiac.

The above scenario is also that of Pope's 'Elegy to the Memory of an Unfortunate Lady', perhaps the most elusive and enigmatic poem he ever wrote. At its opening the speaker confronts the phantom of a young suicide ('What beck'ning ghost, along the moonlight shade / Invites my step, and points to yonder glade?' 1–2); but unlike the ghost of Hamlet's father, this spirit can only gesture, not speak, and her story is never told, just hinted at. The poet raises the possibility of her soul's release from the body:

> Most souls, 'tis true, but peep out once an age,
> Dull sullen pris'ners in the body's cage:
> Dim lights of life that burn a length of years,
> Useless, unseen, as lamps in sepulchres . . . (17–20)

But far from releasing her spirit, the poet becomes concerned with her burial in the earth, and comments stoically that 'A heap of dust alone remains of thee; / 'Tis all thou art, and all the proud shall be!' (73–4). For a moment she seemed to be palpably 'here' ('See on these ruby lips the trembling breath, / These cheeks, now fading at the blast of death', 31–2), but as the poet's emotions move centre-stage the lady herself fades from view, and the poet's memory takes over, offering fragmentary allusions to a narrative that never gets told. We finally don't know who she was, or what happened to her. The poem offers a romantic aspect to this elusiveness: as readers, we feel the text's truth locked away beyond our reach in a subjective area that the writer hints at but never opens up. The text moves between an objectively 'real' physical world and an interior mental one, between perception and memory, between emotional outburst and formal epitaph, between the immediate/dramatic and the distanced/elegiac. Everything about the lady is equivocal, and the poet remains secretive to the last, treasuring her as an image in his own mind, and vowing only to surrender her when he himself dies ('Then from his closing eyes thy form shall part, / And the last pang shall tear thee from his heart',

79–80). There is no final answer to the question the poem seems to be asking – Is the 'real' lady the buried dust, or the Lockean idea within him? Such equivocation about the nature of perceived reality is at the heart of the early eighteenth-century romantic mode.

If Pope's 'Elegy' raises in the reader's mind this question of the 'real', there is a closely related poem that poses it directly. It is written by someone who has clearly admired both *Eloisa to Abelard* and the 'Elegy', and understands how they complement each other. George Woodward's 'An Evening Slumber' (published in his *Poems on Several Occasions*, 1730) is set at night among the ruins of Godstow Nunnery, near Oxford, where the poet has fallen asleep, lulled by the stream and the sound of the wind in the trees. As his imagination wanders, he sees approaching him from the tomb, a phantom figure of the fair Rosamond, hand in hand with her lover, King Henry the Second ('Down from her Head her Night-veil flow'd behind, / Decent, and graceful, sporting with the Wind', 14–15). As Woodward's unfortunate lady begins to recall their doomed love, she invokes in turn the full range of romantic ingredients, which gradually coalesce into an ambient atmosphere of sympathy – the whole scene is whispering and murmuring around them, from the music of flutes and trumpets that 'floated on the Air', to the sound of 'yon soft Cascade', 'the Falling of the drowsy Floods', the 'tender Nightingales' and 'moaning Halcyons'. The lovers' remembered intimacies ('Oft thro' the Gloom I'd steal a tender Sigh, / But then methought I heard thy Soul reply', 44–5) are now being repeated all around them ('Sweet are the whispers of the midnight Breeze, / That gently pants upon the trembling Trees', 58–9). Past and present have fused, and the landscape is suffused with this intangible soul-music. It is as though the lady, like Eloisa, cannot let memory go, but has to bring her hidden world to us:

> Deep in low Vaults I keep eternal Night,
> Shut up from Day, and ev'ry dear delight,
> Where pale-ey'd Virgins sit beneath the Ground,
> And pensive watch the dying Lamps around:
> Whence hollow Sounds are heard, and Shapes are seen
> Gliding athwart the melancholy Green. (76–81)

In his churchyard elegy, Gray declined to release this hidden world of the imagined dead. His turf *heaves*, but nothing more (Johnson, for one, was grateful). As we read Woodward's poem, we too begin to feel suffocated by the way Rosamond's reality becomes our dream. It is the heady essence of the early eighteenth-century romantic.

But like Isaac Thompson in his 'Pastoral VI', the obscure George Woodward knows what he is doing. He understands the mechanisms of the romantic mode, and in the final lines the ghostly Rosamond acknowledges her frustration at the disembodied. The imagined is certainly not the *real*; but the poem has shown how the emotions can alter our sense of it:

> Tho' vanish'd Joys by Fancy we restore,
> Melt in false Love, and act past Pleasures o'er,

Yet how do we our real Passion prove?
Where's the Embrace, the real Soul of Love?
I can no more—for Lo! the Morning Ray
Peeps o'er yon Eastern Hill; I must away.
She said; and, like some Phantom of the Night,
Or Air impassive, vanish'd from the Sight. (102–9)

Rosamond's final pertinent questions about the *real* tackle the limitations of imagination-as-memory. How quickly the immediate becomes the mediated, as the 'idea' is detached from the 'now' of actual experience and seems to have only a posthumous life (*Where's the Embrace . . . ?*). The reach of mind eludes the grasp of body. With that single powerful word *impassive* (meaning both 'without suffering' and 'inanimate') Woodward catches the irony of the moment when the emotional phantom becomes mere *Air*.

At its best, the 'romantic' mode of the 1700–1730 period, as I've been attempting to characterise it, was not self-indulgently subjective, but a way of thinking about issues of subjectivity, especially the relationship between a 'self' (its sensations and emotions) and the physical world. This philosophically aware mode allowed poets to explore current questions regarding the nature of human perceptions and thought-processes, and how far individual experience is involved with identity, memory, truth and reality. These are fundamental topics for any poet.

Notes

1. See David Perkins, *Is Literary History Possible?* (Baltimore and London, 1992), chapter 5 ('The Construction of English Romantic Poetry as a Literary Classification').

2. See Raymond Immerwahr, ' "Romantic" and its Cognates in England, Germany, and France before 1790', in *'Romantic' and Its Cognates: The European History of a Word*, ed. Hans Eichner (Manchester, 1972), pp. 17–97.

3. See David Fairer, 'Organizing Verse: Burke's *Reflections* and Eighteenth-Century Poetry', *Romanticisim*, 3 (1997), 1–19.

4. See, for example, Helen Maria Williams, 'Epistle to Dr Moore' (1792), 53–70.

5. Isaac Thompson, 'The Letter. Pastoral VI', from *A Collection of Poems* (Newcastle, 1731).

6. Thomson – Mallet, 20 September 1729. *James Thomson (1700–1748): Letters and Documents*, ed. A.D. McKillop (Lawrence, Kansas, 1958), pp. 65–6.

7. 'Empiricism' can be defined as the philosophic principle that we are born with no innate ideas, and that everything we experience and know comes originally through the senses. Locke, for example, sees the human mind at birth as a blank sheet of paper on which all our sense experiences register as ideas. Empiricism is not to be equated with materialism: although the 'materialist' Thomas Hobbes (1588–1679) built on this principle, so did the 'idealist' George Berkeley (1685–1753), for whom there is no such thing as material substance. Locke's 'primary' and 'secondary' qualities place him in an ambivalent position.

8. Joshua Oldfield, *An Essay Towards the Improvement of Reason* (1707), II, xix, 23. Oldfield distinguishes '*Objective* certainty, or that of the thing, as it really is in it self'

from 'a *Subjective* certainty of it in the infinite Mind, which beholds all things immediately in themselves, and exactly as they are by intuitive Knowledge; when yet those things may appear to us only Possible and Doubtful, or Probable, or Certain, whether in themselves or by Means of some assuring Evidence and Proof' (p. 216). Oldfield's subjectivity is evidently metaphysically underpinned by *the infinite Mind*.

9. Isaac Watts, *Logick: or the Right Use of Reason in the Enquiry after Truth* (1725), II, ii, 8.

10. Daniel Defoe, 'The Spanish Descent. A Poem', from *A True Collection of the Writings of the Author of the True Born English-man. Corrected by Himself* (1703).

11. Finch's 'Nocturnal Rêverie' may lie behind George Woodward's picture of 'Romantick Sylvia', who 'Soon as the Whisper of the Evening Breeze / Curls on the Lake, or pants upon the Trees, / Far in the Copse she wanders all alone, / And softly listens to the Turtle's Moan: / At ev'ry Note, that murmurs down the Grove, / She fondly Sighs . . .' ('La Belle Romanesque', 19–24. Woodward, *Poems on Several Occasions* (1730).

12. When Comus hears the Lady's song, he comments: 'such a sacred, and home-felt delight, / Such sober certainty of waking bliss / I never heard till now' (Milton, *Ludlow Masque*, 262–4).

13. On the 'Pindaric Ode', see Chapter 7.

14. The sea-god Proteus in Homer's *Odyssey* was able to assume any shape. He reappears in Spenser's *Faerie Queene*, Books III and IV.

15. See David Fairer, *Pope's Imagination* (Manchester, 1984), pp. 26–33.

16. The poem was first printed in *Collected Poems of Thomas Parnell*, ed. Claude Rawson and F.P. Lock (Newark, London and Toronto, 1989), pp. 365–8.

17. See Laurence Babb, *The Elizabethan Malady: A Study of Melancholia in English Literature from 1580 to 1642* (East Lansing, 1951), and Raymond Klibansky, Erwin Panofsky and Fritz Saxl, *Saturn and Melancholy* (London, 1964).

18. See Myrddin Jones, 'Gray, Jaques, and the Man of Feeling', *Review of English Studies*, n.s. 25 (1974), 39–48.

19. The term 'grotesque' seems to have developed from Italian *grottesca* ('grotto-painting') to describe the fanciful wall-paintings of excavated Roman houses. See Arthur Clayborough, *The Grotesque in English Literature* (Oxford, 1965), p. 2.

20. Browning's short poem, 'Love in a Life' (1855) is the 'romantic' version in which the poet celebrates his lover's elusiveness. She is absent, but leaves her *intangible* traces behind.

21. Johnson, *Lives of the Poets*, ed. Hill, II, 315 (Hammond).

22. Locke stresses the practical importance of human 'Judgment' as being 'the faculty which God has given man to supply the want of clear and certain knowledge, in cases where that cannot be had' (*Essay*, IV. xiv.1).

23. *The Works of the Right Honourable Joseph Addison*, ed. Thomas Tickell, 4 vols. (London: Jacob Tonson, 1721), I, xvii–xxi. The poem is addressed 'To the Right Honourable the Earl of Warwick' (Addison had married his mother, the Dowager Countess).

24. In Gray's original line 47 ('Hands that the reins of empire might have swayed', Eton MS) *reins* was altered to *rod* for the printed version – an emendation perhaps made to avoid the direct echo of Tickell. See *The Poems of Gray, Collins, and Goldsmith*, ed. Roger Lonsdale (London and Harlow, 1969), p. 126.

25. William Broome (1689–1745) was one of Pope's helpers in translating the *Odyssey* 'Melancholy. An Ode' was published in Broome's *Poems on Several Occasions* (1727), p. 45.

26. Shakespeare, *The Tempset*, III. iii. 61. Gray uses the phrase in his 'Ode on a Distant Prospect of Eton College', 56. Lonsdale ed., p. 60.

27. See R.D. Havens, *The Influence of Milton on English Poetry* (Cambridge, Mass., 1922).

28. John Norris, *A Collection of Miscellanies: Consisting of Poems, Essays, Discourses & Letters*, 2nd ed. Corrected (London, 1692), pp. 130–1.

29. "'Tis God certainly that is the Author of all my Sensations, as well as of my Ideas' (John Norris, 'Cursory Reflections upon a Book call'd, An Essay Concerning Human Understanding', p. 32). The pamphlet was appended to Norris's *Christian Blessedness* (1690).

30. Delphi, Dardanus, Cumae.

31. Sir Richard Blackmore, *A Collection of Poems on Various Subjects* (1718), pp. 339–45.

32. 'Imagination therefore is nothing but *decaying sense* . . . But when we would express the *decay*, and signifie that the Sense is fading, old, and past, it is called *Memory*. So that *Imagination* and *Memory*, are but one thing' (Thomas Hobbes, *Leviathan* [1651], I. 2).

33. Addison uses the *camera obscura* to illustrate one of the 'Pleasures of the Imagination', *Spectator* 414 (25 June 1712).

Chapter 7

Sublimity, Nature, and God

> Hover no more, my muse! o'er idle themes,
> Sliding shadows! slipp'ry dreams!
> By heaven's high call, from humane byas freed,
> Imagination climbs with dreadful speed!
> Unfetter'd, from earth's humble heights I rise,
> And stretch sublime, a dang'rous flight, which none, untrembling, tries. (1–6)

We now move from hovering ghosts to soaring spirits. Opening his poem *The Judgment-Day* (1721), Aaron Hill contrasts his sublime imagination with the shadowy landscapes of romance. The poet spurns the romantic mode, with its 'human bias' hovering around earthly things like the ghost of Pope's unfortunate lady and exploring the self-conscious inner world. Instead he braces himself for a transcendent flight that will take him outside time, history, and the solar system. For enthusiasts of the sublime at this period, the romantic was to be rejected as creating self-pleasing fictions, a point that the poet Samuel Cobb expressed very neatly: 'The Bard sees Visions, but Romancers dream'.[1] This distinction is an important one for recognising the diversity of early eighteenth-century poetry, and the particular character of the bardic vision. In Aaron Hill's images of release and flight, speed, height, and danger we are meant to register the poet's aspirations and admire his daring reach into the beyond through the seven stresses of that long final line. If Hill sounds a little like the boastful Satan in *Paradise Lost* (1667) ready to launch himself into the void, then the parallel is appropriate, since it is the spirit of Milton's epic that presides here. The blind poet at the beginning of his enterprise had sought inspiration from Urania, the muse of divine poetry: 'What in mee is dark / Illumin, what is low raise and support' (I, 22–3), and Aaron Hill pleads in the same voice: 'Arm my aking eyes, / Aid and support, O God! my failing power' (7–8). On ambitious poetic flights it helped to have a supernatural sponsor.

The sublime Milton was also fully engaged with the political and intellectual debates of his time, and it is the argumentative aspect of visionary poetry that forms the subject of this chapter. Milton's imagination may have taken him into unknown regions ('Things unattempted yet in Prose or Rime', I, 16), but he soared through the universe in order to argue about things on earth. To enter Milton's Heaven, Paradise, and Hell, and understand the principles of each, is to gain insight into earthly constitutions; and when he argues about cosmologies he is also thinking of state power and divine authority in the Britain of Charles the Second. For the Miltonic poets of the early eighteenth century, who wrote just as the wider implications of Newtonian physics were being recognised, the relationship between God and his creation gained a new dimension.

The concept of 'Nature' became contentious, and the status of the natural world changed. At the same time, unprecedented constitutional shifts affected the socio-political system. Both these developments were far reaching, and this chapter will look at how some of the poetic visions of the age engaged with them.

Towards the beginning of the eighteenth century two critical developments occurred simultaneously: Milton's reputation soared, and the reading public came to be fascinated by the sublime. This was no coincidence, as the poet and the theory seemed made for each other. They come together, for example, in Isaac Watts's ode, 'The Adventurous Muse' (1709), in which the poet, led by Urania, breaks free of earth and mounts heavenward in her chariot. On his journey he imagines looking down on conventional poets as if they are tiny boats bobbing around in the shallows ('little Skiffs along the mortal Shores / With humble Toyl in Order creep, / Coasting in sight of one anothers Oars, / Nor venture thro' the boundless Deep', 17–20). Watts, however, is not coasting, but soaring towards Paradise where the immortal Milton himself is waiting. The 'advent'rous Genius' who 'built his Verse sublime' now passes his time entertaining the heavenly host on his lyre ('All Heav'n sits silent . . .', 58). Milton the divine lyric poet has become an inspiration to others.

The theory of the sublime also made an impact among critics. In a ground-breaking discussion, Addison devoted a series of eighteen *Spectator* papers between January and May 1712 to an appreciation of *Paradise Lost*, and it was as a work of 'Sublime Genius' that he particularly praised it, stressing Milton's ability to 'raise and terrifie the Reader's Imagination'[2] and create astonishment with his bold thoughts and descriptions. This kind of critical language which emphasises poetry's imaginative potential was drawn from Longinus' *Peri Hypsous* ('On Soaring'), popularly known as *On the Sublime*,[3] an ancient text that since Boileau's French translation (1674) had become established as a classic to set beside the magisterial critical writings of Aristotle (the *Poetics*) and Horace. Where they stress matters of literary genre, notably epic and tragedy, and the formal and stylistic qualities appropriate to them, Longinus' rhetorical treatise considers how to rouse, move, and inspire. Where Aristotle and Horace tend to value poetry's responsibility to human experience, Longinus stresses imaginative exploration ('the whole universe is not enough to satisfy our minds . . . our ideas often reach beyond the frontiers that enclose us', ch. 35). Placing poetry alongside the art of oratory, Longinus is concerned with seizing the attention of an audience and tapping into an inspirational force that can break through the proprieties of good writing. To reach the sublime a poet takes risks and plays for high stakes:

> What transports us with wonder is more effective than what merely persuades or pleases us. The extent to which we can be persuaded is usually under our control, but sublime passages exert an irresistible force and mastery over every hearer . . . a well-timed stroke of sublimity scatters all before it like a thunderbolt, and in a flash reveals the full power of the speaker. (ch. 1)

The implications for literary form are significant. Sublimity works in the intensity of the moment and therefore transcends structure, decorum and probability (the concerns of Aristotle and Horace). Paradoxically, the sublime allows the reader to feel a sudden access of power whilst not being in control. Rather than gratify our expectations, it gives us a shock – the flash of vision short-circuits the reason.

Longinus's Greek treatise made a strong impression on British critics, several of whom received it enthusiastically. Pope's *Essay on Criticism* (1711) thoughtfully balances Longinus and Horace, recognising the greatness of each, and weighing the powers of creative 'genius' against the principles of correctness and decorum. Where Pope draws them into an argument, Addison in his *Paradise Lost* papers politely accommodates Aristotle, Horace and Longinus without setting them against each other. He defers to the twin authorities who had guided literary criticism for centuries; but when he wants to express his excitement at the poem's imaginative power, then the Longinian sublime is invoked. More boldly, Samuel Cobb uses Longinus to support his notion of 'the Liberty of Writing'. In his view, 'an over curious Study of being correct enervates the Vigour of the Mind, slackens the Spirits, and cramps the Genius of a Free Writer . . . we ought to lay aside those common Rules with our Leading strings'.[4]

One critic stood apart from others in the intellectual rigour with which he combined Longinus's principles and Milton's practice in a theory of poetry that had a major influence on later developments. John Dennis (1657–1734) was satirised by Pope and Gay in their play *Three Hours After Marriage* (1717) as 'Sir Tremendous Longinus', but he was also an admirer of Aristotle and rejected the view that poetry's formal qualities were a constraint on genius. Dennis is a fine critic because he avoids simple binaries of this kind: he refuses to be either an 'ancient' or a 'modern', draws material from different sources, argues out his ideas from principle, and tests them by literary judgment. It was chiefly through him that the sublime was assimilated into British criticism and the native tradition of poetry. The fact that some of his ideas still surprise (and seem a hundred years ahead of their time) is a sign that modern criticism has not fully registered the adventurousness of English poetic theory during the 1700–1750 period. Before looking at how the sublime mode worked in practice, we ought to listen for a while to the voice of John Dennis:

> Poetry is Poetry, because it is more Passionate and Sensual than Prose. A Discourse that is writ in very good Numbers [= verses], if it wants Passion, can be but measur'd [= metrical] Prose. But a Discourse that is every where bold and figurative, is certainly Poetry without Numbers. . . . Passion then, is the Characteristical Mark of Poetry, and consequently, must be every where: For . . . without Passion there can be no Poetry . . .

These words in Chapter 5 of Dennis's *Advancement and Reformation of Poetry* (1701) throw down the gauntlet. Poetry is defined not by metre but by its strong feelings and vivid images, and the logical outcome of this thought is a linked notion of both poetic intensity, and the prose-poem. In his *Grounds of Criticism in Poetry* (1704) Dennis develops the idea in terms of a distinction between 'vulgar' and 'enthusiastic' passion. Under the former we are moved, as 'in the ordinary course of life', by our perception of 'objects themselves' (this is the imagination in its everyday function of registering experience); but under the influence of 'enthusiastic passion' (wonder, terror, horror, joy, sadness, and desire) we see things 'in meditation' and the result is very different:

> Ideas in Meditation are often very different from what Ideas of the same Objects are, in the course of common Conversation. As for example, the Sun mention'd in ordinary conversation, gives the Idea of a round flat shining Body, of about two foot diameter. But the Sun occurring to us in Meditation, gives the Idea of a vast and glorious Body, and the top of all the visible Creation, and the brightest material Image of the Divinity. (ch. 4)[5]

In this mode the imagination creates 'that Spirit, that Passion, and that Fire, which so wonderfully please'. Dennis acknowledges that the province of most poetry is 'vulgar passion', but there are two notable exceptions: the epic invocation (such as Milton's address to Urania), and the 'greater' or 'Pindaric' ode. In these two the 'enthusiastic passion' holds sway.

The Pindaric ode, named after the Greek poet Pindar (518–c. 438 BC), was the favourite medium for the sublime. It had been naturalised into English by Abraham Cowley (1618–67) and John Dryden (1631–1700), and soon became popular with aspiring younger poets, partly because it offered maximum *kudos* without demanding (as epic did) years of concentrated effort. It had become associated with poetic 'genius', a brilliance that broke the rules, and indeed a certain impatience, recklessness, even indiscipline, were regarded as appropriate. In his influential *Essay upon Poetry* (1682) the Duke of Buckingham described the Pindaric ode as 'the Muses' most unruly Horse; / That bounds so fierce, the Rider has no rest, / But foams at mouth, and speaks like one possest'.[6] This idea that the poet is not fully in control of his vehicle goes back to Horace's tribute to Pindar as an overflowing river that 'swells, and ferments with fury'.[7] English 'Pindaricks', as they were called, tried to reproduce the imaginative daring, sudden transitions, and flights of eloquence of their Greek original, but many missed his metrical vitality and complexity, thinking that unpredictable shifts in line-length were enough. Addison criticised such verse as having 'the Distortion, Grimace, and outward Figure, but nothing of that divine Impulse which raises the Mind above it self',[8] and Pope satirised their pretensions in his parody of Longinian excesses, *Peri Bathous: Of the Art of Sinking in Poetry* (1728). Not until Collins and Gray at mid-century would the Pindaric ode recapture the emphatic lyric rhythms of Dryden, and remind the reader that the Greek originals were sung to the lyre.

For Dennis, however, Pindar also had a darker power, an ability to convey 'something dreadful, something which terribly shakes us, at the very same time it transports us'.[9] Here Dennis touches on the notion of ambivalent terror, an idea that was to influence the theories of the sublime later developed by Addison and especially Burke. Where Longinus speaks of astonishment and awe, Dennis extends this into terror, especially the kind we experience when confronted by 'the wrath and vengeance of an angry God'. Given that for Dennis, 'the greatest Sublimity is to be deriv'd from Religious Ideas', then the terrible power of the deity becomes the sublimest ingredient poetry can have. At the climax of his discussion he cannot resist offering a list of ideas that are especially effective in producing what he calls *enthusiastic terror*: 'Gods, Daemons, Hell, Spirits and Souls of Men, Miracles, Prodigies, Enchantments, Witchcrafts, Thunder, Tempests, raging Seas, Inundations, Torrents, Earthquakes, Volcanos, Monsters, Serpents, Lions, Tygers, Fire, War, Pestilence, Famine, etc.'[10] The sublime, in other words, draws creative power from scenarios of destruction when forces are released that threaten civilisation. Faith, hope and love are replaced by awe and fear, as if a providential God has reverted to a primal force that might loosen its hold at any moment and uncreate what he created.

It is this apocalyptic world that Aaron Hill explores in *The Judgment-Day* (1721), a poem that assaults the reader's imagination with images of a universe suddenly released from all laws. Each constituent part is dismantled, inverted, and then mixed into an incongruous jumble. In the following passage fire and water wrestle for supremacy, and the result is a kind of witty paradox projected onto a huge sublime canvas:

> Deep-swallow'd earth, mean while, still loos'ning more,
> Lets in old ocean, to her central fires;
> Th'astonish'd deluge, ne'er so check'd before,
> Shrinks from the pain, and in loud roar, retires!
> Close in pursuit, the bursting flame breaks thro' th'unusual vent,
> O'ertakes the rolling floods slow flight, and climbs th'immense extent!
> On all sides, now, the fire-assaulted waves,
> Feel themselves boil; and curl to shun the heat;
> A night of steam climbs, dark and broad, from their voracious graves,
> And plunging Whales, which no cool comfort meet,
> Spout the hot flood to heaven, in rage, and the froth'd billows beat . . .
>   (120–30)

The *night of steam* mounting from the earth's core anticipates the universal darkness shortly to come, and the whales scalding from inside perform a last gesture on behalf of living things. The galactic system forms a liquid magma ('One firey deluge, wasteful, boils below, / And crumbled worlds, in liquid millions, flow', 216–7), and the scattered remains of the human dead turn to steam ('Bodies of men, in ages, long since past, / Whose wand'ring dust has chang'd a thousand forms, / Purg'd, by the boiling fires, evaporate fast, / And, steaming upward, rise, in misty swarms!', 266–9). Then, in mid-air the miracle occurs, as each atom seeks its rightful place and human bodies reconstitute themselves ('Atoms join atoms, and lost forms renew!'). A 'sublime' voice is heard commanding souls to return, and the 'soft squadrons' pour down to fill every waiting body ('each strikes his own, / And smiles, to fill his long-lost home again', 288–9).

Hill's ode illustrates how a poet could respond to the imaginative possibilities that the critics had found in the sublime. But there is another dimension to the poem beyond its descriptive effects, which reminds us how apocalyptic prophecy can be a way of intervening in history and politics. Poets saw that the theoretical 'licence' of the sublime could be extended, and that bardic prophecy might involve danger and daring of a non-literary kind. The careful Edward Young, in his poem *On the Last Day* (1713) dedicated to Queen Anne, admitted a little ruefully that at the Apocalypse even Great Britain ('where the Stuarts fill'd an awful throne') would be consumed, and her seas burst into flame. But he was careful to add that Time and Nature would be extinguished at the same time (III, 66–8). In contrast, Hill's *Judgment-Day* is vividly unapologetic, sweeping together with relish the atomised fragments of 'the ruler's sceptre, and the captive's chains' (156), as 'Kings, slaves, and patriots, undistinguish'd flow' (272). (The *patriots*, it seems, are those who refuse to be *slaves* to *kings*.) For Hill, the disintegration of an ordered system comes 'when the sov'reign sun forgets his care', and without his influence 'Dependant worlds, in sympathetic woe, / Halt in their course . . . / And roll, in devious mischief' (174–8). The horrified poet watches 'th'escaping sun', and what follows from that sovereign's departure:

> Worlds, by his absence, from dependance freed,
> Scud, in loose liberty, along the sky . . .
> So, rebel kingdoms struggling to be free,
> Shun regal power, and split on anarchy! (189–94)

To us this reads like a metaphor, but in 1721 Hill's image was unsettlingly close to reality. At a moment of renewed crisis he could look back on Britain's eighty-year struggle over the Stuart monarchy – three generations of debate (interspersed with bitter fighting) over the nature of state authority. Did a sovereign rule by divine sanction or by the people's (or parliament's) consent? On what basis was there a national constitution? Could a people kill or exile their king? The fierce political disagreements of the 1700–1750 period continued to centre on these questions, and on the events that gave rise to them. The history of the 'Stuart Cause' was a narrative about which no agreement or neutrality was possible. Even naming the people and events raises problems of interpretation that divide the United Kingdom to this day: the 'Great Rebellion' (or 'Civil War of Parliament against King') 1642–9, culminating in the murder (or execution) of the divinely constituted Stuart sovereign (or betrayer of his people) Charles the First; the usurpation (or interregnum) of Cromwell; the Stuart Restoration of Charles the Second in 1660; the succession of his Roman Catholic brother James the Second, who fled to France in 1688 (was he overthrown or did he abdicate?); and the crown seized by (or given to) the Dutch Protestant Prince of Orange as William the Third, who reigned jointly with his wife, Mary Stuart (James's daughter), then singly after Mary's death; William succeeded in 1702 by Mary's sister, Queen Anne, the last Stuart ruler; and on Anne's death without children in 1714, the throne being dubiously offered (or passing peacefully) to the German Elector of Hanover as George the First; and in the following year the first unsuccessful pro-Stuart Uprising (or Jacobite Rebellion) to restore the Stuart succession in the person of a Catholic 'James the Third'. With a history so disputed, and meanings so contested, it is little wonder that allegory and arcane symbolism became a means of political expression.[11]

The situation in 1721, the year of Hill's *The Judgment-Day*, was tense and dangerous: the state was under threat from financial collapse after the 'South-Sea Bubble', and yet another invasion plot was being hatched to bring over the Stuart 'Pretender'. There was a growing conviction among the Tories that a Stuart restoration was their only hope of 'breaking the Whig stranglehold on church and state'.[12] The first minister, Walpole, suspended the Habeas Corpus Act (the equivalent of declaring a state of emergency) and the leader of Jacobite opinion, the Bishop of Rochester, was arrested and sent to the Tower. A Whig M.P. wrote that if the Pretender had landed, 'he might have rode to St James's with very few hands held up against him'.[13]

It is in this context that we can read the climax of Hill's *Judgment-Day* as presenting a miraculous *restoration*. As the chaos subsides and human souls claim their reconstituted bodies, the mistakes of history can be put right. Quarrels are settled, murderers are confronted by their victims, and one figure is singled out:

> Majestic, in the solemn front, of Stuart's injur'd race,
>   The kingly martyr rears his awful brow!
> Pierc'd by the force of his forgiving face,
>   A gloomy host of back'ning rebels bow!
> And fear, too late, that sovereign pow'r, they never own'd till now! (305–9)

In Hill's vision, Charles the First will regain his authority, and 'Usurpers fly from kings, whose thrones they fill'd' (316). Is this, then, a poem advocating the overthrow of King George and the restoration of the Stuarts? Or is it the vision of a sublime restoration that at the end of time will reassert divine providence over history? Or is one contained in the other? By using the sublime, a political poet in this period was able to embrace seditious earthly meanings within universal ones. Being a transcendent mode did not steer sublime poetry away from political ideas – it enabled poetry to express them.

In the 1720s thinking the unthinkable, and expressing the unexpressible, was the 'sublime' predicament of opposition poets with a Jacobite agenda.[14] To celebrate 'Charles the Martyr' as Christ, to see monarchy as transcending human constitutions, and to imagine a restored order sanctioned by God, encouraged a poet like Hill to find his own sanction in divine vision. There was a decorum in this: the 'bard' was above the sordid *status quo* and took his truths from a higher authority. This lofty position was adopted by Hill's friend, Richard Savage, in *The Wanderer* (1729), a long poem full of Jacobite iconography.[15] Surrounded by vice, folly, faction, and villainy, Savage's poet 'glows impassion'd for his Country's Good' and in doing so he becomes transformed into an image of the inspired bard:

> He takes his *gifted Quill* from *Hands divine*,
> Around his Temples Rays refulgent shine!
> Now rapt! now more than Man!—I see him climb,
> To view this Speck of Earth from Worlds sublime!
> I see him now o'er Nature's Works preside!
> How clear the Vision! and the Scene how wide! (III, 195–200)

Radiant transfigurations of this kind were the very stuff of opposition visionary poetry in the 1720s, but it could be seen as part of a wider agenda of poetic 'restoration' such as James Thomson (another member of Hill's circle) had called for three years earlier in his preface to *Winter* (1726): 'Let POETRY, once more, be restored to her antient Truth, and Purity'. Thomson instanced Hill's *The Judgment-Day* as the perfect expression of this reawakened sense of '*Poetical Ambition*'.[16]

In any argument it also helped to have God on your side, and sublime poetry had the advantage of being able to draw naturally from the language of the Hebrew Bible. It was recognised that God's creating word was the original sublime statement. Longinus had praised Genesis 1:3 (*And God said, Let there be light: and there was light*) for expressing the essence of divine power. Poetry's origins were traced back to Adam and Eve celebrating the wonders of creation. Charles Gildon declared that poetry was 'most sublime in its cause . . . for poetry is as old as mankind, coeval with human race, and was invented as soon as man thought of addressing either his prayers or his praise to heaven'.[17] Dennis, an admirer of the classics, nevertheless claimed he could produce a hundred passages from the Bible 'which are infinitely superior to any Thing that can be brought upon the same Subject, from the *Grecian* and *Roman* Poets', and he compared Psalm 18 (*He bowed the Heavens and came down, and Darkness was under his Feet . . .*) with a passage from Virgil's *Georgics*, concluding: 'how great, how lofty, how terrible, is that . . . How much stronger than that of *Virgil* . . . ?'[18] If King David the Psalmist was a great poet, then so too were the Old Testament prophets: 'For the Prophets were Poets by the Institution of their Order, and Poetry was one of the Prophetick Functions'.[19] Thanks to his appreciation of impassioned and figurative writing, Dennis was able to embrace the 'poetry' of the Bible in its expressions of praise, thanksgiving, prophecy, prayer, and wonder.

All these aspects of biblical poetry were brought together by Anne Finch in 'Upon the Hurricane' (published 1713), one of her most ambitious and startling works. Although best known for the contemplative 'Nocturnal Rêverie' (discussed in the previous chapter) expressing the 'sedate Content' of a human soul at peace in the natural world, Finch also understood nature's potential for terror and destruction. In fact the two poems gain from being read alongside each other, the sublime public ode set against the romantic private meditation. 'Upon the Hurricane' (completed in 1704) engages with the 'Rage' and 'Clamours' that are excluded from the 'Rêverie' (where 'every louder Wind / Is to its distant Cavern safe confin'd', 1–2). Like Aaron Hill's *Judgment-Day*, Finch's sublime encounter with the wrath of God delivers a political message, and in doing so claims the authority and language of biblical prophecy.

Finch's subject is the Great Storm that devastated southern Britain in 1703 (it would not be matched until October 1987). For her it is a timely reminder that the nation's existence is conditional on God's divine sanction, and like all human structures can be swept away if he chooses. Her prophetic warrant is announced by the extended title: '*A Pindarick Poem Upon the Hurricane in* November 1703, *referring to this Text in* Psalm 148. ver. 8. Winds and Storms fulfilling his Word' (in the 1713 volume Finch follows her ode with a verse paraphrase of the psalm). The ode's opening lines recur at various points like a nagging conscience recalling God's displeasure: 'You have obey'd, you WINDS, that must fulfill / The Great Disposer's righteous Will'. It is clear that Finch's Creator can choose to intervene in the natural world and reveal himself at any time. This stress on divine revelation draws Finch into the major theological debate of the age. Put simply, this centred on a challenge to traditional *Revealed Religion* (God has revealed himself to this sinful world through the Bible and Jesus Christ) from an emergent *Natural Religion* partly inspired by modern science (God has designed the world as a perfect system that embodies his purposes). What confirms 'Upon the Hurricane' as a poem of public significance is its insight into the political implications of this encounter between orthodox faith and scientific system.

In Finch's poem, the devastation bears witness to the fact that 'Nature' is subject to a higher authority. She is not a benign order holding everything in place, but an uncaring parent:

> Your Mother Earth, thro' long preceding Rains,
>   (Which undermining sink below)
>   No more her wonted Strength retains;
> Nor you so fix'd within her Bosom grow,
> That for your sakes she can resolve to bear
>   These furious Shocks of hurrying Air (41–6)

This has not been the sudden cataclysm it appears – the roots had already been loosened, so that even mighty cedar-trees could be twisted round like willows. Old inherited structures that seemed enduring have been brought down; 'loftier Palaces' of 'deep Foundation' have collapsed with their 'superfluous Load' of 'costly Fretwork':

>   The present Owner lifts his Eyes,
> And the swift Change with sad Affrightment spies:
>   The Cieling gone, that late the Roof conceal'd;
>   The Roof untyl'd, thro' which the Heav'ns revealed,
> Exposes now his Head, when all Defence has fail'd. (77–81)

From the heaven-revealing storm of 1703 Finch could look back on twenty years of jarring changes in Church and State that had affected her and her husband directly. After the 'bloodless revolution' of 1688 the Finches, with other so-called 'non-jurors', refused to take the oath of allegiance to King William. She lost her position at the Stuart court, and he was arrested and charged with Jacobitism. The pair were forced to take refuge at the houses of their friends. As Finch remarks in another poem, she found herself 'Blasted by a Storm of Fate, / Felt thro' all the *British* State'. She became, she says, like an unsupported vine, trailing on the ground and 'living only in the Root'.[20] But unlike the roots of many trees in the storm, hers remained firm. Another nonjuror who did not adapt to the new dispensation was Bishop Thomas Ken, evicted from his see of Bath and Wells. The fact that his replacement was crushed to death in his palace bedroom allows Finch to see a link between that tottering building and the state of the established Anglican Church:

> Yet strictly pious *KEN!* had'st Thou been there,
> This Fate, we think, had not become thy share;
>   Nor had that awful Fabrick bow'd,
>   Sliding from its loosen'd Bands;
>   Nor yielding Timbers been allow'd
>   To crush thy ever-lifted Hands ... (100–105)

Finch surveys a public world where nothing has remained in place. Her images through the poem are of sliding, bending, varying, twisting, undermining, loosening, yielding, and resigning. It becomes clear that the hurricane has issued a challenge to the state of things in the Britain of 1703, testing the system, putting pressure on the ties and joints with which men have tried to hold the established constitution together. The hurricane has questioned the basis on which the nation's structures stand.

The storm also seems to parody human institutions and party agendas ('Nor WHIG, nor TORY now'). Like statesmen disputing for power, the four winds conspire and struggle with each other in a parody of a rowdy cabinet ('Meeting now, they all contend, / Those assail, while These defend', 127–8). Overriding the laws of parliament, the 'juster Tempest' has swept away the legal fences that enclosed 'another's Right', and the land has reverted to a common ('The Earth agen one general Scene appears', 200). But this return to nature is no Garden of Eden. For Finch it is a glimpse of the natural rights invoked by the radical Diggers and Levellers, closer to the brutish State of Nature feared by Hobbes: 'Free as the Men, who wild Confusion love, / And lawless Liberty approve, / Their Fellow-Brutes pursue their way' (204–6).

'Upon the Hurricane' thus stages an encounter between divine revelation and the two competing 'philosophies of Nature' of the early eighteenth century – the deists' rational System of Nature with its optimistic and benevolist implications, and Thomas Hobbes's analysis of the brutish Nature into which all individuals relapse unless held together by an authorised power. Finch's poem declares that both are false, as are all earthly constitutions that place human arrangements above those of God. Against the deists, she asserts divine revelation and human sin, and against Hobbes she asserts God's sanction above human institutions. In her poem, both the Platonic and materialist systems give way to a humble acceptance of the inscrutable power of God. Her argument is close to that of Dryden in *Religio Laici* (1682): '*Reason* saw not, till *Faith* sprung the Light. / Hence all thy *Natural Worship* takes the *Source*: / 'Tis *Revelation* what thou thinkst *Discourse*' (69–71).

Away from the storm, however, a different nature can be explored, like that celebrated in her 'Nocturnal Rêverie' or her 'Petition for an Absolute Retreat' – an inner principle to be found at moments of quiet thought. Like Wyatt and Marvell, those other poets who had watched the manoeuvrings of state politics close at hand, Finch is sensitive to ideas of alteration and deception. Like them, she comments on public morality by writing about personal integrity. In her hands a poem focused on privacy and retreat has an unspoken political resonance, more powerful because disengaged from the busy world it rejects:

> Be no Tidings thither brought,
> But Silent, as a Midnight Thought,
> Where the World may ne'er invade,
> Be those Windings, and that Shade! ('Petition', 18–21)

This kind of local meditation drawing strength from an internalised nature is very different from the deists' 'Natural Worship' with its celebration of the universal 'Book of Nature'. In place of their confident image of God's text lying open to all, Finch offers silent prayer.

Although Natural Religion was condemned by orthodox churchmen (a sermon against deism was sure to find approval in the right quarters), it proved extremely influential on eighteenth-century poetry. Some resisted nature's divine claims, like the Rev. Isaac Watts who in his imitations of the Psalms set out to 'shew the excellency of the book of Scripture above the book of Nature'.[21] But in poetry the tide was flowing the other way. As a manifestation of the power and providence of God, external nature offered more than descriptive possibilities: it became an important subject in its own right, as significant as anything from history or the Bible. Nature's variety and power, its mood-swings and harsh challenges, could be read as a spiritual dialogue between creator and created, and it was one in which all living things could join. The language of 'Natural Worship' at its most rapturous and expansive can be heard in the voice of Theocles, one of the speakers in Lord Shaftesbury's dialogue, *The Moralists* (1709):

> O GLORIOUS *Nature*! supremely Fair, and sovereignly Good! All-loving and All-lovely, All-divine! . . . whose every single Work affords an ampler Scene, and is a nobler Spectacle than all which ever Art presented! O mighty *Nature*! Wise Substitute of *Providence*! impower'd *Creatress*! Or Thou impowering DEITY, Supreme Creator! (III. i)

The *Creator* seems something of an afterthought here. Nature has assumed Christ's role as God's creating Word[22] to become Earth's delegated *Creatress*. She is also a substitute *Providence* – meaning that God's providential scheme for humanity is being continuously manifested in the natural world. Nature's Trinity of attributes (*All-loving and All-lovely, All-divine*) almost parodies the traditional attributes of God (omnipotent, omniscient, omnipresent). Shaftesbury's tutor, John Locke, argued that 'The works of Nature everywhere sufficiently evidence a deity',[23] and in that word *sufficiently* lies the difference between seeing nature as God's handiwork and celebrating it as a means of knowing God directly.

For many at this time, the man who had come closest to such immediate knowledge was Sir Isaac Newton, whose theory of universal gravitation (expounded in his *Principia*, 1687) struck with the force of revelation. It seemed that Newton had looked into the mind of God, and had revealed the hidden science by which the universe moved. A stone falling from a human hand, the menstrual rhythms of the tides, the planetary orbits, the track of comets – all obeyed the same Law of Gravity. The forces acting on distant suns, and on a dew-drop, were the same. The meanest flower bowed its head according to the mathematics that guided the moons of Jupiter. For an early eighteenth-century poet there were imaginative riches here. Nevertheless, thanks partly to William Blake (writing more than a century after the *Principia*), it has become conventional to think of Newton's influence as a triumph of reason over imagination, with the universe reduced to a static order. From our perspective of eighteenth-century poetry, however, nothing could be further from the truth. (In any case, Blake's 'Newton' is of course late eighteenth-century Newtonianism, not Newton himself.[24]) In connecting ideas together, Newton's theory was analogous to the workings of imagination. All creation could be seen as an interlinked fabric, and with the analogies now possible it was natural to speak of Newton's 'vision', and to find that vision stimulating and spiritually uplifting. It is also important to understand that Newton's is a dynamic system, not a static one. In his *Principia* he shows that Descartes' competing system of swirling vortices will eventually run down and lose all its energy, whereas in his own gravitational theory the energy can be infinitely sustained.[25] Newtonian 'order' is maintained not by stasis but by an interplay of dynamic forces.

It was the sublimity and wonder of the Newtonian universe that struck his contemporaries. Roger Cotes, Professor of Astronomy at Cambridge, celebrated the author's 'sublime genius', and declared: 'The gates are now set open, and by the passage he has revealed we may freely enter into the knowledge of the hidden secrets and wonders of natural things'.[26] Newton's text was no mere explanation, but a revelation, opening up a world of potential discoveries. Others could go boldly in Newton's tracks, and the poets went with imagination as their vehicle. John Hughes in *The Ecstasy. An Ode* (1720) projects his mind onto a sublime pathway through the solar system ('What Pow'r unknown my Course still upwards guides . . . ?') travelling past Mars, Jupiter and Saturn, and out towards the Milky Way. But then he suddenly notices a meteoric form sweeping through space towards him:

> But lo!—what's this I see appear?
> It seems far off a pointed Flame;
> From Earth-wards too the shining Meteor came.
> How swift it climbs th'aerial Space!
> And now it traverses each Sphere,
> And seems some living Guest, familiar to the Place.
> 'Tis He—as I approach more near
> The great *Columbus* of the Skies I know!
> 'Tis NEWTON's Soul that daily travels here
> In Search of Knowledge for Mankind below.
> O stay, thou happy Spirit, stay,
> And lead me on thro' all th'unbeaten Wilds of Day . . . (169–80)

Newton's own *ecstasy* ('escape of soul from body') has inspired the poet's. Even the wit in the passage inverts a sublime idea: Earth's daring adventurer (*great Columbus*) is here just a familiar guest who calls round *daily*. What is awesome to us is routine for him.

Newtonian poetry, far from recording an abstract construct, celebrates an animated system. Writers repeatedly remark that the universe has now been revealed as a living thing. In *A Poem Sacred to the Memory of Sir Isaac Newton* published on Newton's death in 1727, James Thomson stresses the great scientist's life-giving role. 'Every STAR', he writes,

> at his approach
> Blaz'd into SUNS, the living centre each
> Of an harmonious system: all combin'd,
> And rul'd unerring by that single Power,
> Which draws the stone projected to the ground. (63–7)

The sublime bathos of that last line places the universe in a human perspective. Here is a new image for how power works within a system. No longer is there a 'sovereign' sun, the symbol of a divinely ordained ruler (we recall Aaron Hill's lament that 'the sov'reign sun forgets his care'). Our sun, like other stars and planets, is subject to laws – it doesn't transcend them. Rather than standing supreme above a lower creation, this ancient image of sovereignty is now part of a wider dispensation, a mathematically demonstrable settlement. The divine has been demythologised, but also extended and humanised. In this passage Thomson wittily uses the language of tyranny (*rul'd unerring by that single Power*) about something that is beneficent and available to all. The God of gravitation no longer sits shrouded in mystery, but has become the active organiser of the world around us, maintaining its intricate balance of forces. He therefore fulfils a role comparable to Sir Robert Walpole, Prime Minister of Great Britain – a point Thomson himself makes in dedicating his poem to the man who is 'gloriously employ'd' in state affairs: 'You are engag'd in the highest and most active Scenes of Life, balancing the Power of *Europe*, watching over our common Welfare, informing the whole Body of Society and Commerce, and even like Heaven dispensing Happiness to the Discontented and Ungrateful'.[27] Walpole, champion and preserver of the Whig Hanoverian settlement, fulfils a remit remarkably similar to that of the Newtonian God: *balancing, watching over, informing the whole, dispensing*.

At this period the nature of the British state was a living issue in the minds of poets and politicians. Following the reorganisations marked by the Declaration of Rights (1689), the Act of Settlement (1701), and the Act of Union between England and Scotland (1707), it was natural to ask how, and on what principles, the new nation was functioning. Neither subject to tyranny, nor defined by a single written constitution, 'Great Britain' as a working system depended on a variety of elements: both *custom* ('natural' rights, and precedents from an ancient tradition of common law) and constitutional and civil *legislation* (regulating the monarchy, or imposing socio-religious conformity); both *authority* (divided between God, the Crown, Parliament, and Church) and *power* (wealth and influence; trade and business; and the hungry mob).

This potentially volatile mixture depended on achieving some kind of 'settlement' that would encourage competing interests to sustain the system rather than blow it apart. Once again, the model is a dynamic one: an autocratically imposed stability was to be avoided as much as an unlicensed anarchy.

Many poets found these matters fascinating. Whether their primary topic was economics, ethics, the natural world, philosophy, or religion, some of the most influential visionary poems of the period explored how a system could harness competing forces and interests. The remainder of this chapter will consider a group of poems from this viewpoint. They were published between 1714 (year of the Hanoverian succession) and 1746 (the Battle of Culloden), and are very diverse in their poetic language (from doggerel to the sublime), but each of them raises large questions of this kind in terms of the dynamics of nature, society, the self, and God. All are interested in what drives a system, and how it is governed (or not) for the best.

Bernard Mandeville's verse fable 'The Grumbling Hive' (1714)[28] was written to oppose, or more exactly invert, the philosophical system of Lord Shaftesbury ('The attentive Reader', he notes, 'will soon perceive that two Systems cannot be more opposite than his Lordship's and mine').[29] Shaftesbury's idealising model of human society, which we encountered in Chapter 2, assumes a concept of 'Natural Virtue' in which all members find happiness through acting in accordance with their 'Natural Affections' for the public good. Indeed there is no individual 'good' that is not in harmony with the good of all, i.e. 'universal Nature' as expressed in God's best-possible 'SYSTEM of all things'. In Shaftesbury's benevolent system (reminiscent of Milton's Heaven in *Paradise Lost*) all voices are naturally attuned, and to put self in opposition to society is entirely against reason. The system is of course a circular one, in which each term (good, virtue, nature, reason) defines the other, and it is hard to break into without smashing it. Mandeville aimed to do just that. The driving-force of his flourishing beehive is Hobbesian self-interest: it is a ruthless society of dirty dealings, bribery, cheating, theft, and hypocrisy of all kinds, in which lawyers and fixers are kept busy – but it flourishes economically ('Thus every Part was full of Vice, / Yet the whole Mass a Paradise'). This was the world that Walpole would later master. The whole functions successfully through the dynamic relations between its antagonistic parts. A system of 'public virtue' is industriously sustained by 'private vices'. But once Heaven decrees that every bee in the hive shall be honest, their society disintegrates. Without the motive force of selfishness, the energy and ingenuity of the hive are lost; prices fall, trade declines, and the population is decimated. With rigorous logic, Mandeville takes Shaftesbury's harmonious economy and shows it running down, sinking to its satiric apocalypse through a failure of nerve and energy.

What Mandeville cleverly offers is an untranscendent picture in which the poet turns away from the sublime universals of a Shaftesburian God of Nature to record the dirty doings of *human* nature. This exercise in the anti-sublime suggests that idealism makes fine theory but bad practice. A self-driven society at ground level may not look very nice, he implies, but it works. The message is carried in a suitably functional kind of verse, a low jingle (like coins in a pocket) which resists all poetic ambition: 'I do not dignify these few loose Lines with the Name of Poem . . . All I can say of them is, that they are a Story told in Dogrel . . . The Reader shall be welcome to call them what he pleases.'[30] In other words, the fable will speak for itself – the writer offers unpolished 'honesty', not pleasing fiction. The constitutional settlement of the beehive is a similarly practical one, stripped of any ceremonial aspect or higher sanction:

> No Bees had better Government,
> More Fickleness, or less Content:
> They were not Slaves to Tyranny,
> Nor rul'd by wild *Democracy*;
> But Kings, that could not wrong, because
> Their Power was circumscrib'd by Laws. (7–12)

Religious principles, oaths of allegiance, issues of 'right', legitimacy, or divine authority, carry no weight here – the *Laws* apply to criminal and King alike. Mandeville's system is a materialist and pragmatic one. The 'good' is what works best.

Pope shared the pragmatism ('For Forms of Government let fools contest; / Whate'er is best administer'd is best', *Essay on Man*, III, 303–4); but it is typical of his creative need to draw opposites together that he should place this statement within a sublime and divinely inspired system – 'the World's great harmony' (III, 295). There are a host of such seeming contradictions in Pope's *Essay on Man* (1733–4) because it is partly about articulating and reconciling contradiction. It is a poem in which an absolute statement ('Whatever is, is RIGHT', I, 294) is likely to be countered or relativised elsewhere ('"Whatever is, is RIGHT."—This world, 'tis true, / Was made for Caesar— but for Titus too', IV, 145–6). In Pope's world, pragmatism and idealism must live together. In the *Essay* he acknowledges that the 'mighty maze' of the world has a 'plan', but for us humans it is a place of restless searching – there is nothing so simple as a *status quo*. Individual needs, passions and interests keep the puzzling system in motion and drive human life along. For Pope, the passions are 'Modes of Self-love' (II, 93) and are the motive force, but not the end, of life. Similarly, although higher 'reason' understands ends and the wider good, it is itself inert. We need both of them if we are to get anywhere, just like a ship needs wind and a map ('card'): 'On life's vast ocean diversely we sail, / Reason's the card, but Passion is the gale', II, 107–8). A system based on just one of these will be inadequate, so that for Pope, both the idealist system of Shaftesbury, and the materialist system of Hobbes and Mandeville, are seeing only a partial picture. A human being who lacks the driving-force of passion will have no inner impulse and simply be a vegetable ('Fix'd like a plant on his peculiar spot, / To draw nutrition, propagate, and rot', II, 63–4). But if passion possesses him/her to the exclusion of reasonable, sociable feelings, then these egotistical motions will destroy that self along with others ('Or, meteor-like, flame lawless thro' the void, / Destroying others, by himself destroy'd', II, 65–6). Both alternatives fail to harness energy – one is a collapse into a static centre, and the other is a flight outwards that dissipates the energy expanded. Left on their own, centripetal and centrifugal forces will spend themselves.

It is therefore in Newtonian gravity – a meeting of opposing forces – that Pope finds an image for reconciling these impulses within his own dynamic system ('reconcile' not in the sense of a compromise, but as finding an active *modus vivendi* between them):

> On their own Axis as the Planets run,
> Yet make at once their circle round the Sun:
> So two consistent motions act the Soul;
> And one regards Itself, and one the Whole.
>   Thus God and Nature link'd the gen'ral frame,
> And bade Self-love and Social be the same. (III, 313–8)

Order and energy are often thought to be opposed, but Pope shows that without order there can be no energy. Energy needs a structure to harness it, just as a dam or a windmill work to resist, and thereby release, the power of the elements. It would be wonderful if we could all exist in a state of harmony and virtue, but the Nature we inhabit is a turbulent one – hurricanes disrupt the outer world, and fierce passions the inner. If we look for 'order' it is not within our individual experience, but in the vast scheme of things beyond:

> Better for Us, perhaps, it might appear,
> Were there all harmony, all virtue here;
> That never air or ocean felt the wind;
> That never passion discompos'd the mind:
> But ALL subsists by elemental strife;
> And Passions are the elements of Life.
> The gen'ral ORDER, since the whole began,
> Is kept in Nature, and is kept in Man. (I, 165–72)

It is the relationship between the *elemental strife* of our world and a notion of an all-embracing *order* that is the subject of James Thomson's *The Seasons* (1730–46).[31] In this poem, however, the link between the two terms is stretched almost to breaking-point. We remain in the 'harmonious system' celebrated in his *Poem Sacred to the Memory of Sir Isaac Newton*, with its awesome 'world-revolving Power' holding everything on course; but in *The Seasons* the system is a more complex and strife-torn one, and spread over a broader earthly canvas. The poem roves geographically across the created world, encompassing its deserts, polar regions, mountains and oceans, while repeatedly returning to a 'living centre' in the English rural scene. Similarly, contained in its wide temporal sweep is a single farming year followed through from early Spring ploughing to Autumn harvest and Winter storms. Thomson's ambition is to do justice to the universal, but without taking refuge in distance and generality, and so in each scene the details of colour, texture, and sound are insisted on, and we are repeatedly brought close to the physical sense-experience. Here nature is the dynamic principle of life in all its forms and moods. Every scene, however calm, is full of actual or potential movement. It also carries a degree of emotional reverberation, so that we are conscious of an internal dimension to the landscape.

Here, for example, is Thomson's picture of the moment when the icy grip of Winter relents:

> Muttering, the Winds at Eve, with blunted Point,
> Blow hollow-blustering from the South. Subdu'd,
> The Frost resolves into a trickling Thaw.
> Spotted the Mountains shine; loose Sleet descends,
> And floods the Country round. The Rivers swell,
> Of Bonds impatient. Sudden from the Hills,
> O'er Rocks and Woods, in broad brown Cataracts,
> A thousand snow-fed Torrents shoot at once . . . ('Winter', 988–95)

In this characteristically restless passage we are conscious not just of a change of mood, but of a shift in dynamics. We register it, I think, as turning from relaxation to tension, from dispersal to convergence, emptying to filling, loosening to tightening, from the gradual to the sudden. Nature's contrary movements are played out as we read (silently or aloud). At first her forces seem depleted. The sharp violence of the wind has become *hollow-blustering*, and its *blunted Point* is now, like *muttering*, just an empty gesture. The words *subdu'd* and *resolves* suggest that the threat is past and nature has relented; and the verb *trickling* (the third half-hearted present participle) seems to confirm the loss of energy. But out of that word a counter-movement begins, which gathers power as the verbs become active. The swelling forces meet resistance (*Of Bonds impatient*); but just as the word *Sudden* promises release, the verb of the sentence (*shoot*) is held back for two lines until it can make maximum impact in a burst of energy, as everything converges to a single sharp point.

This seems reminiscent of Anne Finch's picture in 'Upon the Hurricane' of a fickle 'Mother Nature' that turns round on mankind and destroys human structures. *The Seasons* contains vivid scenes of nature's destructiveness, everything from the pestilence breeding in her 'Recesses foul' ('Summer', 1031), to lovers struck by lightning ('that moment, to the Ground, / A blacken'd Corse, was struck the beauteous Maid', 'Summer', 1215–6), or a flood sweeping life away ('before whose rushing Tide, / Herds, Flocks, and Harvests, Cottages, and Swains, / Roll mingled down', 'Autumn', 339–41). But in *The Seasons* each picture of horror is counterpoised by moments when nature restores and grows. The sharp frosts of Winter are a 'renovating Force' (704); Autumn also means fruition and stores of food; and in 'Summer' just a few lines after the deadly thunderstorm we see a boy bathing in a pool, an image of nature embracing human life. The youth

> plunges headlong down the circling Flood.
> His ebon Tresses, and his rosy Cheek
> Instant emerge; and thro' th'obedient Wave,
> At each short Breathing by his Lip repell'd,
> With Arms and Legs according well, he makes,
> As Humour leads, an easy-winding Path . . . ('Summer', 1249–54)

After the shock of that opening line recalling the sublime fall of Satan in *Paradise Lost* ('Him the Almighty Power / Hurld headlong ... down / To bottomless perdition', I, 44–7) the downward movement is instantly reversed, and life re-emerges. The *circling Flood* becomes an *obedient Wave*, and by the last line there has been a transformation of mood and movement, with the boy (*As Humour leads*) curving an arabesque through the stream.

In Finch's 'Upon the Hurricane' nature becomes sportive, almost a grotesque anti-nature, playing games with the world and distorting things in 'wild Confusion' (204). But scattered within the chaos are little emblems of divine justice (the miser 'bury'd with his Coin', 172), showing that although nature may be treacherous, God is always watching and judging. We are allowed to glimpse the true text through the tears in nature's fabric. *The Seasons* again works very differently. With its strong deistical tendencies, the poem refuses to separate nature and God in this way. Thomson's passages of elemental chaos stress the sufferer's innocence. The shepherd who dies in the snowdrift while he thinks of his wife and children, is bewildered by a landscape that is very like Finch's sportive nature ('In his own loose-revolving Fields, the Swain / Disaster'd stands; sees other Hills ascend', 'Winter', 278–9). But here we move from his children peering anxiously through the cottage window, to their father's body, and we watch as Winter 'Lays him along the Snows, a stiffen'd Corse, / Stretch'd out, and bleaching in the northern Blast' (320–1). Thomson's natural religion offers no easy optimism. This is what Winter does. There is no saviour watching over him, no 'particular' providence to intervene. But as we move through the panorama of *The Seasons*, this episode, like many others, takes its place in the larger pattern. A few pages later we encounter a different shepherd in a wintry scene where nature has been playing tricks with frozen drifts; but this time the encrusted snow is 'sounding to the Tread / Of early Shepherd, as he pensive seeks / His pining Flock'. On his way down the mountain this shepherd moves easily over the surface, and 'Pleas'd with the slippery Surface, swift descends' (756–9).

In Thomson's system, what could be an ironic contrast becomes something more organic. There are two shepherds, two fates; but instead of being ironically juxtaposed they are both absorbed into the sublime 'mysterious Round' within 'the mighty Hand, / That, ever-busy, wheels the silent Spheres' ('A Hymn on the Seasons', 21–30). In *The Seasons* nothing keeps still enough to be measured independently, and everything becomes part of a cycle. From vortices of many kinds (destructive swirlings and benign wheelings) to the slow recycling of the Earth's waters ('Autumn', 773–835), *The Seasons* is committed to the idea of circulation, and to reaching finally for a vantage-point that will show us the whole encircling vision:

> yet bear up a While,
> And what your bounded View, which only saw
> A little Part, deem'd *Evil* is no more:
> The Storms of WINTRY TIME will quickly pass,
> And one unbounded SPRING encircle All. ('Winter'; 1065–9)

The three dynamic systems of Mandeville, Pope, and Thomson offer an increasingly wide picture of the individual in society. Mandeville's materialist bees have no concerns beyond their grumbling hive: driven by self-interest, they are subject to an economic model of success and failure, and the hive's destiny is in its own hands. In his *Essay on Man* Pope makes this selfish impulse part of a dynamics of contradiction, and tries to construct a sociable ethics that will reconcile the individual to a common 'good' of a more idealistic kind. In *The Seasons* Thomson draws back yet further to place his toiling humans in a providential scheme they cannot themselves experience, and to which they might individually be sacrificed. To find a meaning the poems move increasingly away from the self, and both Pope and Thomson recognise the paradoxical possibilities when a material order and a spiritual order meet. For them, the natural world is subject to physical laws, but 'value' is more intangible. It is not the negotiable commodity that Mandeville defined.

Turning to the final poetic system, Mark Akenside's *The Pleasures of Imagination* (1744), we enter the heady world of youthful Platonism, in which the intangible becomes pre-eminent. In this three-book poem the life-force is not 'Self' or 'Nature', but 'Mind' ('MIND, MIND alone, bear witness, earth and heav'n! / The living fountains in itself contains / Of beauteous and sublime', I, 481–3). For Akenside, these fountains are the human imagination – the vital link between the external world of sense and the internal world of idea. Without it, the senses are a 'superficial impulse', 'not reaching to the heart' (I, 529–30). Mind is therefore redemptive and literally *inspirational* (in the sense of 'breathing life into'). It re-enacts at the human level God's original creativity, which was itself a mental act that extended idea into the dimension of sense – i.e. God *thought* Creation into existence. In his primal imagination he viewed the ideal forms of all potential life, and the organic system unfolded like a germinating seed out of his loving Mind:

> Then liv'd th'eternal ONE: then deep-retir'd
> In his unfathom'd essence, view'd at large
> The uncreated images of things . . .
>   From the first
> Of days, on them his love divine he fix'd,
> His admiration: till in time compleat,
> What he admir'd and lov'd, his vital smile
> Unfolded into being. Hence the breath
> Of life informing each organic frame . . . (I, 64–74)

The Pleasures of Imagination is concerned with ideas of interconnectedness and organic development, and here God's sublime *fiat* is not an authoritative declaration of the Word, but a generous and loving awakening to life. Behind Akenside the neoplatonic scholar is the twenty-two-year-old who later the same year submitted his doctoral thesis on 'The Origin and Growth of the Human Foetus'.

Akenside's subject is human potential ('what high, capacious pow'rs / Lie folded up in man', I, 222–3), and it is this theme that gives the poem a sharp political edge. (Dr Johnson remarked disapprovingly that in his youth the poet was 'no friend to any thing established',[32] and indeed at the age of sixteen, in 'A British Philippic', Akenside had furiously attacked Walpole's foreign policy.) Underpinning the poem's philosophic discussion is the principled idealism of Ancient Greece and republican Rome, with their visions of democratic freedom and public virtue. In Book One Akenside reaches beyond the distant galaxies 'wheeling unshaken thro' the void immense' to find a more powerful inspiration in the death-scene of the tyrant Caesar. Even the Newtonian universe at its most awe-inspiring, he says, falls short of that sublime moment when Brutus, 'amid the croud of patriots', shouted 'Rome again is free' (I, 494–500). The true sublime is the human mind at its noblest and most selfless. Akenside's ideal combines patriotism and friendship ('The toil of patriots, the delight of friends', II, 382), a fusion embodied in the two champions of Greek democratic freedom, Harmodius and Aristogeiton (soon to be celebrated in William Collins's 'Ode to Liberty', 1746), and it is 'Harmodius', the poet's wise teacher, who is the narrator of the visionary allegory in Book Two. He explores the question posed in the final chapter of Longinus's *On the Sublime*: is human liberty essential for a flourishing political and artistic culture? Akenside imagines the dawn of a 'radiant æra' in Britain when political morality and artistic excellence will embrace beneath 'freedom's ample fabric' (II, 43). Harmodius relates how the True and the Beautiful can be joined by bringing Virtue and Pleasure together. During his vision a divine voice declares that the 'harmonious frame' of the universe ('From the mute shell-fish gasping on the shore, / To men, to angels, to cœlestial minds', II, 344–5) is an interconnected whole – not static, but with each stage refining to a higher state of being as it aspires to the ideal:

> As flame ascends,
> As bodies to their proper center move,
> As the pois'd ocean to th'attracting moon
> Obedient swells, and every headlong stream
> Devolves its winding waters to the main;
> So all things which have life aspire to GOD . . . (II, 350–5)

For Akenside this is the true image of the System of Nature – gravity neoplatonised. His fluid lines recall Raphael's speech to Adam in *Paradise Lost* when the archangel explains how the first human pair can aspire from body up to spirit, 'by gradual scale sublim'd' (V, 483). It is this concept of the sublime as 'sublimation' that gives Akenside's system its dynamics, and relates his aesthetic theory to his youthful zeal for liberty. Here the imagination is no mere lumber-room of decaying experience (as it was for Hobbes and Locke), but an active moral force that delights in its freedom and energy. Against the grubby mechanisms of the materialists ('servile custom' and 'sordid policies', III, 616–7) Akenside proposes a view of human potential that will harness its 'energy divine' (III, 625). Functional *Realpolitik* will give way to a 'beneficent and active' idealism.

The early eighteenth-century sublime went beyond issues of taste and aesthetics to become a vehicle for ideas at a time when so much was being controversially re-organised. The natural world, the mental world, and the socio-political world were all reassessed to accommodate new discoveries, principles, and settlements. In different ways, Newton, Shaftesbury, and Walpole each represented a system that brought as many questions as answers, and poets were eager to enter the debate. The emergent theory of the sublime licensed poetry to contemplate things in their fullest extent or deepest essence, and to announce its visions. The final phrase is significant. Where the romantic mode of the early decades turned the imagination inward and stressed the subjective colouring of experience, the sublime comprehended large economies of thought. Confidence and ambition were required, and all the poets in this chapter shared a belief that their voice on the big public issues was important. When Thomson declares in the preface to *Winter* (2nd ed. 1726): 'I know no Subject more elevating, more amusing; more ready to awake the poetical Enthusiasm, the philosophical Reflection, and the moral Sentiment, than the *Works of Nature*', he is setting himself a virtually limitless agenda. It is as though Newton's great modern mind had challenged others to comprehend the world as he had done, and that poetry should not be allowed to fall behind mathematics in its aspirations. But Thomson also saw that poetic ambition had a historical status that needed to be recovered. In following John Dennis by declaring that poetry must be 'restored to her antient Truth, and Purity', he was aware that modern ideas could fruitfully combine with truths of the past. By mid-century this historical dimension would link romantic and sublime modes to the work of earlier English poets.

Notes

1. Samuel Cobb, *Callipaedia* (1712), IV, 389.
2. *Spectator* 303 (16 Feb. 1712). Bond, III, 85, 89.
3. This anonymous Greek rhetorical treatise from the first century AD was wrongly attributed to 'Longinus'. See *Classical Literary Criticism,* transl. T.S. Dorsch (Harmondsworth, 1965), pp. 24–6.
4. Samuel Cobb, 'A Discourse on Criticism and the Liberty of Writing', prefixed to his *Poems on Several Occasions . . . The Third Edition* (London, 1710), sigs. A5^v–A6^v.
5. *The Critical Works of John Dennis*, ed. Edward Niles Hooker, 2 vols. (Baltimore, 1939–43), I, 329.
6. John Sheffield, Earl of Mulgrave and Duke of Buckingham, *An Essay upon Poetry* (1682), 116–18.
7. Horace, *Odes*, IV.ii. 5–8. Dennis translates Horace's lines into a prose poem (what he calls 'English Poetical paraphrastick Prose'): 'As a stream that is lifted above its usual banks by the influx of celestial waters, comes rowling headlong from some Mountains Top, so *Pindar* rais'd by influence divine, ev'n above his own exalted Genius; grows vehement, swells, and ferments with fury, then precipitately flows with a mighty sound, and knows no bounds to his impetuous course' (Preface to *The Court of Death* [1695]. Hooker, I, 43).
8. Addison, *Spectator* 160 (3 Sept. 1711). Bond, II, 129.
9. Dennis, Preface to *The Court of Death* (1695). Hooker, I. 43.

10. Dennis, *The Grounds of Criticism in Poetry*, ch. 4. Hooker, I, 358, 361.

11. See Howard Erskine-Hill, *Poetry of Opposition and Revolution: Dryden to Wordsworth* (Oxford, 1996).

12. Maynard Mack, *Alexander Pope: A Life* (New York and London, 1985), p. 394.

13. See Bruce Lenman, *The Jacobite Risings in Britain, 1689–1746* (London, 1980), p. 258.

14. The sublime at this period was not an exclusively opposition mode. See Christine Gerrard, 'Pope, *Peri Bathous*, and the Whig Sublime', in *Cultures of Whiggism*, ed. David Womersley (Newark, 2003).

15. See Christine Gerrard, *The Patriot Opposition to Walpole: Politics, Poetry, and National Myth, 1725–1742* (Oxford, 1994), p. 236.

16. James Thomson, *The Seasons*, ed. James Sambrook (Oxford, 1981), p. 304.

17. Charles Gildon, *The Laws of Poetry* (London, 1721), p. 14.

18. John Dennis, *The Advancement and Reformation of Poetry* (1701), II. ii. Hooker, I, 268–71. On Dennis and the sublime, see David B. Morris, *The Religious Sublime: Christian Poetry and Critical Tradition in 18th-Century England* (Lexington, 1972), pp. 47–78.

19. John Dennis, *The Grounds of Criticism in Poetry* (1704), ch. 5. Hooker, I, 370.

20. 'The Petition for an Absolute Retreat', 152–61.

21. Isaac Watts, *The Psalms of David, Imitated in the Language of the New Testament, and Applied to the Christian State and Worship*, note to Psalm 19.

22. Jesus Christ's role as the Neoplatonic *Logos* (Word), agent of the Creation, is accepted by Milton in *Paradise Lost*, VII, 162–75.

23. Quoted by Basil Willey, *The Eighteenth Century Background* (London, 1949), no reference given.

24. See Peter Fisher, *The Valley of Vision* (Toronto, Buffalo and London: 1971 ed.), p. 109.

25. See Alexander Koyré, *Newton Studies* (London, 1965), p. 99.

26. Roger Cotes, Introduction *Principia* (2nd ed., 1713).

27. James Thomson, *Liberty, The Castle of Indolence, and Other Poems*, ed. James Sambrook (Oxford, 1986), p. 6.

28. 'The Grumbling Hive: or, Knaves turn'd Honest' had been printed in a pirated edition in 1705. The poem formed part of Mandeville's book *The Fable of the Bees* (1714), which served to gloss and develop ideas in the poem. The whole went through several later revisions and expansions.

29. *The Fable of the Bees*, ed. F.B. Kaye, 2 vols (Oxford, 1924), I, 324.

30. 'Preface', Ibid., I, 5.

31. After the success of *Winter. A Poem* (1726), Thomson published *Summer* (1727), *Spring* (1728), and then gathered them into a subscription edition of *The Seasons* (1730) which incorporated 'Autumn'. The poem was continually revised and expanded during the next twenty years by a further thousand lines. The latest revisions were made for the 1746 edition.

32. Johnson, *Lives of the Poets*, ed. Hill, III, 413. Johnson adds that Akenside 'certainly retained an unnecessary and outrageous zeal for what he called and thought liberty . . . [of which] the immediate tendency is innovation and anarchy, an impetuous eagerness to subvert and confound, with very little care what shall be established' (III, 411–2).

Chapter 8

Recovering the Past

In April 1710 four Iroquois sachems, or 'Kings', from Britain's American colonies visited London. They had an audience with Queen Anne and were shown the sights of the metropolis, which included the newly completed St Paul's Cathedral standing proudly on Ludgate Hill. In a *Spectator* essay the following year Joseph Addison put himself into the mind of one of them recording his impressions of the building in his 'diary':

> It was probably at first an huge mis-shapen Rock that grew upon the Top of the Hill, which the Natives of the Country (after having cut it into a kind of regular Figure) bored and hollowed with incredible Pains and Industry, till they had wrought in it all those beautiful Vaults and Caverns into which it is divided at this Day. As soon as this Rock was thus curiously scooped to their Liking, a prodigious Number of Hands must have been employed in chipping the Outside of it, which is now as smooth as the Surface of a Pebble, and is in several Places hewn out into Pillars that stand like the Trunks of so many Trees . . .[1]

The Iroquois King gives us an appropriate visual emblem for this chapter. As he looks at the mighty edifice, the interior becomes a series of *Vaults and Caverns*, and its art seems less the result of construction than of a process of discovery. This object was not placed there or built up from individual parts, but has been hewn out of an ancient natural feature and re-shaped through the centuries ('This great work', he notes, must have commenced 'many Hundred Years ago'). Addison's imagination reaches beyond Sir Christopher Wren's *neo*-classical building to recover an underlying primal form, something of great power that has borne the imprint of generations of human skill and ingenuity. The cathedral has been scooped out of the massive outcrop of stone, its caverns emerging from the *huge mis-shapen Rock*, as if to suggest continuity between a classical form, with its *regular Figure* and *smooth Surface*, and a native Gothic source. Through the eyes of his Iroquois King, Addison visualises an organic work of art that is no temporary imported feature, but is rooted in a primary original. To describe this idea we reach for words like 'genuine', 'authentic', 'monumental', and 'natural', which express how we value the work's historical dimension and its integrity with the local landscape. The emphasis shifts from a concept of shaping by art to one of recovery through exploration.

This sort of imagery and critical language will recur throughout the present chapter, which takes for its subject the ways in which British poets towards the middle of the eighteenth century became increasingly conscious of belonging to a native historic canon. We can think of them beginning to look at poetry much as the Iroquois King looked at St Paul's, feeling excitement at the possibility of returning to work with primary materials, of rediscovering an older poetic language, regaining a sense of wonder and power, and a more permanent notion of value. They became interested in the idea of a national literary history, and in placing their own work within it.

The concept of a poetic canon is a very old one, and poets have always been conscious of illustrious predecessors among whom they hoped to find a place. Chaucer's position as the 'Father' of English poetry had long been a common-place, and by 1700 Spenser and Milton were seen as completing a Pantheon of great writers, with Dryden beginning to emerge as a modern 'classic'. Pope's remark to Joseph Spence in 1736 was offered as a truism: "'Tis easy to mark out the general course of our poetry. Chaucer, Spenser, Milton, and Dryden are the great landmarks for it'.[2] But of those 'landmarks' Chaucer was virtu-ally unread in the original, and Spenser very little. Their status as canonical English classics was based on reputation rather than reading;[3] their language was generally regarded as outdated and even barbarous, and when being sub-jected to parody, imitation, or modernisation, it was their distance from the present that was being exploited. In 1700 (the year of his death) Dryden remarked: 'We can only say that [Chaucer] liv'd in the Infancy of our Poetry, and that nothing is brought to Perfection at the first. We must be Children before we grow Men'.[4] With this in mind he criticised Milton for 'digging from the Mines of *Chaucer* and *Spencer*' to find 'Antiquated words', rather than use the verbal currency of the present; and in his own modernisations of Chaucer's *The Wife of Bath's Tale*, *The Knight's Tale*, and *The Nun's Priest's Tale* he thought of himself as rescuing the old poet from oblivion. Thanks to Dryden, wrote one poet of the time, '*Chaucer* shall again with Joy be Read, / Whose Language with its Master lay for Dead'.[5] If nothing could be done to resuscitate the language of the old poet, then at least his 'sense' could be preserved before it entirely disappeared.

In a similar way, by 1700 the language and intricate stanza form of Spenser's *Faerie Queene* were viewed as disabling difficulties which only the poet's genius had overcome – they were certainly not to be copied. In 1687 an anonymous 'Person of Quality' published *Spenser Redivivus* ('Spenser Renov-ated') which rewrote the whole of Book One in heroic couplets. The preface commented that Spenser's 'obsolete Language and manner of Verse' had been removed, so that he could join the modern polite world on the arm of his translator 'in more fashionable *English*'. Such modernisings of the English classics were symptomatic of a widespread embarrassment at the barbarity of the native literary past. As Addison elegantly wrote in his 'Account of the Greatest English Poets' (1694):

> Old *Spenser* next, warm'd with poetick rage,
> In ancient tales amus'd a barb'rous age . . .
> But now the mystick tale, that pleas'd of yore,
> Can charm an understanding age no more.[6]

Typically, Spenser is being simultaneously canonised and discarded. His epic *Faerie Queene*, like the old medieval romances, is just a *mystick tale* that cannot appeal to the *understanding*, and therefore belongs to an earlier stage of human development nearer to Dryden's *Infancy of our Poetry*. After the Restoration of 1660 this 'Progress of Refinement' narrative soon became predominant, and to many who looked into the literary past from the civilised elegance of the new century, the Elizabethan age of Sidney, Spenser and Shakespeare had not yet emerged from Gothic barbarity.

Towards the middle of the century, however, a different attitude is noticeable, particularly in Spenserian imitations. The art of imitation seems to become something closer to absorption as poets discover new possibilities of subject, vocabulary, and rhythm. William Thompson's *Hymn to May* (1746), for example, in a seven-line version of the Spenserian stanza weaves a rich descriptive tapestry with images of returning life and love:

> Her hair (but rather threads of light it seems)
> With the gay honours of the spring intwind,
> Copious, unbound, in nectar'd ringlets streams,
> Floats glitt'ring on the sun, and scents the wind,
> Lovesick with odours!—Now to order roll'd,
> It melts upon her bosom's dainty mould,
> Or, curling round her waist, disparts its wavy gold. (64–70)

This erotic picture recalls Belinda and her sylphs in *The Rape of the Lock*. But Thompson also reaches beyond Pope to his sources in the figures of Milton's Eve (her *ringlets*), Spenser's Florimell (her streaming hair and gold-encircled waist) and Shakespeare's Cleopatra (the *lovesick* wind), and even further back to the classic original in Virgil's description of Venus ('From her head ambrosial tresses breathed celestial fragrance'). In just seven lines Thompson has placed himself within a literary history: Virgil-Spenser-Shakespeare-Milton-Pope.[7]

The *Faerie Queene* stanza (eight iambic pentameters followed by a final six-stress 'alexandrine'), or variations on it, began to develop a life of its own beyond the parodic. One of the most popular imitations of the century, William Shenstone's *The School-Mistress* (1737–48) is a case in point. The earliest twelve-stanza version (1737) draws amusement from its quaint language ('In evrich Village less y-known to Fame, / Dwells there, in Cot uncouth, a far renown'd, / A Matron old, whom we *School-Mistress* name'). This opening sounds patronising and self-conscious (an Oxford student putting on a funny voice). But something begins to happen as Shenstone revisits his childhood in the leisurely pace of the Spenserian stanza, which like Thompson's May encourages what is *intwind, copious, unbound*. The Elizabethan burnish of the language begins to suggest both the encrustations of memory, and the magic of a child's perspective. The nine lines give him room to ponder and notice things – as if he has been freed from the tighter responsibilities of the heroic couplet where each thought tends to be shaped into a point. In extending his poem over the years Shenstone exploited this tendency to *copia*. In the final thirty-five stanza version (1748) he offers three stanzas of suggestive detail on the herbs found in the schoolmistress's garden, and in the process transforms her cottage into a place of wonder:

> Lavender, whose spikes of azure bloom
> Shall be, ere-while, in arid bundles bound;
> To lurk amidst the labours of her loom,
> And crown her kerchiefs clean, with mickle rare perfume.[8]

Something that might seem old and dry has been given a rich new life.

The seductive fullness poets seem to have found in Spenser was exploited most memorably in James Thomson's *The Castle of Indolence* (1748) which began as a few stanzas 'in the way of raillery' on himself and his friends, but grew into a two-canto exploration of poetry's delights and responsibilities. In the first canto a Spenserian wealth of description is lavished on the castle and its pampered guests. Thomson leaves direct imitation behind and begins to absorb the allegorical world of enchantment to create a romantic spell of his own:

> Aereal Music in the warbling Wind,
> At Distance rising oft, by small Degrees,
> Nearer and nearer came, till o'er the Trees
> It hung, and breath'd such Soul-dissolving Airs,
> As did, alas! with soft Perdition please:
> Entangled deep in its enchanting Snares,
> The listening Heart forgot all Duties and all Cares. (I, 345–51)

This is Spenser filtered through the dangerous poetry of Milton's *Masque*. If the first canto recognises how Spenser's imagination can create a world of alluring artifice, then the second canto challenges that world by moving towards Spenser the moralist (the 'sage and serious' poet whom Milton admired[9]). With a sudden change of mood, Thomson introduces the 'Knight of Arts and Industry' who is determined to destroy the 'soul-enfeebling' corruptions of the castle. In this he is helped by a Bard who, singing to a '*British* Harp', celebrates his native poetic tradition. Without the achievement of Spenser, Shakespeare, and Milton, he sings, 'the Wits of modern Time had told their Beads, / And monkish Legends been their only Strains' (II, 464–5). Thomson's message is that a thriving and morally healthy nation needs a literary history. But Spenser's position is ambiguous. In this two-part poem Thomson draws out of *The Faerie Queene* both its pleasurable magic and its spiritual and moral dimension. *The Castle of Indolence* combines the world of Spenser's dangerous Bower of Bliss with that of its destroyer, Sir Guyon (Temperance). Thomson understands the complexity of his source and employs Spenser the moralist to challenge Spenser the enchanter.

The awareness that Spenser's poetic character included both imagination and native vigour made him ideal as an instrument of education. He could capture the young with his romantic Fairy-land, but also lead them on to public responsibility and social morality. A Spenserian style would often include severer tones and a national dimension. Gilbert West used it in his poem *Education* (1751) to call for educational reform and the renewal of the nation's self-confidence; and in Robert Bedingfield's *The Education of Achilles* (1747) the future Greek hero absorbs his lessons from various allegorical

figures such as Modesty, Exercise, and Temperance, who (in a duality charac-
teristic of Spenserian writing) 'temper stern behests with pleasaunce gay'. It is
also the theme of James Beattie's *The Minstrel* (1771–4) which in a dual
structure similar to *The Castle of Indolence* traces the education of Edwin the
harpist, a child of nature steeped in his native verse ('Whate'er of lore tradi-
tion could supply / From Gothic tale or song, or fable old'). In Book Two the
youth meets a philosophical hermit who leads him towards a more rigorous
poetry, which requires Beattie himself to 'smite the Gothic lyre [i.e. the
Spenserian stanza] with harsher hand' (II, 21). Such returns to Spenserian
poetry should not be seen as nostalgic. For these poets it was a way to engage
with educative notions of continuity and onward development – to locate a
path leading out from the past to the future, with memory and experience
guiding your footsteps.

It used to be thought that many mid-century poets fell under the 'spell' of
Spenser and Milton, with all that implies of surrendering to another's power.
Concepts such as 'the burden of the past' or 'the anxiety of influence' tended
to represent the phenomenon as sapping the strength of eighteenth-century
verse and turning what had been confident and clear into something gloomy,
indolent, and self-indulgent. It is implied that Spenser and Milton's 'children'
were helpless and unable to find their own voice or direction.[10] This model
will no longer do. Once we widen the issue and speak of a national tradition
of English poetry ('English' in linguistic terms only, as it tended to be British
in outlook) we can see the poets' engagement with it as a token of their
curiosity and confidence rather than their weakness.

More than any other, it was the heroic figure of Milton that helped to define
and strengthen the concept of a national poetry in the mid-eighteenth century.
The previous chapter showed how during the earlier decades the poet of *Para-
dise Lost* came to embody the sublime. By the 1760s he had become, along
with Shakespeare, a universal favourite with all classes of reader. *Paradise
Lost* was 'read with Pleasure and Admiration by every Degree and Condition',
and Dr Johnson had to concede grudgingly that Milton was an author 'with
whom readers of every class think it necessary to be pleased'.[11] *Paradise Lost*
was published over a hundred times between 1705 and 1800, and as well as
scholarly editions and popular reprints there were grammatically simplified
versions, prose versions, and some editions especially for children, many of
whom read the poem at school. The War in Heaven in Book VI was evidently
popular for younger readers.[12] To his admirers at the beginning of the century
Milton was the one English poet fit to stand in the company of Homer and
Virgil as having created an epic poem that was both national and universal. As
if to make this very point, Joseph Trapp, Oxford's Professor of Poetry, trans-
lated Virgil's *Aeneid* into Miltonic blank verse, and then *Paradise Lost* into
Virgilian Latin hexameters.[13]

During the decades after Milton's death in 1674 the rhymed 'heroic' couplet
(along with the irregular Pindaric ode) was supreme, and in earlier chapters we
have seen how powerfully the verse form could be used. It was through Milton's
early admirers, however, that blank verse (unrhymed iambic pentameters)

began to find a niche for itself in non-dramatic poetry. By the 1740s, 'blank verse' and 'Miltonic verse' were practically synonymous.[14] The poet who did most to establish it as a popular poetic medium was John Philips, who came to be thought of as Milton's poetic 'son'. A friend remarked that in *Paradise Lost* Philips found the gateway to 'the Force and Elegancy of his Mother-Tongue'; and he recalled how 'by the Example of his Darling *Milton*, [Philips] searched backwards into the Works of our Old *English* Poets, to furnish himself with proper, sounding, and significant Expressions, and prove the due Extent, and Compass of the *Language*. For this purpose he carefully read over *Chaucer* and *Spenser*'.[15] Milton therefore gave Philips an avenue into literary history, and others later took the same route. Poets found that through Spenser and Milton they could connect themselves to the earlier tradition of English verse.

In his three best-known poems Philips showed how blank verse might be used successfully for a wide variety of modes. In his mock-heroic *The Splendid Shilling* (1701) it transforms the daily routine of a down-at-heel student into an epic struggle with the forces of nature. His worn breeches 'An horrid Chasm disclose, with Orifice / Wide, Discontinuous; at which the Winds / *Eurus* and *Auster* . . . / Tumultuous enter' (124–8). Rather like the young Shenstone in his *School-Mistress*, Philips seems to gain in rhythmic confidence as his poem develops, until with the final description of a shipwreck the verse has a genuine intensity ('Horrors seize / The Mariners, Death in their Eyes appears . . .'). This note is continued in the battle-scene of *Blenheim* (1705), a poem admired for its 'sublime and nervous style' (*nervous* in the sense of 'sinewy' – a combination of strength and flexibility), qualities appropriate for celebrating Marlborough's victory. Perhaps the most influential of the three was *Cyder* (1708), which set a fashion for English blank-verse Georgic (see Chapter 5), by showing how a less heroic and more varied strain could be drawn from *Paradise Lost*, particularly its human scenes. Through this genre patriotic fervour worked a quieter seam during the century.

Thanks to Milton and Philips, blank verse came to be associated with British liberty and with the nation's recovery of a genuine classical style untainted by Frenchified rhyme. Indeed, one poet celebrated Philips's *Blenheim* as the literary equivalent of Marlborough's victory: 'His nervous Verse great *Boileau*'s Strength transcends, / And *France* to *Philips*, as to *Churchill* [i.e. Marlborough], bends'.[16] In choosing blank verse for *The Seasons*, James Thomson happily associated himself with the 'British' tradition of Milton and his poetical heir: 'PHILIPS . . . the second thou / Who nobly durst, in Rhyme-unfetter'd Verse, / With BRITISH Freedom sing the BRITISH song' (*Autumn*, 645–7). Milton himself had given warrant for this by declaring in a prefatory note to *Paradise Lost* that his poem was 'an example set, the first in *English*, of ancient liberty recoverd to Heroic Poem from the troublesom and modern bondage of Rimeing'. The proponents of blank verse at mid-century did not fail to point out that not one of the great primary texts of the classical world that underpinned so much eighteenth-century poetry – Hesiod, Homer, Theocritus, Virgil, Horace, Ovid, Juvenal – was in rhyme. The neo-classical rhymed couplet (like the neo-classical St Paul's) did not exhibit the genuine antique style, and the blank-verse poets of the 1730s and 40s thought of themselves as recovering something closer to the original classical hexameter, and with it their *ancient liberty*. One poet praised Milton's blank-verse followers as those 'Bold British Bards, who re-assume / The free-born Rights of Greece and Rome; / While slavish France in jingling Strain / Drags on, yet hugs, the servile Chain'.[17]

From the 1740s ambitious young poets were becoming, through their reading of Spenser and Milton, increasingly conscious of the body of English poetry that antedated the Restoration of 1660, when a French neo-classicism had become pre-eminent. They felt they wanted to widen poetry's scope and recapture the more daring imagery of the past. They wanted especially to be able to 'hear' verse again – to be surprised by its rhythms and harmonies. In locating the bedrock of their native tradition, poets like the Wartons, Gray, Collins, and Akenside felt they were simultaneously recovering a more pristine poetry that had become overlaid by the prescriptions of the 'petits maîtres' of French criticism. Just as a romance/Gothic line of inheritance was waiting to be rediscovered, so the primal Doric of the Parthenon was somewhere to be found under the grandiloquent façade of Versailles – or St Paul's. The mid-century return to the literary tradition of Spenser and Milton was not a move away from the classical, but towards a 'classic' literary past of great originals. For the new generation of skilled classicists, the recovery of what Thomson called poetry's 'antient Truth, and Purity' meant accommodating both the Druid and the Dryad.

Pope's position in this literary history was an uneasy one. A delighted reader of Chaucer and Spenser from his early teens, he learned his craft by reworking them as well as Homer and Virgil. But to the generation that followed him there seemed to be two Popes: the poet of the 1717 *Works* (especially the author of *Eloisa to Abelard*) and the political/moral satirist of the 1730s, when he could look back on his early verse as a youthful diversion 'in Fancy's maze' before he had 'stoop'd to Truth, and moraliz'd his song'.[18] The awkwardness of placing Pope within the emergent native tradition is fascinatingly dramatised in *Musaeus: a Monody to the Memory of Mr Pope* (1747) by the twenty-three-year-old Cambridge poet William Mason. He imagines the dying Pope being visited in his grotto by Chaucer, Spenser, and Milton. Each in turn offers Musaeus (Pope) generous praise: Chaucer thanks the poet for preserving his reputation through elegant modernisations of his work; Spenser concedes that Pope's Belinda outshines his own Una and Florimell; and Milton withdraws his attack on the bondage of rhyme. Each poet speaks, however, in his own distinctive poetic language – Milton, for example, praises Pope's rhyming couplets in mellifluous blank verse ('at thy magic touch the chains / Off dropt, and (passing strange!) soft-wreathed bands / Of flow'rs their place supply'd', 174–6). The incongruity increases when Milton remembers the youthful freshness he and Pope had shown in their early verses. At this, Pope jolts into life and interrupts Milton disapprovingly in rather preachy heroic couplets:

> Ah! why recall the toys of thoughtless youth?
> When flow'ry fiction held the place of truth;
> When fancy rul'd; when trill'd each trivial strain,
> But idly sweet, and elegantly vain. (197–200)

Rather than welcoming his three visitors (who are not heard from again), Pope disowns the verse he wrote under their influence. All that is left is for the allegorical figure of Virtue to sweep down and embrace him, and the poet dies in her arms. Looking back, we can see that the generous concessions the three poets make (Chaucer on Pope's modernisations, Spenser on his sophisticated Belinda, Milton on his rhyming couplets) point to the eighteenth-century poet's *difference* from them. Ostensibly a warm tribute, Mason's monody serves in fact to isolate the Pope of the 1730s. It is Mason himself who is bidding to inherit the English poetic tradition. Chaucer, Spenser, and Milton speak through him, and he is able to show off his mastery of their individual rhythms, vocabulary, phrasing, and imagery. By the end of the poem it seems as if this skilful young poet is more the true heir of the immortals than Pope himself.

Mason was just one of several young men in the 1740s who stepped forward to claim the mantle of the old poets. In the same month as *Musaeus*, and via the same publisher, the nineteen-year-old Thomas Warton published a poem suffused with the imagery of Spenser and Milton, *The Pleasures of Melancholy* (1747), in which the speaker turns away from civilised society and finds imaginative excitement in searching out traces of the 'Antick' and 'Barb'rous' at a series of abandoned places. As if reaching back beyond a century of sociable civility to the uncouth poetic language of the past, Warton's melancholy man looks for inspiration in caves, ruins, and charnel-houses (where the bones of the dead were kept), places that seem to speak only of loss and decay, but which can re-animate the poet. For him they represent excited discovery and imaginative arousal. This is what the recovered old poetry came to mean for many young writers of mid century. Far from being mere decoration ('Trickt in Antique Ruff and Bonnet', as Dr Johnson sneeringly remarked[19]) it represented an imaginative stimulus that challenged the tastes of the former generation, Addison's so-called 'understanding age':

> Thro' POPE's soft song tho' all the Graces breathe,
> And happiest art adorn his Attic page;
> Yet does my mind with sweeter transport glow,
> . As at the root of mossy trunk reclin'd,
> In magic SPENSER's wildly-warbled song
> I see deserted Una wander wide
> Thro' wasteful solitudes, and lurid heaths,
> Weary, forlorn, than when the fated fair,
> Upon the bosom bright of silver Thames,
> Launches in all the lustre of brocade . . . (153–62)

The glitter of Pope's Belinda belongs to art, not nature. For Warton in his guise as the melancholy visionary it is the Elizabethan poet who opens the magic casement onto a world of romance. His response to Spenser is not passive, but argumentative and experimental. There is a kind of daring in the way Warton seizes on the most unanimating ideas – the aimless, wasteful and weary – to show that poetry need not be full of busy present things, but can stretch the imagination to something more distant. In his delicious solitude he wants to replace the immediacy of the 'now' and 'here' with what is attenuated in time and space, so he can sense things reaching him from a distance ('let me sit / Far in sequester'd iles of the deep dome, / There lonesome listen to the sacred sounds, / Which, as they lengthen thro' the Gothic vaults, / In hollow murmurs reach my ravish'd ear', 201–5). The sounds may begin as loud and communal ones, but by the time they reach his hiding-place they have become intimate whispers. Distance in time and space has brought them closer to him. Warton's poet of sensibility therefore finds his soul-mate in an old hermit, who experiences 'truer joys'

> As from the cliff that o'er his cavern hangs,
> He views the piles of fall'n Persepolis
> In deep arrangement hide the darksome plain.
> Unbounded waste! the mould'ring obelisc
> Here, like a blasted oak, ascends the clouds;
> Here Parian domes their vaulted halls disclose
> Horrid with thorn . . . (260–6)

Ruination somehow reveals the *deep arrangement* beneath human structures. The fallen stones of the city are settling into the bedrock; the *mould'ring obelisc* is becoming an organic form; and the *vaulted halls* are reverting to a *cavern*. Like Addison's Iroquois King, the Wartonian poet looks beyond the arts of civilisation to locate the eternal matrix of nature. In this scene, the neo-classical principle that nature is the 'end' of art attains a deeper truth – it is the form to which all artefacts will finally return.

This reaching back to original forms is also the subject of his brother Joseph Warton's *The Enthusiast: Or The Lover of Nature* (1744), in which the speaker is led out of civilisation into the primal scene to recover what has been overlaid by art. From the décor of Stowe's neo-classical gardens the Dryads lead him to the 'naked roots' of a 'hollow oak'; the fountains at Versailles with their 'tortur'd' artifice give way to the River Anio tumbling over a 'pine-top'd precipice'; even the shepherd is taken from his artful Arcadia (no sheep or pasture here) and is seen 'idly stretch'd on the rude rock' listening to the ocean and watching the dolphins dance. The poem visits the Roman world not at its Augustan zenith, or even its republican prime, but in its earliest moments just as history is emerging from myth. We glimpse the creator of her religious institutions, King Numa, consulting the nymph Egeria at her holy spring ('to a secret grot Ægeria stole / With patriot Numa, and in silent night / Whisper'd him sacred laws', 21–3), and we see Rome's mythical founder, Aeneas, not in heroic guise but sleeping soundly in Evander's cottage ('On shaggy skins, lull'd by sweet nightingales', 82) on the spot where the city will eventually be built. Warton seeks out the foundational materials from which the classical tradition would emerge.

152

These scenes eventually bring the eighteenth-century poet to his own history, and to a question that has already been answered: 'What are the lays of artful Addison, / Coldly correct, to Shakespear's warblings wild?' (168–9). Appropriately taking a hint from Milton,[20] Warton visits English poetry's holy site at the moment when the infant Shakespeare was discovered on the banks of the Avon by the figure of Imagination, who

> ... bore the smiling babe
> To a close cavern: (still the shepherds shew
> The sacred place, whence with religious awe
> They hear, returning from the field at eve,
> Strange whisp'ring of sweet musick thro' the air)
> Here, as with honey gather'd from the rock,
> She fed the little prattler, and with songs
> Oft' sooth'd his wondering ears, with deep delight
> On her soft lap he sat, and caught the sounds. (171–9)

Warton turns the hackneyed notion of Shakespeare the 'child of nature' into a sacred myth. The idea is easily misunderstood as suggesting the young man was not educated, that he took nothing from books. But the import of Warton's lines is subtler. In returning to this primal rocky landscape he is trying to locate both Shakespeare's genius and his humanity. The baby is an emerging consciousness and a *little prattler*, a poet who will conjure sounds and images out of the air, but also reach to the heart of the human experience. At mention of the *close cavern* (prophetic cave and maternal womb) the parenthesis creates a suspended moment within the sentence that aims to catch the sense of magic that Shakespeare will bring to the world. A similar mythic nurturing occurs in his brother's *The Pleasures of Melancholy* when the infant Contemplation is discovered by a Druid during his evening walk in the woods. The baby is carried to 'the close shelter of his oaken bow'r' where she is taught the sounds of nature ('For when a smiling babe, you lov'd to lie / Oft deeply list'ning to the rapid roar / Of wood-hung Meinei, stream of Druids old', 313–5). For the Wartons this secret spot is the place of romantic creativity.

It was partly through the Wartons that a concept of literary history began to have an impact on poetry during the 1740s and 1750s. Along with their verse, the brothers' scholarship and literary criticism helped redirect poetic taste towards the romance tradition. It could even be said that they had a joint project to turn the tide against politeness and wit. Thomas Warton's *Observations on the Faerie Queene* (1754) represents the earliest full-scale example of English historical criticism, discussing Spenser's poem sympathetically within its period context of Elizabethan courtly entertainments and romance narratives. Rather than judge Spenser by classical rules, Warton recontextualises him as a 'ROMANTIC POET' (he puts this phrase in capital letters) who draws on sources in myth and legend, medieval metrical romances, Ariosto, and the Arthurian story. In a thirteen-page digression Warton offers a brief narrative of literary history, placing *The Faerie Queene* at the apex of a visionary allegorical tradition stretching from Chaucer through Shakespeare and the early Milton to the Restoration of 1660, at which point, he says, 'imagination gave way to correctness; sublimity of description to delicacy of sentiment, and striking imagery to conceit and epigram'.[21]

It was in this romance tradition that Thomas Warton placed his own verse. His poems are conscious of cells, caverns, root-systems, springs and sources, sacred removed places where a mouldering text is still partly visible, or where an ancient language can be heard, recovered from an older work. His 'Sonnet Written in a Blank Leaf of Dugdale's Monasticon' sees in that historical record an inspiration for the modern poet: 'While cloyster'd Piety displays / Her mouldering roll, the piercing eye explores / New manners, and the pomp of elder days, / Whence culls the pensive bard his pictur'd stores'. Where we might expect the word 'old', Warton gives us the *new* – he searches for pristine things backwards in time, and finds the writings of the *elder days* a source for the modern poet. Repeatedly in Warton's verse we encounter a lost text, worn away by time, covered in mould, dimly discernible, and usually housed in a remote and concealed place. In the 'Ode written at Vale-Royal Abbey' he goes 'within the deep fane's inmost cell, / To pluck the grey moss from the mantled stone, / Some holy founder's mouldering name to spell' (74–6), and in his 'Ode on the Approach of Summer' he enters a mystical space with similar intent: 'As thro' the caverns dim I wind, / Might I that holy legend find, / By fairies spelt in mystic rhymes, / To teach enquiring later times' (249–52). The texts are *holy* because they are original and revelatory, and his search is for the *founder* of a native tradition. The 'Sonnet on King Arthur's Round Table at Winchester' finds him engaging with yet another text waiting to be recovered:

> on the capacious round
> Some British pen has sketch'd the names renown'd,
> In marks obscure, of his immortal peers.
> Though join'd by magic skill, with many a rime,
> The Druid-frame, unhonour'd, falls a prey
> To the slow vengeance of the wisard Time,
> And fade the British characters away . . .[22]

The table carries a text that is disappearing from view. It is a poetic language that is fading, taking with it the *British characters* – both the words themselves and the men who once sat around that table. But they live on, Warton ends by saying, in 'Spenser's page'. Warton's unspoken boast is that he himself, in his *Observations on the Faerie Queene*, had for the first time shown that the Arthurian world of Malory's *Morte Darthur* was one of Spenser's chief sources. The sonnet is completed with that silent link to his own work as critic and scholar.

Where his brother advanced the cause of Spenser, Joseph Warton set out to demote Pope (in particular the Pope who had been embraced by 'Virtue' in Mason's *Monody*). In his *Essay on the Writings and Genius of Pope* (1756) Warton argues that by pursuing the didactic and moral vein he cut himself off from the 'first class' of English poets, 'our only three sublime and pathetic poets; Spenser, Shakespeare, Milton'. It was they who embodied what Warton liked to call 'pure poetry'.[23] In making this judgment Warton was developing views he had expressed in the 'Advertisement' to his *Odes on Various Subjects* (1746): 'as [the author] looks upon Invention and Imagination to be the chief faculties of a Poet, so he will be happy if the following Odes may be look'd upon as an attempt to bring back Poetry into its right channel'. In describing his poems as 'fanciful and descriptive' Warton hardly needed to mention Spenser and the early Milton in order to define what the 'right channel' was, and to suggest that the nation's poetry had largely lost its way over the previous hundred years. If many at the beginning of the century had rejected the language of Spenser and Milton as being no longer 'current', Warton intends to show that it is they who have cut themselves off from the current of true poetry. His dynamic image presents the task as rechannelling poetry in order to connect it with its true sources.

Joseph Warton's opening 'Ode to Fancy' ('Fancy' and 'Imagination' were interchangeable at this period) celebrates the volume's presiding spirit. His immediate model is Milton's 'L'Allegro' and 'Il Penseroso', and in reworking these youthful poems, which are themselves a tissue of allusions to earlier poets, including Chaucer, Spenser, Shakespeare, Jonson, and Drayton, Warton is also tapping into the native poetic line. Imagination is the connecting idea: 'Then lay me by the haunted stream / Wrapt in some wild, poetic dream, / In converse while methinks I rove / With SPENSER thro' a fairy grove' (41–4). In imitating Milton the poet feels he is conversing with Spenser and being introduced to the spirit of romance, to 'Such sights as youthfull Poets dream / On summer eeves by haunted stream' ('L'Allegro', 129–30). As Warton's imagination guides him through various scenes and emotions he beckons Fancy away from Shakespeare's tomb ('On which thou lov'st to sit at eve, / Musing o'er your darling's grave') towards the present age so that she can inspire some eighteenth-century poet, who 'May boldly smite the sounding lyre, / Who with some new, unequall'd song, / May rise above the rhyming throng'. The poem ends with Warton's vision of a revived national poetry:

> Teach him to scorn with frigid art
> Feebly to touch th'unraptur'd heart . . .
> With native beauties win applause,
> Beyond cold critic's studied laws:
> O let each Muse's fame encrease,
> O bid BRITANNIA rival GREECE! (115–20)

The Wartonian agenda for a national poetry on the ancient Greek model was shared by Akenside and Collins. It can only be achieved, he suggests, by reviving the *native beauties* of the Chaucer-Spenser-Shakespeare-Milton tradition. The Wartons' poetry of echoes plays repeatedly across this stave, as if to define a lost music which they want people to hear again.

In Chapter 6 I argued that a 'romantic mode' was available to English poets of the 1700–1730 period, and went on to characterise it in terms of an encounter between the seventeenth-century tradition of 'philosophic melancholy' and the modern Lockean mind, with its implications for a notion of subjective experience. This argument seems to underplay the innovatory nature of the work of the young poets of the 1740s. But if they did not inaugurate the romantic mode, it becomes clear that they developed it in crucial ways. Perhaps the most important was this campaign, in which the Warton brothers were pre-eminent, to see it as part of English literary history. To the Wartons, the romantic represented something wider and deeper than a 'mode', or particular cast of writing. It was integral to poetry's early, and future, development when *Invention and Imagination* were, and would once again be, supreme. For Thomas Warton, Spenser was specifically a romantic poet because he drew material from medieval romance and aroused the imagination of his reader. It was this linking of romance sources to romantic 'affect' that was the vital move in legitimising romance for the eighteenth-century poet. The connection is made in the opening phrases of a fragmentary 'Essay on Romantic Poetry' which the seventeen-year-old Thomas jotted into a notebook in 1745 (the year *The Pleasures of Melancholy* was written):

> The principal use which the ancients made of poëtry, as appears by their writings, was to imitate human actions & passions, or intermix here & there descriptions of Nature. Several modern authors have employed a manner of poëtry entirely different from this, I mean in imitating the actions of spir[i]ts, in describing imaginary Scenes, & making persons of abstracted things, such as Solitude, Innocence, & many others. A Kind of Poëtry which perhap[s] it would not be improper to call a Romantic Kind of Poëtry, as it [is] altogether conceived in the spirit, (tho with more Judgment & less extravagant) & affects the Imagination in the same Manner, with the old Romances.[24]

Warton's 'Romantic Poetry' is *conceived in the spirit* and *affects the Imagination*, and he finds an analogue for that impulse in the romance tradition of the past. The romantic opens up a temporal dimension for him: the new is at the same time a kind of recovery of a past text, of a romantic response. His brother Joseph's meditation, *The Enthusiast*, published the previous year, had featured a pageant of 'awful forms' that included Solitude and Innocence, and it is clear that Thomas is thinking of the kind of poetry being written by themselves, and by their friend Collins, at this time.

If the Wartons helped to give the romantic a literary history, a strategic contemporary role, and a degree of theoretical justification, other poets of the 1740s were also influential in different ways. In light of the previous chapter's discussion of Akenside's *The Pleasures of Imagination*, it is clear that he reached beyond the Wartonian romantic spirit to the Shaftesburian Platonic idea, and celebrated imagination's lofty ideals and philosophical seriousness. In Akenside's mind, being *conceived in the spirit* meant bringing delightful fiction into partnership with sublime truth. For Akenside, simply 'to muse . . . amid the ghostly gloom / Of graves, and hoary vaults, and cloister'd cells' (I. 396–7) was to be lost in the servile, earthbound imagination. The Wartons might engage with the depredations of *the wisard Time*, but Akenside prefers to look directly toward truth's 'eternal shrine'. His mentor is not a Druid in his cave, but 'th'eternal ONE . . . deep-retir'd / In his unfathom'd essence' (I. 64–5). For Akenside, truth is not located in the past and recoverable through history, but is eternally present to the mind. This contrast between the Wartons and Akenside in terms of time and eternity also has relevance when considering the distinctive work of Thomas Gray and William Collins.

For Gray, recovering the past is both complex and difficult. Like the Wartons', his poetry is rooted in the Spenser-Milton tradition (he would always read Spenser before starting to compose[25]), but he is uncertain about placing his own poetic achievement within it. In a plan he drew up for a history of English poetry, Gray divides literary history into separate 'schools', according to which Spenser and Milton belonged to the 'Second Italian School', terminating with Milton himself ('this school ends in Milton', he notes firmly). It was superseded by the 'School of France' (of Dryden and Pope) which, says Gray, 'has continued down to our own times'.[26] This picture of literary history (of categories, discontinuities, and endings) is especially strange given the character of his own poetry. Where the Wartons campaigned to establish a literary history that would link their work with the line of Spenser and Milton, Gray strangely sees Milton as marking a closure. It is as though he cannot find a continuity between himself and his own sources.

One of the most powerful elements in Gray's poetry is its engagement not with history, but with memory and memorialisation (its marker in the present). This is a more personal concept, and one (for Gray) more subject to uncertainties and discontinuities. In Gray, narratives that might connect the present with the past tend to become diverted, ironised, or broken. The idea of mediation itself is usually a difficult one. Where the Wartons celebrate educative and nurturing presences (like Fancy or Contemplation) who mediate between past and present or body and spirit, Gray finds such encounters fraught and disturbing – in his poetry allegorical figures tend to estrange or threaten. Similarly, voices or texts that are potentially mediating often fail to communicate. Thankfully, the long tradition of seeing Gray's poetry in terms of neurotic frustration and personal failure no longer holds sway. Instead, it is possible to see his work as exploring problems of continuity and connectedness.

Throughout Gray's most famous poem, *Elegy Written in a Country Church Yard* (1751), the speaker is conscious of repressed energies and narrowed possibilities:

> Perhaps in this neglected spot is laid
> Some heart once pregnant with celestial fire,
> Hands, that the rod of empire might have sway'd,
> Or wak'd to extasy the living lyre.
>
> But Knowledge to their eyes her ample page
> Rich with the spoils of time did ne'er unroll;
> Chill Penury repress'd their noble rage,
> And froze the genial current of the soul. (45–52)

These two stanzas show a pattern that is repeated throughout the poem, in which living potential is denied. The energy of Gray's vocabulary (he always seems to choose the most active idea) is repeatedly checked, just as here *pregnant*, *extasy*, and *rage* are all repressed as soon as uttered. In this poem, the personifications don't extend human powers, they obstruct them. The figure of *Knowledge*, in a poem by Akenside or the Wartons, would be an expression of that idea, but here it denies itself and acts the part of Secrecy. Her *ample page / Rich with the spoils of time*, that text which so delighted Thomas Warton, is never unrolled. *Penury* is not a personified condition but a malign frustrater of life's passions. Elsewhere in the poem, *Ambition* doesn't rouse the spirit, but enters to 'mock their useful toil' (29). *Grandeur* is ready to regard the poor 'with a disdainful smile' (31) – where we might expect *Greatness* (a term embodying distinction of status) Gray gives us something more expansive and therefore incongruous. Other figures find their way into the poem to be frustrated themselves: 'Can Honour's voice provoke the silent dust, / Or Flatt'ry sooth the dull cold ear of Death?' (43–4). Here, instead of the more predictable word *disturb*, Gray's *provoke* demands a response that can never come. *Flattery*'s encounter with *Death* is made more eerie with the word *sooth* encountering the *cold ear* – again there can be no response to the active human verb. Gray's personifications cannot even communicate with each other.

In Gray's churchyard there is a variety of old texts – storied urns, frail memorials, artless tales, and uncouth rhymes – strewn around and begging to be read, imploring 'the passing tribute of a sigh' (80). They commemorate the dead villagers: 'Their name, their years, spelt by th'unletter'd muse, / The place of fame and elegy supply: / And many a holy text around she strews, / That teach the rustic moralist to dye' (81–4). But the role of Gray's speaker is not to recover and animate these texts. Where Thomas Warton would scrape the moss away and try to glean some history from them, Gray builds up a sense of frustration, of indignant possibility left interred and repressed, however much the turf 'heaves' about him. At the emotional climax of the poem all the quiet sounds that have been so far heard are gathered into a single urgent, but inaudible, cry: 'Ev'n from the tomb the voice of Nature cries' (91); but there is no response, just a parallel image of living death: 'Ev'n in our Ashes live their wonted Fires' (92). At this point of the poem, with that word *our*, we seem to be approaching the moment when we can re-enter the consciousness of the speaker for some personal response to the scene, and we wait for the 'I' of the text to register (the nearest we have come so far is the 'me' of line 4). But the *Elegy* is not a traditional meditation, and at this point the poem is taken out of the first speaker's hands. Rather than resuming with 'I', the next stanza begins: 'For thee . . .', and we find that the voice has turned unsettlingly on itself. When we finally reach the 'I' it is an old countryman remembering the poet, and even that is a failed encounter ('One morn I miss'd him', 109), and the poem ends with the poet's own 'Epitaph', a text separated from the rest of the poem by its own sub-title.

Another text that draws power from its inability to recover the past and give it meaning in the present is Gray's 'Sonnet on the Death of Richard West'. Here the first person 'I' is trapped in the present, and in place of an elegiac imaginative retrospect there is an endless cycle of present-tense activity in which the poet cannot join:

In vain to me the smileing Mornings shine,
And redning Phœbus lifts his golden Fire:
The Birds in vain their amorous Descant joyn;
Or chearful Fields resume their green Attire:
These Ears, alas! for other Notes repine,
A different Object do these Eyes require. (1–6)

In this poem there is no past to contemplate. Surrounding the poet is a busy scene of recovery and resumption, by the sun, the fields and birds (*resume*, rather than *assume*, makes the idea cyclical). This only serves to throw into ironic relief his own inability to stage any kind of retrieval from the past: 'I fruitless mourn to him, that cannot hear' (13). Where the *Elegy* was haunted by the disturbing notion of 'dumb Forgetfulness' (85), this sonnet creates a gap between a present that cannot speak and a past that cannot hear.

In the 'Ode on a Distant Prospect of Eton College' Gray's difficulties in negotiating between past and present are expressed through the gulf between youth and age, innocence and experience. The poet remains a silent voyeur who watches the schoolchildren at play where he once played, and is trapped in a knowledge of what awaits them ('the vulturs of the mind, / Disdainful Anger, pallid Fear, / And Shame that sculks behind', 62–4). But it is a fallen knowledge that he declines to share ('Yet ah! why should they know their fate?' 95). This gulf becomes especially ironic through the handling of the personified River Thames, a symbol of continuity whose flowing waters have seen countless generations of children come and go. The speaker questions him ('Say, Father THAMES, for thou hast seen / Full many a sprightly race / Disporting on thy margent green / The paths of pleasure trace . . .', 21–4). But this figure is evidently indifferent to the youth educated on his banks – unlike the Wartons' benign foster-parents, with their nurturing routine of learning, listening and feeding. Father Thames does not respond to the poet's curiosity and contributes nothing to the poem. The questions hang in the air, unanswered. The river refuses the role of mediator, and so the poet assumes the place of the allegorical parent-figure ready to impart knowledge to the children; but he realises he can teach them nothing but the misery of maturity. For him, knowledge is *fate*, and *thought* a fall from innocence ('Thought would destroy their paradise', 98). And so the infant, the parent-figure, and the poet, which in the Wartonian model would have converged, go their separate ways. There is no communication between them.

The one poem of Gray's which seems to be consciously attempting a retrieval of the past to re-animate the present is his ambitious Pindaric ode, 'The Progress of Poesy' (1757), originally entitled 'Ode in the Greek Manner'. It takes for its theme, after all, the progress of lyric verse from the ancient Greece of Pindar, to Rome, and on to Britain, and it includes what at first sight appears a perfect example of the Wartonian fostering of a child of nature, in this case the baby Shakespeare. Gray's passage is directly drawn from Joseph Warton's cameo in *The Enthusiast* where Imagination nurses the infant poet; but it is the contrast between the passages that is significant. Gray's version in 'The Progress of Poesy' is:

> In thy green lap was Nature's Darling laid,
> What time, where lucid Avon stray'd,
> To Him the mighty Mother did unveil
> Her aweful face: The dauntless Child
> Stretch'd forth his little arms, and smiled.
> This pencil take (she said) whose colours clear
> Richly paint the vernal year:
> Thine too these golden keys, immortal Boy! (84–91)

Where Joseph Warton's kindly foster-mother, Fancy, feeds and soothes the infant Shakespeare in her lap while she sings to him, Gray's figure is a slightly alarming *mighty Mother* who unveils her *aweful face* before the baby, and in entrusting him with the *golden keys* she seems to be imposing a responsibility upon him rather than awakening a divine gift within him. In face of this, the *dauntless* infant's stretching forth *his little arms* is as much an act of courage as a response to maternal love.

The hints at sublime awe that have found their way into this episode are present also at the end of the poem, where Gray reaches the present day, having himself to be the climax of this handing-on of poetic power. But the act of transfer is signalled instead by a moment of loss, followed by a timid question. He is talking of Dryden's odes:

> Hark, his hands the lyre explore!
> Bright-eyed Fancy hovering o'er
> Scatters from her pictur'd urn
> Thoughts, that breath[e], and words, that burn.
> But ah! 'tis heard no more—
> Oh! Lyre divine, what daring Spirit
> Wakes thee now? (107–113)

It is as if the *Thoughts, that breath[e], and words, that burn* have to cease (as they almost do from over-punctuation) before Gray can bring himself forward. Even as he does so, he disclaims the 'ample pinion' of the 'Theban Eagle' Pindar – the founder of the poetic form he is using (114–5). Gray's 'progress' in this way beautifully collapses into self-questioning and uncertainty. After this, however, Gray's final determined 'Yet shall he mount . . .' has a kind of heroic independence that strikes a deeper note. Gray's recognition of the difficulties in establishing continuities with the past makes him from our vantage point a modern figure, a poet of anxieties and disconnections as opposed to the Wartons' reassuring connectedness. Gray is at his most powerful and interesting when confronting disruptions and loss, texts that find no sympathetic reader, voices that echo with a momentary chill, break off, or expire.

Several poets of the 1740s, as we have seen, were eager to trace the origins of their art. Like Thomson they felt the need to locate its 'antient Truth, and Purity', and to recover its original inspiration and divine sanction. In their different ways, Akenside, the Wartons, and Gray all raise the question of where poetic power comes from, and how a modern poet can access it. The most mystical answer came from William Collins, whose 'Ode on the Poetical Character' (1746) offers simultaneously a myth of poetry's origin, and a literary genealogy for himself. The poem is a fascinating mix of youthful confidence and sobering uncertainty, a vision in which he discovers his ideal, declares his poetic allegiances, and finds a path; but finally recognises the gap between divine aspiration and human achievement. Once again, it is Spenser who unlocks the poet's vision for him. Collins takes as his symbol of poetic power Venus's magic belt in *The Faerie Queene*, which only the chosen can wear. It was woven, says Collins, on the day the Creator formed the earth and sky; and in a mystical scene recalling Akenside's recent *Pleasures of Imagination* he imagines God and 'Young *Fancy*' (the imagination) meeting in loving communion, and giving birth to the sun of poetry – a 'rich-hair'd Youth of Morn', who fuses, Apollo-like, youth and beauty with poetry and prophecy. Since then the belt has been in Fancy's keeping, and she grants 'the God-like Gift' to very few.

As a picture of poetry's seminal moment this takes some beating. Collins has set a fearsome challenge for himself and others. Only one poet, it seems, has succeeded, and that is Milton. If the ode began with *The Faerie Queene*, it moves on appropriately to *Paradise Lost*, and a vision of an Edenic garden perched inaccessibly on a high rock. There Collins can see in his own imagination the oak-tree 'by which as *Milton* lay, His Ev'ning Ear . . / . . its native Strains could hear' (64–6). Collins merges the landscape of poetic romance with Zeus's sanctuary at Dodona, where the oracle's prophecies came from a sacred oak. By the end of his poem, then, Collins has negotiated his way from Spenserian romance to Miltonic epic. He holds Milton's image before him, but the path gives out:

> My trembling Feet his guiding Steps pursue;
> In vain—Such Bliss to One alone,
> Of all the Sons of Soul was known,
> And Heav'n, and *Fancy*, kindred Pow'rs,
> Have now o'erturn'd th'inspiring Bow'rs,
> Or curtain'd close such Scene from ev'ry future View. (71–6)

As the speaker stops in his tracks (or rather in Milton's) we are drawn back into the world of *The Faerie Queene*. The vision of Milton's Paradise is followed by a glimpse of Spenser's tempting artificial paradise, the 'Bower of Bliss', overturned by Sir Guyon in Book Two – a hint at how imagination may indulge itself in false shows. But the final line, offered as an alternative, keeps the mystery intact, and leaves us with the image of a curtained sanctuary shielded from profane eyes. Prophetic vision and romantic mystery combine ambivalently in this poem. It is a dense and allusive fabric, like an allegorical tapestry, a dark conceit that leaves us pondering. The ode is not a record of anxiety or failure, but a complex meditation on poetic choice and aspiration.

Collins's *Odes on Several Descriptive and Allegorical Subjects* ('1747'), the volume which includes this poem, has become a *cause célèbre* for how critics view the eighteenth-century Spenser-Milton tradition. He has been represented in terms of an emergent Romanticism (failing to be Coleridge or Blake), or as a compromised 'Late Augustan' (failing to be Pope or Dr Johnson). Critics have celebrated Collins's intense visionary powers, or deplored his obscurity, vagueness and confusion. His later life has often been projected forwards to give the *Odes* a context of madness, or debilitating uncertainty. 'Poor Collins' tended to be the refrain, until Richard Wendorf's masterly rehabilitation of 1981, though the phrase has recently returned in a critique that sees Collins as having neither a clear vision nor a hold on real experience.[27] A poetic language so allusive and multi-layered as Collins's, and comprised of such densely inter- woven images, can easily seem confused or fraught; and his chameleon-like play with literary influences can be read as hesitancy and lack of 'direction'. Like Akenside, Collins is a poet of ideals and essences, with a zeal for liberty expressed both imaginatively and prosodically. Where Akenside found free- dom in his fluid paragraphs of blank verse, Collins seized on the ode's capa- city to challenge and surprise the hearer with sudden shifts of thought. Dr Johnson disapproved of both. For him, Collins indulged in 'peculiar habits of thought, [and] was eminently delighted with those flights of imagination which pass the bounds of nature'.[28] To recover a sense of the daringness of Collins's book of odes, perhaps it is best to look at the volume as a whole, and to suggest that it might be read in terms of 'performance', as a verse-collection that uses a repertoire of voices and visions, boldly orchestrated with varied tones and dynamics, to express a series of conflicting emotions – a perform- ance that also has an immediate public dimension. Rather than revealing his own hesitancy, perhaps Collins is demonstrating his range and youthful confid- ence in response to a mood of national uncertainty.

Published in December 1746, the volume was being assembled at a time of European war and in the aftermath of a nationwide emergency (the Jacobite rising of 1745–6), and the book is interspersed with reminders of this – images of heroic struggles for freedom, of cruel violence, of unfocused fear, of loss and mourning. Around this core of a present crisis it weaves a fabric of con- trasting responses, of mental and emotional states. It moves amongst ideals and realities, from figures of confrontation to those of reconciliation; it swings between violence and peace, and its many allegorical figures create a restless and occasionally disturbing scene. Taken as a whole, this suite of poems, as arranged for publication, asks how the human passions can work together to create, rather than destroy. The book makes its way eventually to a *Catharsis* – raising human emotions in order finally to calm them.

This is of course the scenario of Aristotelian tragedy, and the volume begins with tragedy's defining emotions: Pity and Fear, the subjects of the first two odes. The opening words invoking Pity introduce images of wounds and car- ing hands that will reappear in later poems transposed in significant ways: 'O Thou, the Friend of Man assign'd, / With balmy Hands his Wounds to bind'. This healing female form will be tested and tormented throughout the book. The following 'Ode to Fear' provides the most direct emotional assault in the whole volume with the speaker himself becoming possessed by a violent pas- sion ('Ah *Fear*! Ah frantic *Fear*! / I see, I see Thee near. / I know thy hurried Step, thy haggard Eye! / Like Thee I start, like Thee disorder'd fly'). It is a crucial moment in the book, establishing a terror that will eventually be exorcised. The poet is distracted (and this ode has always been the prime incriminating evidence for the 'Poor Collins' myth), but as the volume proceeds he will find new perspectives on the emotions he invokes, and show how a conscious artist can make them do his bidding. After this, the 'Ode to Simplicity' marks a new starting-point, a place to find a pure beginning in nature ('O Thou by *Nature* taught, / To breathe her genuine Thought'). In the 'Ode to Fear', *Fancy* had dangerously 'lift[ed] the Veil between' image and reality; but now in Simplicity's poem the poetic imagination has regained her innocence as '*Fancy* loveliest Child'. It is after these contrasts and contradictions that the 'Ode on the Poetical Character' is placed, and we can now see why the nature and role of the poetic imagination needs to be addressed at this point. Following a performance of the tragic emotions, and via the simplicity of nature, the poet questions his own character.

After this vision of a spirit-world, the poet locates the here and now, the wartime present that demands attention. The title, 'Ode, Written in the beginning of the Year 1746', marks this immediacy. The speaker sees the soldiers' newly dug graves and looks forward to the Spring, pictured as a silent female mourner who 'with dewy Fingers cold, / Returns to deck their hallow'd Mold' (those damp and chill fingers remind us that she is touching death). 'Ode to Mercy' immediately follows, whose opening lines ('O Thou, who sit'st a smiling Bride / By *Valour*'s arm'd and awful Side') recall a moment when a soldier and his bride were together. Mercy is silent too, but also active and indignant; she is a figure of protest who can stop the machinery of War with just her gaze ('Thy Form, from out thy sweet Abode, / O'ertook Him on his blasted Road, / And stop'd his Wheels, and look'd his Rage away'). The following 'Ode to Liberty' recalls its origins in ancient Greece, and pictures the young Spartan soldiers ritually combing their hair ('like vernal Hyacinths in sullen Hue') as they prepare to defend freedom; and Collins's opening phrase ('Who shall awake the *Spartan* Fife') sounds their call to arms. The reader is reminded how often liberties have had to be fought for, as the poem swiftly traces the spirit of European freedom across the centuries, to end in the Britain of Autumn 1746 and the current peace negotiations. Collins's final vision is of Liberty transformed to her 'social Form', Concord, a figure of reconciliation ('*Concord*, whose Myrtle Wand can steep / Ev'n *Anger*'s blood-shot Eyes in Sleep'). Once again, the notes change, not just to signal a shift in mood, but to express the urgency of the poem's message about human passions. Fittingly, the next poem, 'Ode, to a Lady, on the Death of Colonel Ross in the Action of Fontenoy' is a vivid reminder of the European war, opening with the image of a distracted country in May 1745 (the month of the battle):

> While, lost to all his former Mirth,
> *Britannia*'s Genius bends to Earth,
>   And mourns the fatal Day:
> While stain'd with Blood he strives to tear
> Unseemly from his Sea-green Hair
>   The Wreaths of chearful *May* (1–6)

163

Britain can no longer be just an island – the sea-green is stained with blood, and the *Wreaths* in his hair are turning into a funereal image as we watch. The poem revisits the turf graves and the mourning female of the earlier ode, but here we see, not a figure of calm, but *Freedom* again, now a picture of Despair, 'Her matted Tresses madly spread, / To ev'ry Sod, which wraps the Dead, / She turns her joyless Eyes' (hair is once again expressively used). The poem ends with the news of Ross's death finding its way from the continental battlefield ('By rapid *Scheld*'s descending Wave') to England and the Lady's Sussex home ('Ev'n humble *Harting*'s cottag'd Vale / Shall learn the sad repeated Tale, / And bid her Shepherds weep'). There follows the pastoral song of 'Ode to Evening', a mood-picture of the British landscape in a state of strangely disturbed stillness, in which sudden harsh sounds interrupt the scene without discomposing it ('Now Air is hush'd, save where the weak-ey'd Bat, / With short shrill Shriek flits by on leathern Wing'). This is followed by the last of the invocations, 'Ode to Peace', suitably placed here, with its direct message that the nation waits for her 'blest Return' after war's depredations.

Collins's penultimate ode, 'The Manners', opens in a fresh key, and a new mood: 'Farewell, for clearer Ken design'd, / The dim-discover'd Tracts of Mind'. The mystical imagination has been superseded by keen Observation (a 'Youth of the quick uncheated Sight'); *Fancy* is now domesticated in a 'thoughtful Cell' from where she can observe the comic scene of social life, in which Humour and Wit (both suitably costumed) are on stage giving their performances. 'The Manners' declares that Collins's volume from its beginning in tragedy has moved to the eternal human comedy, and life goes on. The volume's finale is a communal performance of 'The Passions. An Ode for Music', in which each emotion takes its appropriate instrument and performs a characteristic solo. A session that begins with a comic reminder of conflict as instruments are 'snatch'd', moves in the end to harmony. Fear takes the lead, but this time frightens himself into silence; Anger and Despair sing in turn, followed by a more expansive Hope, who is interrupted by the impatient notes of Revenge in a duet with pleading Pity. In the end, Joy and Mirth assert themselves, and the poem ends by celebrating the divine power of music in ancient Greece. ('The Passions' was publicly performed in various musical settings from 1750.) Collins harmonises the jarring emotions that have sounded throughout the volume. At the same time he brings to a climax his theme of poetic renewal through a return to original sources. Ancient Music's 'all-commanding Pow'r' over the human heart; her combination of strength and simplicity, are needed now, in 'this laggard Age'. She represents a primal classic form that the modern artist has forgotten: 'O bid our vain Endeavors cease, / Revive the just Designs of *Greece*, / Return in all thy simple State!'

Odes on Several Descriptive and Allegorical Subjects represents not just Collins's personal aspirations, but a wider mid-century manifesto for the recovery of poetry's original powers: its lyric roots, its dramatic potential, and its virtuous ideals. As well as Spenser and Milton, Collins invokes Otway's mastery of the pathetic, and Shakespeare's sublimity; and he sees all of them as expressing the original spirit of ancient Greece: the culture of Sophocles,

Euripides, and Pindar. If Spenser's 'descriptive and allegorical' character presides over the volume,[29] it is because Collins found in the Elizabethan 'romantic' poet, as many others did at mid-century, a creative release into Britain's literary history, and saw beneath it a bedrock of classical strength. A key idea in the recovery of the past (it was not at this stage a *return to* the past – that is the story of the next chapter) was to retrieve the essential element of Greek *poesis* (the poet as *maker*), and Spenser and Milton helped poets locate its source. It was not nostalgia, but a glimpse of *ancient liberty*. Whether seen in terms of mystical idea or lost text, this fundamental principle guided them towards the concept of a national poetry.

Notes

1. *Spectator* 50 (27 April 1711). Bond, I, 212–3.

2. Joseph Spence, *Observations*, ed. James M. Osborn, 2 vols (Oxford, 1966), I, 178.

3. Trevor Ross, in *The Making of the English Literary Canon* (Montreal and Kingston, 1998), charts the shift from a 'rhetorical' to an 'objectivist' canon for 'consumers'.

4. John Dryden, Preface to *Fables Ancient and Modern* (1700), sig. B2ᵛ.

5. 'To Dr Samuel Garth' (anon), in *Luctus Britannici: or the Tears of the British Muses; for the Death of John Dryden, Esq.* (1700), p. 55.

6. *The Miscellaneous Works of Joseph Addison*, ed. A.C. Guthkelch (London, 1914), I, 31–2.

7. *Aeneid*, I, 403–4; *Faerie Queene*, III. i. 16; *Antony and Cleopatra*, II. ii. 193–4; *Paradise Lost*, IV, 306.

8. [Dodsley] *Collection of Poems* (2nd ed., 1748), I, 252.

9. Milton, *Areopagitica* (1644). *Complete Prose Works of John Milton*, ed. Don M. Wolfe and others, 8 vols. (New Haven, 1953–82), II, 516.

10. For Paul Sherwin, for example, 'there is no purer instance of the adolescent experience in English literature than Collins's poetic life (and death) cycle' (*Precious Bane: Collins and the Miltonic Legacy* [Austin, 1977], p. 4. See also W. Jackson Bate, *The Burden of the Past and the English Poet* (Cambridge, Mass., 1970), and Harold Bloom, *The Anxiety of Influence: A Theory of Poetry* (New York, 1973).

11. William Massey, *Remarks upon Paradise Lost* (1761), p. iii, quoted by R.D. Havens, *The Influence of Milton on English Poetry* (Cambridge, Mass., 1922), p. 25; Samuel Johnson, *Lives of the English Poets*, ed. George Birkbeck Hill, 3 vols (Oxford, 1905), II, 147 (Addison).

12. See Havens, *The Influence of Milton*, pp. 3–43.

13. Joseph Trapp, *The Æneis of Virgil*, 2 vols (1718–20); *Johannis Miltoni Paradisus amissus*, 2 vols (1741–4).

14. Havens, *The Influence of Milton*, p. 78.

15. *Poems Attempted in the Style of Milton. By Mr John Philips. With his Life by Dr. [George] Sewell*, 10th ed. (London: E. Curll, 1744), p. vii.

16. *The Works of Mr. Edmund Smith* (1714), p. 78.

17. [Anon], 'To the Hon. Lieut. Gen'l Cholmondeley', quoted by J.W. Good, *Studies in the Milton Tradition* (Urbana: University of Illinois Press, 1915), pp. 66–7. Isaac Watts spoke of Milton as 'the noble Hater of degenerate Rhyme' who 'shook off the Chains, and built his Verse sublime, / A monument too high for coupled Sounds to climb' ('The Adventurous Muse' [1709], 48–50).

18. *Epistle to Dr Arbuthnot*, 340–1.

19. 'Phrase that Time has flung away, / Uncouth Words in Disarray: / Trickt in Antique Ruff and Bonnet, / Ode and Elegy and Sonnet' (Samuel Johnson, 'Lines on Thomas Warton's Poems', in *Samuel Johnson. The Complete English Poems*, ed. J.D. Fleeman [Harmondsworth, 1971], p. 132).

20. '. . . sweetest *Shakespear* fancies childe, / Warble his native Wood-notes wilde' (Milton, 'L'Allegro', 133–4).

21. Thomas Warton, *Observations on the Faerie Queene* (1754), p. 237.

22. *The Poetical Works of the Late Thomas Warton, B.D.*, ed. Richard Mant, 2 vols. (Oxford, 1802), II, 150; I, 138; II, 27; II, 158–9.

23. *Essay*, pp. xi, iv. Joseph Warton admired, however, Pope's great example of the 'sublime and pathetic', *Eloisa to Abelard*.

24. MS Trinity College Oxford. Bodleian MS dep. d. 611, fol. 5ᵛ.

25. Norton Nicholls's 'Reminiscences' of Gray (1805). *Correspondence of Thomas Gray*, ed. Paget Toynbee and Leonard Whibley, 3 vols. (Oxford, 1935), III, 1290.

26. Gray-Thomas Warton, 15 April 1770 (Eton College MS 316). *Correspondence*, III, 1122–5.

27. See Richard Wendorf, *William Collins and Eighteenth-Century English Poetry* (Minneapolis, 1981), especially chapter one ('"Poor Collins" Reconsidered'). The phrase has been reinstated by Patricia Meyer Spacks, 'The Eighteenth-Century Collins', in *Early Romantics*, ed. Thomas Woodman (Houndmills, 1998), pp. 70–90 (p. 88).

28. Johnson, *Lives of the Poets*, ed. Hill, III, 310 (Collins). Johnson concluded of Collins: 'his diction was often harsh, unskilfully laboured, and injudiciously selected. He affected the obsolete when it was not worthy of revival'. In his 'Life of Akenside' Johnson sums up his dislike of blank verse: 'Blank verse will, therefore, I fear, be too often found in description exuberant, in argument loquacious, and in narration tiresome' (III, 415).

29. The volume's title alludes to the poetic character of Spenser as he was seen at midcentury: his descriptive powers were frequently praised (by Shenstone and William Thompson, among others) and his allegory puzzled over. See *Edmund Spenser: The Critical Heritage*, ed. R.M. Cummings (New York, 1971). Thomas Warton's *Observations* (1754) included a chapter on 'Spenser's Allegorical Character'.

Chapter 9

Genuine Voices

What did poetry originally sound like? The question came naturally to writers interested in literary history, but it was not easy to answer. The idea that poetry was an inspired art which had existed in the earliest human societies was a commonplace, and we have seen how certain eighteenth-century poets wanted to recover the invention and imagination associated with its bardic genealogy. But during the 1740s little of Britain's old poetry was actually known, even by scholars; and beyond the landmarks of Spenser, Shakespeare, and Milton the terrain was largely unexplored. Twenty years later this ignorance was being enthusiastically remedied, and readers of poetry were being introduced to a range of material that claimed to speak with the tones of their ancestors. Voices from the past were echoing in drawing rooms and across tea-tables throughout the land. But were they 'genuine' ones?

This chapter is shaped by the ambiguous implications of that word. As with its synonym *authentic*, to call something *genuine* could have reference either to its nature or its origins, and the two were not always compatible. It might mean 'of genuine character', or 'from a genuine source'. In the context of mid-eighteenth century poetry such shades of meaning became problematic and the two were bound to clash. The 'genuine' was thought to be present whenever the heart was moved by a direct and natural simplicity. In Akenside's *The Pleasures of Imagination* (1744) 'the feeling heart' responds when 'nature speaks / Her genuine language' (II, 149–50), and Collins (1746) invokes Simplicity as 'Thou by *Nature* taught, / To breathe her genuine Thought' ('Ode to Simplicity', 1–2). The 'genuine' was in this sense artless and inspirational, an unforced power that reached the heart. Readers who were directly aroused by a passage of poetry came to understand that they were in the presence of the 'genuine'. But by the 1750s, at a time when 'genuine poetry' was gaining currency as a critical term, literary scholars were discovering important manuscripts of old verse. The genuine voice and the genuine text could sometimes gloriously coincide – but the two ideas were also set on a collision course.

Within the pages of Spenser, Milton, and the Bible, eighteenth-century readers were given glimpses of poetry's origins in an oral culture where metrical language had a special power. Whether the figure was Spenser's Merlin unfolding his prophetic vision of British history, or Adam and Eve spontaneously hymning the beauty of Paradise, or King David bewailing Jonathan's death, poetry was the natural vehicle for an utterance that was memorable, intense, or solemn. For a reader of 1760, to ask if Merlin's history was myth; whether Adam and Eve spoke in blank verse; or who actually transcribed David's words, was beside the point. This was primal poetry coming from the human spirit, a genuine inner vision. But for scholars in a sophisticated written culture the issue became more complicated, especially at a moment when they were attempting to map out a national literary history for the first time. The demands for genuine history and for genuine poetry might not coincide.

If Spenser and Milton introduced poets to their inheritance from the past, they also aroused curiosity about what old texts might still survive in libraries and private collections. Some poets were also literary historians, and in the 1750s both Thomas Warton and Thomas Gray began researches into the history of English poetry. Warton explored the Oxford libraries for the medieval and Tudor verse that Spenser had known, and in Cambridge Gray began studying the recorded remains of Old Norse and Old Welsh poetry. Gray, however, abandoned his project, and it was not until Warton's *History of English Poetry* (3 vols., 1774–81) that Britain had a full-scale history of its own literature from the Norman Conquest to the end of the sixteenth century, based on original documents. Before that date the picture was a confused and patchy one, and the fact that poets might be simultaneously writing, editing, translating, adapting, and imitating 'genuine poetry' meant that the public's growing appetite for older verse was being satisfied in ways that broke down clear demarcations.

This chapter is written out of a conviction that such confusions were fruitful for the development of English poetry during the 1760s and beyond. All the works discussed here are in different ways touched by the issue of the genuine or authentic, and I want the ambiguities of those words to remain.[1] They can help to characterise the poetic landscape of the period, while allowing for the distinct individual voices that made themselves heard. The aural dimension is important for a poetry that looked for its models to traditions where a more spontaneous and improvisatory mode was the norm. Readers appreciated hearing beneath the voice of the eighteenth-century poet the genuine notes of bard, minstrel, prophet, and psalmist.

In the Spring of 1757 Thomas Gray thought he had heard the genuine sounds of ancient British poetry. The blind Welsh harpist, John Parry, visited Cambridge and (as Gray reported to his friend William Mason) 'scratch'd out such ravishing blind Harmony, such tunes of a thousand year old with names enough to choak you, as have set all this learned body a'dancing'.[2] Inspired by his encounter with the bardic tradition, Gray took up and completed a poem he had set aside eighteen months earlier. In *The Bard. A Pindaric Ode*, he aimed to catch the sound of the Welsh poetry he had been studying in connection with his 'History'. He was making extensive notes on ancient metre and the old Celtic language, and in the voice of his own bard he imitated its pulse and timbre in the roll-call of the poets slaughtered by the English king:

> 'Cold is Cadwallo's tongue,
> That hush'd the stormy main:
> Brave Urien sleeps upon his craggy bed:
> Mountains, ye mourn in vain
> Modred, whose magic song
> Made huge Plinlimmon bow his cloud-top'd head.' (29–34)

The music of the Welsh names (*Cadwallo, Urien, Modred, Plinlimmon*) establishes the tones he works with. But beyond the interwoven assonance and alliteration, the hearer can pick up the reverberant head-notes, the *m*, *n*, and *ng* sounds, like a vibrating string.

Gray's bard, the last of his race, declaims his swan-song from the edge of a cliff ('On a rock, whose haughty brow / Frowns o'er old Conway's foaming flood, / Robed in the sable garb of woe, / With haggard eyes the Poet stood; / (Loose his beard, and hoary hair / Stream'd, like a meteor, to the troubled air)', 15–20). This image of the wild-eyed poet driven to the edge caught the public imagination, and helped to popularise the bard-figure as a poetic motif. But in the context of this chapter it is important to appreciate what meanings the 'bard' had for eighteenth-century poets and readers. The bard did not represent an unsocialised primitivism, or a private vision – if he claimed liberty it was on behalf of others. He offered his voice as a communal one that focused joys, hopes, or fears and gave them expression. Ideas of cultural regeneration or national unity were therefore never far away. The popular anthem 'Rule, Britannia' was first sung by a blind bard in Thomson and Mallet's *Alfred*, performed before the Prince of Wales in 1740, which showed the hero being called from a humble cottage to save and unify the nation. Corin the shepherd knows that his disguised lodger is something special – 'He steals, I know not how, into the heart'. Alfred, in other words, is *genuine*. The climactic anthem is delivered by a figure who represents the common voice; he is '*our* venerable Bard, / Aged and blind',[3] and through him the link is made between a personal and a national integrity.

For eighteenth-century poets, the bard was a social phenomenon (an 'institution'), a celebrator, a means of linking communities, preserving cultural memory, recording events, and embodying continuities between past and future. He might be alone, desperate, the last of the line – but he preserved these principles within himself. Goldsmith describes such a figure in his essay, 'The History of Carolan, the last Irish Bard' (1760):

> Of all the bards this country ever produced, the last and the greatest was Carolan the blind. He was at once a poet, a musician, a composer, and sung his own verses to his harp. The original natives never mention his name without rapture; both his poetry and music they have by heart . . .[4]

It is the final phrase that confirms Carolan too as genuine. The old man becomes the *heart* of the company ('Whenever any of the original natives of distinction were assembled at feasting or revelling, Carolan was generally there, where he was always ready with his harp'). Goldsmith insists that the bard gives the *original natives* a voice. But this popular folk-poet who died in 1738 was not the last of any line. It is just that for Goldsmith, as for others, the bard-figure with his store of songs is always the 'last bard'.

Gray's Celtic bard comes out of a similar culture that is being destroyed by the English invaders. Before leaping to his death he laments a lost tradition and a dispersed community ('Dear lost companions of my tuneful art'); but then his imagination reanimates them and subsumes their voices into his ('With me in dreadful harmony they join', 47). Together the bards offer a vision of the nation's future. A curse on the Plantagenet line is followed by his prophecy of a united country under the Welsh Tudors, which will allow the arts to flourish again. A literary Golden Age of Spenser, Shakespeare, and Milton will one day re-animate the original genius of British poetry ('Hear from the grave, great Taliessin, hear; / They breathe a soul to animate thy clay', 121–2). The living soul, the life within, will return. The genuine bardic voice is always lying dormant and waiting to return. The last bard is never the final one.

It was not long before the literary world was aroused by the discovery of an even older voice than the sixth-century Taliesin. *Fragments of Ancient Poetry* (1760) offered the public the 'genuine remains of ancient Scottish poetry' associated with the third-century bard, Ossian,[5] collected in the north-west of Scotland and 'translated' from the original Gaelic by James Macpherson. Gray, who had been sent specimens in manuscript, was '*extasié* with their infinite beauty', and though he had doubts about the provenance, he considered their creator to be 'the very Demon of Poetry'.[6] In the voice of this pre-Saxon poet he perhaps heard the original of his own bard:

> By the side of a rock on the hill, beneath the aged trees, old Oscian sat on the moss; the last of the race of Fingal. Sightless are his aged eyes; his beard is waving in the wind. Dull through the leafless trees he heard the voice of the north. Sorrow revived in his soul: he began and lamented the dead.[7]

For its first readers, this seemed to catch the genuine notes of bardic poetry. They reach us like the wind in the trees reaches the old man, as a distant voice which begins to stir the senses and revive a memory that must be given expression. It is calculatedly numinous. Macpherson's poetic rhythmical prose is meant to haunt the ear and form an incantatory pulse that is the equivalent of a verse-line or a sweep of a harp-string. (One of his 'translations', *The Six Bards*, survives in both prose and verse versions – the unrhymed verse text is prosaic and flat in a way the prose is not.[8])

After a further journey gathering Gaelic materials Macpherson rapidly produced two full-scale heroic epics, *Fingal* (six books, 1761) and *Temora* (eight books, 1763), and these were collected with some shorter episodes into *The Works of Ossian* (1765). It soon became clear that Macpherson's role had been a remarkably creative one, and that his 'translations' were part invention and part imaginative reconstruction.[9] Many people were sceptical, some contemptuous, and Macpherson came under pressure to produce his originals. As Nick Groom has shown, he became caught in a disastrously compromising position. At first he maintained that the pedigree of his Celtic materials was an ancient oral one (thus giving his Scottish Ossian priority over the Irish manuscript tradition); but then in 1763 he published a twenty-page 'Specimen of the Original of Temora. Book Seventh'.[10] This brought requests to see his manuscript. 'The demand could not be met and, after an extended public controversy, *Ossian* was denounced as a forgery'.[11] Many had considered that the lack of a written source was a mark of the poetry's genuineness – it went from heart to heart, not from pen to parchment. At the time of Macpherson's journeys a tradition of oral poetry lived on in the communities of north-west Scotland, and old ballads and fragments of heroic tales handed down through generations were still being sung in the strong rhythms of the native Gaelic. Those who had encountered the aural experience felt that Macpherson had captured its essence. Even his rival and scholarly opponent, Thomas Percy, was for a while convinced when he heard a young Highlander perform some Ossianic passages in the original Gaelic. He told his friend, Evan Evans: 'I am forced to believe them, as to the main, genuine in spite of my teeth'.[12] This was how genuine poetry worked – it appealed directly without depending on the judgment.

Macpherson's Ossianic poems deserve to be taken seriously as poetry. Those who still employ the term 'forgery' to describe them have to concede that they seeped into the consciousness of many later writers across Europe, and changed the way poetry – and music – sounded. A text became a phenomenon; and this idea can help the reader to find meaning in a poetic language that appears to have little substance beyond sounds and images. It is useful to regard these pieces as an eighteenth-century attempt to locate the 'genuine' by expressing the essence of the sublime and pathetic, those qualities which for Joseph Warton were 'the two chief nerves of all genuine poetry'.[13] Echoing this in his *Critical Dissertation on the Poems of Ossian* (1763), Hugh Blair argued that 'the two great characteristics of Ossian's poetry are, tenderness and sublimity', and he concluded emphatically that 'His poetry, more perhaps than that of any other writer, deserves to be stiled, *The Poetry of the Heart*'. To Blair this was crucial evidence for its authenticity: 'It is a heart penetrated with noble sentiments, and with sublime and tender passions; a heart that glows, and kindles the fancy; a heart that is full, and pours itself forth. Ossian did not write, like modern poets, to please readers and critics'.[14] But the tastes of *readers and critics* were already changing, and poets (including Macpherson) were responding to critics of the late 1750s like Warton, Burke, and Young,[15] for whom sublimity and pathos marked the highest kinds of poetry. Macpherson's Ossian was in tune with the latest critical and readerly trends.

Edmund Burke's characterisation of the sublime as 'the strongest emotion which the mind is capable of feeling'[16] offered a challenge to poets and painters, and many of his ingredients (vastness, darkness, solitude, silence, obscurity, power, privation, intermittent or sudden effects of sound and light) characterise Ossian's eerily disconnected landscapes, and help to create what Burke calls 'a great and aweful sensation in the mind' (II, xvii). As for the pathetic, Macpherson's scenes of tender feeling between fathers and children, lovers and friends are indebted to contemporary stage tragedies such as Home's *Douglas* (1756) and recent fiction like Fielding's *Amelia* (1751) or Richardson's *Sir Charles Grandison* (1753–4). In the Ossian poems these two qualities highlight one another. Incidents of noble or tender sentiment gain in pathos from the dark primal backdrop against which they are played. Sometimes the sublime and pathetic are effectively fused together: 'Her face was pale like the mist of Cromla; and dark were the tears of her cheek. She often raised her dim hand from her robe; her robe which was of the clouds of the desart'.[17]

171

Beyond their direct emotive appeal to the reader, the poems also exemplify the dual nature of the bardic role. An awareness of loss and dispersal combines with a creative spirit that works to find and collect. The mind of Ossian thus becomes the focal point for things that have become inarticulate and fragmented – sounds, people, natural objects, memories, virtues, individual acts and thoughts over time. Rather than observing society from his own viewpoint, the poet allows dispersed and distant things to register in himself, as though the whole wide landscape is being reconstructed in the bard's consciousness. It is in that way a text of sensibility. This idea of the text as a sensorium that registers things dispersed in time and space and gives meaning to them, suggests a parallel (in spite of their very different voices) between *Ossian* and that other 1760s 'phenomenon' *Tristram Shandy*.[18]

To find the 'genuine' in Macpherson-as-Ossian it helps to think about how he uses the idea of song. He identifies it with the continuities and rhythms of nature as the expressive impulse itself, which comes out of the silence and darkness as naturally as the leaves to a tree, or like a stream scarce heard:

> Loud, at once, from the hundred bards, rose the song of the tomb. Carril strode before them, they are the murmur of streams behind him. Silence dwells in the vales of Moi-lena, where each, with its own dark stream, is winding between the hills. I heard the voice of the bards, lessening, as they moved along. I leaned forward from my shield, and felt the kindling of my soul. Half-formed the words of my song, burst forth upon the wind. So hears a tree, on the vale, the voice of spring around; it pours its green leaves to the sun, and shakes its lonely head. The hum of the mountain bee is near it; the hunter sees it, with joy, from the blasted heath.[19]

For the bards and Ossian himself, hearing and speaking are virtually the same process. Song is simultaneously responsive and expressive. It doesn't signal a private self or personal experience, but something communally remembered – a ritual commemoration that moves from heart to heart. In the Ossianic world the 'genuine' is a shared experience. It tends to be fragmentary (*half-formed*) and spontaneous (*burst forth*); it is absorbed into nature (like air and water). The *stream* of consciousness moves, mixed with natural sounds, from the *hundred bards* to Ossian, and on to the *hunter* wandering on the heath.

Ossian's landscapes slip in and out of the metaphorical, hovering between permanence and transience. Isolated trees and rocks are used as emotional landmarks, signalling endurance, transitoriness, death, hope, or memory. Waters roll and roar, and expressive winds brood, rush, blast, or shake. Clouds catch evanescent moods of many kinds. Things dark and silent are momentarily caught by light or make sudden sounds. Occasionally a spear, sword, or shield come to life as they clang or glitter. Always there is a sense of space across which things move or sounds reach. Within an oral culture that lives on sound and memory and takes meanings out of the air, this landscape is used to guarantee the bard's authentic voice – there is nothing else to hold on to: 'The sons of song are gone to rest: my voice remains, like a blast, that roars, lonely, on a sea-surrounded rock, after the winds are laid. The dark moss whistles there, and the distant mariner sees the waving trees'.[20]

If a manuscript was the sole guarantor of authenticity, then it was Evan Evans who produced the genuine bardic text the year after Macpherson's *Temora*. Evans was hoping that in the wake of the sensational popularity of *Ossian*, his translations of 'antient and genuine pieces' of the Welsh bards would have some success. These were, after all, the true originals of Gray's doomed thirteenth-century poets. But *Some Specimens of the Poetry of the Antient Welsh Bards* (1764) made little impression. Evans worked carefully from medieval manuscripts in private collections, attached scholarly historical notes with dates and identifications, and printed his Welsh originals at the end of the volume. But the public were not interested. It was as if the more he demonstrated the authenticity of his materials, the more they seemed dusty old library texts – of antiquarian interest, but lacking that genuine voice:

> How naked and forlorn is our condition! We are exposed to anxious toils and cares. O how heavy is the Almighty's punishment, that the crimson sword cannot be drawn! I remember how great it's size was, and how wide it's havock; numerous are now the oppressed captives who languish in gnashing indignation. Our native Bards are excluded from their accustomed entertainments.[21]

Compared with the expressive force and emphasis of *Ossian*, this reads like a flat paraphrase lacking the essence of 'genuine poetry'. The language has missed the spirit and is reporting on a corpse. It was left to Gray to give Evans's materials a voice when he translated four of the fragments into sounding verse: 'There the Norman sails afar / Catch the winds, and join the war: / Black and huge along they sweep, / Burthens of the angry deep'[22]. For eighteenth-century readers it was lines like these from 'The Triumphs of Owen' that were the stuff of ancient British poetry, tones that stirred an old cultural memory. Paradoxically, the more they resembled echoes of something lost, the more genuine seemed to be the effect.

The public's curiosity about the original voice of poetry was also leading to a renewed interest in the ballad form. As early as 1711, Addison had caused a stir by praising the popular old ballad of *Chevy Chase* as being 'extremely natural and poetical, and full of the majestick Simplicity which we admire in the greatest of the ancient Poets'. But Addison felt that in order to demonstrate its qualities he had to measure the ballad against the classical criteria of Homer and Virgil.[23] By 1723, however, the anonymous editor of *A Collection of Old Ballads* turned such a comparison on its head:

> . . . the very Prince of Poets, old *Homer*, if we may trust ancient Records, was nothing more than a blind *Ballad-singer*, who writ Songs of the Siege of *Troy*, and the Adventures of *Ulysses*; and playing the Tunes upon his Harp, sung from Door to Door, till at his Death somebody thought fit to collect all his Ballads, and by a little connecting 'em, gave us the *Iliad* and *Odysses*, which since that Time have been so much admired.[24]

This picture of Homer as an itinerant singer is intended not to belittle him, but to authenticate his poetic powers. Homer's is the genuine voice of the balladeer in touch with the natural sources of poetry. It was an idea picked up by Thomas

Blackwell in his influential *Enquiry into the Life and Writings of Homer* (1735), in which he argued that 'Homer's being born poor, and living a wandering indigent Bard, was, in relation to his Poetry, the greatest Happiness that cou'd befall him'. Blackwell maintains that this true poet 'took his plain natural Images from *Life* . . . For so unaffected and simple were the Manners of those Times, that the Folds and Windings of the human Breast lay open to the Eye'. Unlike the work of modern writers who 'live within Doors, cover'd, as it were, from *Nature's Face*', the 'old Poetry' struck the notes of truth. It did not 'disguise Nature' or 'dissemble' human behaviour.[25]

A poem that exemplified this image of an older heroic simplicity was the Scottish ballad, *Hardyknute*, a 42-stanza fragment first published in 1719, and frequently reprinted. This story of the defeat of a Norse invasion was a favourite of Gray's, and was admired by Thomas Warton as 'a striking representation of our antient martial manners, that prevailed, before alterations in government, and the conveniencies of civilised life'.[26] To its eighteenth-century readers the ballad offered vivid glimpses of an old feudal society based on loyalty, nobility, and courage. These ancient virtues are given simple and striking images, as at the moment when Hardyknute receives the Scottish King's summons to help save his country:

> Then reid, reid grew his dark-brown cheiks,
>   Sae did his dark-brown brow;
> His luiks grew kene, as they were wont,
>   In dangers great to do;
> He hes tane a horn as grene as grass,
>   And gien five sounds sae shrill,
> That treis in grene wode schuke thereat,
>   Sae loud rang ilka hill. (57–64)[27]

Hardyknute answers the call to arms like a force of nature. His virtues of courage and loyalty rise spontaneously to his face, and his horn's immediate response is bold, strong, and natural. The poem sounds the genuine notes of what Blackwell called 'the Emotions of an artless Mind' (p. 24).

But this poem admired by readers and scholars alike was eventually discovered to be an eighteenth-century production. In 1760 Gray heard rumours but maintained that he still thought highly of it. Warton was told the truth but remarked: 'I am apt to think that the first stanza is old and gave a hint for writing the rest'.[28] Percy received the disappointing news while collecting materials for his *Reliques of Ancient English Poetry* (1765); but he included the ballad all the same as 'a fine morsel of heroic poetry', noting its modern provenance while adding that he thought part of it could be ancient, and that the writer (Elizabeth Wardlaw) might have 'retouched and much enlarged' it – after all, this was no more than Percy himself had done to some of his materials in the *Reliques*.[29] He had also written a contribution of his own ('The Friar of Orders Gray') by combining 'innumerable little fragments of ancient ballads' scattered throughout Shakespeare's plays. It was difficult for scholars to believe that *Hardyknute* had not grown in a similar way from a genuine root, however small. The poem had already accumulated mythical origins: Lady Wardlaw, it was said, had found the relic 'written on shreds of paper' being used for winding thread (*Reliques*, II, 88); or 'she had taken them down in writing from an old woman, who sung them while she was spinning at her distaff.'[30] What is more, a Scottish musician 'declared he had heard fragments of it repeated during his infancy: before ever Mrs. Wardlaw's copy was heard of'.[31] In such ways, a poem so obviously 'genuine' to its readers was preserved in the literary canon. The piece fitted too well into the image of old poetry being projected by eighteenth-century literary history.

By the late 1760s the picture of Britain's early poetic tradition was a fragmentary one, and it was confused by the theories of critics and the awakening interest of contemporary poets. To be told, for example, by William Duff in his *Essay on Original Genius* (1767) that 'the early and uncultivated periods of society are peculiarly favourable to the display of original Poetic Genius, and that this quality will seldom appear in a very high degree in cultivated life'[32] seemed to invite any ambitious poet to project himself into the past in order to find the creative spark. One young man who did this more wholeheartedly than anyone was Thomas Chatterton, whose brief career was devoted to reconstructing the literary history of his native Bristol and thereby changing the whole story of English poetry. As a 'phenomenon' (yet another), he grew from the root system sketched in the previous pages.

Dead at the age of seventeen in a London garret, Chatterton left behind him a substantial literary legacy, and also a large number of unanswered questions. He was a 'charity boy' apprenticed at fourteen to a Bristol attorney, but spent much of his time pursuing a fascination for old poetry. He pored over Chaucer and Elizabethan verse, and with the help of glossaries he was drawn into the linguistic world of the late Middle Ages. The sounds and spellings delighted him, and his imagination was stirred by descriptions, inventories and heraldries. A bundle of parchments that his father had removed from a chest in his local church introduced him to the touch and smell of the past, and he began copying the old writing. Soon the lad was inventing his own texts and supplying Bristol antiquaries with important 'discoveries' about the city's history. Out of these experiments he began to create an imagined version of fifteenth-century Bristol. He himself became 'Thomas Rowley', secular priest,[33] a poet and playwright in the service of his patron, William Canynge (d. 1474), a wealthy merchant, M.P. for Bristol, and five times mayor of the city. Chatterton's 'transcriptions' of Rowley's poems began to cause a stir, and some Rowley manuscripts, written on old parchment in specially concocted ink, were being handed around. But four months after moving to London, and on the threshold of a career as a political writer and satirist, the precocious Chatterton was dead, and 'Rowley' was beginning his brief controversial existence. A full edition of *Poems, Supposed to have been Written at Bristol, by Thomas Rowley, and Others, in the Fifteenth Century* (1777) reopened the question of authorship, and there followed a fierce debate between the scholarly establishment (to whom Rowley was a fiction but Chatterton a genuine 'genius') and the antiquarian believers (to whom Rowley was genuine and Chatterton just an 'illiterate charity-boy'). Only in 1782 was it demonstrated to public satisfaction that Chatterton and Rowley were one and the same.

Once again, the nature of the 'genuine' was crucial, but with the added ingredient of 'genius' to complicate the matter. In 1778 Thomas Warton, who believed the poems to be spurious, nonetheless devoted a chapter of his *History of English Poetry* to them, and was full of praise for their true author: 'This youth . . . was a prodigy of genius: and would have proved the first of English poets, had he reached a maturer age' (II, 157). Warton knew that if they were genuine, Rowley's writings would redeem English poetry from the dark age into which it had sunk after Chaucer's death in 1400. For Warton, the Rowley poems embodied a 'genius' that would not reappear until the Tudor Age. Chaucer had been, he says, 'a genial day in an English spring' after which 'winter returns with redoubled horrors' (II, 51); and it was this lost quality of 'geniality' (in the sense of 'youthful freshness and creativity') that Chatterton's pieces represented for him.[34] Warton saw the Rowley poems as linking the idea of Poetic Genius with the *genial* (i.e. 'generative') principle, and the idea also underpins William Duff's conception of *Original Genius*. As words from the same root, *genuine*, *genial*, and *genius* were naturally drawn together at a time when interest was being rekindled in the early development of the arts. People were hungry for originals. In his manifesto, *Conjectures on Original Composition* (1759), Edward Young remarked that '*Imitators* only give us a sort of Duplicates of what we had . . . The pen of an *Original* Writer, like *Armida*'s wand, out of a barren waste calls a blooming spring' (p. 10), and he added significantly: 'An *Original* may be said to be of a *vegetable* nature; it rises spontaneously from the vital root of Genius; it *grows*, it is not *made*' (p. 12).

These linked ideas take us to the heart of Chatterton's creativeness. Through the character of Rowley he developed an organic awareness of English poetry and set about making texts that fitted into his conception of its early development. He offered connections, completed fragments, and provided origins.[35] He had the knack of supplying just what ought to have been there but wasn't. Amongst the Rowley material were the earliest English *Eclogues*, the first native classical epic (*Battle of Hastynges*), and the first heroic verse tragedy (*Ælla*) complete with Anglo-Saxon 'minstrels'.[36] In the chorus from the dramatic fragment *Goddwyn* we are given a direct ancestor of the English Pindaric ode, as the figure of Freedom is confronted by the violent threats of Power:

> Power, wythe his Heafod straughte ynto the Skyes,   *head stretched*
> Hys Speere a Sonne beame and his Sheelde a Starre;
> Alyche twaie brendeynge Gronfyres rolls hys Eyes,   *like two flaming meteors*
> Chaftes with hys Yronne feete, and soundes to War—   *stamps*
> > She syttes upon a Rocke,
> > She bendes before hys Speere:
> > She ryses from the Shocke,
> > Wieldynge her owne yn Ayre . . . (210–17)

Chatterton's rhythmic resourcefulness can be striking. Although Freedom's lines are shrunk, their simple strength and contained energy hint that she will triumph over Power's blusterings. We find contrast, not compromise; and this is also true of the imagery. Power may invoke the whole heavenly system to enforce his aggressiveness, but really he is a child stamping his feet. Freedom on her rock has strength rather than power (Chatterton understands the difference), a capacity for patient endurance (*syttes*), for resourceful flexibility (*bendes*), and for growth and initiative (*ryses*). He takes us to the heart of the eternal struggle between the threatening system and the grounded principle, oppressor and oppressed. What became known in the Romantic period as Chatterton's 'Ode to Freedom'[37] remains powerful because it gets to the root of the matter.

Chatterton was committed to giving the imagination a physical form, designing and building from the foundations up. For him, the strength of any conception was how firmly grounded it was in the culture. He created a full archival context around Rowley's writings. Crucial to this was the figure of William Canynge, his friend and patron, who combined the ideal and the practical, and who had built the magnificent church of St Mary Redcliffe.[38] This building (the source of his 'found' manuscripts) was at the centre of Chatterton's imagined world, and in his *Discorse on Brystowe* he fabricated a thousand-year history for it, with the drawing of a previous Anglo-Saxon church on the site. To convey the glory of Canynge's newly completed Gothic church, Rowley breaks into verse that in its simple strength conveys his sense of how history is built, and how imagination can make it palpable:

> Stay, curyous traveller, and pass not bye,
> Until this fetive pile astounde thine eye.   *elegant building*
> Whole rocks on rocks with yron joynd surveie,
> And okes with okes entremed disponed lie.   *intermingled, disposed*
> This mightie pile, that keeps the wyndes at baie,
> Fyre-levyn and the mokie storme defie,   *lightening*
> That shootes aloofe into the realmes of daie,
> Shall be the record of the Buylders fame for aie. (1–8)

Rowley's building has the natural strength of a mountain surmounted with oaks. The stones and beams are firmly knitted together (*joynd*, *entremed*), just like his simpler ancestor of the Spenserian stanza, with its two rhymes (*aababbb*) melded into a strong unit. Once again endurance and defiance are the key ideas. The structure defies the storm by an answering gesture that mimics the lightening (*shootes aloofe into the realmes of daie*), just as Saxon Freedom answered Norman Power in the *Goddwyn* chorus. As a *record* it becomes the ideal image for the Rowleyan world, which Chatterton intended to be solid and true to Anglo-Saxon tradition, a defiant response to Norman depredations. He wrote in a draft letter to Horace Walpole: 'the Normans destroy'd all the Saxon MSS, Paintings &c that fell in their Way: endeavoring to suppress the very Language'.[39] In this conviction Rowley became Canynge's agent for recovering Anglo-Saxon manuscripts and translating them. His own poetry reflects his defiant commitment to pre-Conquest culture by repeatedly exposing the Anglo-Saxon foundations of the English language. It was this quality that John Keats singled out for praise: 'Chatterton . . . is the purest writer in the English Language. He has no French idiom, or particles like Chaucer—'tis genuine English Idiom in English Words.'[40]

Chatterton also associated the Anglo-Saxon roots of language with the *genuine*. This comes across vividly in Rowley's 'An Excelente Balade of Charitie', a poem about religious hypocrisy and social inequality, where the poor pilgrim is caught in a very English thunderstorm packed with native words ('the bigge drops falle; / The forswat meadowes smethe, and drenche the raine', 29–30). In these honest drops there is nothing Latin or French. But when the Abbot of St Godwin's rides into view, Rowley notes that 'His chapournette was drented with the reine' (45), and Chatterton enjoys giving the French *chapournette* (a hat worn by churchmen and lawyers) a good Anglo-Saxon *drenching*. This ecclesiastic is a figure with expensive accoutrements: his *autremete* (priestly robe) is edged with gold, and the *trammels* (Old French *tramails*) of his *palfrye* have been decorated by a horse-*millanare* (the word too is an exotic Italian import). When the hungry pilgrim asks him for alms, the abbot invokes *honour*, calls him a *faitour* (Anglo-French for 'beggar'), and rides away. It is left to a poor charitable friar to give the pilgrim his cloak and a silver groat in impeccable Anglo-Saxon: 'Here take this silver, it maie eathe thie care' (83).

This parable of human charity ends with a prayer and a threat: 'Virgynne and hallie Seyncte, who sitte yn gloure, / Or [*either*] give the mittee [*mighty*] will, or *give the gode man power*' (91), and in that last phrase (my italics) we hear the voice of Chatterton the satirist, the outspoken young man who was in 1770 seeking the patronage of the radical John Wilkes. It is helpful to remember that Rowley's creator was a political writer who set simple feeling and natural description against systems of war and power. Chatterton's 'Nature' was a liberating and egalitarian force (we have seen it expose the wealthy abbot), a principle that informed him as a poet and a lover:

> But ever in my Love-lorn flights
> Nature untouch'd by Art delights
>   Art ever gives disgust:
> 'Why?' says some Priest, of mystic Thought.
> The Bard alone by Nature taught,
>   Is to that Nature just. ('To Miss Lydia C[otto]n', 19–24)

This poem to a Bristol girlfriend extends his youthful sexuality ('Nature's rising Fires', 30) to the freedom of the mind: 'In Natural Religion free, / I, to no other bow the Knee, / Nature's the God I own' (31–3). It is clear that to embrace the principle of Nature is to assert an authentic untrammelled self and defy the establishment.

Chatterton, the bard of nature, is voicing the confident independence of character that Thomas Blackwell had identified in a Homer who found in his unsettled society the freedom to express his own mind: 'the Times of such Struggles have a kind of Liberty peculiar to themselves: They raise a free and active Spirit, which over spreads the Country: Every Man finds himself on such occasions his own Master, and that he *may be* whatever he can *make* himself . . . He finds his own Weight, tries his own Strength'.[41] It was this kind of world, where a man could be himself and take his own measure, which Robert Burns celebrated so memorably:

> What though on hamely fare we dine,
>   Wear hoddin [*homespun*] grey, and a' that.
> Gie fools their silks, and knaves their wine,
>   A Man's a Man for a' that.
>   For a' that, and a' that,
>   Their tinsel show, and a' that;
> The honest man, though e'er sae poor,
>   Is king o'men for a' that.—(9–16)

In this poem, as elsewhere in Burns, we hear a man as he *finds his own Weight*. Blackwell's phrase is suggestive in thinking about the strength of Burns's speaking voice, which is sinewy and doesn't carry a decorative surplus. Throughout the poem the repeated *a' that* ('all that') marks out what the 'genuine' life can dispense with – the stuff that weighs the poor down, or the stuffing that bolsters the rich ('The man of independent mind, / He looks and laughs at a' that.—', 23–4). In 1787 Burns recollected his earlier poetic ambitions: 'To know myself had been all along my constant study.—I weighed myself alone; I balanced myself with others'.[42] For Burns, the state in which you can know, and be, what you really are, is 'Liberty'. As he says in 'The Tree of Liberty' (his poem welcoming the French Revolution): 'Upo' this tree there grows sic fruit, / Its virtues a' can tell, man; / It raises man aboon [*above*] the brute, / It maks him ken [*know*] himsel, man' (9–12).[43]

Such a self-aware, independent voice with radical potential had to be carefully handled; and in Burns's first verse collection, *Poems, Chiefly in the Scottish Dialect* (Kilmarnock, 1786), this led to tensions in the way the image of the new poet was being projected. A strong and original personality wanted to find authentic expression; but at the same time it needed to speak directly to the readers' hearts. In Burns, two aspects of the 'genuine' were therefore in danger of clashing – a genuine voice had to have a genuine effect. Knowing yourself had to go along with knowing your audience.

In the Kilmarnock volume the poet is presented as a 'rustic bard', an 'artless' son of the Scottish soil born in obscure poverty, who expresses the simple, natural and spontaneous feelings of the human heart. Expectations are set by the verse motto on the title-page, which his readers would recognise as announcing an untaught 'genius': 'The Simple Bard, unbroke by rules of Art, / He pours the wild effusions of the heart . . .' But if Burns is being marketed here as a humble self-taught poet, it is clear that he is uneasy about the full implications of the idea. There is a danger that he will be regarded in a patronising way by his readers, a fate suffered by generations of labouring-class poets since Stephen Duck in the 1730s. This is clear from passages in the preface (written in the third person) where a pompous editorial style takes over: 'Unacquainted with the necessary requisites for commencing Poet by rule, he sings the sentiments and manners, he felt and saw in himself and his rustic compeers around him, in his and their native language' (iii). The phrase *rustic compeers* might be reassuringly polite, but it strikes a note of condescension that drives a wedge between the poet and his audience. Perhaps with this in mind, Burns is careful to offer his 'sincere thanks' to his subscribers in a way that claims a direct emotional bond with them – it is 'not the mercenary bow over a counter,' he says, 'but the heart-throbbing gratitude of the Bard'(v). The choice of words is interesting. That symbol of class-difference, the shop-keeper's *counter*, is an obstacle to his intimacy with the reader. Rather than be patronised by a customer, he wants to break down the barrier and have a *sincere* relationship.

Readers have always warmed to this impulse, and the fact that generations of Scots have taken Burns's poems into their hearts (and memories), performing them on convivial occasions of haggis-eating or whisky-drinking, links him indisputably to the bardic tradition. This sociable bard gave a nation songs to sing. Genuineness is Burns's appropriate theme, and the critical tradition has valued his poetry for a range of qualities that express that ideal: spontaneity, honesty, naturalness, truth, universality. There are many anecdotes of his extempore genius, and memories of hearing him try out poems as he walked through a field or worked in the garden, declaiming verses to himself, or whistling a tune as he tried to fit words to it. These originary moments are part of a longstanding concern for what Nicholas Roe has called 'Authenticating Robert Burns', in which the poet's 'native' qualities have been insisted upon, his genealogy obsessively verified, and his birth in an 'auld clay biggin' repeatedly invoked in 'nativity naratives'. Roe writes that 'the need to authenticate his claim to be the poet of his native culture . . . was shadowed by Ossian and Thomas Rowley – ghostly witnesses to the contrary possibility that Burns's obscurity might be a cover for the literary fake, with the "Scottish Bard" revealed as an imposter'.[44]

Not being Ossian was therefore important to Burns (however much he admired that 'prince of Poets'[45]). There could hardly be a greater stylistic contrast than that between the sounding paragraphs of Macpherson's prose-poetry and Burns's tightly spun rhymes. It is the difference between far off echoes and intimate conversation, between the landscape of memory and the responsive 'now'. But for Burns the choice of a poetic language was not a straightforward one. Where Chatterton was able to enter at will into the Rowleyan linguistic world, and Macpherson discovered one single consistent voice for Ossian, Burns faced a conundrum. What was his own 'genuine' language?

The challenge of finding an authentic voice raised social as well as linguistic questions for a young man who had an enviable range open to him. Dugald Stewart, Professor of Moral Philosophy at Edinburgh University, recalled that 'when [Burns] spoke in company . . . he aimed at purity in his turn of expression, and avoided, more successfully than most Scotchmen, the peculiarities of Scottish phraseology'.[46] It is clear that Burns could communicate with the 'great folks' in their own style. Indeed, the 'Heaven-taught ploughman' acclaimed by the reviewers[47] was in fact a tenant-farmer well educated at local schools and by private tutors, knowledgeable in French and mathematics, who by the age of eighteen was a keen reader of English poetry. Burns's admiration for writers like Thomson, Gray, Shenstone, and Goldsmith is evident in the group of non-dialect poems in the Kilmarnock collection. In 'Despondency, An Ode', for example, he seems to be experimenting with a mode of subjective melancholy distilled from Gray: 'Oh, enviable, early days, / When dancing thoughtless Pleasure's maze, / To Care, to Guilt unknown! / How ill exchang'd for riper times, / To feel the follies, or the crimes, / Of others, or my own!' (57–62). This strain of refined self-consciousness appropriately exploits the more 'universal' voice that English gave him.[48] In other poems he will turn from a thickly textured dialect at moments when he needs simplicity and pathos, as in 'The Death and Dying Words of Poor Mailie', where the author's pet ewe trapped in a ditch is speaking to her lambs:

> O, may thou ne'er forgather up,   *get together*
> Wi' onie blastet, moorlan *toop*;   *worthless moorland ram*
> But ay keep mind to moop an' mell,   *nibble and meddle*
> Wi' sheep o' credit like thysel!
>   And now, *my bairns*, wi' my last breath,
> I lea'e my blessin wi' you baith:
> An' when ye think upo' your Mither,
> Mind to be kind to ane anither. (53–60)

The Scottish accent is preserved; but the move into a common vocabulary allows Burns to make a more direct appeal to the sentimental emotions – to tune his notes to a simpler pathos. This is not a shift between art and nature (both styles are artful), but perhaps from one notion of the 'genuine' to another. The working vocabulary of the hill-farmer is followed by the 'language of the heart'. This 'unco' mournfu' tale', as Burns terms it, has just the right element of humour to engage the reader's tender feelings without satirising them.

It seems natural to divide the Burns canon into the 'dialect' poems and those in 'standard English'. But this overlooks the degree to which his dialect poems have standard features. In a classic article, Raymond Bentman demonstrates Burns's linguistic impurity: 'he wrote no poems in pure vernacular Scottish. The "Scottish" poems are written in a literary language, which was mostly, although not entirely English, in grammar and syntax, and, in varying proportions, both Scottish and English in vocabulary'.[49] The phrase *varying proportions* is significant, since the 'dialect' poems vary greatly in the degree of their Scottishness. The clear division, however, persists, along with the opinion that Burns is only really himself when writing in Scots. Alan Bold, for example, argues that 'when he was most honest as a poet, he was most Scottish', and that while 'Burns's poems in Scots were inspirational, his poems in English were occasional'.[50] Such judgments engage head-on with the question of Burns's authentic voice, and suggest that only in Scots was he being 'genuine'.

Burns himself, however, particularly in his debut collection, had a more complex notion of what 'honest' poetry was. This is clear from a group of poems concerned with what kind of poet he could or should be, and the range of positions is considerable. As he negotiates questions of inspiration, subject-matter, style, and audience, he moves between Scots and English in ways that suggest he regards 'genuineness' as dependent not on a single register, but on his ability to move when appropriate across the linguistic range. The reader is struck by the variety of voices, amongst which 'honesty' finds different tones.

In 'A Dream' Burns does indeed use 'honest' dialect to satirise poetic flattery, when he takes on the role of Great Britain's Poet Laureate. He has just fallen asleep while reading Thomas Warton's Birthday Ode to the King, and he imagines himself at court in his fine clothes giving the Royal Family something to sing about. This North British laureate enjoys breaking through the veneer of formality to deliver a colloquial ballad rather than a lofty laureate ode. It is the very indecorum of his voice 'on sic a day' that makes it carry weight. He punctures pretension and treats Prime Minister 'Willie Pit' and others like objects of tavern gossip ('I muckle doubt, my SIRE, / Ye've trusted "Ministration, / To chaps, wha, in a *barn* or *byre*, / Wad better fill'd their station"', 41–4). This satiric poem featuring an over-familiar address, is clearly an example of Burns exploiting dialect for tactical truth-telling; and part of the effect is a slippage in and out of the official vocabulary of "fealty an" subjection'.

'A Dream', however, is immediately followed by 'The Vision' (an interesting contrast in titles). From the humorous fantasy of being the Nation's Laureate, Burns moves on to consider what his genuine poetic role might be. Here he opens with eight stanzas in dialect (1–48) only to continue from that point in standard English – and it is the arrival of the 'vision' that brings the linguistic change. The fact that his caller is a local girl makes the shift even more intriguing. The poem begins with Burns sitting in his chimney-corner lamenting the time he has wasted in writing verses (what he calls 'stringing blethers ["babble"] up in rhyme / For fools to sing', 23–4). He is about to renounce poetry for ever, when his guiding spirit lifts the latch of the cottage door. At first he takes the figure to be an 'outlandish *Hizzie*' ('wench'), but she stops him in his tracks:

> Ye need na doubt, I held my whisht;   *kept quiet*
> The infant aith, half-form'd, was crusht;   *oath*
> I glowr'd as eerie's I'd been dusht,   *I stared with fright as if I'd been butted*
>   In some wild glen;
> When sweet, like *modest Worth*, she blusht,
>   And stepped ben (43–8)   *inside*

The moment he notices her true nature (47) he slips into standard English, in spontaneous response to the polite visitor (the italics are his). Given the context, this is a fascinating move, since the figure who confronts him is Coila, the guardian angel of Kyle (Burns's native district of Ayrshire) who has watched over him from birth and followed 'the embryotic trace, / Of *rustic*

Bard' (147–8). She speaks throughout in impeccable English: 'With future hope,' she tells him, 'I oft would gaze, / Fond, on thy little, early ways, / Thy rudely-caroll'd, chiming phrase, / In uncouth rhymes' (157–60). She has come to declare his genuineness, and to guarantee his destiny as a regional poet. But this well spoken Ayrshire spirit serves only to curtail Burns's Scottish voice. Her poetic ideals obviously transcend the local, and she tells him that, although he will prove to be no Thomson, Shenstone, or Gray, he will find his own bardic voice within his '*humble* sphere' (212). Coila crowns him with a garland of Ayrshire holly, and vanishes. As Burns becomes conscious of his destiny, however, he does not return to dialect, but ends the poem in the standard English she introduced:

> '*And wear thou this*'—She solemn said,
> And bound the *Holly* round my head:
> The polish'd leaves, and berries red,
>   Did rustling play;
> And, like a passing thought, she fled,
>   In light away. (223–8)

He is caught between an evanescent *passing thought* and the tangible *rustling* of the holly round his head – a token that something real has happened to him. It cannot be said that this graceful language is inauthentic. If anything, these final lines are prophetic of Burns's later collections of songs, in which he will make such polished lyricism his own.

Questions of poetic language are also to the fore in Burns's verse letters to other local poets. In the first 'Epistle to J. L[aprai]k, an Old Scotch Bard' he at once strikes up a friendly intimacy in a lively broad Scots, and this carries him naturally into an attack on their common enemy, those learned 'Critic-folk' who speak in 'your jargon o' your Schools'. Here the dialect voice is effective in conveying a scorn for poetic rules: 'What sairs ["serves"] your Grammars? / Ye'd better taen up *spades* and *shools* ["shovels"], / Or *knappin-hammers* [tools for stone-breaking]' (64–6). But the instant Burns begins to express his own ideal of a poetry based on nature and simplicity, the tone of voice changes, and the dialect speech subsides:

> Gie me ae spark o' Nature's fire,
> That's a' the learning I desire;
> Then tho' I drudge thro' dub an ' mire
>   At pleugh or cart,
> My Muse, tho' hamely in attire,
>   May touch the heart. (73–8)

At this honest moment the defiant dialect gives way to a language of *the heart*. Burns's self-image of the humble ploughman trudging through the mud is conveyed as directly as possible. But here he is less an individual Ayrshire labourer, than a representative of common humanity. Perhaps this awareness – of how the localised, immediate and intimate can speak to the universal human condition – is the key to the way some of Burns's poems fluctuate across the linguistic scale between dialect and standard English.

Nevertheless, the moment he turns to poetry as a spontaneous inspiration – a sheer rush of words – there is only one appropriate vocabulary: 'The words come skelpan ["rushing"], rank and file, / Amaist before I ken!', he declares towards the end of 'Epistle to Davie. A Brother Poet'. Scots is Burns's medium when he's thoroughly *het* ('heated up') and in his stride. He tells Davie: 'My spavet ["lame"] *Pegasus* will limp, / Till ance he's fairly het; / And then he'll hilch, and stilt, and jump, / And rin an unco ["odd"] fit' (147–50). The poem ends with a sprint to the finish; and as Burns prepares to leave his friend's company, he dismounts a poetic horse that has covered a lot of ground and needs to be thoroughly rubbed down ('dight'): 'But least then, the beast then, / Should rue this hasty ride, / I'll light now, and dight now, / His sweaty, wizen'd hide' (151–4). It is typical of Burns's poetry that his *Pegasus* (the inspirational steed ridden by poets since the time of Pindar) is a living, sweaty animal. Burns is always sensitive to surges of energy, and his rhythms will pick up the pace in response to the body's promptings, as they do in the witches' reel in 'Tam o'Shanter' – 'The dancers quick and quicker flew; / They reel'd, they set, they cross'd, they cleekit, / Till ilka carlin swat and reekit' (146–8). Moments of light-headedness are also well caught, like Tam's 'glorious' tipsiness, when the narrator brilliantly slips into standard English as if to mimic the maudlin sentimentality of the drunk as he stands up and heads for home:

> But pleasures are like poppies spread,
> You seize the flower, its bloom is shed;
> Or like the snow falls in the river,
> A moment white—then melts for ever;
> Or like the borealis race . . . (59–63)

Burns catches the embarrassment as Tam is guided towards the door. The English lines come to life if we imagine a drunken man saying them (with perhaps a hiccup for the dash). It is a heady lyrical 'glory' before Tam's demons descend ('. . . Or like the rainbow's lovely form / Evanishing amid the storm . . .'). Thank you Tam – we'll see you next market-day.

It is at expressive moments like these that Burns's aural imagination comes into its own. His linguistic range helps him to be alert for lines that 'ring true', when thought and language are at play together. Such happy coincidences are another aspect of 'genuineness' in its ideal lyric trajectory from the heart to the heart. Burns's increasing interest in song-writing during the 1790s gets him closer to this smooth transition from sincerity of feeling, into rightness of language, to immediacy of response: 'O my Luve's like a red, red rose, / That's newly sprung in June; / O my Luve's like the melodie / That's sweetly play'd in tune'. This is not a song about love, but a love-song. The feeling (*my Luve*) and its object (*my Luve*) fuse together in the well tuned melody. Burns's poems and songs are still frequently performed because they encourage what might be called 'lyric appropriation' – the reader or singer makes them his/her own and becomes the medium for the experience. In such a way their genuineness is forever being reconfirmed by being freshly appropriated. With this in mind we can understand how Thomas Percy's encounter with the young high-lander, or Gray's with the blind harpist turned out to be experiences of the 'genuine'.

Athanasius, the fourth-century Bishop of Alexandria, conceived of the Psalms in a similar way: 'he who recites the Psalms is uttering [them] as his own words, and each sings them as if they were written concerning himself'. The individual Christian was encouraged to draw the scriptural text into the soul, which 'gaining its composure by the singing of the phrases . . . becomes forget-ful of the passions and, while rejoicing, sees in accordance with the mind of Christ'. [51] In this religious context issues of genuineness give way to immediate conviction as words become sanctioned by the spirit:

> As in the spirit I repeat
> His praise, my musings shall be sweet,
>   To just refinement wrought;
> Yea, while I yet suppress my voice,
> To thee, O Lord, will I rejoice
>   In melody of thought. (199–204)

In this stanza from Christopher Smart's translation of Psalm 104 ('Bless the Lord, O my soul') the poet allows the sacred text to germinate in him as a *melody of thought*, a lyric appropriation. The lines are themselves an expan-sion of verse 34 of the psalm ('My meditation of him shall be sweet: I will be glad in the Lord'). The act of suppressing his individual voice allows him to be articulate *in the spirit*, becoming the instrument on which the melody is played.

Being *glad in the Lord* (with the emphasis on 'in') is the essence of Smart's religious poetry. Jesus Christ, the humanity of God, possesses him and is in turn his own possession:

> Take ye therefore what ye give him,
>   Of his fulness grace for grace,
> Strive to think him, speak him, live him,
>   Till you find him face to face.[52] ('New Year', 33–6)

In this reciprocal relationship between God and the human heart, the lyric outpouring offers back what has been received. Smart's Epiphany hymn (mark-ing the moment God revealed himself to mankind) appropriately expresses a simultaneous filling and pouring out:

> Fill my heart with genuine treasures,
>   Pour them out before his feet,
> High conceptions, mystic measures,
>   Springing strong and flowing sweet. ('Epiphany', 29–32)

In Smart, the *genuine* is thus relieved of any problematic involvement with questions of authentic sources, individual human genius, or linguistic choices. Where Macpherson, Chatterton, and Burns, in seeking to express the genuine, had to negotiate these problems, Smart resolves them by fusing together past and present, self and object, idea and word.

'Expression' therefore becomes literally the 'pressing out' of what is within, and for Smart this takes on a strongly vocal character. He insists on the spiritual urgency of giving voice, because true prayer is the clear and forceful expression of your God-given character:

> For the AIR is purified by prayer which is made aloud and with all our might.
> For loud prayer is good for weak lungs and for a vitiated throat.
> For SOUND is propagated in the spirit and in all directions.
> For the VOICE of a figure is compleat in all its parts.
> For a man speaks HIMSELF from the crown of his head to the sole of his feet.
> For a LION roars HIMSELF compleat from head to tail.
> For all these things are seen in the spirit which makes the beauty of prayer.
> For all whispers and unmusical sounds in general are of the Adversary.
>
> (*Jubilate Agno*, B 224–31)

Significantly, it is Satan (*the Adversary*) who speaks in jarring hints and whispers. That whole 'romantic' dimension of the subjective, obscure, ambivalent, and suggestive, is consigned by Smart to a secretive half-life in which truths that are mediated or glimpsed remain only half-truths. Genuine truth, by contrast, is unmediated, bold, open, and direct. Smart's is therefore the poetry of declaration, of speaking out, because the voice represents the whole character in its active spiritual state, *compleat in all its parts*, offering itself to its maker. In Smart's poetry there is much that is intimate and personal, but it tends to be declared openly, not filtered through a private consciousness. The unknown or the dimly known have no force in Smart's world, which is the reverse of Keats's romantic fascination with 'the burden of the Mystery' located in the 'dark Passages' of human experience.[53] Smart's poetic language breaks through things that veil or enclose. In the words of his Victorian admirer, Robert Browning, he 'pierced the screen / 'Twixt thing and word, lit language straight from soul'.[54]

Balancing the concept of 'expression' is that of 'impression' (they are two sides of the one coin), and the word is again specific – this is no vague impression, but an energetic 'pressing in'. Smart is aware of using language in a forceful and tactile way, imprinting a sense that the reader will take up. Once again there are no subjective mediations involved here, but an exact and direct transfer of meaning from the poet to us: 'For my talent is to give an impression upon words by punching, that when the reader casts his eye upon 'em, he takes up the image from the mould which I have made' (B 404). The word is a matrix or 'pattern' that allows the specific idea to be reproduced. What is impressed is then expressed.

In Smart, self-expression is by definition *praise*, and his poetry takes delight in the way every created thing plays its part. His most startling work, *Jubilate Agno* ('Rejoice in the Lamb'), a fragmentary manuscript first printed in 1939, is a sustained song of praise (what Smart called his 'Magnificat'), an offering back to God of his own creation in which Smart assumes the role of Psalmist: 'Rejoice in God, O ye Tongues: give the glory to the Lord, and the Lamb. / Nations, and languages, and every Creature, in which is the breath of Life' (A1–2). The universal life-force is nowhere more evident than in his cat, Jeoffry, a being who exemplifies the active Christian who expresses the divine in all his moods and activities:

> For he keeps the Lord's watch in the night against the adversary.
> For he counteracts the powers of darkness by his electrical skin and glaring eyes.
> For he counteracts the Devil, who is death, by brisking about the life.
> For in his morning orisons he loves the sun and the sun loves him.
> For he is of the tribe of Tiger. (B720–4)

Jeoffry represents the living energy that fills the created world ('For by stroaking of him I have found out electricity. / . . . For the Electrical fire is the spiritual substance, which God sends from heaven to sustain the bodies both of man and beast', B762–4). But we see in the above passage how Jeoffry also serves a moral purpose. From what has been said, it might be thought that Smart regards all energies as good, and all potential as positive. But this notion would empty life of its spiritual struggle and result in a Utopian self-indulgence. Smart avoids this trap in the way Milton does in *Paradise Lost*, by placing Jeoffry in a world of will and choice. He is the one creature in the poem who, like Adam and Eve in Paradise, has an active goodness that depends on a degree of self-restraint, on holding back from mere impulse:

> For he has the subtlety and hissing of a serpent, which in goodness he suppresses.
> For he will not do destruction, if he is well-fed, neither will he spit without provocation.
> For he purrs in thankfulness, when God tells him he's a good Cat. (B726–8)

Jeoffry could be the serpent in the Garden, but chooses not to be. With this self-prohibition he not only expresses Good, but suppresses Evil. Hence God's special message to him that *he's a good Cat*. In several ways, therefore, Jeoffry is the model of an active Christian, a pattern that repays our attention: 'For he is good to think on, if a man would express himself neatly' (B757).

Smart is concerned throughout his religious poetry with the idea of 'pattern' in its different senses, whether finding models for emulation, or discerning patterns and correspondences of many kinds. In his work these meanings tend to coincide. When he builds poems from the patterns of the liturgy or the church year it is to help his reader see the wider design and accumulate spiritual understanding; while in his fascination with numerological or cabbalistic patterning he seems to be reaching for underlying structures of a symbolic nature.[55] Smart loves collecting, enumerating, and cataloguing, and he tends to build up his poems by grouping individual units together to form sections for meditation. *A Song to David* (1763) is the most striking example of this architectural awareness, with its series of symmetrical sections gathered round a central block of ten stanzas (nos. 39–48 in a poem of 86 stanzas). This 'exercise upon the decalogue [i.e. the Ten Commandments]' as he calls it – one of several 'exercises' in the poem – acts structurally like the keystone of an arch, with these central faith-sustaining principles given a median position in the whole work. Another structural element is a seven-stanza unit (31–37) which superimposes the seven days of creation onto the Seven Pillars of

Wisdom, and shows the world taking shape like a massive church. To choose one example, the third pillar, *Eta* (each is given a Greek letter), corresponds to the third day of creation when the earth was planted ('Let the earth bring forth grass, the herb yielding seed, and the fruit-tree yielding fruit'):

> Eta with living sculpture breathes,
> With verdant carvings, flow'ry wreathes
>   Of never-wasting bloom;
> In strong relief his goodly base
> All instruments of labour grace,
>   The trowel, spade, and loom. (193–8)

This pillar puts Smart in mind of the relationship between divine and human art. God's *living* sculpture is literally so, and his *verdant carvings* are the work of the supreme creative artist. Represented on the pillar they form its decorative capital, from which the eye moves to its base, boldly carved *in strong relief* to remind us of mankind's eternal struggle to exploit (by building, digging, and weaving) the powers of nature that were inaugurated on that day. Smart creates a context in which the *never-wasting bloom* of art is balanced by implements representing human labour after the fall. But here, with a witty turn, *base labour* is entwined with *goodly grace*. This pillar is one of those from which, as the Bible says, 'Wisdom hath builded her house' (*Proverbs*, 9:1).

The poem finds its ultimate pattern in King David himself, considered in his combined role as poet of the Psalms and planner of the temple at Jerusalem. According to Robert Lowth in his *Lectures on the Sacred Poetry of the Hebrews* (1753), a book well known to Smart, David ruled Israel at a time when 'the arts of music and poetry were in their most flourishing state'. Lowth identifies the Jewish 'prophet' (*nabi*) as the original poet-musician: 'the prophetic office had a most strict connexion with the poetic art. They had one common name, one common origin, one common author, the Holy Spirit'. These divinely inspired proto-bards were trained in 'colleges of prophets' where they 'devoted themselves entirely to the exercises and study of religion . . . celebrating the praises of Almighty God in hymns and poetry'.[56] In *A Song to David* Smart seems to be presenting himself as a *nabi* in these terms. But in his own 'exercises' he is also taking on the architectural challenge, as if filling the role of Solomon, David's son, who was entrusted with the temple's building: 'Take heed now', David tells Solomon, 'for the Lord hath chosen thee to build an house for the sanctuary: be strong, and do it. Then David gave to Solomon his son the pattern of the porch, and of the houses thereof . . . the pattern of all that he had by the spirit' (1 Chron. 28:10–12); 'And David said to Solomon his son, Be strong and of good courage, and do it' (28:20). It is with an evident sense of triumph at the completion of his own structure that Smart declares in the final lines of the poem: 'And now the matchless deed's atchiev'd, / DETERMIN'D, DAR'D, and DONE' (515–6).

In choosing King David as his pattern, Smart was returning to the ultimate origins of his art. He accepted the contemporary theory that the historical David was the original for Orpheus (the mythic poet who could charm inanimate objects with his harp), and that in the Hebrew Bible was to be found the primary 'spirit' of poetry. In his poem *On the Goodness of the Supreme Being* (1756) Smart invoked this cluster of ideas to inspire himself for his great subject: 'ORPHEUS, for so the Gentiles call'd thy name, / Israel's sweet Psalmist, . . . / . . . in this breast / Some portion of thy genuine spirit breathe' (1–11). As we have seen in this chapter, the conviction that poetry was a *genuine spirit*, an animating 'breath' coeval with the first human breath on earth, led a number of eighteenth-century poets to find inspiration in the ancient oral tradition where it had been preserved, and to associate poetry especially with the vocal powers. Taking on variously the voices of bard, minstrel, psalmist and prophet they wanted their readers to become an audience and to hear verse in a fresh way. The poets' aims were not modest, their motives and methods might raise questions, but each of them developed a strong individual identity and extended poetic language in new directions.

Notes

1. Towards the end of the century some writers were wishing to distinguish the *genuine* from the *authentic*. Richard Watson, Bishop of Llandaff, wrote: 'A genuine book, is that which was written by the person whose name it bears, as the author of it. An authentic book, is that which relates matters of fact, as they really happened' (*An Apology for the Bible* [1796], II, 33. See *OED* 'genuine' 3.

2. Gray – Mason. *Correspondence*, ed. Toynbee and Whibley, II, 502.

3. James Thomson and David Mallet, *Alfred: A Masque Represented before Their Royal Highnesses the Prince and Princess of Wales, at Clifden, On the First of August, 1740* (London, 1740), pp. 42–3.

4. *British Magazine*, July 1760. *Collected Works of Oliver Goldsmith*, ed. Arthur Friedman (Oxford, 1966), III, 119. On Carolan, see Fiona Stafford, *The Last of The Race: The Growth of a Myth from Milton to Darwin* (Oxford, 1994), pp. 84–7.

5. Preface to *Fragments of Ancient Poetry* (2nd ed. 1760). Many oral ballads were attributed to Oisin mac Fhinn, the legendary Gaelic bard and warrior, whose mythical history features in Irish manuscripts from the twelfth century onwards.

6. Gray – Wharton [c. 20 June 1760]. *Correspondence*, II, 680.

7. Fragment 8. *The Poems of Ossian and Related Works*, ed. Howard Gaskill, with an introduction by Fiona Stafford (Edinburgh, 1996) p. 18.

8. For parallel texts of 'The Six Bards', see *The Poems of Ossian*, ed. Malcolm Laing, 2 vols (Edinburgh, 1805), II, 414–42. There are some verbal adjustments between the versions.

9. For a full account of Macpherson and the 'Ossian' controversy, see Fiona Stafford, *The Sublime Savage. A Study of James Macpherson and the Poems of Ossian* (Edinburgh, 1988).

10. Printed in *The Poems of Ossian and Related Works*, pp. 329–41.

11. Nick Groom, *The Making of Percy's Reliques* (Oxford, 1999), p. 92.

12. Percy – Evans, 24 December 1765. *The Correspondence of Thomas Percy & Evan Evans*, ed. Aneirin Lewis (Baton Rouge, 1957), p. 117. See Groom, p. 80.

13. Joseph Warton, *Essay on the Writings and Genius of Pope* (1756), p. x. The statement forms part of Warton's prefatory letter to Edward Young, to whom the volume is dedicated.

14. *The Poems of Ossian and Related Works*, p. 356.

15. Sublimity and pathos are poetic ideals in Young's *Conjectures on Original Composition* (1759).

16. Burke, *A Philosophical Enquiry into the Origin of Our Ideas of the Sublime and Beautiful* (1757), I. vii.

17. *Fingal*, Book IV. *The Poems of Ossian and Related Works*, p. 84.

18. Tom Keymer reveals fascinating links between the two texts: 'both document the obsessive yet finally unavailing struggles of their presiding voices to recover and transmit, in memory and language, this otherwise fugitive past' ('Narratives of Loss: The *Poems of Ossian* and *Tristram Shandy*', in *From Gaelic to Romantic*, ed. Fiona Stafford and Howard Gaskill [Amsterdam and Atlanta, 1998], pp. 79–96).

19. *Temora*, Book III. *The Poems of Ossian and Related Works*, pp. 249–50.

20. 'The Songs of Selma' (end). *The Poems of Ossian and Related Works*, p. 170.

21. 'Ode of the Months, composed by Gwilym Ddu of Arfon, to Sir Gruffudd Llwyd, of Tregarnedd and Dinorweg', in Evan Evans, *Some Specimens of the Poetry of the Antient Welsh Bards. Translated into English, with Explanatory Notes on the Historical Passages . . .* (London: R. and J. Dodsley, 1764), p. 47.

22. 'The Triumphs of Owen. A Fragment', 15–18, first published in Gray's *Poems* (1768). The three others were printed in 1775 after his death.

23. See *Spectator* 70 and 74 (21, 25 May 1711). Bond, I, 297–322. At the end of no. 74 Addison conceded: 'I feared my own Judgment would have looked too singular on such a Subject, had not I supported it by the Practice and Authority of *Virgil*'.

24. *A Collection of Old Ballads, Corrected from the Best and most Ancient Copies Extant*, 3 vols (London: James Roberts, 1723–5), I, iii–iv. See Albert B. Friedman, *The Ballad Revival* (Chicago, 1961), pp. 146–54.

25. Thomas Blackwell, *An Enquiry into the Life and Writings of Homer. The Second Edition* (London, 1736), pp. 105, 34–5, 25.

26. *Observations on the Faerie Queene* (1754), p. 114. Warton printed *Hardyknute* in his verse anthology *The Union* (1753).

27. Text from *The Union*, ed. Thomas Warton, 3rd ed. (1766), p. 166.

28. Gray – Horace Walpole, [April 1760]. *Correspondence*, ed. Toynbee and Whibley, II, 665; Warton, *Observations on the Fairy Queen* (2nd ed. 1762), I, 156.

29. On Percy's 'inventive editing', see Groom, *The Making of Percy's Reliques*, pp. 164, 226.

30. See *The Works of Allan Ramsay*, ed. Burns Martin, 6 vols (Edinburgh and London, 1951–74), IV, 71. I am grateful to Dr Melvin Kersey for this reference.

31. *Reliques*, II, 88. This was William Thomson, who published *Orpheus Caledonius or a Collection of the best Scotch Songs* (1722). In the 1770s Sir Walter Scott was taught to recite *Hardyknute* before he could read (J.G. Lockhart, *Memoirs of the Life of Sir Walter Scott*, 7 vols [1837–8], I, 83).

32. William Duff, *An Essay on Original Genius* (London, 1767), pp. viii–ix.

33. See Nick Groom, 'Thomas Rowlie Preeste', in *Early Romantics: Perspectives in British Poetry from Pope to Wordsworth*, ed. Thomas Woodman (Houndmills, 1998), pp. 242–55.

34. 'But a want of genius will be no longer imputed to this period of our poetical history, if the poems . . . are genuine' (*History*, II, 139).

35. One fragment showed that Rowley thought of the printing press twenty years before Caxton introduced it to England. See *Works*, ed. Taylor, p. 60.

36. With the 'Mynstrelles Song' from *Ælla* Rowley illustrated Thomas Percy's argument in the prefatory essay to the *Reliques* (1765) that medieval minstrels were 'the genuine successors of the ancient Bards' (I, xv).

37. See Nicholas Roe, *John Keats and the Culture of Dissent* (Oxford, 1997), p. 95.

38. In fact, St Mary Redcliffe was completed c. 1380, and the historical William Canynge (d. 1474) had been only its repairer and improver.

39. Chatterton – Walpole, 14 April 1769 [first draft]. *Works*, ed. Taylor, p. 272.

40. Keats – Reynolds, 21 September 1819. One example of Chatterton's avoidance of 'French idiom' may be his reluctance to place an adjective after the noun (as in *Orders Gray*).

41. *Enquiry into the Life and Writings of Homer* (1736 ed.), pp. 65–6.

42. Burns – Dr John Moore, 2 August 1787. *The Letters of Robert Burns*, ed. G. Ross Roy (Oxford, 1985), I, 144.

43. On the authorship of this disputed poem, see *The Poems and Songs of Robert Burns*, ed. James Kinsley, 2 vols (Oxford, 1968), p. 1528; and Alan Bold, *A Burns Companion* (Houndmills, 1991), pp. 281–5.

44. Nicholas Roe, 'Authenticating Robert Burns', *Essays in Criticism*, 46 (1996), 195–218 (p. 202). The essay is reprinted in *Critical Essays on Robert Burns*, ed. Carol McGuirk (New York, 1998), pp. 208–24.

45. Burns – Agnes M'Lehose, 18 March 1788. *Letters*, I, 265.

46. Quoted by James Mackay, *A Biography of Robert Burns* (Edinburgh, 1992), p. 243. Stewart also noted that 'his dread of anything approaching meanness or servility rendered his manner somewhat decided and hard'.

47. Henry Mackenzie's phrase in his review of the Kilmarnock volume in *The Lounger*, 9 December 1786 (*Robert Burns: The Critical Heritage*, ed. Donald A Low [London, 1974], p. 70).

48. In the Kilmarnock glossary Burns says he has omitted 'words that are universally known' (p. 236).

49. Raymond Bentman, 'Robert Burns's Use of Scottish Diction', in *From Sensibility to Romanticism: Essays Presented to Frederick A. Pottle*, ed. Frederick W. Hilles and Harold Bloom (New York, 1965), pp. 239–58; reprinted in *Critical Essays on Robert Burns*, pp. 79–94 (p. 79).

50. Alan Bold, *A Burns Companion*, pp. 81, 87.

51. Quoted by Mark W. Booth, *The Experience of Songs* (New Haven and London, 1981), p. 127.

52. Christopher Smart, 'Hymn 1: New Year', from 'Hymns and Spiritual Songs for the Fasts and Festivals of the Church of England', in *A Translation of the Psalms of David* (1765).

53. Keats – Reynolds, 3 May 1818.

54. Robert Browning, 'With Christopher Smart', 114–5, from *Parleyings with Certain People* (1887).

55. See Chris Mounsey, *Christopher Smart, Clown of God* (Lewisburg, 2001), pp. 229–30.

56. Robert Lowth, *Lectures on the Sacred Poetry of the Hebrews*, trans. G. Gregory, 2 vols (London, 1787), II, 194; II, 18; II, 12. Lowth's lectures were delivered while Professor of Poetry at Oxford, 1741–50, and first published as *De sacra poesi Hebraeorum praelectiones* (1753).

Chapter 10

Economies of Landscape

Traditionally the eighteenth-century landscape has always seemed to offer a neatly disposed and settled prospect, one of foreground pastoral (usually with nibbling sheep or a crystal stream), a middle-distance picturesque (perhaps with a grot or ruined abbey), and a distant sublime (of mountains that are far enough away not to be threatening – and certainly not to be walked over). In this stereotyped picture the landscape is irredeemably pastoralised, with a matching poetic diction that populates the scene with the 'sportive train', the 'feathery people', or Thomas Maude's 'fleecy bleaters'.[1] The age that conceived of landscape gardening as one of the liberal arts[2] might seem to be longing for a nature that is restrained and bounded, like the Reverend John Pomfret's prescription for his ideal country estate (it is not too deep in the country, we notice):

> Near some fair Town I'd have a private Seat,
> Built Uniform, not little, nor too great:
> Better, if on a rising Ground it stood,
> Fields on this side, on that a Neighb'ring Wood.
> It shou'd within no other Things contain,
> But what are Useful, Necessary, Plain . . .
> A little Garden, grateful to the Eye,
> And a cool Rivulet run Murmuring by . . . (*The Choice*, 5–14)

Pomfret's style, like the style of his estate, is *Useful, Necessary, Plain*. It is an exercise in composure where everything is appropriately positioned and functional, creating an emblem of poetic ease. With Horace and Virgil on his study shelf just a few steps from his riverside walk, Pomfret's landscape captures a life of emotional containment, which as the poem proceeds becomes neurotic in its fastidiousness, its repeated shunning of excess or disturbance ('no surly Care / Wou'd venture to assault my Soul, or dare / Near my Retreat to hide one secret Snare', 131–3). Even the poem's date, 1700, shows perfect decorum. Pomfret is the ideal host to open any anthology of eighteenth-century verse.

But he is so because his picture of a civilised country life (developed from Horace's celebration of his Sabine farm in *Satire II.6*) represents the kind of static composition that eighteenth-century descriptive poetry was to leave behind. Pomfret's scene works like a canvas backdrop on the stage, capturing the essence of a location but unable to respond to the human drama. In contrast, later poets view landscape with a restless and searching eye, and with a mind conscious of its own perceptions. It was James Thomson who brought a dynamic mode of seeing into engagement with an ever-shifting nature, and after reading *The Seasons* (1730) no-one would look at landscape in quite the same way again. Even a century later the great landscape-painters Turner and Constable were attaching quotations from *The Seasons* to some of their best known pictures. Constable's *Hadleigh Castle* (1829) and Turner's *Dunstanborough Castle: Sunrise after a Squally Night* (1798) both take their motto from the same Thomson passage on returning sunlight:

> The Precipice abrupt,
> Projecting Horror on the blacken'd Flood,
> Softens at thy Return. The Desart joys
> Wildly, thro' all his melancholy Bounds.
> Rude Ruins glitter; and the briny Deep,
> Seen from some pointed Promontory's Top,
> Far to the blue Horizon's utmost Verge,
> Restless, reflects a floating Gleam. ('Summer', 163–70)[3]

Thomson's emotional projections and reflections intensify the dynamism of the scene. Throughout *The Seasons* he is interested in movement and change as registered in the medium itself – in light, language, air, sound. As a delighted Newtonian he understands that the play of forces in nature can be extreme, the contrasts stark and even contradictory (the precipice *softens*; the desert *joys*; rudeness *glitters*), but as the *restless* prospect veers between tragedy and hope this energy guarantees the system's continued life.

After Thomson, movement and change were inextricably part of the natural scene, but later descriptive poets tended to shy away from an all-encompassing Nature (capitalised) and sublime sweeps across time and space. Attention turned increasingly to specific and more localised landscapes, where ideas of growth and change were still crucial, but operated in more social terms. In exploring some of the landscape poetry of the second half of the eighteenth century, this chapter will continue to stress the dynamic principle discussed in Chapter 7. But in place of the macrocosm of the Newtonian system and the sublimities of the universe, the focus will be on the economics of the English countryside and the microcosm of the estate, the village, and the local scene. The 'mixed' British constitution will remain a contentious issue, but no longer as a reflection of the System of Nature or divine revelation. By the 1760s the mounting political pressures were coming from a new direction – not from theological dispute but from social change. Divine Right was less of an issue than rural depopulation. In this chapter, therefore, the poet is more of an economist than a visionary, becoming concerned with the way resources are managed and structures organised. This is 'œconomy' in the wider eighteenth-century sense, which included the financial economy (expanding as never before) but also encompassed notions like 'the œconomy of the body', 'the œconomy of the mind', 'the œconomy of nature', and 'the civil œconomy'.[4] The development of these concepts testifies to the century's interest in how forces operate within a system, and how any organised structure manages its resources (the Newtonian system could be understood as an 'economy' in this sense). When Milton, in his introduction to *Samson Agonistes* (1673), discussed the play's 'œconomy, or disposition of the fable', he was anticipating how eighteenth-century poetry would also be conscious of the literary implications of the idea.

Increasingly from mid-century the English landscape was bearing the imprint of rapid commercial expansion. With 'improvement' as the watchword, land use was being reorganised to exploit a national market economy by achieving what we now call 'economies of scale'. The countryside was reshaped by the appropriation and enclosure of common land, the 'engrossing' of smallholdings into larger and more efficient units, and the increasing spread of private estates. The agriculturalist Arthur Young, an enthusiast for the 'improvers', wrote in 1771 that 'Nature takes a new face under their hands; whole counties are converted at once from deserts, into finely cultivated countries'.[5] Young over-dramatises of course, but in individual cases the transformation of the local scene could appear both sudden and complete. In this context, space, being a finite resource, becomes a socio-economic concern; and all the writers considered in this chapter are in different ways conscious of spatial matters, both in the scenes they describe and in the organisation of their poems. Unlike the sublime expanses limited only by the poet's imagination, these economic spaces impose constraints and pressures. Because land is part of a nexus of wealth and property, the idea of landscape itself raises contentious issues. Questions of ownership and use are always in the background, and the concept of 'private space' is here less a subjective realm than an ostentatious 'privatised' lifestyle. Goldsmith in *The Deserted Village* (1770) makes the point bluntly:

> The man of wealth and pride,
> Takes up a space that many poor supplied;
> Space for his lake, his park's extended bounds,
> Space for his horses, equipage, and hounds . . . (277–80)

Set against an older subsistence economy '[w]hen every rood of ground maintained its man' (58), this improved scene has wastefully extended the private at the expense of the social. The happy crowd on the village green pictured at the poem's opening is cramped, but happily so – human sociability enjoys eye contact. Pope understood this when he pictured a mighty landowner shrunk by the vastness of his windswept acres: 'His building is a Town, / His pond an Ocean, his parterre a Down: / Who but must laugh, the Master when he sees, / A puny insect, shiv'ring at a breeze!' (*Epistle to Burlington* [1731], 105–8). Eighteenth-century landscapes bear the imprint of the minds that organise them, and the wealthy Timon is set out on display for us in Pope's poem. We walk through the sad formal emptiness of his life, wondering at the way each feature dissipates human social energies; everything in the scene appears stretched out or rigidified so that nothing is in a living relationship with anything else. But where Pope has a final good word for Timon as an economic stimulus ('A bad Taste employs more hands, and diffuses Expence more than a good one'),[6] Goldsmith's nameless improver cannot accommodate a peasantry. He drives smallholders from the common and forces the villagers to seek a livelihood in the city or in America.

Economic growth at home and colonial expansion abroad meant that traders and speculators became rich. To be a landed gentleman was no longer the preserve of the aristocracy. Income from India or the West Indies built many a country estate, and British 'nabobs' laid out their fortunes in lawns and mansions. It has been calculated that in the Chiltern Hills alone (to the north-west of London) there were in 1760 nearly four hundred enclosed parks, and by 1820 the number had almost doubled.[7] One result was that a new wealthy elite less concerned with local traditions and duties was displacing the village squire – and the squire's son was learning the new 'improving' ways. What Paul Langford has called 'a crisis of paternalism in the 1760s and 1770s'[8] has been seen by others as the inevitable collapse of an old 'feudal' order (in the looser modern sense) that had been crumbling since early Stuart times. The process had become part of poetic tradition too. In the seventeenth-century country-house or 'retirement' poetry that developed in the tradition of Ben Jonson's *To Penshurst* (1616), the celebration of a thriving local estate carried a political message about the dangers of corruption and disunity at national level.[9] If the mid-eighteenth-century landscape was unscarred by civil war or violent revolution, it was being subjected to organic changes that were no less marked, and poets were ready to engage with them. They understood how an expanding economy inevitably brought growth and change. As writers they were interested in whether such forces could be accommodated within existing structures, or whether they needed more flexible poetic economies themselves.

All these matters are brought into focus in Mary Leapor's 'Crumble Hall' (1751), a poem that enacts the eighteenth-century economic revolution with dramatic and satiric effect, and with a keen sense of its spatial implications. Thanks to her experiences as a kitchen maid at Edgcote House, Northamptonshire, Leapor knows this rambling medieval hall from the inside, and while the current owner plans its replacement by an elegant modern mansion she helps us to explore the Gothic labyrinth before it is swept away. She recalls its old generosities:

> *Crumble-Hall*, whose hospitable Door
> Has fed the Stranger, and reliev'd the Poor;
> Whose *Gothic* Towers, and whose rusty Spires,
> Were known of old to Knights, and hungry Squires.
> There powder'd Beef, and Warden-Pies, were found;
> And Pudden dwelt within her spacious Bound . . .
> Here came the Wights, who battled for Renown,
> The sable Frier, and the russet Clown:
> The loaded Tables sent a sav'ry Gale,
> And the brown Bowls were crown'd with simp'ring Ale;
> While the Guests ravag'd on the smoking Store,
> Till their stretch'd Girdles would contain no more. (13–28)

The domestic economy of this poem celebrates mixtures of all kinds. What might seem mock-heroic juxtapositions are here friendly associations. The Gothic towers and the pudding in the kitchen define between them the *spacious Bound* that once contained the adventuring knight, the mendicant friar, and the peasant (*Clown*). Like its well supplied guests, the house becomes the embodiment of generous containment. It is crammed full of details, and as Leapor takes us on a tour we notice that there seems to be room for everything to cohabit happily. In the roof of the great hall, above the carved heraldry with its royal associations, 'the pleas'd Spider plants her peaceful Loom' (46). The humblest creatures find a life here, and we ourselves follow in the steps of the mice, who 'safely . . . through yon dark Passage run' (52). When we come to the kitchen with the hanging hams and 'steaming Odours' we know we have reached the heart of the building. It is the kingdom ruled by Sophronia the cook, a figure who embodies this household economy of well-mixed ingredients:

> *Sophronia* sage! whose learned Knuckles know
> To form round Cheese-cakes of the pliant Dough;
> To bruise the Curd, and thro' her Fingers squeeze
> *Ambrosial* Butter with the temper'd Cheese:
> Sweet Tarts and Pudden, too, her Skill declare;
> And the soft Jellies, hid from baneful Air. (115–20)

In Crumble Hall everything is deliciously mixed up together, and just as the curd squeezes between the cook's fingers the reader is expertly twisted and turned through the narrow passageways of the house: 'We count the Stairs, and to the Right ascend . . / . . From hence we turn . . / . . Shall we proceed?— . . .' (72–85)

> Would you go farther?—Stay a little then:
> Back thro' the Passage—down the Steps again;
> Thro' yon dark Room—Be careful how you tread
> Up these steep Stairs—or you may break your Head.
> These Rooms are furnish'd amiably and full:
> Old Shoes, and Sheep-ticks bred in Stacks of Wool . . . (94–9)

In this benign confusion comfortable old things are not thrown away, and even the minute *Sheep-ticks* are part of a Gothic eco-system. The house, like the poem, has no regular plan, and as we move through the cramped spaces we take in its sensuous and vivid life. The only occasion when the verse feels bland and insecure is the moment Leapor ('Mira') emerges from a small door in the roof, and the whole estate is laid out before her: 'Here a gay Prospect meets the ravish'd Eye: / Meads, Fields, and Groves, in beauteous Order lie' (105–6). The couplet is suitably characterless. It is an uneasy glimpse of an expansive order that, unlike the jumbled interior, has no room for her. Refusing the grand survey, it is almost with relief that she hurries down: 'From hence the Muse precipitant is hurl'd, / And drags down *Mira* to the nether World' (107–8).

But if visual command is impossible, back at ground level Leapor can wander 'in frolick Fancy' through the gardens and make them her enchanted grove of romance, populated by elves and nightingales. Suddenly, however, the description is halted by a 'Scream'. To the sound of 'The *Dryads* howling for their threaten'd Shades' (166) she watches the beginning of the improvements that will sweep Edgcote away. The owner is widening his prospects; but in doing so he is cutting himself off from what she suggests was a more natural and humane past:

> And shall those Shades . . .
> Whose rev'rend Oaks have known a hundred Springs;
> Shall these ignobly from their Roots be torn,
> And perish shameful, as the abject Thorn;
> While the slow Carr bears off their aged Limbs,
> To clear the Way for Slopes, and modern Whims;
> Where banish'd Nature leaves a barren Gloom,
> And aukward Art supplies the vacant Room? (169–78)

The phrase *vacant Room* suggests how spiritually empty the new spaces will be.

At this period a combination of *aukward Art* and *modern Whims* was also beginning to shape the suburban landscape of England, as a new class of successful tradespeople and men of business sought the rural life. Around the growing towns, and especially on the outskirts of London, land was being parcelled out into small estates so that the *nouveaux riches* could possess their 'country box', a compact version of a rural mansion. Where Lancelot 'Capability' Brown (1715–83) reshaped the grander landscapes like Nuneham Courtenay and Blenheim, these more contained spaces could be furnished out of the Halfpenny brothers' published design-books featuring the latest custom-made wooden temples and summer-houses in the Gothic or Chinese styles. This is the characteristic landscape of the new market economy exploited by men like 'Sir Thrifty' in Robert Lloyd's 'The Cit's Country Box' (1757). Thrifty is a 'cit' who makes his money in the City of London and drives out at weekends to his suburban retreat:

> The wealthy Cit, grown old in trade,
> Now wishes for the rural shade,
> And buckles to his one-horse chair,
> Old *Dobbin*, or the founder'd mare;
> While wedg'd in closely by his side,
> Sits Madam, his unwieldy bride,
> With *Jacky* on a stool before 'em,
> And out they jog in due decorum. (1–8)

For Thrifty, space (like everything else) is at a premium, and Lloyd reflects this *decorum* in his own poetic management. His jog-trot octosyllabics are tightly packed like neatly stacked shelves. Everything is concise and handy – 'Some three or four mile out of town, / (An hour's ride will bring you down,) . . .' (41–2). When the couple reach their chosen site, Lady Thrifty's language is a compromise of the aesthetic with the practical: 'It is a charming spot of ground; / So sweet a distance for a ride, / And all about so *countrified!* / 'Twould come to but a trifling price / To make it quite a paradise . . .' (59–62). Milton's description of the Garden of Eden lay behind many an eighteenth-century landscaped garden,[10] but the Thriftys (blest mortals) have it easy – the *trifling price* for their regained Paradise is just 'a few hundreds from the stocks' (39).

Lady Thrifty wants to update their property; and in a parody of the language of 'improvement' she insists they enlarge their prospects by a smooth front lawn that will catch the envious eyes of travellers: 'Nothing its views to incommode, / But quite laid open to the road . . .' (77–8). Equipped with the full package of modern 'Taste' ('Genius, Fancy, Judgment, Goût, / Whim, Caprice, Je-ne-scai-quoi, Virtù', 91–2) they set their workmen on:

> The trav'ler with amazement sees
> A temple, Gothic, or Chinese,
> With many a bell, and tawdry rag on,
> And crested with a sprawling dragon;
> A wooden arch is bent astride
> A ditch of water, four foot wide,
> With angles, curves, and zigzag lines,
> From Halfpenny's exact designs. (101–8)

The contours of nature have been forgotten. In this 1750s version of garden-centre aesthetic the lines are strained and awkward (*sprawling, bent, zigzag*), and the fussy haphazardness is amusingly resisted by the closing phrase. In the preface to his *Rural Architecture in the Chinese Taste* (1752) Will Halfpenny had indeed expressed concern for the *exact* erection of his structures:

> The few following Essays are an Attempt to rescue those agreeable Decorations from the many bad Consequences usually attending such slight Structures, when unskilfully erected: Which must often unavoidably happen at a Distance from this Metropolis, without such Help as, I flatter myself, the Workmen will here find laid down . . .

'Taste' was spreading from London to the provinces, and the results were not uniformly happy. Without a 'Capability' Brown or a Repton to guide them, the new middle class had to keep a close watch on their workmen. In attempting to capture this consumerist lifestyle (the modern terms are appropriate here) Lloyd is founding a whole tradition of English suburban poetry culminating in the work of John Betjeman in the Twentieth Century.

Both emptiness and clutter had their drawbacks, and it was not always possible to find a happy medium. To make 'Nature' your guide or to 'consult the Genius of the Place in all', as Pope's *Epistle to Burlington* had recommended, suited the aristocratic estate; but in the practical age of improvement, following nature could easily turn into Lady Thrifty's 'countrifying', and the *Genius of the Place* might be the only thing left when the local villagers had been forcibly rehoused.[11] Goldsmith's attack on this practice in *The Deserted Village* (1770) pointedly leaves the displacing landscape out. As discussed in Chapter 5, the fractured economy of his poem registers a break with the past in terms of structural and stylistic discontinuities. Goldsmith intended to reflect on a national crisis in which both luxury and poverty were intensifying at the expense of social cohesion. In response to his argument (reinforced in the dedication to Sir Joshua Reynolds) the state of English rural life became a political issue.[12]

This is confirmed by a little known reply to Goldsmith in which the thriving English village comes to the nation's rescue. In an anonymous verse pamphlet, *The Frequented Village* (1771), evidently by Anthony King,[13] the poet sets out to recover an idyllic rural community and make the perfect village his model for a contented and stable Britain. King sets it against the evils of the city, where life is lived contrary to 'nature's rules', and 'wanton vices' are linked to 'ill got wealth'. His nameless village is a place 'where nature dwells, and innocency grows', a 'mimic Eden' of health and virtue, where the land is spontaneously productive with 'plenty's crop'. In a lovingly described setting, the young woo and marry, old age is respected, and the villagers indulge their favourite pastimes. Their lives find a focus in the church, where funerals, weddings, and Sunday services draw the people together:

> Mark, with what placid look, becoming air,
> The village circle to the church repair,
> That church, whose hallow'd spires devoutly shine,
> A sacred building, a long worshipp'd shrine . . . (221–4)

The church is at the centre of the *village circle*, just as the village is at the centre of King's nation. Here even the lisping children join in the service, and as the families wend their way home for a 'frugal meal' they discuss the sermon: 'Clean, not superb, with decency they walk, / And of the parson, and his merit talk' (229–30).

To see a gulf between country virtue and city vice was nothing new; but in King's hands they become two alternative models for Britain itself – two financial, social and moral economies that mark out a widening political divide. Rural community is set against metropolitan selfishness; frugality against luxury; British 'plenty' against imported wealth; the villagers' patriotism against the 'foreign hearts' of the urban rich. King puts his faith in 'village morals' (a phrase he uses without irony) as a means of renewing Britain. 'Religion, justice, piety live here', he declares, and his small community guided by 'sacred truth' is a contented nation in miniature. The poet is specific about this parallel. The village is the model for a place where truth's 'pure ensigns, instituted shine, / And stamp a people with a mark divine' (429–30). King hopes this institution will renovate Britain as a whole and make it a place where a genuine liberty dwells. For him it certainly did not dwell in the metropolis, where John Wilkes M.P. was the hero of the London freeholders with their dangerous cry of 'Wilkes and Liberty!'. He concludes that 'freedom properly we see, / When king, and people's sentiments agree' (455–6). The poet is anxious to distinguish his rural England from the political freedoms being sought by the 'friends of liberty' during the 1760s, a decade of rising prices and periodic recession when pressure for parliamentary and social reform was mounting.

A crucial element of King's parochial system is charity. With its description of a sick widow on her 'bed of grief' *The Frequented Village* acknowledges the fact of rural poverty, only to show it being alleviated by a visit from a benevolent 'wealthier dame' who brings charitable relief ('than which, no medicine gives /

Such balmy comfort, to delight our lives', 277–8). The poet's touching faith in the power of individual instincts to activate society seems naïve to us; but it represents his dynamic vision of a moral economy generated from localities like his – an alternative to the corrupt urban machine that drives the national system. He wants a benevolent current to activate all layers of society, much in the way a joyful exchange of kisses runs through his crowd at the wedding-feast:

> So, in electric tryals have I seen,
> When many hands conjointly met have been,
> When once the fire hath seal'd the crackling kiss,
> And the brisk flame communicated is,
> The shock once suffer'd, soon with speed expands,
> And pervious passage, forces thro' the hands. (299–304)

This multiple electric shock provides the poet with an image for a communal energy that could spread through Britain. King is careful to point out that his poem is not recommending rural retreat ('to seek refinement in an humble cell') but the reverse. He wants his village values to expand nationally ('rather let us emulation catch, / And from the peasant, full perfection snatch', 407–8).

Addressed amicably to Goldsmith, *The Frequented Village* offers a patriotic corrective to *The Deserted Village*'s pessimistic vision of Britain's emigrating peasantry ('I see the rural virtues leave the land', says Goldsmith). For all their differences, however, both poets believe there *are* 'rural virtues' worth rescuing. This was not the opinion of George Crabbe. In his two-book poem *The Village* (1783) Crabbe drew on his experiences as an apothecary at Aldeburgh, a fishing community on the flat and exposed Suffolk coast, to create an unrelenting picture of a blighted existence. Crabbe's poem is traditionally (and usefully) discussed as a challenge to Goldsmith's idealised Auburn.[14] But *The Frequented Village*, with its air of complacent optimism, its idealised descriptions, its pastoral rivalry between Tom and 'Corydon', its heart-warming cottage-scene, its reassuring episodes of visiting the sick and a village funeral (both chillingly reworked by Crabbe), make it in several ways an even more appropriate candidate for the anti-text to Crabbe's attack on the pastoral idealisations of village life.

Where King's village represents a nation blessed by a fruitful nature and at peace with itself, Crabbe's village clings to the edge, a place of 'sterile soil' and 'thin harvest' where 'Nature's niggard hand' puts all its power into the weeds that choke off other life:

> Rank weeds, that every art and care defy,
> Reign o'er the land and rob the blighted rye:
> There thistles stretch their prickly arms afar,
> And to the ragged infant threaten war;
> There poppies nodding, mock the hope of toil,
> There the blue bugloss paints the sterile soil;
> Hardy and high, above the slender sheaf,
> The slimy mallow waves her silky leaf;
> O'er the young shoot the charlock throws a shade,
> And the wild tare clings round the sickly blade ... (I, 67–76)

Images of hope, growth, and aspiration all turn negative. Crowding out the scene are a tangle of aggressively expansive *thistles*, hopelessly somnolent *poppies*, artily superficial *bugloss*, loftily flouncing *mallow*, gloomily oppressive *charlock*, cloyingly frustrating *tare*. With a bit of imagination we can find a human equivalent for each of them. Together they form an over rich, competitive, and predatory society, a parody of human energies. There is no harvest expected here, and infant growth is blighted.

Crabbe's poem was probably begun in 1780,[15] and the time of its writing coincides with years of national crisis and instability. Some historians have viewed the years 1779–84 as the period during the century when Britain came closest to revolution.[16] In the words of Ian Gilmour, 'the years 1779–84 saw invasion scares, ignominious defeat in the American war, industrial riots, religious disturbances, near revolt in Ireland, denunciation of the Crown in Parliament, a reform movement in the country, a government so feeble that it seemed bound to collapse, fluctuating ministries and almost every symptom of discontent and decay'.[17] Crabbe's poem was published in 1783, the year of the Peace of Versailles ending the traumatic American War, and it may be no coincidence that his description of unweeded fields recalls the Duke of Burgundy's speech during the final peace negotiations in Shakespeare's *Henry V* with its image of an exhausted land where only weeds flourish ('Wanting the scythe, all uncorrected, rank, / Conceives by idleness, and nothing teems / But hateful docks, rough thistles, kecksies, burrs . . .', V.ii. 50–2). A decade after the poems of Goldsmith and King the nation was if anything less stable and unified. Crabbe had memorably witnessed the Gordon Riots of June 1780 when for a week London was at the mercy of a mob of 60,000 sporting blue cockades, and between eight hundred and a thousand people were killed.[18]

Where King had pictured a contented valley, Crabbe gives us an uneasy seacoast. His villagers turn away from the sterile landscape to look expectantly out to sea – but their thoughts are not on trade. This is no *Windsor-Forest* (Pope's poem celebrating the economic benefits of a peace treaty). They seize what opportunities the ocean offers, which besides fishing consists of looting wrecks and smuggling. These villagers survive by subverting trade and substituting an economy of plunder and exploitation. They are as predatory as the sea itself. Crabbe's coastline becomes an emblem for a land vulnerable to the 'greedy waves' that eat away 'the lessening shore', 'Till some fierce tide, with more imperious sway, / Sweeps the low hut and all it holds away' (I, 127–8). Crabbe in fact confirms Goldsmith's analysis of a land where 'trade's proud empire hastes to swift decay' (*D.V.*, 429).

In *The Frequented Village* King had pictured a society whose communal rituals marked the different stages of the villagers' lives. A venerated old man, for example, is buried with due ceremony ('Up yonder hill, the decent mourners bend, / A crowded train, his funeral pomp attend', 165–6). Crabbe's version of the scene has a verbal echo ('Up yonder hill, behold how sadly slow / The bier moves winding from the vale below, I, 323–4), but there is a difference: Crabbe's crowd are distressed because the busy priest leaves the old man's grave unblessed. His version of the sick-bed visit is equally uncomfortable. Where King describes the arrival of a benevolent lady ('The widow's tears she charitably drys, / And wipes the trickling rivers from her eyes', 269–70), Crabbe's dying invalid finds no such sympathy ('For him no hand the cordial cup applies, / Or wipes the tear that stagnates in his eyes', I, 272–3). In Crabbe there is no charitable economy that helps to hold society together. In its place is the much-resented poor-rate ('the scrap'), a charge imposed on the villagers to support the parish poorhouse:

> Here sorrowing, they each kindred sorrow scan,
> And the cold charities of man to man.
> Whose laws indeed for ruin'd age provide,
> And strong compulsion plucks the scrap from pride;
> But still that scrap is bought with many a sigh,
> And pride embitters what it can't deny. (I, 246–251)

In Crabbe's village the economic system brings the worst out of everybody. It pulls against the grain of human nature and creates a niggardly, grudging quality reflected in the verse, which moves at an implacable steady pace throughout. In the above passage, words tend to restrain each other and positive impulses are negated: *kindred* and *charities* are shackled to *sorrow* and *cold*. The impetus of *provide* hardens into *compulsion*. What can't be denied is seized or dearly *bought*. Nothing is freely given or happily accepted. Crabbe presents a chilling world in which individuals are wary of each other and keep their distance, even in their suffering ('Forsaken wives and mothers never wed; / Dejected widows with unheeded tears', I, 237–8). The poorhouse seems to reflect the itemised, disconnected world outside. If Thomson in *The Seasons* showed the sweeping brush-strokes of a Turner or a Constable, then Crabbe's art is closer to engraving. 'He is his own landscape painter, and engraver too', wrote William Hazlitt in 1818: 'His pastoral scenes seem pricked on paper in little dotted lines'.[19]

Crabbe's landscape is an uneasy one. At the beginning of *The Village* he promises to show 'the real picture' (I, 5); yet his *real* is not what we would call 'observed reality', but is closer to 'the truth about the way things are'. These are not, of course, the same thing. As Gavin Edwards has shown, Crabbe finds it useful to create a village that is both strongly characterised and yet generic, less a visual observation than a timeless record. Edwards notes how the poem employs a 'universalising present tense' that hovers between individual truth and general truth, leaving it unclear how 'typical' his village is.[20] Instead of individual stories there are grainy snapshots, and a 'before' and 'after' picture will substitute for a missing narrative. In this way Crabbe's village is an inorganic concept – nothing is developing or growing except weeds, and we don't discover how things became as they are. Although it gives us a vivid landscape, *The Village* is not, therefore, a topographical poem.

Descriptions of specific places became increasingly popular in the second half of the century. Areas of Britain were being veritably mapped out by poems that connected a local landscape with its history – in 1779 Dr Johnson commented that poets 'have left scarce a corner of the island not dignified either by rhyme or blank verse'.[21] It was this linking of the dimensions of space and time that gave the topographical poem its concern with ideas of continuity and variety. The time-scale of some could be comprehensive. In *Edge-Hill, or, The Rural Prospect Delineated and Moralized* (four books, 1767) Richard Jago surveys his home territory on the Warwickshire-Oxfordshire border in a historical sweep that embraces the creation of the world and the end of time itself. Like many local poets he is fascinated by the processes that have shaped his landscape. He considers what 'furious Shock' must have formed the 'once fluid' hills when they made 'Stranger-Fossils . . / . . Or Shell marine incorp'rate with themselves' (I, 144–6). This image of varied materials organically combining comes naturally to the topographical poem, which incorporates individual local elements (landmarks, people, buildings, events, and institutions) into an idea of nationhood. Topographical poets are interested in how things evolve, decline, or grow. The principle of variety becomes a challenge, and their poems tend to celebrate diversity, as if the more multifarious the text's fabric is, the stronger is the spirit holding it all together.

In Jago's poem, the major country estates of the present (some forty of them) are plotted across a landscape marked with the remains of the past. Myth slides into history, and the land is overwritten with generational layers: Roman features, the Saxon traces of Hengist and Offa, sites associated with the Wars of the Roses, and inevitably Edgehill itself where the first battle of the Civil War was fought in 1642. Like many another topographical poem, Jago's *Edge-Hill* looks back to their literary ancestor, *Coopers Hill* (1642) by the Royalist Sir John Denham, a poem published in that momentous year, and the text which for Johnson had inaugurated the tradition of 'local poetry'. But Denham's survey of the Thames valley was also his vision of a Britain on the brink of terrible factional violence. Once the Civil War was over, the topographical poem had a natural investment in encouraging productive human energies and in showing how competing interests could be usefully accommodated. *Coopers Hill* served as a reminder of what was at stake. By the mid-eighteenth century Great Britain had become a strong and wealthy kingdom, but lurking just beneath the surface were memories of how precarious civil peace could be. As his poem draws to a close Jago comes to the field where the Civil War had begun, 'Yon' Grass-green Mount, where waves the planted Pine, / And whispers to the Winds the mournful Tale' (IV, 559–60). Recalling Virgil's picture in the *Georgics* of the Italian landscape scarred by Rome's civil war, Jago's native soil yields reminders of the past:

> Still as the Plowman breaks the clotted Glebe,
> He ever and anon some Trophy finds,
> The Relicks of the War—or rusty Spear,
> Or canker'd Ball; but, from Sepulchral Soil,
> Cautious he turns aside the lifted Share,
> Lest haply, at its Touch, uncover'd Bones
> Shou'd start to View . . . (IV, 563–9)

The decaying remains of the *rusty Spear* and the *canker'd* cannonball are sinking reassuringly into antiquity, but after a century and a quarter it is still possible to imagine the sudden return of old skeletons.

In the preface Jago declares that he has written his poem out of 'Affection ... for his native Country' (p. vi); but *Country* here means 'local district' (it is 'his native Country, lying at the Foot of this celebrated Mountain'). The momentary ambiguity highlights the subtle way *Edge-Hill* touches on national issues. In mapping out a peaceful and flourishing midlands as an image for Britain, Jago is offering a view of the nation that is politically coloured. A country clergyman with three Warwickshire livings, the Reverend Jago celebrates not only King Charles I's Royalist generals for their 'duteous Loyalty, / With Love of regal Sway' (IV, 401–2), but also the opposing parliamentarians with their 'sacred Love of Liberty, / Dear Liberty! when rightly understood, / Prime social Bliss!' How different, he suggests, from the Wilkite cries for constitutional liberty being heard in 1767: 'Oh! may no Sons of Fraud / Usurp thy Name, to veil their dark Designs / Of vile Ambition, or licentious Rage!' (IV, 409–13). With this hit at the motives of the *licentious* Wilkes we are brought back to the streets of contemporary London. At this period, as we saw in *The Frequented Village*, behind the idyllic country landscape was a noisier and more unruly cityscape.

During the 1770s, under the administration of Lord North, the old Tory squirearchy had a new political lease of life. The bedrock of ministerial support came from independent country gentlemen who, in Paul Langford's words, 'continued to consider themselves true representatives of the old Tory tradition':

> It was their Church and King mentality, their latent royalism and authoritarianism, which did much to create a coherent court politics during these years. They were a source of immense strength to North, himself ... by temperament more a country gentleman than an aristocrat. On major issues of the day he had a better claim to represent the broad body of landed opinion than any other minister of the century.[22]

Not surprisingly, landscape poetry of the period often expressed this *broad body of landed opinion*. The concept of breadth reflected the degree to which local loyalties could be relied upon to reinforce national ones, and it came naturally to the topographical poem, whose 'prospects' presented a Britain rooted in the land, its history and traditions.

These links are seen in Henry James Pye's *Faringdon Hill* (2 books, 1774). Pye, who was later to become a pro-government M.P., occupies a vantage-point overlooking his own inherited estate. From the hilltop he turns through the compass-points to survey the land near and far, present and past. He picks out the individual spires of other villages, Oxford his student home, and various rivers and hills with their historical and literary links. His geographical range overlaps both Windsor Forest and Cooper's Hill, and their associated poems are subsumed into his, along with the more recently celebrated landscape of Gray's Eton. He takes in the groves of the old Druidic religion, the battlefield where Alfred triumphed over the Danes, an abbey with its predatory monks, and the more productive modern cider orchards. At one moment he is looking to the future when a canal will link Bristol with the Thames; at another the fields of Runnymede recall the signing of Magna Carta. Both past and future enhance his theme of British freedom. Pye's is a nation in which a son guards 'the rights his sires have won'; and towards the end of the poem he returns to the foreground of his paternal estate, with its old house scarred by a Civil War skirmish, and the nearby church where 'beneath yon roof by the cold pavement press'd, / My peaceful sires in solemn silence rest' (II, 435–6). He recalls his father and grandfather, and through them his ancestor John Hampden, the champion of English liberty who had fought at Edgehill. Pye places his estate, house, and family at the centre of a wider (spatial and temporal) inheritance, and in doing so he creates an image that Edmund Burke would later use to describe the British constitution:

> We have given to our frame of polity the image of a relation in blood; binding up the constitution of our country with our dearest domestic ties; adopting our fundamental laws into the bosom of our family affections; keeping inseparable, and cherishing with the warmth of all their combined and mutually reflected charities, our state, our hearths, our sepulchres, and our altars.[23]

In 1790, after the fall of the Bastille, Burke's stress on Britain's traditional values and organic constitution harked back to the 1770s rhetoric of the English shires that had shaped poems like *The Frequented Village* and *Faringdon Hill*. The move shocked Burke's former Whig allies, but the principle behind such poems had already been voiced by Burke in 1782: 'a nation is . . . an idea of continuity, which extends in time as well as in numbers and in space'.[24]

Jago and Pye wanted to embrace the extended and continuous in this Burkean sense. In the tradition of Denham and Pope they gave the prospect poem an expansive economy that worked from small localities to identify a wider regional character that could help to constitute a national *idea of continuity*. At least this was their intention. Whether they succeeded partly depends on the politics of the reader. The similarity with Burke's evolutionary (or antirevolutionary) rhetoric places such writing at the conservative end of the spectrum. In these poems we hear the language of the land, not the Wilkite sounds of the street. Liberty is here the constitutional principles of Hampden, not the equality sought by the Levellers. These poems anticipate the Burkean project by offering models of continuous change and localised development in which history is not a discarded past but the sound root-system of the British constitution. When Thomas Warton published the history of his own Oxfordshire parish of Kiddington in 1782 he intended it to serve as a model for a History of Oxfordshire as part of a wider concept of a national parochial history,[25] and being appointed Poet Laureate in 1785 (he was succeeded by Pye in 1790) Warton used his official odes to celebrate Britain through historical and topographical themes. The landscape poem was a constant reminder that London was not the nation.

The conservative cast of this kind of patriotism has encouraged some scholars to split apart what writers like these wanted to draw together. The poets' interest in local history is seen as a fondness for antiquarian remains; memorials to the past become fake reproductions; rich details become detached miniaturisations; imaginative associations become failures to engage; the local becomes the peripheral; the scattered traces slip into random fragments. Stephen Bending's persuasive discussion of *Edge-Hill*, for example, argues that 'Jago's account of the past emerges from scattered fragments and random traces. As such, its grasp on a coherent narrative and its ability to make sense of the disparate is limited'.[26] This indeed was the challenge Jago and others set themselves – to picture the country as holding steadily together, with all its diverse individual interests and associations – in Burke's sense, organically constituted. Jago recognised the problem, but hoped that his poem could persuade its readers that 'a Subject limited in its Nature may become generally interesting by the Force of good Management' (1767 Preface, p. vii). In this regard, his carefully ordered poetic economy might hope to encourage *good Management* at national level.

Of course, there was nothing inherently conservative about a prospect. It all depended on how you looked at the scene. One of the most popular prospect poems in its day was *Lewesdon Hill* (1788) by William Crowe, a carpenter's son who had risen to be a fellow of New College, Oxford, and the university's Public Orator. Crowe's reformist Whig sympathies are evident in his scepticism about regal eminences:

> But what is yonder Hill, whose dusky brow
> Wears, like a regal diadem, the round
> Of antient battlements and ramparts high;
> And frowns upon the vales? I know thee not.
> Thou hast no name, no honourable note,
> No chronicle of all thy warlike pride,
> To testify what once thou wert, how great,
> How glorious, and how fear'd. (358–65)

So much for Eggardon Hill, the proud iron-age hillfort in Dorset. In a footnote Crowe emphasises the uncertainty about the name's derivation and whether or not the remains are Roman. He is refusing to absorb its problematic early history, which reminds him of those 'who seek their greatness in dominion held / Over their fellows' (366–7). Where other topographical poets aim to preserve memory, Crowe celebrates oblivion – he is happy that the fort's builders should 'be as thou forgotten, and their fame / Cancell'd like thine!' (368–9).

Atop Lewesdon Hill, Crowe registers the expansiveness of the prospect, but in his case it is internalised: 'on this height I feel the mind / Expand itself in wider liberty' (69–70). His conviction that 'the mind is free' (184) makes him an interesting and unpredictable observer. His scenes are busy and purposeful, with a sense of direction, like the distant highway with its hurrying coaches. After his climb he thinks about rest, but in doing so his mind turns to two great men who have deserved laurels to rest upon – General Paoli, the Corsican patriot, and General Washington, now the leader of his 'own deliver'd country' (260). From his modest Dorsetshire hill, Crowe reaches for a spirit beyond the national. His little England is part of a wider dispensation.

Whatever its political tendencies, a 'prospect' was usually characterised by a degree of confidence and spatial command. The poet was at liberty to select points of focus and to digress and moralise at will. Jago, Pye and Crowe, like Denham and Pope before them, all suggest that their reading of the scene is both comprehensive and representative of the national spirit. They are also aware that a 'prospect' takes in the future as well as the past. (Jago's interest in Birmingham's industrial growth and Pye's encouragement of canal-projects recognise that Britain is continuing to develop.) There is one 'hill' poem, however, in which all such prospects are closed down, and the topography becomes a disconcerting mixture of observation and introspection. Ann Yearsley's *Clifton Hill* (1785) confronts the problem of finding her place within an economy that is the opposite of expansive and connected. The keynote is set by the opening couplet where a harsh solitariness is established, which the poem never shakes off: 'In this lone hour, when angry storms descend, / And the chill'd soul deplores her distant friend . . .' The prospect looks bleak from the start. Instead of an ascent, it is the descending storm that registers, and distance is equated with separation. This might be appropriate for a nocturnal meditation, but it suggests that this topographical poem will find both height and distance a challenge. When she finally gains a view, the 'I' and 'eye' of the text enter together:

> As o'er the upland hills I take my way,
> My eyes in transport boundless scenes survey:
> Here the neat dome where sacred raptures rise,
> From whence the contrite groan shall pierce the skies;
> Where sin-struck souls bend low in humble prayer,
> And waft that sigh which ne'er is lost in air. (67–72)

The vision is stopped in its tracks and the scene closes in on a penitent sinner bent low by guilt. What are released are only groans and sighs. The prospect has already disappeared, and by the next line Yearsley's eyes are focused on the ground. We find she is in Clifton churchyard standing by her mother's grave: 'Ah! sacred turf! here a fond Parent lies, / How my soul melts while dreadful scenes arise! / The past! Ah! shield me, Mercy!' (73–5). In this poem, the *past* is not something that enriches and integrates the scene. It has become a private memory that works as a counter-movement pulling her downwards ('my bulwark tumbles to the deep, / Amaz'd – alone I climb the craggy steep; / My shrieking soul deserted, sullen views / The depths below', 87–90). The hill is now less a vantage-point than an allegorical pathway, and her bearings are disoriented.

This pattern of frustrated prospects runs through the poem. When she comes to the famous view of the 300-foot Avon Gorge framed on either side by St Vincent's rocks, the panorama once again closes down immediately: 'Ye silent, solemn, strong, stupendous heights, / Whose terror-striking frown the school-boy frights / From the young daw; whilst in your rugged breast / The chattering brood, secured by Horror, rest' (118–121). The sentence ends there, with no main verb. It is as though Yearsley is thankfully turning away from the threatening rocks to peer into a jackdaw's nest, its fledglings safe from schoolboy predators (just one of many uneasy refuges in the poem). In the next lines the narrow Avon becomes a 'low cradle' with those huge stone giants brooding over it – two 'low'ring brothers' looking down with 'their native frown' (122–5). It is like a domestic scene in a disturbing folk-tale. As she moves around the hill, Yearsley is continually looking for shelter, imagining herself at one moment reborn a snail, a creature that avoids the open prospect at all costs: 'The harmless snail, slow-journeying, creeps away, / Sucks the young dew, but shuns the bolder day./ (Alas! if transmigration should prevail, / I fear LACTILLA's soul must house in snail)', 170–3). We could hardly be further from the confident outreach of the prospect poem.

This is an ecology of survival, and it ends with the story of the outcast Louisa (lines 206–96), a foreign refugee who for three years survived on Clifton Hill beneath a haystack. Her tale of disappointed love provides the poem's final bitter retrospect – another personal history that substitutes for the wider national history of the prospect poem. Louisa's distraction gives Yearsley a model for the way human thought becomes disorganised, and instead of shaping and mastering experience exposes a fragmented self:

> THOUGHT, what art thou? of thee she boasts no more,
> O'erwhelm'd, thou dy'st amid the wilder roar
> Of lawless anarchy, which sweeps the soul,
> Whilst her drown'd faculties like pebbles roll,
> Unloos'd, uptorn, by whirlwinds of despair . . . (281–5)

In this poem, Ann Yearsley ('Lactilla'), the Bristol milkwoman who sold her milk from door to door around Clifton Hill (like her mother before her), creates her own very personal topography. In someone else's poem she would have featured as a detail, a piece of local colour – perhaps as a pastoral milkmaid 'caroling blithe' in the distance, or 'tripping' along with her pails – part of a composed scene whose meaning belonged to someone else. But here this unit in the division of labour challenges the wider economy.[27] It is too easy to see *Clifton Hill* as a neurotic text, the product of inabilities and fears. When read against the economies of the 'prospect', it becomes instead a poem of stubborn refusal. Yearsley takes the motifs of the prospect poem and uses them to disturb the notion of landscape as a settled possession or a favourable vantage-point. In her text no-one owns the land over which she walks, and any houses have to be improvised. She may not see a great distance, but she has the survival instinct, and notices what she has to.

Lactilla was 'discovered' by Hannah More, the Bristol poet and educational writer, and the story of their relationship is a fascinating one.[28] It is enough to say that after a well received subscription volume, *Poems, on Several Occasions* (1785), Yearsley quarrelled with her benefactor and had to make her own way to a literary career. (She eventually opened a circulating library at the foot of Clifton Hill.) More was worried about Yearsley's widening prospects, and insisted that 'making of verses' should not interfere with her family responsibilities. It is this notion of a woman's dutiful limitation within a domestic economy that underlies More's belief that extensive landscapes were not appropriate for the female sex:

> A woman sees the world, as it were, from a little elevation in her own garden, where she makes an exact survey of home scenes, but takes not in that wider range of distant prospects which he who stands on a loftier eminence commands.[29]

More's image suggests that the full scope of a topographical poem was beyond a woman's reach. In fact her assumptions had already been challenged by an ambitious work that celebrated a regional terrain of considerable extent and variety. *Teisa* (Newcastle, 1778) by Anne Wilson[30] follows the course of the River Tees from its source near Great Dun Fell in the North Pennines eastward to the North Sea ports. In over sixteen hundred lines Wilson maps out a series of distinct landscapes that taken together represent the life of the region at all levels from the local gentry and clergy to the underpaid labourers. The poem is an example of how the georgic became subsumed into the topographical poem (see Chapter 5), and also of how a series of shifting prospects could move the discussion naturally from locality to nation without making the shires of middle-England its model. This view from the North East is in no way provincial – Wilson finds more common cause with the American colonists than with the government in London.

From a bubbling spring of 'virgin water' (5) to its busy coastal estuary, the Tees represents for Wilson a kind of arterial system. The river's flow provides her with a thematic thread, and she returns to it periodically to shift her mood or move on to another topic. But more than this it acts as a continual reminder of life's natural pace and level – almost a democratising principle. All the landmarks and figures we encounter are treated with equal interest and consideration, and there is no single viewing-point. The miners' thatched cottages get as much attention as the castle or the comfortable vicarage. 'Each thing in common to the muses lies' (390), Wilson pointedly remarks. In her practical economy there should be space and resources for all, but the private landscape garden consumes rather too much of both: 'I often, in large winding walks, lament / To see much ground, and labour vainly spent' (1018–19). At the fortuitously named 'Cooper's Hill' at Coniscliffe, she is put in mind of how unevenly nature's resources are divided:

> Oh! were my Muse to Denham's so ally'd,
> I'd sing each tree that grows along its side;
> Patrician oaks, that like the great o'ershade
> The lowly Plebean wood, along each glade,
> Catching the drops that nursing clouds distil,
> Nor sparing one 'till they have drunk their fill . . . (1241–6)

A hundred and thirty years after the Civil War the lofty few still overshade the humble many; but Wilson proceeds to give the hazel, hawthorn, and briar their deserved space in her poem.

In the world of *Teisa* people are judged by how they use or mis-use nature. Forms of planting, cultivation, or rearing win her approval since these continue and augment life, whereas game-shooting or the farming of wild salmon (which involves building dams to divert the river) are regrettable depredations and disturbances – the 'honest miller' makes do with a natural dam of thorns. Wilson's economy is at heart a self-sustaining one that finds room for traditional skills like cheese-making and land-drainage, and the detail with which both are described suggests she was a curious observer.[31] With the pace of life becoming unnaturally quickened by the stage-coach (those 'destructive flys', she calls them), the natural flow is being disturbed by the river's new competitor, the turnpike road: 'From town to country, from country to town, / All, in vast hurry, bustle up and down' (1083–4). Wilson is witnessing the effects of the national road-building mania between 1750 and 1770, a development that is dramatically evident in Eric Pawson's maps of the turnpike network of England and Wales in each of those years. The second map has become so thickly criss-crossed that it resembles the web of a demented spider, and it shows that Teesdale had recently been opened up westward to Carlisle, Kendal, and Lancashire.[32] For Wilson, speedy transport is in danger of drawing local people off the land: 'The husbandman of useful labour tir'd, / Is by the golden mines of London fir'd; / The ruddy milk-maid, she is weary grown / Of her lot, in the fly she goes to town' (1087–90). Ease of communication was just one factor in an expanding economy, and Wilson notes the effects that the increased competition was bringing. In her view, the wool traders of Barnard Castle have been too eager to embrace the free market:

> Their labours, grateful plenty wou'd reward;
> But selfish views they only here regard:
> Emulous of engrossing all they strive,
> Selling too low their woollen wares, to thrive.
> The weaver hence maugre his work and pains,
> Not just reward, not needful victuals gains;
> Is forc'd to seek from other looms his bread . . .
> By making wages small, thus Barnard forc'd
> Her working people out . . . (573–90)

In this embryonic version of *Monopoly* (*Emulous of engrossing all they strive*) independent weavers lose their livelihood. By deploring such *selfish views,* Wilson is resisting the influential theories of Adam Smith, whose *Wealth of Nations* (1776) celebrated free competition and the efficient market. Smith's brave new world was in the ascendant, and Wilson's economy of happy sufficiency was becoming dated. In her eyes, however, the ambitious undercutting of each other's prices means that a flourishing cottage industry has lost many of its workforce, with especially unfortunate results for women, 'who, in the weaving art, with men wou'd vie' (593).

Wilson is not objecting to expanding trade, but to a breakdown of community and the concentration of growing wealth in fewer hands. If she is suspicious of the artificial acceleration of life she is nevertheless happy to accelerate her own pace as soon as the Tees becomes tidal (the river is again a reminder of a natural dynamics). We are swept through 'busy Yarm' and on to the flourishing port of Stockton with its shipbuilders and merchant 'princes'. The reader is conscious of fresh energies taking over: 'Smooth TEISA gently glides away from hence / . . ships of burden now advance' (1460–1). The poem's onward flow meets a counter-movement, and in describing the dockland scene Wilson reveals the organic principle that has guided the whole of her poem:

> Around we see the little barges float;
> Some busy, take away their foreign store,
> Others, of our own produce, are bringing more:
> Like the muscular heart's velocity,
> Where the systole and the diastole agree,
> By fits to drive away, and to retain
> The crimson blood, while vital pow'rs remain . . . (1463–9)

Here, where the river's current meets the sea's ebb and flow, is the region's beating heart. Exports and imports are the *systole* and *diastole* of its vital system, circulating life through the body's organs. With this simile Wilson suggests that her living landscape will flourish by nurturing local productivity and welcoming external trade – by both sustaining and renewing its resources. The poem's final movement widens this theme of mutual give-and-take to those distant rivers, the St Laurence and the Mississippi, and to the troubled waters of Massachusetts Bay, scene of the notorious Boston Tea Party of 1773 when the 'Sons of Liberty' dumped cargoes of British tea in the harbour. With a nod at Pope's *Windsor-Forest* Wilson looks to the day when American produce will arrive at the Tees, and peace will return. Her hope is that Britain and her overtaxed American colonies ('from their once kind indulgent mother torn', 1550) can be reconciled and the family quarrel ended. Once trade has supplanted war, she comments, 'the fragrant, the soothing balsamic tea, / No more shall perish in the brackish sea' (1548–9). It is a touch of homely common sense. Tea is a natural restorative – but it has to be brewed properly.

Wilson's hopes for the future, however, are dashed with the death on 11 May 1778 of America's British champion, William Pitt, Earl of Chatham. She announces the 'mournful news' with all the shock of a breaking story, and the poem once again shifts its focus to take in the far-reaching implications ('Chatham alive, Britain still hop'd to see / The jarring lands enjoy sweet unity', 1596–7). The politics of *Teisa* finally come into focus as Wilson's opposition to Lord North's Squirearchy becomes clear. All along, her levelling muse has challenged the estate-centred landscapes of Jago and Pye. In her poem, the sense of local identity goes along with a recognition of economic pressures and competing interests. During her final eloquent tribute to Chatham, Wilson creates the vision of a scarred landscape that is wasting its human resources:

> Monstrous crimes in every shape appear,
> While peaceful peasants with the plow-share tear
> The fallow grounds, they to the wars are prest,
> The late useful looms amidst lumber rest,
> While their industrious own'rs, interr'd, now lay
> In America's hospitable clay. (1602–7)

The word *hospitable* offers a strange homecoming for the displaced Teesdale labourer who dies far away. It suggests a kinship with the local earth he left behind. The image of the plough tearing the ground hints at the way productive energies are being perverted and the Bible's language of peace reversed ('and they shall beat their swords into plowshares . . . neither shall they learn war any more').[33] If georgic cultivation was an expression of a land's recovery from internal strife, Wilson is faced with a lapse back into the nearest thing to Civil War Britain had faced since the 1640s – a deadly struggle against her own people.

In the course of its sixteen hundred lines *Teisa* creates the picture of a varied and productive commonwealth that would thrive if only the nation were wisely led and human selfishness were prevented from *engrossing* others' lives. Wilson's landscape cannot be divorced from the many individual interests that have formed it and are served by it. It is this understanding of the socio-political dynamics of the local scene – how it continues to be shaped by a combination of natural energies and external pressures – that makes *Teisa* a fascinating example of the eighteenth-century topographical poem.

Each of the texts discussed in this chapter recognises that landscape is to some degree a human responsibility, a product of culture. Whether it be Lady Thrifty's garden or Pye's estate, a bleak hilltop or a village-green, a ploughed battlefield or an American graveyard, Auburn or Crumble Hall, these are all sites where people have lived and worked, or otherwise left their mark. Eighteenth-century landscapes are not divorced from the social, political, and economic forces that have helped to create them. They are to that degree scenes where 'nature' comes to terms with 'art' (human skills and needs). In the past this contextual awareness has been called a failure of poetic vision. Introducing Crowe's *Lewesdon Hill*, Jonathan Wordsworth talks of Crowe's inability 'to cross the border into the fully imaginative experience of oneness with the God in Nature', and of 'the world of Romanticism that Crowe from his still-Augustan hilltop merely glimpsed'.[34] The landscapes of today, however, tell a more complex story, and egotistical sublimities will not save us. Nature has lost its innocence, and both space and resources are increasingly a cause of conflict. The 'management' of landscape is no longer a negative idea, and our word 'environment' acknowledges shared social surroundings. Later eighteenth-century topographies can be seen to anticipate current concerns such as 'stewardship' and 'sustainability'. Indeed, the title of a recent essay in the journal *Landscape Research* – 'Landscape Dynamics and the Management of Change' – could have been the sub-title of this chapter.[35] Today we are ready to recognise, as these poets did, that every ecology is also an economy.

Notes

1. 'The bearded field, the udder-swelling plain, / Some fleecy bleaters, and a fit domain / For winter forage' (Thomas Maude, *Wensleydale; or Rural Contemplation: A Poem* [1780], p. 55).

2. A useful and concise account of the development of garden landscapes during the century is *The Genius of the Place: The English Landscape Garden 1620–1820*, ed. John Dixon Hunt and Peter Willis (London, 1975), pp. 1–46. See also John Dixon Hunt, *The Figure in the Landscape: Poetry, Painting, and Gardening During the Eighteenth Century* (Baltimore, 1976).

3. See Martin Butlin and Evelyn Joll, *The Paintings of J.M.W. Turner* (New Haven and London, 1977), p. 4; and Graham Reynolds, *The Later Paintings and Drawings of John Constable* (New Haven and London, 1984), p. 199.

4. All these concepts were available by 1752. See *OED*, s.v. 'economy' 8.

5. Arthur Young, *A Six Months Tour through the North of England* (2nd ed., 4 vols, London, 1771), III, 115. Quoted by Paul Langford, *A Polite and Commercial People: England 1727–1783* (London, 1989), p. 439.

6. Pope's note to *Epistle to Burlington*, line 169.

7. Hugh C. Prince, 'Parkland in the Chilterns', *Geographical Review*, 49 (1959), 18–31 (pp. 22, 28–9).

8. Langford, *A Polite and Commercial People*, p. 441.

9. See Alastair Fowler, *The Country House Poem: A Cabinet of Seventeenth-Century Estate Poems and Related Items* (Edinburgh, 1994), p. 21; and Virginia C. Kenny, *The Country-House Ethos in English Literature 1688–1750: Themes of Personal Retreat and National Expansion* (New York, 1984).

10. In an essay on gardening in *The World*, 118 (3 April 1755) the writer recommends Milton as a model: 'the boundless imagination of Milton, in the fourth book of Paradise Lost, struck out a plan of a garden, which I would propose for the entertainment and instruction of my readers, as containing all the views, objects, and ambition of modern gardening'.

11. See Mavis Batey, 'Oliver Goldsmith: An Indictment of Landscape Gardening', in *Furor Hortensis*, ed. Peter Willis (Edinburgh, 1974), pp. 57–71.

12. See *The Poems of Gray, Collins, and Goldsmith*, ed. Roger Lonsdale (London and Harlow, 1969), p. 672.

13. [Anthony King], *The Frequented Village. A Poem. Inscribed to Dr. Oliver Goldsmith. By a Gentleman of the Middle Temple* (London: J. Godwin, [1771]). King authenticated every copy with his initials.

14. For a persuasive comparison between Crabbe and Goldsmith, see John Barrell, *The Dark Side of the Landscape: The Rural Poor in English Painting, 1730–1840* (Cambridge, 1980), pp. 77–85. *The Deserted Village* is quoted ironically in *The Village* I, 305.

15. *George Crabbe. The Complete Poetical Works*, ed. Norma Dalrymple-Champneys and Arthur Pollard, 3 vols (Oxford, 1988), I, 662.

16. See H. Butterfield, *George III, Lord North, and the People, 1779–80* (London, 1949), v–vi, 27; and John Cannon, *The Fox-North Coalition: Crisis of the Constitution, 1782–4* (Cambridge, 1969), p. xi.

17. Ian Gilmour, *Riot, Risings and Revolution: Governance and Violence in Eighteenth-Century England* (London, 1993), pp. 342–3.

18. Gilmour, p. 370. See *The Life of George Crabbe. By His Son*, ed. Edmund Blunden (London, 1947), pp. 71–4.

19. William Hazlitt, 'Lectures on the English Poets', Lecture 5 ('On Thomson and Cowper'). Hazlitt adds: '[Crabbe's] parish ethics are the very worst model for a state'.

20. Gavin Edwards, *George Crabbe's Poetry on Border Land* (Lewiston etc., 1990), pp. 35–55.

21. Samuel Johnson, 'Life of Denham', *The Lives of the English Poets*, ed. George Birkbeck Hill, 3 vols (Oxford, 1905), I, 78. See also Brendan O Hehir, *Expans'd Hieroglyphicks: A Critical Edition of Sir John Denham's Coopers Hill* (Berkeley and Los Angeles, 1969).

22. Langford, *A Polite and Commercial People*, p. 524.

23. Edmund Burke, *Reflections on the Revolution in France* (1790), ed. Conor Cruise O'Brien (Harmondsworth, 1986 ed.), p. 120.

24. Edmund Burke, *On a Motion Made in the House of Commons . . . for a Committee to Enquire into the State of the Representation of the Commons in Parliament* (1782), quoted in J.G.A. Pocock, 'Burke and the Ancient Constitution – A Problem in the History of Ideas', *The Historical Journal*, 3 (1960), 125–43 (p. 140).

25. Thomas Warton, *Specimen of a Parochial History of Oxfordshire* (1782), Preface. This was the model eventually adopted by the Victoria History of the Counties of England, begun in 1899 and still continuing.

26. Stephen Bending, 'Prospects and Trifles: The Views of William Shenstone and Richard Jago', *Qwerty*, 10 (October 2000), 125–31 (p. 129). See also John Barrell, *English Literature in History 1730–80: An Equal Wide Survey* (London, 1983).

27. The division of human labour into efficient units was influentially recommended by the economist Adam Smith in *Wealth of Nations* (1776).

28. See Mary Waldron, *Lactilla, Milkwoman of Clifton* (Athens and London, 1996), pp. 48–78.

29. Hannah More, *Strictures on Female Education*, 2 vols (1799), II, 25–6.

30. *Teisa: A Descriptive Poem of the River Teese, Its Towns and Antiquities. By Anne Wilson* (Newcasle-Upon-Tyne, 1778).

31. See Bridget Keegan, 'Writing Against the Current: Anne Wilson's *Teisa* and the Tradition of British River Poetry', *Women's Studies*, 31 (Summer 2002), 267–85 (p. 275).

32. See Eric Pawson, *Transport and Economy: The Turnpike Roads of Eighteenth Century Britain* (London etc., 1977), pp. 140 and 151.

33. Isaiah, 2:4.

34. Jonathan Wordsworth, 'Introduction' to William Crowe, *Lewesdon Hill. 1788* (Oxford, 1989).

35. Robert Wood and John Handley, 'Landscape Dynamics and the Management of Change', *Landscape Research*, 26:1 (Jan. 2001), 45–54.

Chapter 11

Sensibility: Selves, Friends, Communities

Having reached the mid-point of his long descriptive poem, *Edge-Hill* (1767), Richard Jago suddenly raises an issue that threatens to undermine his whole project – Is there an objective *material world* beyond his own sense perceptions? In other words, does a physical Warwickshire landscape actually exist? For what he thinks is a self-evident answer to this disturbing question he appeals to his readers:

> What say my Friends? Or are ye airy Shapes?
> Or do ye see, and hear, and taste, and smell?
> Do all our Senses make the same Report?
> Or mock we each with Semblances of Sense?
> Are we, or are we not what thus we seem?
> Or is this World, which we material call,
> A visionary Scene, like midnight Dreams,
> Without Existence, save what Fancy gives? (III, 9–16)

It is a remarkable passage because it suggests that Jago's plotting out of his local topography with its people, houses, fields, and layers of human history, is partly meant to stand in defiance of eighteenth-century sceptical philosophy. In Jago's hands the English landscape will refute Enlightenment doubt, and especially the arguments of David Hume (1711–76) who had questioned the existence of both material substance and a continuous self, and thus seemed to undermine everything on which truth, belief, morality, and principle rested. For Jago, such 'Metaphysic Subtleties' (III, 28) can be answered simply by opening the senses to experience. As he watches the sunlight play over the ruins of Kenilworth Castle he is certain that a physical world of 'external Things' does exist. While he registers textures, fragrances, sounds, and colours, his senses 'prove that all this outward Frame of Things / Is what it seems, not unsubstantial Air, / Ideal Vision, or a waking Dream' (III, 2–4). But as if to reassure himself, Jago suddenly embodies his anonymous readers as *Friends*, independent beings who can confirm that his landscape is not a figment of the imagination. The reader's presence becomes part of Jago's claim against *solipsism*, a state in which no objective reality exists beyond one's own mind. This idea has for him become associated with the poetic imagination, which 'paints / Unreal Scenes' and 'reject[s] what sober Sense, / And calmest Thoughts attest' (III, 20–2). Shying away from the visionary excursions of *The Seasons* or *The Pleasures of Imagination*, Jago feels the need for a firmly grasped geography to resist the dangers of perceptual and moral vacancy. An issue that never occurred to James Thomson in 1730 has become in 1767 a nagging question that must be dealt with and 'exploded'.[1]

Some of the most interesting poetry of the second half of the century is marked by these concerns about the relationship between the subjective self and objective 'reality'. As a general topic it was of course nothing new. In Chapter 6 we saw how poets of the period 1700–1730 explored subjectivity, and in Chapter 7 how selfishness and sociability could be reconciled within a moral economy. Indeed, the rippling movement outwards from 'self' to friends, family, society, and 'all human race' was memorably celebrated by Pope in *An Essay on Man* (1734), IV, 361–72. But by the 1760s, as Jago's address to his readers indicates, the matter had become complicated by developments in British empirical philosophy. Teasing new questions had arisen that did not leave poets untouched – Is there a 'self' at all? Is there a set of material phenomena 'out there' that our senses are perceiving? What are the grounds for saying 'I know', 'I believe', or even 'I am'? In an age of restless enquiry this sceptical catechism offered to challenge structures of all kinds, including moral, social, and political ones.

Such thinking represented the radical potential of 'sensibility', a concept that bridged self-consciousness and sense perception, and which could accommodate doubts perhaps more easily than certainties. As previous chapters have argued, poets from the early years of the century like Finch, Pope, and Aaron Hill were fascinated by human sensation and emotion as subjective responses to experience – there was nothing new in sensibility as such.[2] But by the 1760s the term had attracted a cluster of more specific ideas and seemed to be on everyone's lips. There was an increasing interest in the science of the mind, and poets and novelists joined with philosophers and medical writers in being curious about the intricate mechanisms of feeling. In particular, sensibility highlighted the great enigma of the mind-body relationship:[3] how is a body moved by an idea? At what point does a thought become physicalised – as with a blush or a tear, for example? When I wave to a friend I set my arm in *voluntary motion* – a notion that Hume called the most 'mysterious' 'in all nature' because it evinced the meeting of mind and matter.[4] A person of sensibility, embodying a heightened responsiveness to the moment, could therefore be seen as a wonderful machine of feeling that registered the most delicate and elusive sensations. Behind this 'delicacy', however, were two other dimensions of sensibility that exploited the mind/body dynamic in more active ways – an intellectual robustness that tested all abstractions by experience, and a lusty playfulness that relished the self's protean adventures. Sensibility was thus a complex mixture of active and passive, empathy and self-centredness, sociability and solipsism, scepticism and faith. It was not a structure of ideas, but an openness to ideas. If this instability made sensibility unpopular with moralists, it had more appeal for those willing to negotiate ethics.

This final chapter will look at a selection of poets who engaged with this tangle of issues. The groupings may seem odd – three mid-century satirists, two sonneteers of the 1780s, and several poets of strong religious or social conviction – but between them they raise interesting questions about how poetry might work within and beyond the self in an intellectual context where subjectivity was accruing new untested (and perhaps untestable) powers. How far could the self be allowed to create its own truth? Was anything its judge or conscience? In what way might the self be socialised? In the traditional 'faculty psychology'[5] inherited from the Renaissance, imagination could be let out to play, supervised by an amused reason; but in the experimental world of nerve fibres, vibrations, and animal spirits, new psychic organisations broke the old internal hierarchy of the mind. For the poets in this chapter sensibility, with its sceptical implications, made self-consciousness more problematic and intriguing. It also had a social dimension, and by encouraging an identification with others' feelings it became the spur to friendship and human sympathy (if Hume was the philosopher of scepticism, he was also the presiding spirit of sympathetic friendship[6]). Sensibility gave the satirists inventive opportunities, introduced delicacies of sensation to the romantic mode, and for poets with ethical concerns it made 'liberty' the keystone that joined poetic imagination to civic virtue.

Mid-century sensibility gave a fresh impetus to satire. Being a mode of intelligence as well as feeling, sensibility was not necessarily the enemy of the satiric impulse, suffusing judgmental outlines in a glow of generous feeling; rather it encouraged satire's playfulness and gave it a new subject in judgment itself. The authority of satire (its claims on truth) could be twisted round, and modes of authority themselves questioned. Sentimental heroes or heroines were often defined in opposition to the demands of 'the World', and even their naivety or foolishness could be used to indict unsympathetic social norms.[7] A hypersensitive inner life, responsive to the minutest stimuli, might defy the unthinking and unfeeling multitude. Rather than representing social standards in opposition to folly (like Young in *The Universal Passion*, for example), a sentimental satirist could challenge those norms by espousing folly himself. To confine 'the Age of Satire' to the early Scriblerian decades is to risk limiting its range and ignoring how poets later in the century developed the satiric persona in new directions. (It also underestimates the extent to which works like Swift's *Tale of a Tub* or Pope's *Dunciad* toyed imaginatively with unruly subjectivities.) In his novels *Tristram Shandy* (1759–67) and *A Sentimental Journey* (1768) Laurence Sterne brought sensibility and satire into fascinating poise, comically exposing the mechanisms of sensation and thought, and engaging in a sometimes rueful projection of the self in its troubled collisions with material reality. In Sterne's world it is possible for sympathy to be a satire on judgment. Rather than making claims to truth, sentimental satire can expose claim-making as an imposition, a false confidence in structures of belief. The rapid flow of sentimental impressions resists prescriptiveness because it is the opposite of pre-scripted: it is a continuous surprise, a recognition that one's identity is remade at each instant. This is one contribution that Hume made to the languages of sensibility and satire – pushing them away from judgment and towards scepticism, and in the work of Charles Churchill and his friends we can recognise the satiric potential of such a move.

When it was published in 1762, Churchill's long and rambling poem, *The Ghost*, was welcomed by *The Monthly Review* as 'a kind of *Tristram Shandy* in *verse*'.[8] It exhibits the improvisatory and digressive character of Sterne's novel, and its sense that experience is rushing on too quickly to be grasped:

> For our pursuits, be what they will,
> Are little more than shadows still,
> Too swift they fly, too swift and strong,
> For man to catch, or hold them long.
> But Joys which in the FANCY live,
> Each moment to each man may give.
> True to himself, and true to ease,
> He softens Fate's severe decrees,
> And (can a Mortal wish for more?)
> Creates, and makes himself new o'er,
> Mocks boasted vain *Reality*,
> And *Is*, whate'er he wants to Be. (IV, 299–310)

Whereas Jago was unsettled by his *airy Shapes*, Churchill is happy to celebrate the insubstantial, and to live in the imagination of the moment. Conscious of the irony, he asserts the possibility of being *true to himself*, and then an instant later denies the notion of continuous identity (*Creates, and makes himself new o'er*). This echo of Rochester's living-for-the-moment philosophy underlines Churchill's links with the Restoration 'Libertine' tradition, but it also places him alongside his friend John Wilkes. Wilkite political 'Liberty' becomes naturalised into the poem's notion of a generous, unbounded, even sportive 'Nature' ('NATURE, who in her act most free, / Herself delights in Liberty', IV, 227–8). Mocking outdated faculty psychology, Churchill defies those moralists who cling to the defunct constitution of the brain: 'Should She presumptuous joy receive, / Without the Understanding's leave, / They deem it rank and daring Treason / Against the Monarchy of REASON' (IV, 185–8). In Churchill's mental state, that King's prerogative has been ended.

The radical implications of the newer theories of mind are clear, and in the early philosophy of Hume the limitations of reason are further exposed. In his *Treatise of Human Nature* (1739–40)[9] he argues that all our ideas, even of the simplest kind like the shape of a pen, are built up from fleeting 'impressions', forceful and lively units of sense data that succeed each other rapidly in the mind. These immediate impressions may appear to be linked by cause and effect (when I release the pen it falls to the ground), but this is for Hume only a succession of ideas, not one thing causing another (the notion of a 'cause' is something we assume but cannot argue). For him there is no necessary or proveable connection between any ideas, even those that appear to be related (like heat in a flame). As for material things, it is not possible to deduce the existence of matter from an idea. All that exist are collections of swiftly flowing, exceedingly brief impressions, and nothing more (an idea is merely a less vivid – because not immediate – impression). Similarly, to speak of a continuous human identity that is perceiving these is again unwarranted. Previous philosophers had held that there was a unitary 'soul-substance' underlying all our experience; Locke conceived of a material *substratum* that grounded our ideas; and even Berkeley (who denied the existence of matter) believed that our ideas inhered in a substantive 'soul'. But Hume discounts all these attempts to conceptualise a continuous self (I. iv. 6). Any underlying basis for objective 'knowledge' or 'reason' is denied. What, then, about a belief or opinion? Hume's response is the logical one that these can be nothing more than 'a lively idea related to or associated with a present impression' (I. iii. 7). There is, to put it crudely, no added value in a 'belief', or any means of testing it. We can of course *speak* of 'opinions', or *act* on 'beliefs', but Hume disconnects them from knowledge or truth. Certainly they have no claim on anyone else.

In *The Ghost* Churchill welcomes the freedom this scepticism gives:

> Opinions should be free as air;
> No man, whate'er his rank, whate'er
> His Qualities, a claim can found
> That my Opinion must be bound,
> And square with his; such slavish chains
> From foes the lib'ral soul disclaims . . . (IV, 251–6)

Without any regulatory authority or responsible guardian, *Opinion* floats free, to be claimed or disclaimed at will. This could be seen as a liberation of language into a world of signs without referents (a licentious language), and Churchill's poem indeed seems to create its world as it goes, flowing along unpredictably, spurning connectedness, digressing, contradicting itself, and veering from one subject to the next. He is happy to detach himself from others' knowledge and truth, and follow his own imagination: 'Some few in *knowledge* find relief, / I place my comfort in *belief*. / Some for *Reality* may call, / FANCY to me is All in All' (IV, 289–92). Churchill doesn't confuse his *belief* with reality.

The Ghost represents Churchill at his most playful and eccentric. It is partly an exercise in playing the fool with experience – a licence, or natural liberty, traditionally claimed by the satirist (the notion is reminiscent, for example, of Shakespeare's Jaques: 'I must have liberty / Withal, as large a charter as the wind, / To blow on whom I please, for so fools have', *As You Like It*, II, vii, 47–9). In a world of folly the satirist has sometimes to *charter* himself and create a kind of parallel universe in which he has licence to roam. This is to some degree what Churchill does in *Gotham* (1764). Gotham, the land of fools, is an island country (not yet on the maps) that he has discovered, and to which he stakes his claim as its monarch. This is, he says, no more than Europeans have done in claiming rule over 'their' colonies:

> Cast by a tempest on the savage coast,
> Some roving Buccaneer set up a Post;
> A Beam, in proper form transversely laid,
> Of his Redeemer's Cross the figure made . . .
> His royal master's name thereon engrav'd,
> Without more process, the whole race enslav'd,
> Cut off that Charter they from Nature drew,
> And made them Slaves to men they never knew. (I, 13–22)

The satirist is no worse than the pirate, and his *Charter* no more flimsy than the wooden cross claiming a new land for God and King. Losing their natural liberty, the inhabitants become *enslav'd* to somebody else's system, and here the sceptical satirist also attacks the tyranny of mental colonisation, the structure of belief that ties Christ to George III. The native hitherto lived free of imported knowledge, religion, and law: 'No rules he held, but what were made for use; / No Arts he learn'd, nor ills which Arts produce; / False Lights he follow'd, but believ'd them true; / He knew not much, but liv'd to what he knew' (I, 63–6). Their own 'false' belief was preferable to another's truth. The authentic life is to live to what you know. The rest is just bad faith.

Hume recognised that no-one, least of all himself, could live a life of total scepticism and solipsism, and in his 'Conclusion' to the *Treatise* he turns with relief to the everyday habits of mind that take us through our experiences: 'Nature . . . cures me of this philosophical melancholy and delirium . . . I dine, I play a game of backgammon, I converse, and am merry with my friends . . .'. Life, he confesses, will always draw us to what is easy and reassuring; nonetheless 'in all the incidents of life, we ought still to preserve our scepticism. If we believe that fire warms, or water refreshes, it is only because it costs us too much pains to think otherwise' (I. iv. 7). The answer is a good-humoured avoidance of self-assurance and dogma. Because it doubts rather than knows, Hume's scepticism is relaxed and easy about things: 'The conduct of a man who studies philosophy in this careless manner, is more truly sceptical', he notes. He is saved from 'total scepticism' by a certain diffidence and modesty, and especially by his imagination.[10] His intellectual outlook could be summed up in Churchill's words: 'By his own Sense and Feelings taught, / In speech as lib'ral as in thought, / Let ev'ry Man enjoy his whim; / What's He to Me, or I to him?' (*The Ghost*, IV, 213–6). Here the poet is thinking of people whose views he dislikes; but a generous allowance for another's odd turns of mind could also be the basis for conviviality and friendship (aspects of life especially appreciated by Churchill and Hume).

The freedom of a person to *enjoy his whim* is the subject of 'The Whim. An Epistle to Mr. W. Woty' by Churchill's close friend Robert Lloyd. The poem, Lloyd declares, is the 'off'ring of a lazy muse', and he spontaneously decides to 'draw her picture on the spot':

> A perfect ease the dame enjoys;
> Three chairs her indolence employs:
> On one she squats her cushion'd bum,
> Which wou'd not rise, tho' kings should come;
> An arm lolls dangling o'er another,
> A leg lies *couchant* on its brother . . .
> She smokes, and smokes; without all feeling,
> Save as the eddies climb the ceiling,
> And waft about their mild perfume,
> She marks their passage round the room. (59–72)

There is a relaxed anarchy about this, a style that gives a new turn to the informal freedom of the verse letter. In a Pope poem or a Hogarth print this lolling body would demand moral disapproval, but here its odd combination of awkwardness and ease creates a more complex effect. The figure's stubborn carelessness defies authority (*wou'd not rise, tho' kings should come*), while the eddying smoke mimics the arabesques of the imagination in a way that recalls Uncle Toby's pipe in that most whimsical of novels, *Tristram Shandy*. Lloyd's careless muse exemplifies a kind of mental vacancy that is also a more positive openness of mind ('Give me the man whose open mind / Means social good to all mankind', 41–2).

We seem to have moved a long way, crossing over from self to sociability, from the solipsistic implications of sceptical philosophy to ideas of friendship and the good of mankind. But the binary is deceptive. As I have tried to show, both Hume and Churchill negotiate between the two, as other people of sensibility did during this period (a character like Sterne's Toby, although locked into his private mental world, yet has a great capacity for human friendship). The explanation is not far to seek. We can appreciate that in an intellectual world in which notions of reason, identity, matter and causation were all being brought into question, life (as Hume recognised) still had to be lived. Certainly, what seemed to be solid public truths were being undermined; but more uncertain, intimate, and fleeting modes of 'truth' were gaining significance. In this context it was possible to celebrate the individual and personal as against the universal. 'Truer' ideas might even be those that were struggling to be spoken at all, rather than those proclaimed more publicly. Even incoherent beginnings of thought could be shared with a sympathetic listener:

> First, for a thought—since all agree—
> A thought—I have it—let me see—
> 'Tis gone again—Plague on't! I thought
> I had it—but I have it not. (35–8)

This is William Cowper amiably stumbling during his *Epistle to Robert Lloyd* (1754). The elusiveness of his thought (itself an amusing thought) shows us a mind in process. His friend is admitted into his consciousness while an idea is struggling to form and all impressions seem to have been suspended. Cowper, another victim of philosophic melancholy (or 'spleen'), is using his poem to fill a mental space that something else threatens to enter. He tells Lloyd he is writing

> to divert a fierce banditti,
> (Sworn foes to every thing that's witty!)
> That, with a black, infernal train,
> Make cruel inroads in my brain,
> And daily threaten to drive thence
> My little garrison of sense:
> The fierce banditti, which I mean,
> Are gloomy thoughts, led on by spleen. (13–20)

This is a mind that risks ambush at any second, and the ease and spontaneity of his poem suggest how he might be surprised. Where Anne Finch used her poem *The Spleen* wittily to diagnose and characterise her mental state, Cowper is holding off an attack, an idea sharpened by the immediacy of the epistle form. The poem has become part of his mental mechanism as a man of sensibility (anticipating the way Sterne's *Tristram Shandy* will be similarly written hurriedly 'against the spleen'). *Sense* is here the poet's defender from the dark side of his imagination. He addresses Lloyd as 'crony mine', a friend whose presence keeps that darkness at bay.

Churchill, Lloyd and Cowper had been cronies since their days at Westminster School during the 1740s. By the late 1750s they had formed into a group called the 'Nonsense Club', a literary coterie who met each Thursday for drink and humour.[11] The surviving verses exchanged amongst this 'indiscreet fraternity of geniuses', as William Kenrick called them,[12] celebrate vigour and spontaneity, and the 'honesty' of converse between friends ('in writing to a friend / A man may any nonsense send, / And the chief merit to impart, / The honest feelings of his heart').[13] In their own non-sensical company they could turn against the everyday 'sense' that tyrannised others. Their intimacy created a kind of communal self to resist the claims of the public world. This is the subject of Churchill's *Night* (1761), a verse letter addressed to Lloyd that celebrates the nocturnal life they shared ('Oft with thee, LLOYD, I steal an hour from grief, / And in thy social converse find relief', 3–4). Night becomes their vantage-point from which to challenge the values that drive everyone else: they are able to 'see by NIGHT what fools we are by DAY' (122). The daytime life of power and business, prudence and conformity traps people in the mechanical routines of the body – it takes an animated nocturnal sensibility to recognise how life is regimented by its official machinery. Churchill scorns the 'wretch'

> Who ne'er thro' heat of blood was tripping caught,
> Nor guilty deem'd of one eccentric thought,
> Whose soul directed to no use is seen
> Unless to move the body's dull Machine;
> Which, clock-work like, with the same equal pace,
> Still travels on thro' life's insipid space . . . (21–6)

Churchill disrupts these regulatory mechanisms by setting his satiric clock to his own 'temper' – very different from the well-behaved Rupert: 'In diff'rent courses diff'rent tempers run, / He hates the Moon, I sicken at the sun. / Wound up at twelve at noon, *his* clock goes right, / *Mine* better goes, wound up at twelve at night' (81–4). It is characteristic of sentimental satire to exploit the individual sensibility in this way, and to give eccentricity a lever against the normal. According to this inversion, it is day that creates the illusions people live by ('Through a false medium things are shewn by day, / Pomp, wealth, and titles judgment lead astray', 139–40). Beneath 'NIGHT's honest shade', however, 'pomp is buried and false colours fade' (153–4).

As the poem reaches its close, Churchill places himself in the position normally reserved for the satiric victim: a madman trapped in the self and isolated by the world's judgment ('*You* must be wrong' he tells himself, 'the WORLD is in the right', 352). Far from making a broad appeal to common sense, Churchill has shrunk his satiric base to almost nothing. It is the logic of scepticism. He ends as someone clinging to the letter of Hume's text: 'nothing is ever really present to the mind, besides its own perceptions' (*Treatise*, I. iv. 2). With this thought, we can read Churchill's defiant ending as having a solipsistic logic:

> In spite of Dullness, and in spite of Wit,
> If to thyself thou canst thyself acquit,
> Rather stand up assur'd with conscious pride
> Alone, than err with millions on thy side. (379–82)

Here Churchill's satiric self has become a robust singularity, a self-authenticating solitary voice; but it is rescued from solipsism by Lloyd, the friend who will inwardly assent to his words – after all (to quote somebody who knew them both) 'they were inseparable, one sentiment governing the minds, and one purse administring to the wants of both'.[14] It is the nature of the *sentiment* that it is offered in this trusting way to a reader willing to reach out sympathetically to the poet's private world.

Sentimental writing appeals to the few who have minds and hearts tunable enough to understand. The text of sensibility, therefore, is a kind of performance of intimacy. Introducing her *Elegiac Sonnets* (1784) to the public, Charlotte Smith ends by saying: 'I can hope for readers only among the few, who to sensibility of heart, join simplicity of taste'. The fact that by the fifth edition of 1789 she is thanking her 'brilliant assemblage' of subscribers (some of whom ordered ten copies, others more) suggests how many wanted to be counted among the 'few'.

Entering the traditional 'narrow room' of the fourteen-line sonnet, the self of sensibility forfeits its expansive possibilities in favour of reflection.[15] In Smith's hands the 'I' tends to reach out briefly only to be turned back on itself like a reflecting image – a moment usually of confirmation or realisation, rather than a discovery that moves her on. In the nocturnal scene of Sonnet 4 ('To the Moon'), for example, the 'self' of the poem registers a series of transient visual impressions ('Alone and pensive, I delight to stray, / And watch thy shadow trembling in the stream, / Or mark the floating clouds that cross thy way', 2–4); it then moves to a response ('thy mild and placid light / Sheds a soft calm upon my troubled breast', 5–6), then to a reflection of her own ('The sufferers of the earth perhaps may go, / Releas'd by death—to thy benignant sphere', 9–10), but back finally to reality ('Oh! that I soon may reach thy world serene, / Poor wearied pilgrim—in this toiling scene!', 13–14). It is as though, by combining the sense impressions and linking them to an emotion (calm), her imagination has formed an idea, out of which comes a further emotion (hope) before the present returns. A reader of sensibility enters the poem's consciousness as a short-lived 'self', taking on its mood sympathetically, and being made for a moment part of its subjective world. As one sonnet follows another, we are aware of a poetic identity reaffirming itself around a series of impression-led ideas.[16] There is no attempt at a narrative development or organic growth of this consciousness, just a textual self, repeatedly reflecting on, and being reflected by, the natural world.

'When I turn my reflection on *myself*, I never can perceive this *self* without some one or more perceptions; nor can I ever perceive anything but the perceptions. It is the composition of these, therefore, which forms the self'.[17] This is Hume again challenging the concept of an independent continuous self. For him it is rather a series of composed perceptions that allow a self to be *reflected on* (and without which it could not be imaged by the mind). Charlotte Smith's accumulating collection of numbered sonnets (rising eventually to ninety-two) can be thought of in similar terms, with the individual poems representing succession rather than continuity. Hume helps us characterise the sentimental sonnet more generally as a medium that allows perceptions to be reflectively connected, however briefly, so as to form an identity that friendly readers can enter.

> Press'd by the Moon, mute arbitress of tides,
>   While the loud equinox its power combines,
>   The sea no more its swelling surge confines,
> But o'er the shrinking land sublimely rides.
> The wild blast, rising from the Western cave,
>   Drives the huge billows from their heaving bed;
>   Tears from their grassy tombs the village dead,
> And breaks the silent sabbath of the grave!
> With shells and sea-weed mingled, on the shore
>   Lo! their bones whiten in the frequent wave;
>   But vain to them the winds and waters rave;
> *They* hear the warring elements no more:
> While I am doom'd—by life's long storm opprest,
> To gaze with envy, on their gloomy rest.[18]

Here in Sonnet 44 ('Written in the Church Yard at Middleton in Sussex') a self emerges that is no less a spectator than we are. The 'I' is postponed until the penultimate line, by which time the *warring elements* in the natural scene have already become the reader's perceptions. Rather than creating or organising the scene, and using it for a self-exploratory contemplation, this 'I' (when it does enter) is an uneasy respondent like us, reflecting on the sense impressions it has registered. The location of a 'self' is difficult to pin down. We could say that, as the text proceeds, a self-consciousness emerges that finds expression at the end; but the final couplet suddenly refers to the poet's *life* outside the poem. We seem to be witnessing an intense moment of awareness within a much vaguer *long storm* – one that is meant to symbolise her 'continuing' existence. A reader of her 1789 volume, however, would be more vividly aware of a succession of self-realising textual moments.

Charlotte Smith's sonnets are clearly related to the romantic mode discussed in Chapter 6, exploring subjective experience and appealing to the sympathetic imagination of the reader. Indeed, the first sonnet in her collection ends with a rewording of the last line of Pope's *Eloisa to Abelard* about the sympathising poet who will record Eloisa's woes ('He best can paint 'em, who shall feel 'em most'). In a parallel way Smith is fated to be the poet of her own sufferings, '*If those paint sorrow best—who feel it most!*' But, whereas Eloisa's visions fill the darkness of her cell, Smith's sonnets reflect on a series of distinct landscapes and situations that cannot be explained as phantoms of the mind. In fact, her specific sense impressions become a way of talking about the self, and movements between inner and outer worlds are used for ironic effects. Such a difference suggests how 'sensibility' developed a slightly different emphasis from the earlier 'romantic' mode. The natural scene is for Smith a more ambiguous one – less a projection of the poet's subjectivity than an external context to which the poet is uneasily related. Where a 'romantic' scene might be more responsive to the self's imaginings (for good or ill), the scene of 'sensibility' tends toward the accidental or contingent, exploiting the uncertainties of the mind's relation to the outer world. Sensibility is less concerned with dreams or visions and more with the elusiveness of reality.

These are fine distinctions, and perhaps it would be more helpful, rather than striving to distinguish them, to see sensibility as a wider concept that subsumes the romantic mode of the early decades, developing its subjective mechanisms, and finding elements of irony, playfulness or scepticism to exploit. There are moments indeed when Smith shows the romantic mode as no longer sustainable. Sonnet 47 ('To Fancy') bids farewell to the 'glowing tints' of her imagination: 'Thro' thy false medium then, no longer view'd, / May fancied pain and fancied pleasure fly' (9–10). This makes explicit the precariousness of Smith's visions as they encounter the material world. It is evident also in sonnet 63 ('The Gossamer'),[19] in which the imagination's 'schemes' are pictured as an intricate network of spiders' webs covering the landscape. But this image of a responsive sensorium 'waving in every sighing air that stirs' is physically vulnerable: 'the wind rises, and the turf receives / The glittering web' (9–10). The result is disillusionment: 'So vanish schemes of bliss, by Fancy made; / . . . fragile as the fleeting dreams of morn' (12–13). The interconnected threads form only briefly, and must be continually respun.

Such discomposure is typical of Smith's sonnets. Rather than finding a healing harmony with nature, the voice remains uneasy and restless, never quite at home ('Alas! can tranquil nature give *me* rest, / Or scenes of beauty, soothe me to repose?')[20]. Moments of alienation tend to predominate, realisations that she cannot give herself entirely to the scene. In the graveyard sonnet (no. 44) discussed earlier, the human bones bleaching in the sea are more at rest than she is ('*They* hear the warring elements no more'). The delights of Spring in Sonnet 8 can 'soothe awhile', but only by 'bring[ing] life's first delusions once again'. She feels most acclimatised in sonnet 12 ('Written on the Sea Shore') where she contemplates the storm and imagines herself as a shipwrecked mariner beyond help ('Faint and more faint are heard his feeble cries, / 'Till in the rising tide, th'exhausted sufferer dies', 13–14). An accompanying illustration in the 1789 edition shows a bright female form seated by the foot of a dark rock, with a black cloud and the swirling sea about to encroach on her. She holds a white book open to the elements, while her eyes are fixed downwards, looking neither at the book nor at the scene. It is an eerie vignette of an incongruous figure.

With the following sonnet, however, we seem to have emerged into a different world entirely. Its title is 'Written at Tinemouth, Northumberland, After a Tempestuous Voyage':

> As slow I climb the cliff's ascending side,
> Much musing on the track of terror past,
>   When o'er the dark wave rode the howling blast,
> Pleas'd I look back, and view the tranquil tide,
>   That laves the pebbled shore; and now the beam
> Of evening smiles on the grey battlement,
> And yon forsaken tow'r that time has rent:—
>   The lifted oar far off with silver gleam
> Is touch'd, and the hush'd billows seem to sleep!
>   Sooth'd by the scene, ev'n thus on sorrow's breast
>   A kindred stillness steals, and bids her rest;
> Whilst sad airs stilly sigh along the deep,
>   Like melodies which mourn upon the lyre,
>   Wak'd by the breeze, and as they mourn, expire.[21]

This sonnet by William Lisle Bowles (1789) is an exercise in harmonising nature with the individual sensibility. The poem opens with two backward glances – across time and across space – which effectively merge into a single retrospect (*musing on the track of terror past . . . Pleas'd I look back*), so that when the distance is pictured, *the tranquil tide* gains a temporal dimension as well – calm after storm. The surge of private pleasure is externalised when the evening light *smiles* on the grey ruin, and with that object comes a reminder of a far deeper *time* underlying the scene. The evening sunlight then reaches out to sea, touching momentarily a *lifted oar* far below, catching the briefest of impressions like a highlight in a painting. That word *touch'd* (one of those crucial sentimental words that allow physical and emotional to meet) is then given more nuance by its half-echoes, *hush'd* and *sooth'd*. The whole composed landscape is then personally registered (*Sooth'd by the scene . . .*); but just as we expect the 'I' to return, we find that the self has become absorbed into a wider idea (*on sorrow's breast / A kindred stillness steals*). The word *kindred* gathers up the sonnet's various echoes and reflections into a more capacious kinship between humanity and nature, preparing for the final lines to register an all-embracing harmony in the symbol of the wind-harp, imaging the sensibility whose notes we have heard throughout the poem. The sonnet ends appropriately on *expire*, both a 'breathing out' and a last breath or expiration into utter stillness.

In Bowles's hands, nature heals over the spot where spirit and matter join. The meeting of the human mind with the physical world (the location for so many sentimental moments, paradoxes, accidents) seems no longer a problematic or epiphanic encounter, just a natural elision. It was this organic element of Bowles's poetry that so excited the young Coleridge:

> [T]hose Sonnets appear to me the most exquisite, in which moral Sentiments, Affections, or Feelings, are deduced from, and associated with, the scenery of Nature . . .

They create a sweet and indissoluble union between the intellectual and the material world . . . Hence, the Sonnets of BOWLES derive their marked superiority over all other Sonnets; hence they domesticate with the heart, and become, as it were, a part of our identity'.[22]

The fusing of *the intellectual and the material world* dispels the metaphysical aspects of Humean scepticism. In the sonnets, Bowles's organic sensibility expresses itself through images of healing, solace, and recovery. Scenes are left, but also revisited and recollected in absence. Vivid immediate impressions are repeatedly accommodated into the background tones of time and age. When the poet visits Netley Abbey the ruins are 'sunk forlorn', and he begins to meditate on them as an emblem of the 'hard mishap' of life; but just when the reader is expecting a move to the poet's own troubles (such as Charlotte Smith might make) the speaker withdraws and leaves the scene to recompose itself. He sees that the ancient building is

> Yet wearing still a charm, that age and cares
> Cou'd ne'er subdue, decking the silver hairs
>   Of sorrow—as with short-liv'd gleam the morn
> Illumines, whilst it weeps, the refted tower
> That lifts its forehead grey, and smiles beneath the shower. (Sonnet XIX, 10–14)

While the poem's single sentence unfolds, the ruins merge into an image of human age. Once again *silver* bursts out of *grey*, and a brief light effect animates the landscape as the old physical material responds to the impression of the moment. Observation and metaphor, matter and idea, are amicably joined, and no return to the self is needed because it has been absorbed into the scene. In this way the limited space of the sonnet allows generous room for the reader. The experience is not privatised, but opened out to us in friendship. In Coleridge's words, the final lines *domesticate with the heart, and become, as it were, a part of our identity.*

The young Coleridge of the 1790s came to associate the sonnet form, and Bowles's sonnets in particular, with the idea of friendship. The words stayed with you and like a friend they could be turned to in moments of need or pleasant association ('easily remembered from their briefness . . . these are the poems which we can "lay up in our heart, and our soul," and repeat them "when we walk by the way, and when we lie down and when we rise up"').[23] From his first reading of Bowles's sonnets in 1789 Coleridge used them to express his own friendships – he made over forty copies of them for others, and in 1796 he edited a small collection of sonnets, mostly by himself and his friends, to be bound up with those of Bowles, opening the collection with Bowles's sonnet 'To a Friend'.[24] Friendship could thus be given a palpable, communal form.

In *Biographia Literaria* (1817) Coleridge paid tribute to Bowles for having rescued him in adolescence from the 'mental disease' of 'metaphysicks'. As his early mentor, Bowles helped initiate 'a long and blessed interval, during which my natural faculties were allowed to expand and my original tendencies to develop themselves'.[25] This image of the human mind and senses growing naturally into their powers is one that both Coleridge and Wordsworth developed memorably from the late 1790s on. It also forms the subject of a poem addressed to Coleridge in 1797 by Anna Laetitia Barbauld, one that confronts aspects of the relationship between the physical and 'meta-physical', the worlds of matter and idea, which have guided this chapter. Her 'To Mr Coleridge' is simultaneously an encouragement and a warning to a 'romantic' poet of the 1790s.

Barbauld's setting is a grove half way up the allegorical hill of 'science' (i.e. knowledge). It is a place of Spenserian enchantment, which offers a temporary reprieve from the poet's arduous journey where 'each mind / Of finer mould, acute and delicate, / In its high progress to eternal truth / Rests for a space, in fairy bowers entranced' (25–8). In this landscape of ghosts and 'floating gossamer' the young man is drawn into a substanceless dimension where 'dreams hang on every leaf: unearthly forms / Glide through the gloom; and mystic visions swim / Before the cheated sense'. It is, in other words, the essence of the romantic mode. In this delightful place 'things of life, / Obvious to sight and touch' fade into images, and ideas lose contact with the material reality that should support them. Barbauld's warning to Coleridge is clear:

> Youth beloved
> Of science—of the muse beloved, not here,
> Not in the maze of metaphysic lore,
> Build thou thy place of resting! . . . Active scenes
> Shall soon with healthful spirit brace thy mind:
> And fair exertion, for bright fame sustained,
> For friends, for country . . . (32–41)

Outside the self's reflexive images, a physical world is waiting with its opportunities and responsibilities. But *exertion* is needed (here in the older sense of 'force directed outwards') if the youth's potential is to be realised. This is the key to Barbauld's view of the self as a dynamic, God-given power. An individual sensibility expands into a wider sphere by engaging with *friends* and *country*, and its development is sustained by a combination of divine prompting and human nurturing – as Barbauld says in the blessing that ends the poem: 'Now heaven conduct thee with a parent's love!'. These are for her two aspects of a single force.

Barbauld's Unitarianism (shared by Coleridge at this date) is an important element of this and other poems of hers from the 1760s onwards. Its principle of a universal spirit informing and unifying all life finds a continuity between the vast creation and the still small voice within, between the sublime and the domestic. What might be seen as a subjective mental world is in fact a Unitarian 'conscience', a growing knowledge of the world and our place within it, which guides human progress. Barbauld's handling of this idea in 'A Summer Evening's Meditation' (published in her first collection of *Poems*, 1773) combines an imaginative exploration of the solar system with a simultaneous awareness of inner growth. The two are interdependent. Through introspection she locates her infinite potential:

> At this still hour the self-collected soul
> Turns inward, and beholds a stranger there
> Of high descent, and more than mortal rank;
> An embryo GOD, a spark of fire divine,
> Which must burn on for ages . . . (53–7)

The self *turns inward*, but only to find the energy for a poetic journey through the extent of creation. Having reached the far end of the universe she imagines the worlds beyond that God has not yet animated, '[w]here embryo systems and unkindled suns / Sleep in the womb of chaos' (97–8). It is the same image of human possibility with which she started.

The epigraph to the 'Meditation' is taken from Book Nine of Edward Young's *Night Thoughts* (1742–5), a sublime nocturnal meditation on the grandest scale, which soon became the most admired religious poem of the century (and not only in Britain). Barbauld's poem, however, is notable for its different theological and poetic emphasis. Behind Young's visions is an apocalyptic scenario of God's judgment on human sin. There is a degree of relish when Young imagines the final day of reckoning: 'I see the JUDGE inthron'd! The flaming Guard! / The Volume open'd! Open'd every Heart! . . / . . For Guilt no Plea! To Pain, no Pause! no Bound! / Inexorable, All! and All, Extreme!' (IX, 268–74). Lacking this high-decibel emphasis on sin and damnation, Barbauld's Unitarian spirit waits quietly for its eventual revelation: 'Let me here / Content and grateful, wait th'appointed time / And ripen for the skies' ('Meditation', 118–20). In place of Young's momentous sublime she offers a more organic sublimation. Being a development from the Natural Religion of the early eighteenth century, Unitarianism sees nature as expressing the divine essence. Young, however, like Anne Finch in the wake of the 1703 hurricane,[26] makes it powerless before God's decree:

> In various Modes of Emphasis and Awe,
> *He* spoke his Will, and trembling *Nature* heard;
> He spoke it loud, in Thunder and in Storm.
> Witness, Thou *Sinai!* whose Cloud-cover'd Height,
> And shaken Basis, own'd the present GOD: (*Night Thoughts*, VII, 1105–9)

The divine *Will* is spoken through the Ten Commandments of the Hebrew Bible, the basis of God's law, delivered to Moses on Mount Sinai ('And all the people saw the thunderings, and the lightnings').[27] And here in contrast is Barbauld invoking her God in explicit contradiction to the biblical account that Young offers. Her divine force works calmly from within:

> O look with pity down
> On erring guilty man; not in thy names
> Of terrour clad; not with those thunders arm'd
> That conscious Sinai felt, when fear appall'd
> The scatter'd tribes; thou hast a gentler voice,
> That whispers comfort to the swelling heart . . . ('Meditation', 106–11)

For Barbauld, God's voice is an interior one. It does not thunder from a mountain top and deliver moral laws on tablets of stone. Barbauld's holy book is the universal text of nature – a 'mystic tablet, hung on high / To public gaze' (33–4).

The Unitarian language of nature emphasises the communal dimension of the individual life; it tends to see belief and knowledge as growing outward together, and a system of values emerging through personal experience. This provides the basis for an ethical self, the idea of human potential being exerted in a wider context within the physical world. Freedom of the spirit is therefore central, chiefly because it allows the self to communicate with other free spirits, and share intellectual excitements and human sympathies.[28] Where Young's nocturnal thoughts sweep him into a spiritual cosmos that spurns worldly attachments,[29] Barbauld's early poetry written during her Warrington years is fired by actual people and causes that embody this spirit, whether it is a little nation struggling for independence ('Corsica'), a trapped 'free-born' mouse begging for release ('The Mouse's Petition'), or a great scientist unravelling nature's secrets ('A Character of Joseph Priestley') – all are exerting a God-given liberty. Her friend Priestley, a teacher at the Warrington Academy before becoming a Unitarian minister, is celebrated as a spiritual disseminator: 'Pour thy free spirit o'er the breathing page, / And wake the virtue of a careless age!' (11–12). The irony of 'The Mouse's Petition' is that it is directed at Priestley, who had imprisoned the animal 'for the sake of making experiments with different kinds of air'[30] – but this tiny creature is playing a part in Priestley's discovery of oxygen. Its appeal to 'the vital air' that both of them breathe as 'nature's commoners' is a plea to the chemist as much as the egalitarian philosopher.

The growth of large things from small fascinates Barbauld, and nowhere more than in her poem of domestic sublimity, 'To a Little Invisible Being who is expected soon to become visible'.[31] The infant in the womb, a 'germ of new life', is a potential consciousness waiting to engage with the world of sense: 'What powers lie folded in thy curious frame,—/ Senses from objects locked, and mind from thought!' (5–6). This creature will soon establish its own identity within a context of friendship and mutuality, a 'rich inheritance of love' (25). Barbauld takes the attuned sympathies of sensibility (here literally symbiotic) and complicates them by focusing on the separating out of one individual being from another; it is seen, however, not as a severance but as the beginning of an attachment. It will be an expansion of the mother's self into an object of love, a growth in awareness through this new being: 'She longs to fold to her maternal breast / Part of herself, yet to herself unknown' (21–2). Like Priestley the experimental chemist, Barbauld recognises that the smallest new unit within nature can become a vital part of the greater scheme, its value emerging only when its individual powers encounter others. In talking about scientific discovery, Priestley seems to be glossing the thought in Barbauld's poem. He welcomes

> those single facts, which may seem, at first sight, to be the most insignificant, and the most remote from every possible use. Every new fact should be carefully examined, as a treasure of unknown value, the real worth of which time, and the discovery of other kindred powers in nature, may bring to light.[32]

We are back to the Unitarian principle of things unfolding into value. Nothing is so remote and insignificant that it cannot have meaning – but meaning and value develop together when the self recognises *kindred powers in nature*. No fact has meaning for itself alone. Not surprisingly, Barbauld finds the notion of individual 'rights' insufficient for her purposes. In her challenging poem 'The Rights of Woman' she urges a move from a language of self-asserting 'rights' to one that acknowledges a more communal ethos where 'separate rights are lost in mutual love' (32). *Separate* is the negative word here. The divine spirit in each human being guarantees that the fullest self-expression (or rather, self-exertion) is not through subjectivity, but through finding ways of conversing with others. In the dynamics of Barbauld's poetry the physical world offers scope and proper exercise for the 'free spirit'.

This principle of sociable self-exertion is also a guiding motif of William Cowper's *The Task* (1785), a six-book poem that holds the reader's interest through an extraordinary range of topics, from furniture design to religious doctrine, from the slave trade to cucumber-growing. Although Cowper's religious beliefs differed markedly from Barbauld's,[33] in *The Task* he shares her concern with socialising the self, and with developing the poetic voice into a kind of friendly conscience – an active and companionable moral sensibility that the reader can engage with. Earlier in this chapter we heard the twenty-three-year-old Cowper, among his satirical cronies of the Nonsense Club, losing his mental thread as he chatted to his friend Lloyd (''Tis gone again— Plague on't! I thought / I had it—but I have it not'). It seems a very different Cowper three decades later who in *The Task* can hold his multifarious threads together with ease and converse so sanely and wisely with his readers. The sceptical coffee-house wit of the 1750s is certainly a long way from the man in his fifties who has found refuge in domesticity and country retreat – after years of breakdowns and recoveries, religious rebirth and spiritual crisis. Yet it is possible to discern a connecting 'thread' between the two Cowpers in the idea of friendly 'converse' itself (what Coleridge called 'the divine Chit chat of Cowper'[34]), which grows out of a need for the self to reach 'out there' for some kind of meaning, however precarious, and find something with which the heart can *domesticate*. For Cowper, familiarity (in places, friends, routines) was imperative, and *The Task*'s compendious character allowed the poet to introduce his readers to every aspect of his physical, mental and emotional world. We in turn become amicably familiar with his favourite places, his hobbies, his pet hates, his worries and grumbles, the things that make him angry and the things that fill him with joy.

In this way, Cowper's *Task* may help to continue the trajectory of this chapter, which has attempted to trace some of the significant developments in sensibility (and especially in notions of the 'self') during the second half of the century. We have moved from the protean, performative 'self' of mid-century satire, to the reflective 'self' of the sonnet, and the exertions of the ethical self in Barbauld. From a philosophical scepticism that challenged both continuous identity and a material 'reality' we have reached the Unitarian imperative of projecting the free spirit into the living world. Behind all these shifting positions, however, has been a need for human intimacy. It is something that Cowper's *Task* expresses, and the theme has emerged repeatedly in this discussion – in Richard Jago wanting reassurance from his friendly readers, in Hume playing backgammon, in the *social converse* of Churchill and Lloyd, in Charlotte Smith and her sentimental subscribers, in Coleridge making Bowles part of his identity, and in Barbauld's mother and baby. These are not just matters of *address*, but forms of vital connectedness that for some hold off solipsism and vacancy.

Cowper's *Task* is a product of these tensions, and his particular achievement in the poem is to create an identity that can hold his miscellany of topics together without being egocentric or expressing mere personality. He manages to achieve a voice that is simultaneously principled yet accommodating, and with it he is able to substantiate (literally 'stand beneath') the self he is projecting. It gives his words weight and conviction, and as readers we are made to feel that we are not just responding to an individual, but becoming part of an ethical community. Here he is setting out at the beginning of Book Five on a winter morning walk, watching as the low sun plays tricks with his shadow:

> Mine, spindling into longitude immense,
> In spite of gravity and sage remark
> That I myself am but a fleeting shade,
> Provokes me to a smile. With eye askance
> I view the muscular proportion'd limb
> Transform'd to a lean shank. The shapeless pair
> As they design'd to mock me, at my side
> Take step for step . . . (V, 11–18)

This is a poet who understands the games of self and can look *askance* at his own image. How many possible tones and reactions are accommodated here – satiric, playful, moralising, curious, boastful, melancholy, even a touch morbid – all held together by a wry amusement at the moment's ironies. The substantial human microcosm (with his *longitude* and *gravity*) has become a walking shadow. And echoing behind Cowper's words are the intoned phrases of the burial service in the 1662 Anglican prayerbook: 'Behold, thou hast made my days as it were a span long . . . For man walketh in a vain shadow . . .'.[35] The reader becomes conscious that this *doppelgänger* of his own mortality is an intimate friend who will always accompany him – though never so visible again. There is a personal language here, but at the same time a communal one.

In *The Task* we are in the hands not of a meditative ego, but of an alert consciousness on the move. A self is certainly being revealed, but in a more oblique way, like his spindly shadow – and we watch him watching it. Whether taking one of his familiar walks, seated at the fireside, or working in his garden, his attention will focus on natural or domestic details, then expand into any topic that he wishes. Cowper revels in his poem's generic freedom, drawing from the language of Miltonic epic, georgic, mock-heroic, devotional verse, political and moral satire, or parody. In particular he combines the public range of the topographical poem and the relaxed conversational intimacies of the verse letter. The poem was begun as a lighthearted 'task' to write Miltonic verse in praise of the sofa (a subject suggested by his friend, Lady Austen), but after a hundred lines Cowper steers away from this playful exercise of the wit into a full exercise of the sensory, spiritual, and moral faculties. At the beginning he celebrates the sofa in mock-heroic terms for the freedom it gives the human body: 'relaxation of the languid frame / By soft recumbency of outstretch'd limbs' (I, 81–2). But for Cowper freedom is not relaxation.[36] The passage recalls his friend Lloyd's picture of the 'lazy muse' indolently stretching across three chairs ('An arm lolls dangling o'er another'). As if to dismiss this caricature of his old Nonsense Club days and set the character of his new poem, Cowper immediately leaves the sofa behind ('The SOFA suits / The gouty limb', I, 106–7), and goes for a brisk walk, delighting in the physical exercise – 'The play of lungs inhaling and again / Respiring freely the fresh air, that makes / Swift pace or steep ascent no toil to me' (I, 137–9). This is the man we have to follow. There is to be no languid self-indulgence, no idle smoke-rings blown at the ceiling, but a sense of purpose and effort that we are invited to share.

To breathe *freely* is a crucial idea in the poem. Like Barbauld, Cowper is fervently committed to the principle of liberty as being vital for the organic growth of human life. He associates it with the freedom to move, love, create, gain knowledge, and choose one's own path – to be in a state where the self can develop emotionally and mentally. He chose as the poem's motto *Fit surculus arbor* ('The shoot becomes the tree'). For him, the liberty to grow lies behind all creativity. We meet instances of this when we catch up with him on his winter morning walk. He is marvelling at the icicles on the trees, where nature's 'random strokes' take on 'a thousand shapes'. The frost's enchanting, whimsical effects put him in mind of the ice-palace of the Russian Empress, constructed of heavy blocks whose 'well-adjusted parts / Were soon conjoin'd' (146–7). But its freezing rooms, with an ice-bed and furniture correct in every detail, were made to torture a courtier and his bride – a cruel joke played by a tyrant.[37] For Cowper this palace offers a revealing comment 'on human grandeur and the courts of kings':

> 'Twas transient in its nature, as in show
> 'Twas durable. As worthless as it seem'd
> Intrinsically precious. To the foot
> Treach'rous and false, it smil'd, and it was cold. (V, 173–6)

We feel Cowper's shudder at an artistic sensibility turned evil. Unlike nature's organic forms this controlled illusion was created by a malign will, and thus had an *intrinsic* worthlessness and falsity.

These thoughts lead Cowper into an attack on state tyranny and an argument that moves him naturally to its great symbol, the Bastille. This inhuman structure (sadly not so transient as an ice-palace) becomes the focus for his thoughts on the nature of freedom and the horror of its loss. Cowper's liberty is both external and internal, and he is uncompromising about the role that the spirit must play in preserving it: 'Whose freedom is by suff'rance, and at will / Of a superior, he is never free. / Who lives and is not weary of a life / Expos'd to manacles, deserves them well' (363–6). It is the nature of rule to oppress, and the only justification for any state system is the people's love. Without it, 'blind instinct' takes over, which 'crouches to the rod, / And licks the foot that treads it in the dust' (V, 355–6). This is the self-tyranny of the unthinking subject who has lost claim to an autonomous identity. Only when the communal *spirit* has been aroused can an oppressive state be overthrown: 'But slaves that once conceive the glowing thought / Of freedom, in that hope itself possess / All that the contest calls for; spirit, strength, / The scorn of danger, and united hearts' (374–7). It will be an uprising of a people's humanity, and he looks to the day when the Bastille will fall.

But in 1785 the tyranny was still in place. When he enters the prison cell Cowper does not give the reader a picture of a forlorn inmate. There is no dirty bearded figure for us to sympathise with. Instead, his imagination draws us into a horrifying material solipsism. We are made to share a consciousness whose freedom has been destroyed. The mind feels too painfully its own mental reflections on the world outside, and is forced 'to fly for refuge from distracting thought' and seize on the physically palpable. Fourteen lines describe the narrow room into which the senses and emotions have now shrunk:

> To read engraven on the mouldy walls,
> In stagg'ring types, his predecessor's tale,
> A sad memorial, and subjoin his own—
> To turn purveyor to an overgorg'd
> And bloated spider, till the pamper'd pest
> Is made familiar, watches his approach,
> Comes at his call and serves him for a friend—
> To wear out time in numb'ring to and fro
> The studs that thick emboss his iron door,
> Then downward and then upward, then aslant
> And then alternate, with a sickly hope
> By dint of change to give his tasteless task
> Some relish, till the sum exactly found
> In all directions, he begins again—(V, 418–31)

The prisoner is brought ever closer to madness. The text he carves into the wall (struggling to imitate the 'look' of print) will be his epitaph, to be read only by his successor. The need for intimacy with a friend is met by a predatory spider. The eye, no longer able to range through nature, numbers the studs on the door, and Cowper gives us a marching parody of visual variety (*Then downward and then upward, then aslant / And then alternate*). These suffocating obsessions represent everything that Cowper strives to resist. In its dynamic engagement with the world beyond the self, *The Task* asserts that we should value and use the freedom of our minds. Wide-ranging thought represents not just the character of the poem, but its ethical imperative:

'Tis liberty alone that gives the flow'r
Of fleeting life its lustre and perfume,
And we are weeds without it. All constraint,
Except what wisdom lays on evil men,
Is evil, hurts the faculties, impedes
Their progress in the road of science; blinds
The eye sight of discov'ry . . . (V, 446–52)

In his 'Eton College Ode' Gray talked of 'constraint / To sweeten liberty' (33–4), but Cowper feels no ambivalence on this point. Sharing Barbauld's commitment to *the road of science*, he is aware of the extent to which *constraint* is an evil because it blocks off our human *faculties*. In this Bastille scene Cowper is conscious of the paradox by which we project ourselves imaginatively into the mind of a figure deprived of his imagination, and enter sympathetically the world of someone cut off from human sympathies.

In a literary text, sensibility could thus create a frustrating gap between the reader's imaginative freedom (here to reach out and open the prison door) and the plight of a victim in the material world. The radical potential of imaginative sympathy lay in its ability to arouse private emotions of pity, indignation, or anger (perhaps each in turn), which might spread outward from an individual, through networks of sympathetic friends, and into the wider community. Sensibility offered a centrifugal model for the growth of a national conscience.[38] It could be a potent weapon, too, in infusing large public issues with an emotional immediacy, opening a channel between private affect and social effect. Harnessed to the wider principle of the 'brotherhood of man' within a 'universal nature', sentimental mechanisms could make another's plight your own, and show not only how things were but how they might be made different.

Between 1787 and 1791 one national issue helped to politicise sensibility by exploiting this notion of a community of feeling. The campaign to abolish the British slave trade ('human nature's broadest, foulest blot', wrote Cowper[39]) reached a climax in 1788 when hundreds of local petitions circulated all over Britain and became a nationwide voice. For some poets it was a triumphant indication of how far human sympathy could extend. Hannah More in her poem *Slavery* (1788) appreciated the potential: 'From heads to hearts lies Nature's plain appeal, / Tho' few can reason, *all mankind can feel*' (149–50, my italics). Sensibility's organic mechanisms became the model for how benevolent feelings could defy physical boundaries and establish a universal society. There seemed to be no limit to this unleashing of the spirit:

Oh, social love,
Thou universal good, thou that canst fill
The vacuum of immensity, and live
In endless void! Thou that in motion first
set'st the long lazy atoms, by thy force
Quickly assimilating, and restrained
By strong attraction—touch the soul of man;
Subdue him; make a fellow-creature's woe
His own by heartfelt sympathy . . . (414–22)

This is Ann Yearsley in her *Poem on the Inhumanity of the Slave-Trade* (1788) using the enigma of voluntary motion (individual physical atoms stimulated to *touch the soul*) as an image for the boundless possibilities of human love, and for a supreme non-material value. For her, as for William Blake, 'One thought fills immensity';[40] but the question remained whether such a powerful idea could be harnessed to practical realities. For the men of business who resisted reform, the notion was fanciful and utopian. In place of the abolitionists' national spirit, a correspondent of *The Gentleman's Magazine* urged a Hobbesian model of the nation-body, which had to survive in a brutal material world: 'Self-preservation', he remarked, 'is the primary law of nations, as well as nature'. For him, the idea of abolition was 'a visionary system, which never yet existed but in the productions of poetic genius', and he deplored 'those visionary lamentations which the enthusiasm of benevolence has diffused through the nation'.[41] When Hannah More ruefully asked 'Does matter govern spirit?' (*Slavery*, 65) she was exposing the philosophical core of the slavery debate.[42]

Yearsley and other campaigning poets sought literally to 'animate' Great Britain – to give it a soul, a conscience, and a nervous system, make it register the horrors of slavery and rouse itself as a moral being. In Yearsley's poem, the graphic details of the torture and death of Luco the slave are designed to touch the nerves of her readers, who by 'sympathy unseen, shall feel / Another's pang' (406–7). In this way matter and spirit, nerve and soul, will become continuous, and register something of Luco's agony. Hannah More used similar terms to assert the full humanity of the African slave (often denied): 'There needs no logic sure to make us feel. / The nerve, howe'er untutor'd, can sustain / A sharp, unutterable sense of pain; / As exquisitely fashion'd in a slave ...' (*Slavery*, 158–60); and in 'The Negro's Complaint' (1788) Cowper voiced the idea in his slave's direct challenge to the British nation: 'Prove that *You* have Human Feelings / 'Ere ye proudly question *Ours*' (55–6). Britain had to show that she could feel others' pain. It was the country's failure three years later to rise to this challenge that stirred Anna Barbauld to write her *Epistle to William Wilberforce, Esq. on the Rejection of the Bill for abolishing the Slave Trade* (1791). In her text the nation is a callous and unfeeling body that has refused to become fully human:

> Thy Country knows the sin, and stands the shame!
> The Preacher, Poet, Senator in vain
> Has rattled in her sight the Negro's chain ...
> She knows and she persists—Still Afric bleeds,
> Uncheck'd, the human traffic still proceeds;
> She stamps her infamy to future time,
> And on her harden'd forehead seals the crime. (2–18)

It has been a human failure, and Britain carries the guilt of it.

To see the country in personified terms was nothing new; but to equip it not only with a mind and voice but also with a sensibility, an imagination, and a conscience, was risking disappointment. The self and the state were not to be so easily equated. In terms of the self, sensibility allowed mercurial leaps from feeling to thought to action: 'Sweet Sensibility! thou keen delight! / Unprompted moral! sudden sense of right! / Perception exquisite! fair virtue's seed! / Thou quick precursor of the lib'ral deed!' (Hannah More, *Sensibility* [1782], 237–40); but as a model for political action, as More herself came to realise, these rousing spontaneities hinted at a revolutionary agenda, and set a dangerous precedent. Sensibility during the 1790s became associated with radical fervour and the excesses of the French 'Terror',[43] and the *lib'ral deed* of ending the slave trade took another forty years.

If change was to come, then perhaps it had to be accommodated to that recalcitrant tradition of British common sense, which enjoyed checking idealist theories with stubborn actuality. In this chapter we have seen how Richard Jago held off the immaterial 'visionary Scene' by embracing his local landscape and his sensible readers, and also how Bowles's sonnets helped Coleridge to fend off metaphysics. In *The Task*, Cowper identifies what he calls a 'roughness in the grain / Of British natures' (V, 480–1), an aspect of the national character about which he feels ambivalent. To him it is an unpleasing, material stubbornness; but the rough grain is also a sign of rugged independence, part of the awkward constitutional mixture called British freedom ('wanting its excuse / That it belongs to freemen, would disgust / And shock me', V, 481–3). As an amateur carpenter, Cowper knew how the grain in wood could be exploited, and that areas of strength were often located in 'tough knee-timber' where the wood was most gnarled. [44] Writing to a friend about the structure of *The Task*, Cowper spoke of 'the tenons and mortises by which the several passages are connected and let into each other',[45] and this image from carpentry gets us to the heart of his poetic workmanship. Cowper understood the way a natural material could be worked; but there was a wider political lesson in this too. For a state to survive through the centuries it had to accommodate many tensions and individual interests. After the fall of the Bastille in 1789 the British kingdom appeared precarious, a decayed structure waiting to be toppled. An independent America had enshrined its liberties in a written constitution, and the French were beginning the world again. But Britain clung to its traditional compromises, resisting reform, and combining repression at home with a long continental war. For Cowper in 1792, writing his poem 'Yardley Oak', the nation itself seemed like an old oak-tree, hollow and misshapen, but with its roots intact:

> Embowell'd now, and of thy antient self
> Possessing nought but the scoop'd rind that seems
> An huge throat calling to the clouds for drink . . .
> Yet is thy root sincere, sound as the rock,
> A quarry of stout spurs and knotted fangs
> Which crook'd into a thousand whimsies, clasp
> The stubborn soil, and hold thee still erect.
> So stands a Kingdom whose foundations yet
> Fail not, in virtue and in wisdom lay'd,
> Though all the superstructure by the tooth
> Pulverized of venality, a shell
> Stands now, and semblance only of itself. (110–24)

This *antient self*, a grotesque fusion of whim and stubbornness, somehow survives because its spirit is alive, and it continues to draw from its roots. What gives the tree an identity is not the *superstructure* but the life within. We are brought back to David Hume's enigma of the continuous self, and it is Hume who best explains the idea behind Cowper's lines. In his chapter 'Of Personal Identity', Hume writes: 'An oak that grows from a small plant to a large tree is still the same oak, though there be not one particle of matter or figure of its parts the same'.[46] Cowper, however, can also accommodate physical continuity and heroic endurance, turning Hume's sceptical paradox into rooted belief. This kind of organic sensibility, developed as we have seen by poets like Bowles, Barbauld, and Cowper, partly as a reaction to metaphysical scepticism, was taken further by a new generation of poets in the 1790s, for whom the organic growth of a poetic self was a subject with great creative potential.

Notes

1. 'Metaphysical Subtleties exploded' is Jago's boastful claim in the 'Argument' to Book Three (*Edge-Hill* [1767], p. 82). The address to the reader is omitted from the revised text of Book Three in his *Poems* (1784).

2. See earlier, pp.

3. See G.J. Barker-Benfield, *The Culture of Sensibility: Sex and Society in Eighteenth-Century Britain* (Chicago and London, 1992), pp. 1–36; T. Brown, 'From Mechanism to Vitalism in Eighteenth-Century Physiology', *Journal of Human Biology*, 7 (1974), 179–216; L.J. Rather, *Mind and Body in Eighteenth-Century Medicine* (Berkeley and Los Angeles, 1965); and David Fairer, 'Sentimental Translation in Mackenzie and Sterne', *Essays in Criticism*, 49 (1999), 132–51 (pp. 133–7).

4. See David Hume, *An Enquiry Concerning Human Understanding* (1777), Section VII, Part I). In *Edge-Hill* Jago acknowledges that 'Reason strives in vain to tell / How Matter acts on incorporeal Mind' (III, 17–18).

5. The faculties of sense, imagination, and reason, each with its own function and location within the brain. See Lawrence Babb, *The Elizabethan Malady* (East Lansing, 1951), pp. 2–5. Reason's godlike rule is described by Milton's Adam, *Paradise Lost*, V, 100–113. See also Michael DePorte, *Nightmares and Hobbyhorses: Swift, Sterne, and Augustan Ideas of Madness* (San Marino, 1974), pp. 12–14.

6. See John Mullan, *Sentiment and Sociability: The Language of Feeling in the Eighteenth Century* (Oxford, 1988), pp. 1–56.

7. Examples are Harley in Henry Mackenzie's *The Man of Feeling* (1771), Primrose in Goldsmith's *The Vicar of Wakefield* (1766), and most notably the hero of Sterne's *Tristram Shandy* (1759–67).

8. *The Monthly Review*, 26 (1762), 316.

9. Hume's *Treatise* made very little impact on first publication (it 'fell dead-born from the press'). He reworked his ideas in more popular form in *Philosophical Essays concerning Human Understanding* (1748) and *An Enquiry concerning the Principles of Morals* (1751), both of which established his philosophical reputation.

10. 'We save ourselves from this total scepticism only by means of that singular and seemingly trivial property of the fancy, by which we enter with difficulty into remote views of things, and are not able to accompany them with so sensible an impression, as we do those which are more easy and natural' (*Treatise*, I. iv. 7).

11. See Lance Bertelsen, *The Nonsense Club: Literature and Popular Culture, 1749–1764* (Oxford, 1986), especially pp. 91–131. Churchill, though not an original or 'official' member of the group of seven, was intimately part of its activities from 1758 (p. 92).

12. *The Poetical Works of Robert Lloyd, A.M.*, ed. William Kenrick, 2 vols (London, 1774), I, xi.

13. Lloyd, 'Familiar Epistle to * * * * * * ', 131–4 (*Poetical Works*, II, 154).

14. *Poetical Works*, I, xiv (Kenrick is quoting 'Capt. E. Thompson').

15. The quotation is from Wordsworth's sonnet, 'Nuns fret not at their convent's narrow room'. He goes on to remark that 'in sundry moods, 'twas pastime to be bound / Within the Sonnet's scanty spot of ground'.

16. Sonnets 21–25 assume the voice of Goethe's suicidal hero Werther. Each poem is developed from a single image or phrase in the novel (1774), and moves to the idea of death in its final line, so as to form a sequence of emotional cameos.

17. Hume, *Appendix to the Treatise* (1740).

18. *Elegiac Sonnets, by Charlotte Smith. The Fifth Edition, with Additional Sonnets and Other Poems* (London, 1789), p. 44.

19. Added for the two-volume eighth edition of *Elegiac Sonnets* (1797), II, 4.

20. Sonnet 40, from Smith's novel *Emmeline* (1788). *Elegiac Sonnets* (1789), p. 40.

21. William Lisle Bowles, *Sonnets, Written Chiefly on Picturesque Spots, During a Tour*, 2nd ed. (Bath, 1789), p. 12. This is the text Bowles revised from the first edition earlier that year (*Fourteen Sonnets, Elegiac and Descriptive. Written During a Tour*).

22. S.T. Coleridge (ed.), *Sonnets from Various Authors* (1796), preface.

23. Ibid.

24. See the facsimile edition by Paul M. Zall (Glendale, 1968). See also David Fairer, 'Coleridge's *Sonnets from Various Authors* (1796): A Lost Conversation Poem?', *Studies in Romanticism* (2003).

25. S.T. Coleridge, *Biographia Literaria* (1817), ch.1.

26. See Anne Finch, 'Upon the Hurricane', pp. 129–31 above. The voice of Young's 'Nature' also acknowledges a greater power: 'Place, at Nature's Head, / A Sovereign, which o'er all Things rolls His Eye, / Extends His Wing, promulgates His Commands' (*Night Thoughts*, IX, 2024–6).

27. Exodus, 20:18.

28. On the relationship between the domestic and the public/civic in Barbauld's writings, see Harriet Guest, *Small Change: Women, Learning, Patriotism, 1750–1810* (Chicago and London, 2000), pp. 220–51.

29. See Steve Clark, ' "Between Self and Self's Book": Locke and the Poetry of the Early Romantics', in *Early Romantics: Perspectives in British Poetry from Pope to Wordsworth*, ed. Thomas Woodman (Houndmills, 1998), pp. 30–54 (pp. 43–7).

30. Barbauld's footnote in *Poems* (1773).

31. Printed in Barbauld's *Works* (1825), I, 199–201. It is undated, but Barbauld's modern editors note that its position in the *Works* suggests a date c. 1795. See *The Poems of Anna Letitia Barbauld*, ed. William McCarthy and Elizabeth Kraft (Athens and London, 1994), p. 296.

32. Joseph Priestley, *The History and Present State of Discoveries relating to Vision, Light, and Colours*, 2 vols (London, 1772), I, 56. This is quoted by Jane Stabler in her valuable article exploring the links between Barbauld, Priestley, and Coleridge. See 'Space for Speculation: Coleridge, Barbauld, and the Poetics of Priestley', in *Samuel Taylor Coleridge and the Sciences of Life*, ed. Nicholas Roe (Oxford, 2001), pp. 175–204 (p. 184).

33. Cowper came to have a vivid belief in God's judgment on human sin, and in the divine inspiration of the Bible: 'The word is a flaming sword, and he that touches it with unhallowed fingers, thinking to make a tool of it, will find that he has burnt them' (Cowper – John Newton, [April 1783]).

34. S.T. Coleridge – John Thelwall, 17 December 1796.

35. The prayerbook text is based on Psalm 39.

36. He wrote to a friend about his progress on the poem: 'The Sofa is ended but not finish'd . . . Do not imagine however that I lownge over it. On the contrary I find it severe exercise to mould it and fashion it to my mind' (Cowper – William Bull, [3 August 1784]).

37. See P.M.S. Dawson, 'Cowper and the Russian Ice Palace', *Review of English Studies*, 31 (1980), 440–3.

38. 'There, feeling is diffus'd through every part, / Thrills in each nerve, and lives in all the heart' (Hannah More, *Sensibility* [1782], 71–2).

39. *The Task*, II, 22.

40. William Blake, 'Proverbs of Hell', 36 (*The Marriage of Heaven and Hell*, 1790, Plate 8).

41. 'Thoughts on the Abolition of the African Slave Trade, considered chiefly in a prudential and political View' (*The Gentleman's Magazine*, 58 [1788], 407–9). The writer added: 'War is a necessary consequence of human depravity . . . Such is the state of nature' (p. 409).

42. More is referring to the pro-slavery argument that African blacks were not fully human: 'Does then th'immortal principle within / Change with the casual colour of a skin? / Does matter govern spirit?' (*Slavery*, 63–5).

43. James Gillray's anti-radical cartoon 'New Morality' (*The Anti-Jacobin*, 1 August 1798) includes a statue of 'Sensibility' weeping over a dead bird, while her foot rests on the severed head of Louis XVI.

44. '. . . robust and bold, / Warp'd into tough knee-timber' ('Yardley Oak', 98–9). Knee-timber, 'found in the crooked arms of oak', was able to bear counter-stresses, and was used in shipbuilding 'where the deck and the ship-sides meet' (Cowper's note).

45. Cowper – John Newton, 27 November 1784.

46. Hume, *Treatise*, I. iv. 6. Hume took this image from Locke's *Essay Concerning Human Understanding*, II. xxvii. 3–4.

Chronology

DATE	POEMS	OTHER WORKS	HISTORICAL EVENTS
1700	Dryden *Fables* Pomfret *The Choice*	Congreve *The Way of the World*	John Dryden dies (b. 1631) James Thomson born (d. 1748)
1701	John Philips *The Splendid Shilling* Chudleigh *The Ladies Defence* Finch *The Spleen*	Dennis *The Advancement and Reformation of Poetry*	Act of Settlement James II dies (b. 1633)
1702		Centlivre *The Stolen Heiress*	War of the Spanish Succession (–13) William III dies (b. 1650), succeeded by Anne John Pomfret dies (b. 1667) Judith Madan born (d. 1781)
1703	Egerton *Poems on Several Occasions* Chudleigh *Poems*	Hickes *Thesaurus* (–05) Addison and Steele *The Tender Husband*	Great Storm Samuel Pepys dies (b. 1633) Gilbert West born (d. 1756) John Wesley born (d. 1791)
1704		Swift *A Tale of a Tub, The Mechanical Operation of the Spirit* and *The Battle of the Books* Dennis *The Grounds of Criticism in Poetry* Newton *Opticks*	Battle of Blenheim Capture of Gibraltar John Locke dies (b. 1632)
1705	John Philips *Blenheim* Mandeville *The Grumbling Hive* Addison *The Campaign*	Astell *The Christian Religion*	Stephen Duck born (?) (d. 1756)
1706	Watts *Horae Lyricae*	Locke *Essay Concerning Human Understanding* (5th ed.) Farquhar *The Recruiting Officer*	Battle of Ramillies James Miller born (d. 1744) William Pattison born (d. 1727)

241

1707	Watts *Hymns and Spiritual Songs*	Farquhar *The Beaux' Stratagem*	Act of Union between England and Scotland
			Henry Fielding born (d. 1754)
			Mary Jones born (d. 1778)
1708	John Philips *Cyder*	Shaftesbury *A Letter Concerning Enthusiasm*	Samuel Boyse born (d. 1749)
	Ozell *Boileau's Lutrin*		
1709	*Poetical Miscellanies* (includes *Pastorals* by Pope and Ambrose Philips)	Shaftesbury *Sensus Communis*	First copyright law passed
		Steele and others *The Tatler* (–11)	John Philips dies (b. 1676)
	Ambrose Philips *A Winter-Piece*	Manley *New Atalantis*	Walter Harte born (d. 1774)
			John Armstrong born (d. 1779)
	Swift *A Description of the Morning*		Samuel Johnson born (d. 1784)
1710	Swift *A Description of a City Shower*	Swift and others *The Examiner* (–11)	Tories win general election
		Berkeley *Principles of Human Knowledge*	Mary Chudleigh dies (b. 1656)
			Edmund Smith dies (b. 1672)
			Robert Lowth born (d. 1787)
1711	Pope *Essay on Criticism*	Addison, Steele and others *The Spectator* (–14)	John Norris dies (b. 1657)
			David Hume born (d. 1776)
		Shaftesbury *Characteristicks*	
		Handel *Rinaldo*	
1712	Pope *Rape of the Lock* (two cantos)	Addison *The Pleasures of Imagination* (in *The Spectator*)	Handel settles in England
	Diaper *Nereides*		Last conviction for witchcraft in England
	Blackmore *The Creation*		Stamp Act
1713	Pope *Windsor-Forest*	Addison *Cato*	Peace of Utrecht
	Finch *Miscellany Poems*	Steele *The Guardian*	Lord Shaftesbury dies (b. 1671)
	Gay *The Fan*		Laurence Sterne born (d. 1768)
1714	Gay *The Shepherd's Week*	Mandeville *Fable of the Bees* (–29)	Queen Anne dies (b. 1665), succeeded by George I
	Pope *Rape of the Lock* (five cantos)	Locke *Collected Works*	Fall of Tory ministry
		The Ladies Library	Swift retires to Dublin
	Edmund Smith *Works*		William Shenstone born (d. 1763)

1715	Pope's translation of the *Iliad* (–20); *Temple of Fame* Watts *Divine Songs for the Use of Children*	Hughes's edition of Spenser Parnell *An Essay on the Life, Writings and Genius of Homer* Elizabeth Elstob *Anglo-Saxon Grammar*	Jacobite Rebellion Nicholas Rowe appointed Poet Laureate John Brown born (d. 1766) Richard Jago born (d. 1781)
1716	Gay *Trivia* Curll publishes Montagu's *Court Poems*		Thomas Gray born (d. 1771)
1717	Pope *Works* *The Rape of the Smock*	Pope, Gay and Arbuthnot *Three Hours after Marriage*	William Diaper dies (b. 1685)
1718	Prior *Poems on Several Occasions* Blackmore *The Kit-Cats*	Centlivre *A Bold Stroke for a Wife*	Thomas Parnell dies (b. 1679) Nicholas Rowe dies (b. 1674). Laurence Eusden appointed Poet Laureate
1719	Watts *The Psalms of David Imitated* Arbuckle *Snuff* *Hardyknute*	Defoe *Robinson Crusoe* Haywood *Love in Excess*	Joseph Addison dies (b. 1672) Samuel Garth dies (b. 1661) James Cawthorn born (d. 1761)
1720	Gay *Poems on Several Occasions* Hughes *The Ecstasy*		South Sea Bubble War with Spain (–29) Anne Finch dies (b. 1661) John Hughes dies (b. 1677)
1721	Thomas Parnell *A Night Piece on Death* Hill *The Judgment-Day* Arbuckle *Glotta*	Tickell (ed.) *Works of Addison* Gildon *The Laws of Poetry* Montesquieu *Lettres Persanes*	Walpole Prime Minister (–42) Matthew Prior dies (b. 1664) William Collins born (d. 1759) James Grainger born (d. 1766) Mark Akenside born (d. 1770) Tobias Smollett born (d. 1771)
1722	Parnell *Poems on Several Occasions* (ed. by Pope) W. Thomson *Orpheus Caledonius*	Defoe *Moll Flanders* Steele *The Conscious Lovers*	The Atterbury Plot Marlborough dies (b. 1650) Mary Leapor born (d. 1746) Christopher Smart born (d. 1771) Joseph Warton born (d. 1800)
1723	*A Collection of Old Ballads*	Jane Barker *A Patch-work Screen*	Sarah Egerton dies (b. 1670) Joshua Reynolds born (d. 1792)

1724	Ramsay *The Ever Green* Haywood *Poems*	Defoe *A Tour Thro' the Whole Island of Great Britain* Swift *Drapier's Letters*	William Mason born (d. 1797)
1725	Pope, trans., *Odyssey* (–26) Young *The Universal Passion* (–27)		
1726	Dyer *Grongar Hill* Thomson *Winter*	Newton *Principia* (3rd ed.) Swift *Gulliver's Travels*	Voltaire in England (–29)
1727	Gay *Fables* Pope, Swift, Arbuthnot *Miscellanies* (–35) Thomson *Summer* and *To the Memory of Newton* Broome *Poems*	Newton *Principia* trans. into English	George I dies (b. 1660), succeeded by George II Newton dies (b. 1642) William Pattison dies (b. 1706) Thomas Gainsborough born (d. 1788) John Wilkes born (d. 1797)
1728	Pope *Dunciad* (three books) Thomson *Spring*	Gay *Beggar's Opera* Chambers *Cyclopaedia* (–29) Pope *Peri Bathous*	Thomas Warton born (d. 1790)
1729	Pope *Dunciad Variorum* Savage *The Wanderer* Thomson *Britannia*	Swift *A Modest Proposal* Bach *St Matthew Passion*	Methodist Society founded Sir Richard Blackmore dies (b. 1650) William Congreve dies (b. 1670) Sir Richard Steele dies (b. 1672) Edmund Burke born (d. 1797) Thomas Percy born (d. 1811)
1730	Thomson *The Seasons* Duck *Poems on Several Subjects* George Woodward *Poems* Young *Imperium Pelagi*	Bolingbroke *Remarks Upon History* (in *The Craftsman*) Newton *Opticks*, 4th ed.	Oliver Goldsmith born [?] (d. 1774) Laurence Eusden dies (b. 1688). Colley Cibber appointed Poet Laureate
1731	Pope *Epistle to Burlington* Isaac Thompson *Poems*	Edward Cave starts *The Gentleman's Magazine* (–1907) Prévost *Manon Lescaut*	Charles Beckingham dies (b. 1699) Daniel Defoe dies (b. 1660) Charles Churchill born (d. 1764) William Cowper born (d. 1800)

1732	Pope *Epistle to Bathurst* Swift *The Lady's Dressing Room*	Hogarth *A Harlot's Progress*	Vauxhall Gardens open John Gay dies (b. 1685) Haydn born (d. 1809)
1733	Pope *Essay on Man* (–34) and *Imitation of Horace Satire II.1* Montagu *Verses to the Imitator of Horace*	Bolingbroke *Dissertation Upon Parties* (in *The Craftsman*) Voltaire *Letters Concerning the English Nation*	Excise Bill crisis Bernard Mandeville dies (b. 1670) Robert Lloyd born (d. 1764)
1734	Mary Barber *Poems*		John Dennis dies (b. 1657) James Arbuckle dies (?) (b. 1700)
1735	Pope *Epistle to Arbuthnot* and *Epistle to a Lady* Thomson *Liberty* (–1736)	Blackwell *Enquiry into the Life and Writings of Homer* Hogarth *A Rake's Progress*	John Arbuthnot dies (b. 1667) James Beattie born (d. 1803)
1736	Wesley *Psalms and Hymns* Duck *Poems on Several Occasions* Armstrong *Oeconomy of Love* Harte *Essay on Reason*		Porteus Riots in Edinburgh Gin riots James Macpherson born (d. 1796)
1737	Pope *Horace's Epistles*, I. i., vi; II. i, ii Shenstone *Poems*	Montagu *The Nonsense of Common-Sense* (–38)	Theatre Licensing Act Edward Gibbon born (d. 1794) Tom Paine born (d. 1809)
1738	Johnson *London* Pope *Epilogue to Satires*		Herculaneum excavated
1739	Swift *Verses on the Death of Dr. Swift* Collier *The Woman's Labour*	Hume *Treatise of Human Nature* (–40)	War declared on Spain; capture of Porto Bello Foundling Hospital established
1740	Thomson and Mallet *Alfred. A Masque* Sarah Dixon *Poems*	Richardson *Pamela*, Vols I–II (–42)	War of Austrian Succession (–48) Thomas Tickell dies (b. 1686) James Boswell born (d. 1795)

245

1741	Arbuthnot and others *Memoirs of Martinus Scriblerus* James Miller *Of Politeness*	Henry Fielding *Shamela* Richardson *Pamela*, Vols III–IV Hume *Essays* (–42)	Handel's *Messiah*, first performed in Dublin Garrick plays Richard III
1742	Collins *Persian Eclogues* Pope *New Dunciad* (i.e. Book IV) Young *The Complaint, or Night Thoughts* (–45) Shenstone *The School-mistress*	Henry Fielding *Joseph Andrews*	Walpole resigns Anna Seward born (d. 1809)
1743	Blair *The Grave* Pope *Dunciad* (four books)	Henry Fielding *Jonathan Wild*	Battle of Dettingen Pelham ministry Richard Savage dies (b. 1697?) Anna Laetitia Barbauld born (d. 1825)
1744	Akenside *The Pleasures of Imagination* Armstrong *The Art of Preserving Health* Thomson *The Seasons* (rev.) Joseph Warton *The Enthusiast*	Haywood *The Female Spectator* (–46) Sarah Fielding *David Simple*	First Methodist Conference Alexander Pope dies (b. 1688) James Miller dies (b. 1706)
1745	Akenside *Odes on Several Subjects* Thomas Warton *Five Pastoral Eclogues* John Brown *An Essay on Satire*	Hogarth *Marriage-à-la-Mode*	Battle of Fontenoy Jacobite Rebellion Jonathan Swift dies (b. 1667) William Broome dies (b. 1689) Robert Walpole dies (b. 1676) Henry James Pye born (d. 1813) William Crowe born (d. 1829) Hannah More born (d. 1833)
1746	Collins *Odes* [1747 imprint] Joseph Warton *Odes* William Thompson *Hymn to May*	Dodsley *The Museum* (–47)	Battle of Culloden Mary Leapor dies (b. 1724)

1747	Gray *Eton College Ode* Montagu *Six Town Eclogues* Mason *Musaeus* Thomas Warton *The Pleasures of Melancholy* Bedingfield *The Education of Achilles*	Johnson *Plan of a Dictionary* Richardson *Clarissa* (−48) Garrick *Miss in her Teens*	
1748	Gray *Ode on the Spring* Leapor *Poems* Thomson *Castle of Indolence* Dodsley (ed.) *Collection of Poems* (−58)	Smollett *Roderick Random* Montesquieu *L'Esprit des Lois*	Peace of Aix-la-Chapelle Ruins of Pompeii discovered James Thomson dies (b. 1700) Isaac Watts dies (b. 1674)
1749	Johnson *Vanity of Human Wishes* Collins *Ode Occasion'd by the Death of Mr. Thomson* Gilbert West *Odes of Pindar*	Henry Fielding *Tom Jones* Johnson *Irene* Handel *Solomon* *Monthly Review* begins	Ambrose Philips dies (b. 1674) Samuel Boyse dies (b. 1708) Charlotte Smith born (d. 1806)
1750	Mary Jones *Miscellanies*	Johnson *The Rambler* (−52)	Aaron Hill dies (b. 1685)
1751	Gray *Elegy Written in a Country Church Yard* Leapor *Poems* Gilbert West *Education*	Smollett *Peregrine Pickle* Henry Fielding *Amelia* Haywood *Betsy Thoughtless*	Prince of Wales dies (b. 1707) Richard Sheridan born (d. 1816)
1752	Smart *Poems on Several Occasions*	Lennox *The Female Quixote*	Gregorian Calendar adopted in Britain Thomas Chatterton born (d. 1770) Frances Burney born (d. 1840)
1753	Gray *Designs by Mr. R. Bentley for Six Poems by Mr. T. Gray* Dodsley *Agriculture*	Hogarth *The Analysis of Beauty* Lowth *De Sacra Poesi Hebraeorum* *The World* (−56)	Hardwicke's Marriage Act Ann Yearsley born (d. 1806)
1754	Elizabeth Tollet *Poems* Samuel Bowden *Poems*	Thomas Warton *Observations on the Faerie Queene* *The Connoisseur* (−56)	Henry Fielding dies (b. 1707) Elizabeth Tollet dies (b. 1694) George Crabbe born (d. 1832)

247

1755	*Poems by Eminent Ladies*	Johnson *A Dictionary of the English Language*	Lisbon Earthquake
1756	Lloyd *The Cit's Country Box*	Home *Douglas* Joseph Warton *Essay on Pope*, Vol. I *Critical Review* begins	Seven Years War (–63) Stephen Duck dies (b. 1705?)
1757	Collins *Oriental Eclogues* Dyer *The Fleece* Gray *Odes*	Burke *Enquiry into the Origin of our Ideas of the Sublime and Beautiful* Brown *Estimate of the Manners and Principles of the Times*	Battle of Plassey Thomas Blackwell dies (b. 1701) John Dyer dies (b. 1699) Colley Cibber dies (b. 1671). William Whitehead appointed Poet Laureate William Blake born (d. 1827)
1758	Dodsley (ed.) *Collection of Poems* (6 vols)	Hume *Enquiry Concerning Human Understanding* Johnson *The Idler* (–60) Upton's edition of *The Faerie Queene*	Mary Robinson born (d. 1800)
1759		Adam Smith *Theory of Moral Sentiments* Young *Conjectures on Original Composition* Johnson *Rasselas* Voltaire *Candide*	British Museum opens Battle of Quebec William Collins dies (b. 1721) Handel dies (b. 1685) Robert Burns born (d. 1796)
1760	Macpherson *Fragments of Ancient Poetry*	Sterne *Tristram Shandy* (–67)	Death of George II (b. 1683), succeeded by George III
1761	Macpherson, *Fingal* [imprint 1762] Churchill *The Rosciad*	Rousseau *La Nouvelle Héloïse*	Pitt resigns Bridgewater canal opens Samuel Richardson dies (b. 1689) James Cawthorn dies (b. 1719)
1762	Churchill *The Ghost* Collier *Poems* Elizabeth Carter *Poems*	Goldsmith *The Citizen of the World* Hurd *Letters on Chivalry and Romance* Rousseau *Du Contrat Social* and *Emile*	Lady Mary Wortley Montagu dies (b. 1689) Mary Collier dies (?) (b. 1690?) William Lisle Bowles born (d. 1850)

1763	Churchill *Prophecy of Famine*	Montagu *Embassy Letters*	Peace of Paris
	Macpherson *Temora*	Frances Brooke *Julia Mandeville*	John Wilkes arrested
	Smart *Song to David*	Catharine Macaulay *History of England* begun	Johnson and Boswell meet
	Percy *Five Pieces of Runic Poetry*	Blair *Critical Dissertation on Ossian*	William Shenstone dies (b. 1714)
1764	Evans *Specimens of Ancient Welsh Bards*	Walpole *The Castle of Otranto*	Mozart in England (−65)
	Goldsmith *The Traveller*		Charles Churchill dies (b. 1732)
	Churchill *Gotham*		Robert Lloyd dies (b. 1733)
	Grainger *The Sugar-Cane*		Hogarth dies (b. 1697)
1765	Macpherson *The Works of Ossian*	Blackstone *Commentaries on the Laws of England*	American Stamp Act
	Percy *Reliques of Ancient English Poetry*	Johnson's edition of Shakespeare	Edward Young dies (b. 1683)
	Smart *The Psalms of David*	Fordyce *Sermons to Young Ladies*	Sarah Dixon dies (b. 1672)
1766	Anstey *The New Bath Guide*	Goldsmith *The Vicar of Wakefield*	Second Pitt (Chatham) ministry
		Smollett *Travels Through France and Italy*	Food riots
		Colman and Garrick *The Clandestine Marriage*	John Brown dies (b. 1715)
		Lessing *Laokoon*	James Grainger dies (b. 1721)
1767	Jago *Edge-Hill*	Priestley *History of Electricity*	Royal Crescent, Bath, begun
		Duff *Essay on Original Genius*	
1768	Gray *Poems*	*Encyclopaedia Britannica* (−71)	Chatham resigns
		Boswell *Account of Corsica*	Royal Academy founded
		Sterne *A Sentimental Journey*	Sterne dies (b. 1713)
1769	Gray *Ode for Music*	Reynolds's annual *Discourses on Art* begin	Cook at Tahiti
			Shakespeare Jubilee
		Elizabeth Montagu *Essay on Shakespeare*	Wilkes troubles
			Watt patents steam engine

1770	Goldsmith *The Deserted Village*	*London Magazine* begins	North ministry (–82) Mark Akenside dies (b. 1721) Thomas Chatterton dies (b. 1752) William Wordsworth born (d. 1850)
1771	Beattie *The Minstrel* (–74) Cawthorn *Poems* King *The Frequented Village*	Mackenzie *The Man of Feeling* Smollett *Humphry Clinker*	Arkwright's first spinning-mill Thomas Gray dies (b. 1716) Christopher Smart dies (b. 1722) Tobias Smollett dies (b. 1721) Walter Scott born (d. 1833)
1772	Mason *The English Garden* (–81)	Priestley *History of the Present State of Discoveries*	Cook's second voyage (–75) S.T. Coleridge born (d. 1834)
1773	Barbauld *Poems*	Goldsmith *She Stoops to Conquer*	Boston Tea Party Lord Chesterfield dies (b. 1694)
1774	Pye *Faringdon Hill* Lloyd *Poetical Works*	Goethe *The Sorrows of Young Werther* Burke *Speech on American Taxation* Thomas Warton *History of English Poetry* (–81)	Priestley discovers oxygen Goldsmith dies (b. 1730?) Walter Harte dies (b. 1709) Robert Southey born (d. 1843)
1775	Mary Robinson *Poems*	Sheridan *The Rivals* Johnson *Journey to the Western Islands of Scotland* Beaumarchais *Le Barbier de Séville*	Jane Austen born (d. 1817) Charles Lamb born (d. 1834)
1776	Hannah More *Sir Eldred of the Bower*	Gibbon *Decline and Fall of the Roman Empire* (–88) Adam Smith *Wealth of Nations* Charles Burney *History of Music*	American Declaration of Independence Cook's third voyage (–79) David Hume dies (b. 1711)
1777	Chatterton *Poems*, supposed to have been written at Bristol, by Thomas Rowley, and others Thomas Warton *Poems*	Sheridan *School for Scandal*	Burgoyne defeated at Saratoga

1778	Anne Wilson *Teisa*	Frances Burney *Evelina* Reeve *The Old English Baron*	Lord Chatham dies (b. 1708) Rousseau dies (b. 1712) Voltaire dies (b. 1694) Mary Jones dies (b. 1707) William Hazlitt born (d. 1830)
1779	Cowper *Olney Hymns*	Johnson *Lives of the English Poets* (−81) Sheridan *The Critic*	First iron bridge Machine riots James Cook dies (b. 1728) John Armstrong dies (b. 1709) David Garrick dies (b. 1717)
1780	Seward *Elegy on Captain Cook*		Gordon riots Blackstone dies (b. 1723)
1781	Crabbe *The Library*		Cornwallis surrenders at Yorktown Uranus discovered Watt's rotary steam-engine Richard Jago dies (b. 1715)
1782	Cowper *Poems* Thomas Warton *Verses on Reynolds's Window*	Frances Burney *Cecilia* Sir William Jones *The Principles of Government* Rousseau *Confessions* (−89) Laclos *Les Liaisons Dangereuses*	The 'Rowley' controversy
1783	Crabbe *The Village* Blake *Poetical Sketches*	Catharine Macaulay *History of England* completed	Peace of Versailles William Pitt Prime Minister
1784	Charlotte Smith *Elegiac Sonnets*	Beaumarchais *Le Mariage de Figaro*	First balloon ascent in Britain Samuel Johnson dies (b. 1709) Leigh Hunt born (d. 1859)
1785	Cowper *The Task* Yearsley *Poems on Several Occasions*	Boswell *Journal of a Tour to the Hebrides*	William Whitehead dies (b. 1715). Thomas Warton appointed Poet Laureate
1786	Burns *Poems, Chiefly in the Scottish Dialect* Helen Maria Williams *Poems*	Beckford *Vathek* Mozart *The Marriage of Figaro*	Coal gas used for lighting

1787	Yearsley *Poems on Various Subjects* James Johnson (ed.) *Scots Musical Museum* (–1803)	Wollstonecraft *Thoughts on the Education of Daughters*	U.S. constitution signed Anti-Slave Trade Society founded Robert Lowth dies (b. 1710)
1788	Crowe *Lewesdon Hill* Yearsley *A Poem on the Inhumanity of the Slave-Trade* Hannah More *Slavery, A Poem*	Charlotte Smith *Emmeline* Wollstonecraft *Mary, A Fiction*	Anti-Slavery petition Convict settlement at Botany Bay Thomas Gainsborough dies (b. 1727) Lord Byron born (d. 1824)
1789	Blake *Songs of Innocence* and *The Book of Thel* Bowles *Fourteen Sonnets* Charlotte Smith *Elegiac Sonnets* (5th ed.)	Bentham *An Introduction to the Principles of Morals and Legislation* White *Natural History of Selborne*	Fall of the Bastille Mutiny on the *Bounty* Washington becomes President of U.S.A.

General Bibliographies

Bibliographies, Dictionaries, etc.

Case, Arthur E. *A Bibliography of English Poetical Miscellanies, 1521–1750* (Oxford, 1935)

Foxon, David *English Verse, 1701–1750*, 2 vols (Cambridge, 1975)

Mell, Donald C., ed. *English Poetry, 1660–1800* (Detroit, 1982)

Sitter, John, ed. *Eighteenth-Century British Poets: First Series*. Dictionary of Literary Biography 95 (Detroit, 1990)

Sitter, John, ed. *Eighteenth-Century British Poets: Second Series*. Dictionary of Literary Biography 109 (Detroit, 1991)

Todd, Janet, ed. *A Dictionary of British and American Women Writers, 1660–1800* (London, 1984)

Womersley, David, ed. *A Companion to Literature from Milton to Blake* (Oxford, 2000)

Anthologies

Fairer, David, and Christine Gerrard, eds. *Eighteenth-Century Poetry: An Annotated Anthology* (Oxford, 1999)

Foster, Gretchen M., and Robert W. Uphaus, eds. *The 'Other' Eighteenth Century: English Women of Letters 1660–1800* (East Lansing, 1991)

Fullard, Joyce, ed. *British Women Poets 1660–1800: An Anthology* (Troy, NY, 1990)

Lonsdale, Roger *The New Oxford Book of Eighteenth-Century Verse* (Oxford, 1984)

Lonsdale, Roger *Eighteenth-Century Women Poets* (Oxford, 1989)

Rogers, Katharine M., and William McCarthy, eds. *The Meridian Anthology of Early Women Writers: British Literary Women From Aphra Behn to Maria Edgeworth 1660–1800* (New York, 1987)

History and Criticism (general)

Barrell, John *English Literature in History 1730–80: An Equal Wide Survey* (London, 1983)

Blom, T.E. 'Eighteenth-Century Reflexive Process Poetry', *Eighteenth-Century Studies*, 10:1 (1976), 52–72

Bogel, Fredric V. *Literature and Insubstantiality in Later Eighteenth-Century England* (Princeton, 1984)

Brown, Marshall *Preromanticism* (Stanford, 1991)

Carnochan, W.B. 'The Continuity of Eighteenth-Century Poetry: Gray, Cowper, Crabbe, and the Augustans', *Eighteenth-Century Life*, 12 (1988), 119–27

Christmas, William J. *The Lab'ring Muses: Work, Writing and the Social Order in English Plebeian Poetry, 1730–1830* (Newark and London, 2001)

Cox, Stephen *'The Stranger within Thee': Concepts of the Self in Late Eighteenth-Century Literature* (Pittsburgh, 1980)

Doody, Margaret Anne *The Daring Muse: Augustan Poetry Reconsidered* (Cambridge, 1985)

Doody, Margaret Anne 'Women Poets of the Eighteenth Century', in *Women and Literature in Britain, 1700–1800*, ed. Vivien Jones (Cambridge, 1999), pp. 217–37

Dowling, William C. 'Ideology and the Flight from History in Eighteenth-Century Poetry', in *The Profession of Eighteenth-Century Literature: Reflections on an Institution*, ed. Leo Damrosch (Madison, 1992), pp. 135–53

Erskine-Hill, Howard *Poetry of Opposition and Revolution: Dryden to Wordsworth* (Oxford, 1996)

Fox, Christopher, ed. *Teaching Eighteenth-Century Poetry* (New York, 1990)

Griffin, Dustin *Regaining Paradise: Milton and the Eighteenth Century* (Cambridge, 1986)

Griffin, Dustin *Patriotism and Poetry in Eighteenth-Century Britain* (Cambridge, 2002)

Griffin, Robert J. *Wordsworth's Pope: A Study in Literary Historiography* (Cambridge, 1995)

Irlam, Shaun *Elations: The Poetics of Enthusiasm in Eighteenth-Century Britain* (Stanford, 1999)

Parker, Blanford *The Triumph of Augustan Poetics: English Literary Culture from Butler to Johnson* (Cambridge, 1998)

Ross, Marlon B. *The Contours of Masculine Desire: Romanticism and the Rise of Women's Poetry* (New York and Oxford, 1989)

Rothstein, Eric *Restoration and Eighteenth-Century Poetry 1660–1780* (London, 1981)

Sitter, John *Literary Loneliness in Mid-Eighteenth-Century England* (Ithaca, 1982)

Sitter, John, ed. *The Cambridge Companion to Eighteenth-Century Poetry* (Cambridge, 2001)

Terry, Richard 'Transitions and Digressions in the Eighteenth-Century Long Poem', *Studies in English Literature*, 32 (1992), 495–510

Weinbrot, Howard D. *Britannia's Issue: The Rise of British Literature from Dryden to Ossian* (Cambridge, 1993)

Woodman, Thomas *Politeness and Poetry in the Age of Pope* (Rutherford and London, 1989)

Woodman, Thomas, ed. *Early Romantics: Perspectives in British Poetry from Pope to Wordsworth* (Houndmills and New York, 1998)

Historical and Cultural Context

Allen, Robert J. *The Clubs of Augustan London* (Cambridge, Mass., 1933)

Ashton, T.S. *An Economic History of England: The Eighteenth Century* (London, 1955)

Benedict, Barbara M. *Making the Modern Reader: Cultural Mediation in Early Modern Literary Anthologies* (Princeton, 1996)

Black, Jeremy, ed. *Britain in the Age of Walpole* (New York, 1984)

Black, Jeremy *The English Press in the Eighteenth Century* (Aldershot, 1991)

Brewer, John *The Pleasures of the Imagination: English Culture in the Eighteenth Century* (London, 1997)

Colley, Linda *Britons: Forging the Nation 1707–1837* (New Haven, 1992)

Donoghue, Frank *The Fame Machine: Book Reviewing and Eighteenth-Century Literary Careers* (Stanford, 1996)

Ellis, Aytoun *The Penny Universities. A History of the Coffee-houses* (London, 1956)

Feather, John *The Provincial Book Trade in Eighteenth-Century England* (Cambridge, 1985)

Fox, Christopher *Locke and the Scriblerians* (Berkeley, 1989)

Foxon, David *Pope and the Early Eighteenth-Century Book Trade* (Oxford, 1991), rev. and ed. James McLaverty

George, Dorothy M. *London Life in the Eighteenth Century* (Harmondsworth, 1966)

Gerrard, Christine *The Patriot Opposition to Walpole: Politics, Poetry, and National Myth, 1725–1742* (Oxford, 1994)

Griffin, Dustin *Literary Patronage in England, 1650–1800* (Cambridge, 1996)

Hammond, Brean S. *Professional Imaginative Writing in England, 1670–1740: 'Hackney for Bread'* (Oxford, 1997)

Kernan, Alvin *Printing Technology, Letters, and Samuel Johnson* (Princeton, 1987)

Klein, Lawrence E. *Shaftesbury and the Culture of Politeness: Moral Discourse and Cultural Politics in Early Eighteenth-Century England* (Cambridge, 1994)

Langford, Paul *A Polite and Commercial People: England 1727–1783* (London, 1989)

Levine, Joseph M. *The Battle of the Books: History and Literature in the Augustan Age* (Ithaca and London, 1991)

McDowell, Paula *The Women of Grub Street: Press, Politics, and Gender in the London Literary Marketplace 1678–1730* (Oxford, 1998)

Newman, Gerald *The Rise of English Nationalism: A Cultural History 1740–1830* (London, 1987)

Pittock, Murray *Poetry and Jacobite Politics in Eighteenth-Century Britain and Ireland* (Cambridge, 1994)

Pocock, J.G.A. *Virtue, Commerce and History: Essays on Political Thought and History, Chiefly in the Eighteenth Century* (Cambridge and New York, 1985)

Rivers, Isabel, ed. *Books and their Readers in Eighteenth-Century England* (Leicester, 1982)

Rivers, Isabel, ed. *Books and their Readers in Eighteenth-Century England: New Essays* (Leicester, 2001)

Rogers, Pat *Grub Street: Studies in a Subculture* (London, 1972)

Sambrook, James *The Eighteenth Century: The Intellectual and Cultural Context of English Literature, 1700–1789* (London and New York, 1986)

Siskin, Clifford *The Work of Writing: Literature and Social Change in Britain 1700–1830* (Baltimore, 1998)

Speck, W.A. *Society and Literature in England 1700–1760* (Dublin, 1983)

Straus, Ralph *The Unspeakable Curll* (London, 1927)

Wilson, Kathleen *The Sense of the People: Politics, Culture and Imperialism in England, 1715–1785* (Cambridge, 1994)

The Making of the Canon

Armstrong, Isobel, and Virginia Blain, eds. *Women's Poetry in the Enlightenment: The Making of a Canon, 1730–1820* (Basingstoke, 1998)

Kramnick, Jonathan Brody *Making the English Canon: Print-Capitalism and the Cultural Past, 1700–1770* (Cambridge, 1998)

Patey, Douglas Lane 'The Eighteenth Century Invents the Canon', *Modern Language Studies*, 18 (1988), 17–37

Ross, Trevor *The Making of the English Literary Canon: From the Middle Ages to the Late Eighteenth Century* (Montreal, etc., 1998)

Terry, Richard 'The Eighteenth-Century Invention of English Literature: A Truism Revisited', *British Journal for Eighteenth-Century Studies*, 19 (1996), 47–62

Terry, Richard 'Literature, Aesthetics, and Canonicity in the Eighteenth Century', *Eighteenth-Century Life*, 21:1 (1997), 80–101 (see also the ensuing forum, pp. 102–7, and 21:3 (1997), 79–99)

Terry, Richard *Poetry and the Making of the English Literary Past, 1660–1781* (Oxford, 2002)

Weinbrot, Howard D. 'Enlightenment Canon Wars: Anglo-French Views of Literary Greatness', *ELH*, 60 (1993), 79–100

Zionkowski, Linda 'Territorial Disputes in the Republic of Letters: Canon Formation and the Literary Profession', *The Eighteenth Century: Theory and Interpretation*, 31 (1996), 3–22

Satire and Epistle

Bond, Richmond P. *English Burlesque Poetry.* Harvard Studies in English VI (Cambridge, Mass., 1932)

Dowling, William C. *The Epistolary Moment: The Poetics of the Eighteenth-Century Verse Epistle* (Princeton, 1991)

Hammond, Brean 'Scriblerian Self-Fashioning', *Yearbook of English Studies*, 18 (1988), 108–24

Lockwood, Thomas *Post-Augustan Satire* (Seattle, 1979)

Mack, Maynard 'The Muse of Satire', *Yale Review*, 41 (1951), 80–92

Redford, Bruce *The Converse of the Pen: Acts of Intimacy in the Eighteenth-Century Familiar Letter* (Chicago and London, 1986)

Seidel, Michael *Satiric Inheritance: Rabelais to Sterne* (Princeton, 1979)

Stack, Frank *Pope and Horace: Studies in Imitation* (Cambridge, etc., 1985)

Weinbrot, Howard D. 'The Pattern of Formal Verse Satire in the Restoration and the Eighteenth Century', *PMLA*, 80 (1965), 394–401

Weinbrot, Howard D. *The Formal Strain: Studies in Augustan Imitation and Satire* (Chicago, 1969)

Weinbrot, Howard D., ed. *Eighteenth-Century Satire: Essays on Text and Context from Dryden to Peter Pindar* (Cambridge, 1988)

Wood, Marcus *Radical Satire and Print Culture 1700–1822* (Oxford, 1994)

Landscape, Pastoral, and Georgic

Barrell, John *The Idea of Landscape and the Sense of Place, 1730–1840: An Approach to the Poetry of John Clare* (Cambridge, 1972), pp. 1–63

Chalker, John *The English Georgic: A Study in the Development of a Form* (London, 1969)

Congleton, J.E. *Theories of Pastoral Poetry in England 1684–1798* (Gainesville, 1952)

Crawford, Rachel 'English Georgic and British Nationhood', *ELH*, 65 (1998), 123–58

Crawford, Rachel *Poetry, Enclosure, and the Vernacular Landscape, 1700–1830* (Cambridge, 2002)

Durling, Dwight L. *Georgic Tradition in English Poety* (New York, 1935)

Feingold, Richard *Nature and Society: Later Eighteenth-Century Uses of the Pastoral and the Georgic* (Brighton, 1978)

Fulford, Tim *Landscape, Liberty and Authority: Poetry, Criticism and Politics from Thomson to Wordsworth* (Cambridge, 1996)

Heinzelman, Kurt 'Roman Georgic in the Georgian Age: A Theory of Romantic Genre', *Texas Studies in Language and Literature*, 33 (1991), 182–214

Janowitz, Anne *England's Ruins: Poetic Purpose and the National Landscape* (Oxford, 1990)

Landry, Donna *The Invention of the Countryside: Hunting, Walking, and Ecology in English Literature, 1671–1831* (Houndmills and New York, 2001)

Low, Anthony *The Georgic Revolution* (Princeton, 1985)

McKeon, Michael 'Surveying the Frontier of Culture: Pastoralism in Eighteenth-Century England', *Studies in Eighteenth-Century Culture*, 26 (1998), 7–28

Messenger, Ann *Pastoral Tradition and the Female Talent: Studies in Augustan Poetry* (New York, 2001)

Patterson, Annabel *Pastoral and Ideology: Virgil to Valery* (Oxford, 1988)

Radcliffe, David Hill 'Genre and Social Order in Country House Poems of the Eighteenth Century: Four Views of Percy Lodge', *SEL*, 30 (1990), 445–65

Rosenmeyer, Thomas G. *The Green Cabinet: Theocritus and the European Pastoral Lyric* (Berkeley and Los Angeles, 1969)

Williams, Raymond 'Pastoral and Counter-Pastoral', in *The Country and the City* (London, 1973), pp. 13–34

Ballad, Lyric, and Ode

Cohen, Ralph 'The Return to the Ode', in *The Cambridge Companion to Eighteenth-Century Poetry*, ed. John Sitter (Cambridge, 2001), pp. 203–24

Davie, Donald *Augustan Lyric* (London, 1974)

Davie, Donald *The Eighteenth-Century Hymn in England* (Cambridge, 1993)

Dugaw, Dianne 'The Popular Marketing of "Old Ballads": The Ballad Revival and Eighteenth-Century Antiquarianism Reconsidered', *Eighteenth-Century Studies*, 21 (1987), 71–90

Friedman, Albert B. *The Ballad Revival: Studies in the Influence of Popular on Sophisticated Poetry* (Chicago, 1961)

Fry, Paul H. *The Poet's Calling in the English Ode* (New Haven, 1980)

Groom, Nick *The Making of Percy's Reliques* (Oxford, 1999)

Knapp, Steven *Personification and the Sublime: Milton to Coleridge* (Cambridge, Mass., 1985)

Maclean, Norman 'From Action to Image: Theories of the Lyric in the Eighteenth Century', in *Critics and Criticism Ancient and Modern*, ed. R.S. Crane (Chicago, 1952), pp. 408–460

Morris, David B. *The Religious Sublime: Christian Poetry and Critical Tradition in 18th-Century England* (Lexington, 1972)

Price, Martin 'The Sublime Poem: Pictures and Powers', *Yale Review*, 58 (1968–9), 194–213

Shuster, G.N. *The English Ode from Milton to Keats* (New York, 1940)

Tuveson, Ernest 'Space, Deity and the "Natural Sublime"', *Modern Language Quarterly*, 12 (1951), 20–38

Watson, J.R. *The English Hymn: A Critical and Historical Study* (Oxford, 1997)

Elegy and Epitaph

Clymer, Lorna 'Graved in Tropes: The Figural Logic of Epitaphs and Elegies in Blair, Gray, Cowper, and Wordsworth', *ELH*, 62 (1995), 347–86

Sacks, Peter M. *The English Elegy: Studies in the Genre from Spenser to Yeats* (Baltimore, 1985)

Scodel, Joshua *The English Poetic Epitaph: Commemoration and Conflict from Jonson to Wordsworth* (Ithaca and London, 1991)

Smith, Eric *By Mourning Tongues. Studies in English Elegy* (Ipswich, 1977)

Sensibility

Barker-Benfield, G.J. *The Culture of Sensibility: Sex and Society in Eighteenth-Century Britain* (Chicago, 1992)

Conger, Syndy McMillan *Sensibility in Transformation: Creative Resistance to Sentiment from the Augustans to the Romantics* (London and Toronto, 1989)

Frye, Northrop 'Towards Defining an Age of Sensibility', *ELH*, 23 (1956), 144–52

Hagstrum, Jean H. *Sex and Sensibility: Ideal and Erotic Love from Milton to Mozart* (Chicago and London, 1980)

Johnson, Claudia L. *Equivocal Beings: Politics, Gender, and Sentimentality in the 1780s* (Chicago and London, 1995)

Jones, Chris *Radical Sensibility: Literature and Ideas in the 1790s* (London and New York, 1993), pp. 20–58

McGann, Jerome *The Poetics of Sensibility: A Revolution in Literary Style* (Oxford, 1996)

Mullan, John *Sentiment and Sociability: The Language of Feeling in the Eighteenth Century* (Oxford, 1988)

Todd, Janet *Sensibility: An Introduction* (London and New York, 1986)

Aesthetics and Imagination

Dickie, George 'The Myth of the Aesthetic Attitude', *American Philosophical Quarterly*, 1 (1964), 56–65

Engell, James *The Creative Imagination: Enlightenment to Romanticism* (Cambridge, Mass., and London, 1981)

Jones, Robert W. *Gender and the Formation of Taste in Eighteenth-Century Britain: The Analysis of Beauty* (Cambridge, 1998)

Mattick, Paul *Eighteenth-Century Aesthetics and the Reconstruction of Art* (Cambridge, 1993)

Patey, Douglas Lane ' "Aesthetics" and the Rise of Lyric in the Eighteenth Century', *Studies in English Literature*, 33 (1993), 587–608

Paulson, Ronald *Breaking and Remaking: Aesthetic Practice in England, 1700–1822* (New Brunswick, 1989)

Sharpe, Kevin, and Steven N. Zwicker, eds. *Refiguring Revolutions: Aesthetics and Politics from the English Revolution to the Romantic Revolution* (Berkeley, etc., 1998)

Tuveson, Ernest Lee *The Imagination as a Means of Grace: Locke and the Aesthetics of Romanticism* (Berkeley and Los Angeles, 1960)

Woodmansee, Martha *The Author, Art, and the Market: Rereading the History of Aesthetics* (New York, 1994)

Individual Poets

ADDISON, Joseph (1672–1719) Educated at Charterhouse and Queen's College, Oxford, he became a Fellow of Magdalen College 1697–1711. A distinguished classicist, he gained notice early through his Latin poems, and received a government pension to travel abroad 1699–1703; he was commissioned to write *The Campaign* (1705) celebrating Marlborough's victory of Blenheim; under-secretary of state 1706; M.P. for Malmesbury 1709–19 and member of the Whig Kit-Cat Club. He helped his friend Sir Richard Steele with *The Tatler* (1709–11), and together they started *The Spectator* (1711–12, revived 1714); his verse tragedy *Cato* was a spectacular success in 1713. At the centre of London's cultural elite, Addison encouraged and patronised aspiring poets who included Thomas Tickell, Edward Young, and Ambrose Philips. He married the Countess of Warwick 1716. His critical essays in *The Spectator* introduced the new aesthetics of beauty and sublimity to a wide public, and he helped to shape the tastes of the century.

Guthkelch, A.C., ed., *The Miscellaneous Works of Joseph Addison* (London, 1914).

AKENSIDE, Mark (1721–70) Son of a Newcastle butcher, he was educated at the grammar school, then at a school attached to his local Unitarian chapel. During 1737–8 he had poems published in *The Gentleman's Magazine*, and in *The Voice of Liberty* (1738) he attacked Walpole's foreign policy with patriotic fervour. He entered Edinburgh University 1739 with a view to becoming a minister, but changed to the study of medicine and took the degree of M.D. from Leyden in Holland 1744. In January of that year his three-book poem *The Pleasures of Imagination* was successfully published by Dodsley, the leading poetry publisher of the period, and reached a fourth edition by November. Akenside was a fine Greek scholar, and his poetry is strongly marked both by his early unitarianism and his deep study of Plato. Akenside's *Odes* (1745) disappointed the public, but as editor of Dodsley's *Museum* (1746–7) he gave opportunities to other young poets like the Warton brothers. During the 1750s his professional medical career took over and he rose to be Principal Physician at St Thomas's Hospital 1759 and one of the Queen's physicians 1761. He began a comprehensive reworking of *The Pleasures of the Imagination* (its new title) in five books, left incomplete at his death.

Aldridge, A.O. 'Akenside and Imagination', *Studies in Philology*, 42 (1945), 769–92.
Dix, Robin, ed., *The Poetical Works of Mark Akenside* (Madison and Teaneck, 1996).
Hart, Jeffrey, 'Akenside's Revision of *The Pleasures of Imagination*', *PMLA*, 74 (1959), 67–74.
Houpt, Charles T., *Mark Akenside: A Biographical and Critical Study* (Philadelphia, 1944; repr. New York, 1970).
Jump, Harriet Devine, 'High Sentiments of Liberty: Coleridge's Unacknowledged Debt to Akenside', *Studies in Romanticism*, 28 (1989), 207–24.
Kallich, Martin, 'The Association of Ideas and Akenside's Pleasures of Imagination', *Modern Language Notes*, 62 (1947), 166–73.
Marsh, Robert, 'Akenside and Addison: The Problem of Ideational Debt', *Modern Philology*, 59 (1961–2), 36–48.
Marsh, Robert, 'Akenside and the Powers of Imagination', in his *Four Dialectical Theories of Poetry* (Chicago, 1965), pp. 48–86.
Meehan, Michael, *Liberty and Poetics in Eighteenth Century England* (London, 1986), pp. 52–63.

Norton, John Francis, 'Akenside's *The Pleasures of Imagination*: An Exercise in Poetics', *Eighteenth-Century Studies*, 3 (1969–70), 366–83.

Sitter, John, 'Theodicy at Mid-Century: Young, Akenside, and Hume', *Eighteenth-Century Studies*, 12 (1978), 90–106.

ARBUCKLE, James (b. 1700) Son of the Rev. James Arbuckle (d. 1720), Presbyterian minister at Dublin. Entered Glasgow University and was a precocious poet, publishing *Snuff* (Glasgow, 1717; Edinburgh, 1719); *Epistle to Thomas, Earl of Haddington, on the Death of Joseph Addison, Esq.* (1719), and *Glotta* (1721), featuring the landscape of the River Clyde near Glasgow. Arbuckle settled as a schoolmaster in the north of Ireland, and as 'Hibernicus' (1725–7) he ran a miscellany of prose and verse in *The Dublin Journal*, gathered as *A Collection of Letters and Essays* (2 vols, 1729). Wrote *Momus Mistaken* (Dublin, 1735), a satirical panegyric on Swift.

Coleborne, Bryan, 'James Arbuckle and Jonathan Swift: New Light on Swift's Biography', *Eighteenth-Century Life*, 11 (1987), 170–80.

Williams, Aubrey L., ' "A Vile Encomium", That "Panegyric on the Revered D-n S-t" ', in Fischer, John Irwin, and Donald C. Mell, Jr., eds. (assoc. ed. David M. Vieth), *Contemporary Studies of Swift's Poetry* (Newark, 1981), pp. 178–90.

Woolley, James, 'Arbuckle's "Panegyric" and Swift's Scrub Libel: The Documentary Evidence', in *Contemporary Studies of Swift's Poetry*, pp. 191–209.

Woznak, John F., 'James Arbuckle and the Dublin Weekly Journal', *Journal of Irish Literature*, 22 (1993), 46–52.

ARMSTRONG, John (1709–79) Born at Castleton, Roxburghshire, Scotland. He pursued a medical career and gained his M.D. from Edinburgh University 1732, but his touchy, shy and splenetic character hampered his professional advancement; published medical works and became Physician to the Army in Germany 1760. *The Oeconomy of Love: A Poetical Essay* (1736) was a daring attempt to write about human sexuality in georgic form. Armstrong gained fame with *The Art of Preserving Health* (four books, 1744), a poem often reprinted throughout the century.

Boehrer, Bruce, 'English Bards and Scotch Physicians: John Armstrong's Debt to *Paradise Lost* and the Dynamics of Literary Reception', *Milton Quarterly*, 32 (1998) 98–104.

Knapp, Lewis M. 'Dr. John Armstrong, Litterateur, and Associate of Smollett, Thomson, Wilkes, and Other Celebrities', *PMLA*, 59 (1944), 1019–58.

BARBAULD, Anna Laetitia (1743–1825) She was born into a prominent dissenting family at Kibworth, Leicestershire. From 1758, when her father was appointed a teacher at the Warrington Academy, the young Anna flourished in a stimulating and enlightened intellectual regime that included scientific learning and modern languages as well as the classics. The unitarian polymath Dr Joseph Priestley was also a tutor there and encouraged her writing. Her volume of *Poems* (1773) soon ran into a fourth edition, and with her brother John she brought out *Miscellaneous Pieces, in Prose* (1773). In 1774 she married the Rev. Rochemont Barbauld, and they set up a boy's school at Palgrave, Suffolk, for which she wrote the popular *Lessons for Children* (1778) and similar works. The couple moved to Hampstead near London in 1786. Poems of hers appeared in the *Monthly Magazine*, of which her brother was literary editor, and she edited Akenside's *The Pleasures of Imagination* (1794) and the poems of William Collins (1797). She published a number of radical pamphlets during the early years of the French Revolution, including her anti-slavery poem, *Epistle to William Wilberforce* (1791). After her husband's death in 1808 Barbauld took on many literary projects, compiling the massive *British Novelists* in fifty volumes (1810). Her poetry was collected into her *Works* (2 vols, 1825) edited by her niece, Lucy Aikin.

Bradshaw, Penny, 'Gendering the Enlightenment: Conflicting Images of Progress in the Poetry of Anna Laetitia Barbauld', *Women's Writing*, 5 (1998), 353–71.

Guest, Harriet, *Small Change: Women, Learning, Patriotism, 1750–1810* (Chicago and London, 2000), pp. 220–51.

Keach, William, 'Barbauld, Romanticism, and the Survival of Dissent', *Essays and Studies*, 51 (1998), 44–61.

McCarthy, William, ' "We Hoped the Woman Was Going to Appear": Repression, Desire, and Gender in Anna Laetitia Barbauld's Early Poems', in Feldman, Paula R., and Theresa M. Kelley, eds., *Romantic Women Writers: Voices and Countervoices* (Hanover, 1995), pp. 113–37.

McCarthy, William, and Elizabeth Kraft, eds., *The Poems of Anna Laetitia Barbauld* (Athens, 1994).

McDonagh, Josephine, 'Barbauld's Domestic Economy', *Essays and Studies*, 51 (1998), 62–77.

Shankman, Steven, 'Anna Barbauld, William Collins, and the Rhetoric of the Sublime', *Hellas*, 7 (1996), 159–67.

Stabler, Jane, 'Space for Speculation: Coleridge, Barbauld, and the Poetics of Priestley', in Roe, Nicholas, ed., *Samuel Taylor Coleridge and the Sciences of Life* (Oxford, 2001), pp. 175–204.

Vargo, Lisa, 'The Case of Anna Laetitia Barbauld's "To Mr C[olerid]ge," ' *The Charles Lamb Bulletin*, 102 (April 1998), 55–63.

BEATTIE, James (1735–1803) The poet, essayist and moral philosopher was born at Laurencekirk, Kincardine, Scotland, son of a shopkeeper and small farmer. He attended Marischal College, Aberdeen, where he studied Greek under Thomas Blackwell, and on taking his degree he returned to his native district as a schoolmaster. By 1760, however, he was back in Aberdeen as Professor of Moral Philosophy and Logic, and he continued to lecture for over thirty years. On his periodic visits to London Beattie was fêted for his *Essay on Truth* (1770), a 'common sense' attack on Hume's sceptical philosophy, which brought him an honorary degree from Oxford and a pension from George III in 1773. His popular Spenserian poem, *The Minstrel* (two books, 1771, 4), celebrated the natural education of a young poet, but also the claims of virtue and duty.

Brunstrom, Conrad, 'James Beattie and the Great Outdoors: Common Sense Philosophy and the Pious Imagination', *Romanticism*, 3 (1997), pp. 20–34.

King, Everard H., 'James Beattie's *The Minstrel*: Its Influence on Wordsworth', *Studies in Scottish Literature*, 8 (1970), 3–29.

King, Everard H., 'James Beattie's "The Castle of Scepticism" (1767): A Suppressed Satire on Eighteenth-Century Sceptical Philosophy', *Scottish Literary Journal*, 2 (1975), 18–35.

King, Everard H., *James Beattie* (Boston, 1977).

Robinson, Roger, 'The Origins and Composition of James Beattie's *The Minstrel*', *Romanticism*, 4 (1998), 224–40.

BECKINGHAM, Charles (1699–1731) Son of a Fleet Street linen-draper, and educated at Merchant Taylors' School. By the age of twenty he had two historical tragedies produced on the London stage, but thereafter seems to have done editing and miscellaneous work for the publisher Edmund Curll, as well as addressing poems to possible patrons, such as his *Ode to the Right Honorable Sir Robert Walpole* (1725).

BEDINGFIELD, Robert (c. 1720–68) Matriculated from Hart Hall, Oxford, taking his M.A. 1743. A friend of the Warton brothers, his Spenserian poem 'The Education of Achilles' appeared in *The Museum* (1747) and in Dodsley's *Collection of Poems* (1748).

BLACKMORE, Sir Richard (c. 1655–1729) Son of an attorney, educated at Westminster School and St Edmund Hall, Oxford. Took his M.D. at Padua. Physician to both William III and Queen Anne; knighted 1697. Author of a popular philosophical poem, *Creation* (7 books, 1712), much admired by Dennis and Johnson, and several ambitious epics including *Prince Arthur* (1695), *Eliza* (1705) and *Alfred* (1723). His 'Satyr against Wit' (1700) made Blackmore many poetical enemies, and he became a favourite target of the Scriblerians.

Moore, J.R., 'Gay's Burlesque of Blackmore's Poetry', *Journal of English and Germanic Philology*, 50 (1951), 83–9.
Rosenberg A., *Sir Richard Blackmore: A Poet and Physician of the Augustan Age* (Lincoln, Neb., 1953).
Solomon, Harry M., *Sir Richard Blackmore* (Boston, 1980).

BOWLES, William Lisle (1762–1850) A protégé of the Warton brothers, Bowles studied at Winchester College with Joseph and at Trinity College, Oxford, with Thomas. After leaving Trinity in 1787 and travelling on the continent he returned to publish at Bath a small edition of *Fourteen Sonnets* (1789) which were so successful that he revised and added to them later that year as *Sonnets, Written Chiefly on Picturesque Spots, During a Tour*. They were excitedly read by Coleridge, Wordsworth, and Southey. There followed the elegiac poems, *Monody Written at Matlock* (1791) and *Elegy Written at the Hot-Wells, Bristol* (1791). Taking orders in 1792, Bowles became in 1804 Vicar of Bremhill, Wiltshire, where he lived until the end of his life. His later works included longer historical poems.

Bamborough, J.B., 'William Lisle Bowles and the Riparian Muse', in *Essays & Poems Presented to Lord David Cecil*, ed. W.W. Robson (London, 1970), pp. 93–108.
Bauschatz, Paul, 'Coleridge, Wordsworth, and Bowles', *Style*, 27 (1993), 17–40.
Fairer, David, 'Coleridge's *Sonnets from Various Authors*: A Lost Conversation Poem?', *Studies in Romanticism*, 42 (2003).
Gilfillan, George, ed., *The Poetical Works of William Lisle Bowles*, 2 vols (Edinburgh, 1855).
Greever, Garland, ed., *A Wiltshire Parson and his Friends. The Correspondence of W.L. Bowles* (London, 1926).
Ruddick, William, ' "Genius of the Sacred Fountain of Tears": A Bicentenary Tribute to the Sonnets of William Lisle Bowles', *Charles Lamb Bulletin*, 72 (October, 1990), 276–84.

BOYSE, Samuel (1708–49) Son of a Presbyterian minister in Dublin, he was educated at Glasgow University. He lived for several years in Edinburgh and published *Translations and Poems* (1731) and *The Tears of the Muses* (1736). Debts forced him to migrate to London where he published *Deity: a Poem* (1739). He was befriended by Samuel Johnson and shared the great writer's precarious existence as a writer for *The Gentleman's Magazine*. Boyse ended his days destitute.

Hart, Edward, 'Portrait of a Grub: Samuel Boyse', *Studies in English Literature, 1500–1900*, 7 (1967), 415–425.

BROOME, William (1689–1745) Born at Haslington, Cheshire, son of a poor farmer; educated at Eton and St John's College, Cambridge. A fine Greek scholar and deep admirer of Pope, Broome acted as the poet's research assistant for his translation of Homer. Many of the notes and a third of the Odyssey (1725–6) are his. Broome's *Poems on Several Occasions* (1727) gathered his own verse together, including 'Melancholy', written on the death of his daughter in 1723.

BROWN, John (1715–66) 'Estimate' Brown, son of the Vicar of Wigton, Cumberland, attended the local grammar school and graduated B.A. from St John's College, Cambridge, 1735, then took holy orders. His *Essay on Satire* (1745) was included in Dodsley's *Collection* (1748). After writing two tragedies for the London stage, Brown caused a public stir with an attack on modern luxury, *An Estimate of the Manners and Principles of the Times* (1757). He committed suicide in 1766.

Eddy, Donald D., *A Bibliography of John Brown* (New York, 1971).
Roberts, William, *A Dawn of Imaginative Feeling: The Contribution of John Brown (1715–66) to Eighteenth Century Thought and Literature* (Carlisle, 1996).

BURNS, Robert (1759–96) Son of an Ayrshire tenant farmer, Burns had a literary education at the village school followed by some private tutoring. He worked on the family farm and read the poetry of Pope, Thomson, Shakespeare, and Allan Ramsay, gaining a local reputation for his own verses. These early works were collected in a subscription edition of *Poems, Chiefly in the Scottish Dialect* published at Kilmarnock in 1786 with the aim of defraying the expenses of his emigration to Jamaica. This was abandoned when Burns was acclaimed in Edinburgh as the 'heaven-taught ploughman', and a second subscription edition published there sold 2,876 copies. His poems were published in London in 1787. In 1788 he became an exciseman (tax collector) and later moved to Dumfries with his young family. In 1787 he met James Johnson and began supplying material for the latter's *Scots Musical Museum*, collecting and revising traditional Scottish songs and writing original lyrics himself. Burns's two-volume *Poems* (1793) included the popular 'Tam o'Shanter' and other recent work. Being a national poet did little to alleviate Burns's financial worries, and he died of rheumatic fever. Burns's dialect poetry is in the Scottish tradition of Dunbar, Douglas, Ramsay and Fergusson, but he deeply admired English poets such as Thomson, Gray, Shenstone and Cowper.

Bold, Alan, *A Burns Companion* (Houndmills and London, 1991).
Brown, Mary Ellen, *Burns and Tradition* (London, 1984).
Campbell, Ian, 'Burns's Poems and their Audience' in Low, Donald A., ed., *Critical Essays on Robert Burns* (London and Boston, 1975), pp. 39–53.
Crawford, Robert, ed., *Robert Burns and Cultural Authority* (Iowa City, 1997).
Crawford, Thomas, *Burns: A Study of the Poems & Songs* (Edinburgh and London, 1960).
Ferguson, J. De Lancey, and G. Ross Roy, eds., *The Letters of Robert Burns*, 2 vols (Oxford, 1985).
Jack, R.D.S., and Andrew Noble, eds., *The Art of Robert Burns* (London, 1982).
Kinsley, James, ed., *The Poems and Songs of Robert Burns*, 3 vols (Oxford, 1968).
McGuirk, Carol, *Robert Burns and the Sentimental Era* (Athens, 1985).
McGuirk, Carol, ed., *Critical Essays on Robert Burns* (New York, etc., 1998).
McGuirk, Carol, 'Burns, Bakhtin, and the Opposition of Poetic and Novelistic Discourse: A Reply to David Morris, *The Eighteenth Century: Theory and Interpretation*, 32 (1991), 58–72.
Mackay, James, *A Biography of Robert Burns* (Edinburgh, 1992).
Morris, David, 'Burns and Heteroglossia', *The Eighteenth Century: Theory and Interpretation*, 28 (1987), 3–27.
Roe, Nicholas, 'Authenticating Robert Burns', *Essays in Criticism*, 46 (1996), 195–218.

CAWTHORN, James (1719–61) Son of a Sheffield upholsterer; educated at the local grammar school. At 18 he matriculated at Clare Hall, Cambridge, but did not reside and became a schoolmaster in London. As Headmaster of Tonbridge Grammar School he gained a local reputation for his poetry, publishing a heroic epistle, *Abelard to Eloisa* (1747). Cawthorn was killed in a riding accident. His verses were finally collected in *Poems* (1771).

CHATTERTON, Thomas (1752–70) His father, a Bristol writing-master, died before he was born, and he was supported by his mother's work as a seamstress. He attended Colston's Charity School in Bristol, and at fourteen was apprenticed to an attorney. He read Chaucer and Spenser, and became fascinated by the poetic language of the past. His imagination was also stirred by old parchments that his father had collected from a chest in St Mary Redcliffe Church, and Chatterton began writing his own fifteenth-century poetry under the assumed character of 'Thomas Rowley'. These were part of a wider concern with recovering a lost medieval literary inheritance based on Bristol, and on Rowley's patron William Canynge. While 'Rowley' was creating an idealised civic culture, Chatterton was anonymously attacking the corruptions of modern government and court in a stream of satiric poems and essays in the newspapers. Released from his apprenticeship in 1770, he went to London, but felt rebuffed by the literary establishment, notably James Dodsley and Horace Walpole. He died by his own hand in a Holborn garret at the age of seventeen, just as his talents were becoming recognised. The Rowley poems were published in 1777, and doubts about their authenticity came to a head in the 'Rowley Controversy' of 1782, when Thomas Warton and other scholars proved them to be modern productions.

Barry, Jonathan, 'Chatterton in Bristol', *Angelaki* 1:2 (Winter 1993–4), 55–81.
Groom, Nick, ed., *Thomas Chatterton and Romantic Culture* (Houndmills, 1999).
Kelly, Linda, *The Marvellous Boy: The Life and Myth of Thomas Chatterton* (London, 1971).
Lockwood, Thomas, *Post-Augustan Satire* (Seattle, 1979).
Meyerstein, E.H.W., *A Life of Thomas Chatterton* (London, 1930).
Taylor, Donald S., ed., in association with Benjamin B. Hoover, *The Complete Works of Thomas Chatterton*, 2 vols (Oxford, 1971).
Taylor, Donald S., *Thomas Chatterton's Art: Experiments in Imagined History* (Princeton, 1978).
Warren, Murray, *A Bibliography of Thomas Chatterton* (New York, 1977).

CHUDLEIGH, Mary (1656–1710) Born Mary Lee, at Winslade, Devon, she married a local baronet, Sir George Chudleigh, in 1685. Lady Chudleigh was widely read in the classics and English verse, but nothing is known of her education. In her best known poem, *The Ladies Defence* (1701), she defended women from attack by a nonconformist clergyman who had denigrated the female sex as superficial, weak and unruly. She published under her own name *Poems on Several Occasions* (1703), dedicated to Queen Anne, and *Essays upon Several Subjects* (1710).

Barash, Carol, ' "The Native Liberty . . . of the Subject": Configurations of Gender and Authority in the Works of Mary Chudleigh, Sarah Fyge Egerton, and Mary Astell', in Grundy, Isobel, and Susan Wiseman, eds., *Women, Writing, History: 1640–1799* (Athens, 1992), pp. 55–69.
Coleman, Antony, ' "The Provok'd Wife" and "The Ladies Defence" ', *Notes and Queries*, 17 (1970), 88–91.
Ezell, Margaret J.M., ed., *The Poems and Prose of Mary, Lady Chudleigh* (New York and Oxford, 1993).

CHURCHILL, Charles (1731–64) At Westminster School he formed life-long friendships with a group of poetical young men who later became the Nonsense Club (Lloyd, Colman, Thornton and Cowper). On his father's death in 1758 Churchill succeeded to his curacy of St John's Westminster, supporting his wife and children on a meagre stipend supplemented by earnings from his verse satires. *The Rosciad* (1761), a critique of the acting profession, brought him popular acclaim, and his reputation as a subversive and unpredictable genius was confirmed by a succession of satires that included *Night* (1762), *The Prophecy of Famine* (1763), and *Gotham* (1764). A close alliance with the radical John Wilkes enhanced his anti-establishment credentials. His heroic couplets have a vivid energy that places him in the Popean line, but he stamps his more expansive and improvisatory character on them. A collected edition of *Poems* appeared in 1763. Churchill died of a fever in Boulogne, where he had gone to meet Wilkes.

Bertelsen, Lance, *The Nonsense Club: Literature and Popular Culture, 1749–1764* (Oxford, 1986).

Caretta, Vincent, *The Snarling Muse: Verbal and Visual Political Satire from Pope to Churchill* (Philadelphia, 1983).

Carnochan, W.B., 'Satire, Sublimity, and Sentiment: Theory and Practice in Post-Augustan Satire', *PMLA*, 85 (1970), 260–7.

Fisher, Alan S., 'The Stretching of Augustan Satire: Charles Churchill's "Dedication to Warburton"', *Journal of English and Germanic Philology*, 72 (1973), 360–77.

Golden, Morris, 'Sterility and Eminence in the Poetry of Charles Churchill', *Journal of English and Germanic Philology*, 66 (1967), 333–46.

Grant, Douglas, ed., *The Poetical Works of Charles Churchill* (Oxford, 1956).

Hammond, Brean S., and Martin Malone, 'Pope and Churchill', in Nicholson, Colin, ed., *Alexander Pope: Essays for the Tercentenary* (Aberdeen, 1988), pp. 22–38.

Lockwood, Thomas, *Post-Augustan Satire: Charles Churchill and Satirical Poetry 1750–1800* (Seattle, 1979).

Smith, Raymond J., *Charles Churchill* (Boston, 1977).

COLLIER, Mary (?1690–c. 1762) Born near Midhurst, Sussex, Collier never attended school, but was taught to read by her parents. She supported herself by various menial jobs in the district, borrowing books and reading for amusement, and moved to Petersfield 'where my chief Employment was, Washing, Brewing and such labour'. She knew by heart Stephen Duck's *The Thresher's Labour* (1730) and responded to his attack on lazy females with *The Woman's Labour* (1739), printed at her own charge. Collier continued to live by her physical labours, and at the age of sixty-three she moved to Alton where she ended her days 'in Piety, Purity, Peace, and an Old Maid'. An edition of her *Poems* with an autobiographical memoir was published at Winchester in 1762.

Christmas, William J., *The Lab'ring Muses: Work, Writing and the Social Order in English Plebeian Poetry, 1730–1830* (Newark and London, 2001), pp. 115–29.

Ferguson, Moira, introd., Duck, *The Thresher's Labour*, and Collier, *The Woman's Labour* (facsimile ed.). Augustan Reprint Society, vol. 230 (William Andrews Clark Memorial Library, 1985).

Ferguson, Moira, *Eighteenth-Century Women Poets: Nation, Class, and Gender* (Albany, 1995), pp. 7–25.

Goodridge, John, *Rural Life in Eighteenth-Century Poetry* (Cambridge, 1995), pp. 1–88.

Landry, Donna, *The Muses of Resistance: Laboring-Class Women's Poetry in Britain, 1739–1796* (Cambridge, 1990), pp. 56–77.

Thompson, E.P., and Marian Sugden, eds., *The Thresher's Labour by Stephen Duck. The Woman's Labour by Mary Collier* (London, 1989).

COLLINS, William (1721–59) Son of the Mayor of Chichester, Collins attended Winchester College and Magdalen College, Oxford. He was a close friend of the Warton brothers, and like them published his first volume (the exotic *Persian Eclogues*, 1742) while an undergraduate. He settled in London full of literary ambitions, but little came of his plans. His *Odes* (Dec. 1746) failed to sell. A bequest from his uncle in 1749 lifted financial worries, but his poetic output was minimal. Three of Collins's odes were included in the second edition of Dodsley's *Collection* (1748), and he published *Ode Occasion'd by the Death of Mr Thomson* (1749). His longest poem, *Ode on the Popular Superstitions of the Highlands* was not printed till 1788. During 1751–3 Collins evidently became ill and travelled in France to restore his health, but by 1754 he was beginning to suffer from mental illness. He moved back to Chichester where he lived in the Cathedral cloisters with his sister. John Langhorne's edition of his *Poetical Works* (1765) initiated Collins's high posthumous reputation.

Barry, Kevin, *Language, Music and the Sign: A Study in Aesthetics, Poetics and Poetic Practice from Collins to Coleridge* (Cambridge, 1987), pp. 27–55.

Carver, P.L., *The Life of a Poet. A Biographical Sketch of William Collins* (London, 1967).

Hagstrum, Jean H., *The Sister Arts: The Tradition of Literary Pictorialism and English Poetry from Dryden to Gray* (Chicago and London, 1958), pp. 268–86.

Johnston, Arthur, 'The Poetry of William Collins', *Proceedings of the British Academy*, 59 (1973), 321–40.

Lonsdale, Roger, ed., *The Poems of Gray, Collins and Goldsmith* (London and Harlow, 1969).

McKillop, Alan D., 'Collins's *Ode to Evening* – Background and Structure', *Tennessee Studies in Literature*, 5 (1960), 73–83.

Sherwin, Paul S., *Precious Bane: Collins and the Mid-Century Legacy* (Austin, 1977).

Sigworth, Oliver F., *William Collins* (New York, 1965).

Wasserman, Earl R., 'Collins's "Ode on the Poetical Character," ' *ELH*, 34 (1967), 92–115.

Wendorf, Richard, and Charles Ryskamp, eds., *The Works of William Collins* (Oxford, 1979).

Wendorf, Richard, *William Collins and Eighteenth-Century English Poetry* (Minneapolis, 1981).

Woodhouse, A.S.P., 'The Poetry of Collins Reconsidered', in Hilles, F.W., and Harold Bloom, eds., *From Sensibility to Romanticism: Essays Presented to Frederick A. Pottle* (New York, 1965), pp. 93–137.

COWPER, William (1731–1800) Son of the Rector of Berkhamsted, Hertfordshire, he attended Westminster School, a contemporary and close friend of Churchill and Lloyd. Abandoning a law career, he developed the knack of humorous light verse and contributed satirical essays to *The Connoisseur* (1754–6). His life among the coffee-house wits ended in 1763 when he had the first of several breakdowns, and he recovered at a house for the insane at St Albans. Cowper was 'born again' to evangelical religion and moved to Huntingdon where he lived with the Unwin family. In 1767 he and the widowed Mary Unwin (1724–96) moved to Olney, Buckinghamshire, where he began writing hymns for prayer meetings presided over by the Rev. John Newton. After a severe relapse in 1773 Cowper became convinced he was damned and he remained under that shadow for life. Having established a quiet routine, he contributed sixty-six hymns to *Olney Hymns* (1779) and published a collection of *Poems* (1782). *The Task* (1785) brought him national popularity. His blank-verse translation of Homer (1791) was intended to challenge Pope's couplet version. Severe depression closed in, and Cowper spent the last five years of his life at his cousin's house in Norfolk, where he wrote his final poems.

Baird, John D., and Charles Ryskamp, eds., *The Poems of William Cowper*, 3 vols (Oxford, 1980–95).

Fulford, Tim, 'Wordsworth, Cowper and the Language of Eighteenth-Century Politics', in Woodman, Thomas, ed., *The Early Romantics: Perspectives in British Poetry from Pope to Wordsworth* (Houndmills, 1998), pp. 117–33.

Golden, Morris, *In Search of Stability: The Poetry of William Cowper* (New York, 1960).

Griffin, Dustin, 'Cowper, Milton and the Recovery of Paradise', *Essays in Criticism*, 31 (1981), 15–26.

Griffin, Dustin, 'Redefining Georgic: Cowper's *Task*', *ELH*, 57 (1990), 865–79.

Hutchings, Bill, *The Poetry of William Cowper* (London and Canberra, 1983).

King, James, and Charles Ryskamp, eds., *The Letters and Prose Writings of William Cowper*, 5 vols (Oxford, 1979–86).

King, James, *William Cowper. A Biography* (Durham, NC, 1986).

Matheson, Ann, 'The Influence of Cowper's *The Task* on Coleridge's Conversational Poems', in Sultana, Donald, ed., *New Approaches to Coleridge* (London, 1981), pp. 137–50.

Newey, Vincent, *Cowper's Poetry: A Critical Study and Reassessment* (Liverpool, 1982).

Newey, Vincent, 'William Cowper and the Condition of England', in Newey, Vincent, and Ann Thompson, eds., *Literature and Nationalism* (Liverpool, 1991), pp. 120–39.

Priestman, Martin, *Cowper's 'Task': Structure and Influence* (Cambridge and New York, 1983).

Sambrook, James, ed., *William Cowper: The Task and Selected Other Poems* (London and New York, 1994).

Spacks, Patricia Meyer, *The Poetry of Vision: Five Eighteenth-Century Poets* (Cambridge, Mass., 1967), pp. 165–206.

Terry, Richard, ' "Meaner themes": Mock-heroic and Providentialism in Cowper's Poetry', *Studies in English Literature*, 34 (1994), 617–34.

CRABBE, George (1754–1832) Son of a customs officer in the Suffolk fishing town of Aldeburgh, he worked as a dock-hand and an apothecary until his poetry found a patron in Edmund Burke, who arranged for the publication of *The Library* (1781). In 1782 Crabbe was ordained and became chaplain to the Duke of Rutland. At Belvoir Castle he wrote *The Village* (1783), the success of which enabled him to marry. He pursued his duties as a rural clergyman, and after a long silence published his *Poems* (1807), which included a collection of verse tales, 'The Parish Register'. He perfected the brief heroic-couplet narrative in *The Borough* (1810) and *Tales* (1812). Prone to depression, Crabbe moved in 1813, on the death of his wife, to Trowbridge, Wiltshire. He ended his days as a notable figure in London literary society.

Dalrymple-Champneys, Norma, and Arthur Pollard, eds., *George Crabbe: The Complete Poetical Works*, 3 vols (Oxford, 1988).

Edwards, Gavin, 'Crabbe's So-Called Realism', *Essays in Criticism*, 37 (1987), 303–20.

Edwards, Gavin, *George Crabbe's Poetry on Border Land* (Lewiston etc, 1990).

Faulkner, Thomas C., ed., with the assistance of Rhonda L. Blair, *Selected Letters and Journals of George Crabbe* (Oxford, 1985).

Hatch, Ronald B., *Crabbe's Arabesque: Social Drama in the Poetry of George Crabbe* (Montreal, 1976).

Huchon, René, *George Crabbe and his Times 1754–1832. A Critical and Biographical Study*, trans. by Frederick Clarke (London, 1907).

McGann, Jerome J., 'The Anachronism of George Crabbe', *ELH*, 48 (1981), 555–72.

Nelson, Beth, *George Crabbe and the Progress of Eighteenth-Century Narrative Verse* (Lewisburg, 1976).

Sigworth, Oliver, *Nature's Sternest Painter: Five Essays on the Poetry of George Crabbe* (Tucson, 1965).

CROWE, William (1745–1829) Born at Midgham, Berkshire. His father was a carpenter at Winchester, and in 1758 William was elected a 'poor scholar' of Winchester College, where Joseph Warton was second master. Crowe entered New College, Oxford, 1765, where he became fellow and tutor 1767–83. As Public Orator of the University 1784–1829 Crowe was noted for his rustic simplicity, impressive voice, and popular sermons. He commuted on foot between Oxford and his Wiltshire parish. His most popular poem *Lewesdon Hill* (1788) was later enlarged and republished with his other poems in 1804 and 1827.

Martin, C.G., 'Coleridge and William Crowe's "Lewesdon Hill,"' *Modern Language Review*, 62 (1967), 400–6.

DIAPER, William (1685–1717) Little is known of Diaper. Of humble origins, he was born at Bridgwater, Somerset, and entered Balliol College, Oxford, as a poor scholar 1699. He became a country curate, but seems never to have been ordained priest. Coming to London in 1712 to seek patronage, he saw published in that year both his *Nereides* and *Dryades*, the latter declaring its author's Tory loyalties. He met Swift, who thought the *Nereides* original and 'very pretty' but their author 'a poor little short Wretch'. He and his friends gave Diaper financial support, but the young curate's chances of patronage were lost when the Tory ministry collapsed in 1714. Diaper seems to have died in obscurity.

Broughton, Dorothy, ed., *William Diaper: The Complete Works* (London, 1951).
Kupersmith, William, 'William Diaper and Two Others Imitate Swift Imitating Horace', *Swift Studies*, 10 (1995), 26–36.

DIXON, Sarah (1671–1765) Born in Rochester, Kent, the daughter of James Dixon (d. 1716), an attorney for the Dean and Chapter of Rochester Cathedral. The family moved to rural Newnham (between Rochester and Canterbury) when her father remarried. An idyllic friendship with a daughter of Lord Teynham of nearby Lynsted Park was ended when her beloved 'Stella' married. Thereafter Dixon appears to have been her family's poor relation, perhaps living with a wealthy aunt in London. Her only published volume, *Poems on Several Occasions* (Canterbury, 1740), was issued by subscription to bring her financial support. (Pope was one of the subscribers.) Dixon continued writing poetry at least into her seventies, and died at the age of 93.

Messenger, Ann, *Pastoral Tradition and the Female Talent: Studies in Augustan Poetry* (New York, 2001), pp. 135–55.

DUCK, Stephen (?1705–56) A farm labourer born at Charlton St Peter, Wiltshire, Duck attended the local charity school until the age of fourteen. At nineteen he married, but continued to study in his spare time, collecting with a friend a small library of poetry that included Shakespeare, *The Spectator*, *Paradise Lost*, and Dryden's *Virgil*. His early poems, including 'The Thresher's Labour', were pirated as *Poems on Several Subjects* (1730), and Queen Caroline summoned this newly discovered prodigy to court. Duck was given a pension and a house at Richmond. He became keeper of Merlin's Cave, Caroline's gothic folly, and married his royal patroness's housekeeper. His *Poems on Several Occasions* (1736) had a formidable subscription list. In 1746 Duck took holy orders, and eventually became Rector of Byfleet, Surrey. He drowned himself in 1756.

Christmas, William J., *The Lab'ring Muses: Work, Writing and the Social Order in English Plebeian Poetry, 1730–1830* (Newark and London, 2001), pp. 73–95.
Ferguson, Moira, introd., Duck, *The Thresher's Labour*, and Collier, *The Woman's Labour* (facsimile ed.). Augustan Reprint Society, vol. 230 (William Andrews Clark Memorial Library, 1985).
Goodridge, John, *Rural Life in Eighteenth-Century Poetry* (Cambridge, 1995), pp. 1–88.
Keegan, Bridget, 'Georgic Transformations and Stephen Duck's "The Thresher's Labour,"' *Studies in English Literature*, 41 (2001), 545–562.
Thompson, E.P., and Marian Sugden, eds., *The Thresher's Labour by Stephen Duck. The Woman's Labour by Mary Collier* (London, 1989).
Zionkowski, Linda, 'Strategies of Containment: Stephen Duck, Ann Yearsley, and the Problem of Polite Culture', *Eighteenth-Century Life*, 13 (1989), 91–108.

DYER, John (1699–1757) Son of a Welsh attorney, Dyer attended Westminster School, but left early to work in his father's office. When his father died in 1720 Dyer was able to abandon his legal studies and follow his twin loves of poetry and art. He moved to London to study painting, being drawn into Aaron Hill's circle, which at this time included James Thomson and Richard Savage. Six of his early poems, including 'Grongar Hill', appeared in Savage's *Miscellany* (1726). In 1724 Dyer, like many young artists, travelled to Italy, where he wrote *The Ruins of Rome* (not published until 1740). In his thirtieth year he moved to rural Herefordshire, and began another phase of his life as a successful and practically-minded farmer. In 1741 he took holy orders and became a country parson. Under the encouragement of his patron, the Earl of Hardwicke, he produced his major work, *The Fleece* (1757).

Barrell, John, *English Literature in History: An Equal Wide Survey* (London, 1993), pp. 90–109.
Feingold, Richard, *Nature and Society: Later Eighteenth-Century Uses of the Pastoral and Georgic* (Hassocks, 1978), pp. 83–119.
Goldstein, Laurence, *Ruins and Empire: The Evolution of a Theme in Augustan and Romantic Literature* (Pittsburgh, 1977), pp. 25–58.
Goodridge, John, *Rural Life in Eighteenth-Century Poetry* (Cambridge, 1995), pp. 91–180.
Goodridge, John, ed., *John Dyer: Selected Poetry and Prose* (Nottingham, 2000).
Humfrey, Belinda, *John Dyer* (Cardiff, 1980).
Patey, Douglas Lane, 'Anne Finch, John Dyer, and the Syntax of Nature', in Rivero, Albert J., ed., *Augustan Subjects: Essays in Honor of Martin C. Battestin* (Newark and London, 1997), pp. 29–46.
Williams, Ralph M., *Poet, Painter and Parson: The Life of John Dyer* (New York, 1956).

EGERTON, Sarah Fyge (1670–1723) Born in London, daughter of Thomas Fyge (d. 1706) and Mary Beacham (d. 1704). Like Mary Chudleigh, she first came to public notice with a spirited defence of the female sex. In her case *The Female Advocate* (1686) responded to Robert Gould's predictable satire in *Love Given O're* (1682). Such precocity brought parental displeasure, and Sarah was dispatched to live with relatives in the country. She was married twice, first to an attorney, and after his death to the Rev. Thomas Egerton (d. 1720), whom she unsuccessfully sued for divorce. Her *Poems on Several Occasions* (1703), dedicated to the prominent Whig patron, Lord Halifax, exhibits her strong personality and impatience with form and custom.

Barash, Carol, '"The Native Liberty . . . of the Subject": Configurations of Gender and Authority in the Works of Mary Chudleigh, Sarah Fyge Egerton, and Mary Astell', in Grundy, Isobel, and Susan Wiseman, eds., *Women, Writing, History: 1640–1799* (Athens, 1992), pp. 55–69.

EUSDEN, Laurence (1688–1730) Son of the Rector of Spofforth, Yorkshire, he attended St Peter's School, York, and Trinity College, Cambridge, of which he became a fellow 1711. Well directed poetic flattery brought him the powerful patronage of the Earl of Halifax and the Duke of Newcastle, and Eusden was repaid by being made the nation's Poet Laureate 1718, an appointment that raised eyebrows and hackles, but suited his obsequious muse. He died as Rector of Coningsby, Lincolnshire, leaving an unfinished translation of Tasso.

FINCH, Anne (1661–1720) Daughter of Sir William Kingsmill, she became in her early twenties a Maid of Honour to Mary of Modena, wife of James, Duke of York (Charles II's brother) and lived at St James's Palace. In 1684 she married Captain Heneage Finch

(1657–1726), and the couple became prominent courtiers when the Roman Catholic James became King the following year. The 'bloodless revolution' of 1688 affected both their lives. Refusing to swear the oath of allegiance to the Protestant William III, the Catholic Finches were forced into country retirement. Anne Finch lived the rest of her life at Eastwell Park, Kent, home of her husband's nephew the young Earl of Winchilsea. She returned to court as a Lady of the Bedchamber to Queen Anne, and her husband inherited the family title in 1712. The Countess of Winchilsea's poems circulated in manuscript and some, like 'The Spleen', found their way into published collections. With some reluctance she brought out her own volume of *Miscellany Poems* (1713), which included *Aristomenes, a Tragedy*.

Barash, Carol, *English Women's Poetry, 1649–1714: Politics, Community, and Linguistic Authority* (Oxford, 1996), pp. 259–87.

Brower, Reuben A., 'Lady Winchilsea and the Poetic Tradition of the Seventeenth Century', *Studies in Philology*, 42 (1945), 61–80.

Hinnant, Charles H., *The Poetry of Anne Finch: An Essay in Interpretation* (Newark, etc., 1994).

Keith, Jennifer, 'The Poetics of Anne Finch', *Studies in English Literature*, 38 (1998), 465–80.

Mallinson, Jean, 'Anne Finch: A Woman Poet and the Tradition', in Messenger, Ann, ed., *Gender at Work: Four Women Writers of the Eighteenth Century* (Detroit, 1990), pp. 34–76.

McGovern, Barbara, *Anne Finch and Her Poetry: A Critical Biography* (Athens, 1992).

McGovern, Barbara, 'Finch, Pope, and Swift: The Bond of Displacement', in Mell, Donald C., ed., *Pope, Swift, and Women Writers* (Newark and London, 1996), pp. 105–24.

McGovern, Barbara, and Charles H. Hinnant, eds., *The Anne Finch Wellesley Manuscript Poems* (Athens, 1998).

Messenger, Ann, 'Publishing without Perishing: Lady Winchilsea's Miscellany Poems of 1713', *Restoration*, 5 (1981), 27–37.

Patey, Douglas Lane, 'Anne Finch, John Dyer, and the Syntax of Nature', in Rivero, Albert J., ed., *Augustan Subjects: Essays in Honor of Martin C. Battestin* (Newark and London, 1997), pp. 29–46.

Reynolds, Myra, ed., *Poems* (Chicago, 1903).

Sena, John F., 'Melancholy in Anne Finch and Elizabeth Carter: The Ambivalence of an Idea', *Yearbook of English Studies*, 1 (1971), 108–19.

GARTH, Samuel (1661–1719) Garth attended school at Ingleton, Yorkshire, and entered Peterhouse, Cambridge, 1676. He studied medicine at Leyden and received his M.D. 1691. He was elected a fellow of the Royal Society of Physicians 1693. A supporter of William III and member of the Whig Kit-Cat Club, Garth lobbied on behalf of free medical care for the London poor, a scheme naturally opposed by the apothecaries. The battle is given mock-heroic treatment in Garth's popular poem, *The Dispensary* (1699 and much reprinted). Dr Garth, 'the best natured of men' according to Pope, was knighted in 1714. His later verse includes the descriptive poem *Claremont* (1715), and a share in the translation of Ovid's *Metamorphoses* (1717).

Ackerman, Stephen J., 'The "Infant Atoms" of Garth's Dispensary', *Modern Language Review*, 74 (1979), 513–23.

Cook, Richard I., *Sir Samuel Garth* (Boston, 1980).

Daly, Patrick J., 'Monarchy, the Disbanding Crisis, and Samuel Garth's Dispensary', *Restoration*, 25 (2001), 35–52.

Sena, John F., *The Best-Natured Man: Sir Samuel Garth, Physician and Poet* (New York, 1986).

GAY, John (1685–1732) Born into a merchant family at Barnstaple, Devon, Gay was apprenticed to a London silk-tradesman, but was eventually drawn into the literary world of the coffee-house wits. He did magazine-work for his old schoolfellow, Aaron Hill, before publishing *Wine* (1708), a comic georgic. Gay formed a close literary bond with Pope, Swift and Arbuthnot through the Scriblerus Club, of which he acted as secretary. *Rural Sports* (1713) and *The Shepherd's Week* (1714) confirmed his talent for catching the humorous details of country life, and in the three-book *Trivia* (1716) he turned his attention to the city. This was followed by his collaboration with Pope and Swift on a farce, *Three Hours After Marriage* (1717), and a successful subscription edition of his *Poems* (1720). Gay felt frustrated by his many bids for patronage, but with his *Fables* (1727) and the wildly successful staging of *The Beggar's Opera* (1728), he showed his infallible knack of breathing life into old genres and creating new ones.

Ames, Dianne S., 'Gay's *Trivia* and the Art of Allusion', *Studies in Philology*, 75 (1978), 199–222.

Beckwith, Charles E., 'The Languages of Gay's *Trivia*', *Eighteenth-Century Life*, 10 (1986), 27–43.

Burgess, C.F., ed., *The Letters of John Gay* (Oxford, 1966).

Fischer, John Irwin, 'Never on Sunday: John Gay's *The Shepherd's Week*', *Studies in Eighteenth-Century Culture*, 10 (1981), 191–203.

Lewis, Peter, and Nigel Wood, eds., *John Gay and the Scriblerians* (London and New York, 1989).

Dearing, Vinton A., ed. with Charles E. Beckwith, *John Gay. Poetry and Prose*, 2 vols (Oxford, 1974).

Nokes, David, *John Gay: A Profession of Friendship. A Critical Biography* (Oxford, 1995).

GOLDSMITH, Oliver (?1730–74) Son of an Irish clergyman, he studied at Trinity College, Dublin, but then drifted irresolutely in search of a career. Returning from a trip round Europe in 1756 he worked as a physician and a schoolmaster. Ralph Griffiths, editor of the *Monthly Review* gave him his chance as a reviewer, and Goldsmith himself became editor of a weekly journal, *The Bee* (1759). He immersed himself industriously in many literary projects. His poem *The Traveller* (1764) drew on his observation of other nations and showed his skill in shaping pointed and memorable couplets. His novel, *The Vicar of Wakefield* (1766), combined pictures of domestic and country life with sentimental and dramatic description; and in *She Stoops to Conquer* (1773) he mastered stage comedy. A close friend of Dr Johnson, Goldsmith was a valued, if at times exasperating, member of the 'Club'. His best known poem, *The Deserted Village* (1770) became an instant classic, with its indignant picture of lost rural virtues.

Friedman, Arthur, ed., *Collected Works of Oliver Goldsmith*, 5 vols (Oxford, 1966).

Ginger, John, *The Notable Man: The Life and Times of Oliver Goldsmith* (London, 1977).

Lonsdale, Roger, ed., *The Poems of Gray, Collins and Goldsmith* (London and Harlow, 1969).

Lonsdale, Roger, ' "A Garden and a Grave": The Poetry of Oliver Goldsmith', in Martz, Louis L., and Aubrey Williams, eds., *The Poet in his Work: Essays on a Problem in Criticism* (New Haven and London, 1978), pp. 3–30.

Mahony, Robert, 'Lyrical Antithesis: The Moral Style of *The Deserted Village*', *Ariel*, 8 (1977), 33–47.

Newey, Vincent, 'Goldsmith's "Pensive Plain": Re-viewing *The Deserted Village*', in Woodman, Thomas, ed., *Early Romantics: Perspectives in British Poetry from Pope to Wordsworth* (Houndmills, 1998), pp. 93–116.

Storm, Leo, 'Literary Convention in Goldsmith's *Deserted Village*', *Huntington Library Quarterly*, 33 (1969–70), 243–56.

Swarbrick, Andrew, ed., *The Art of Oliver Goldsmith* (London, 1984).
Wardle, Ralph M., *Oliver Goldsmith* (Lawrence, 1957).

GRAINGER, James (?1725–66) Grainger seems to have been born at Duns, Berwickshire, Scotland, the son of a customs officer. He was educated at a school in North Berwick before studying medicine at Edinburgh University. As a British army surgeon he was present at the battle of Culloden (1746) when the Jacobite uprising was ended. After the Peace of 1748 he evidently toured Europe. Taking his M.D. from Edinburgh 1753 he left the army and began practising medicine in London. He had a Wartonian poem, 'Solitude', printed in Dodsley's 1755 *Collection* and began writing regular reviews for the *Monthly Review* 1756–8, becoming a friend of Thomas Percy, Dr Johnson, and Goldsmith. In 1759 he accompanied a wealthy young pupil to St Kitts in the Caribbean, where he married and settled as a physician. He returned to Britain for six months 1763–4 with the manuscript of *The Sugar-Cane*, his georgic of the sugar plantations, published by Dodsley in 1764. Grainger died in the West Indies.

Gilmore, John, *The Poetics of Empire: A Study of James Grainger's The Sugar-Cane* (London, 2000).
Irlam, Shaun, ' "Wish You Were Here": Exporting England in James Grainger's *The Sugar-Cane*', *ELH*, 68 (2001), 377–96.
Spate, O.H.K., 'The Muse of Mercantilism: Jago, Grainger and Dyer', in *Studies in the Eighteenth Century* (Canberra, 1968), pp. 119–31.

GRAY, Thomas (1716–71) Son of a London scrivener, Gray was educated at Eton and Peterhouse, Cambridge. Intending originally to enter the legal profession, he was invited to accompany his schoolfriend Horace Walpole, son of the Prime Minister, on the Grand Tour to Italy, 1739–41. Back in England he found a poetic soulmate in another Etonian, Richard West, whose death in 1742 affected Gray deeply. Thereafter he moved back to Peterhouse as a Fellow-Commoner, pursuing scholarly studies and spending vacations during the 1740s and 50s with his mother and aunts at the village of Stoke Poges, Buckinghamshire. Like other poets of the period he was brought into the limelight by Robert Dodsley, who published his 'Ode on a Distant Prospect of Eton College' (1747) and included Gray's work in his *Collection of Poems* (1748). Publication of *Elegy Written in a Country Church Yard* (1751) brought the shy poet instant and unwelcome fame. Gray's *Odes* (1757) mastered the lofty Pindaric style and became along with the elegy his most admired work. In 1756 Gray had moved to Pembroke College, where he remained for the rest of his life studying the old northern languages, music, botany, and antiquities. But he was also an eager picturesque traveller, and a delightful letter-writer. In 1768 he was appointed Regius Professor of Modern History, but never gave any lectures. By his death only fourteen short poems of his had appeared in print.

Clark, S.H., ' "Pendet Homo Incertus": Gray's Response to Locke', *Eighteenth-Century Studies*, 24 (1991), 273–91, 484–503.
Griffin, Dustin, 'Gray's Audiences', *Essays in Criticism*, 28 (1978), 208–15.
Hutchings, W.B., and William Ruddick, eds., *Thomas Gray: Contemporary Essays* (Liverpool, 1993).
Jackson, Wallace, 'Thomas Gray and the Dedicatory Muse', *ELH*, 54 (1987), 277–98.
Kaul, Suvir, *Thomas Gray and Literary Authority: Ideology and Poetics in Eighteenth-Century England* (Delhi and Oxford, 1992).
Ketton-Cremer, R.W., *Thomas Gray. A Biography* (Cambridge, 1955).
Lonsdale, Roger, ed., *The Poems of Gray, Collins and Goldsmith* (London and Harlow, 1969).
Lonsdale, Roger, 'The Poetry of Thomas Gray: Versions of the Self', *Proceedings of the British Academy*, 59 (1973), 105–23.

Spacks, Patricia Meyer, ' "Artful Strife": Conflict in Gray's Poetry', *PMLA*, 81 (1966), 63–9.

Starr, H.W., and J.R. Hendrickson, eds., *The Complete Poems of Thomas Gray* (Oxford, 1966).

Toynbee, Paget, and Leonard Whibley, eds., *Correspondence of Thomas Gray*, 3 vols (Oxford, 1935; repr. with additions by Herbert Starr, 1971).

Weinbrot, Howard D., 'Gray's *Elegy*: A Poem of Moral Choice and Resolution', *Studies in English Literature 1500–1900*, 18 (1978), 537–51.

Weinfeld, Henry, *The Poet without a Name: Gray's 'Elegy' and the Problem of History* (Carbondale and Edwardsville, 1991).

Zionkowski, Linda, 'Bridging the Gulf Between: The Poet and the Audience in the Work of Gray', *ELH*, 58 (1991), 13–38.

HARTE, Walter (1709–74) Son of a non-juror clergyman, Harte was educated at Marlborough Grammar School and St Mary Hall, Oxford, where he later became tutor and Vice-Principal. His youthful *Poems on Several Occasions* (1727) were issued by subscription, and Pope ordered four copies. Harte was already his warm admirer and the pair became friends. Harte's adulation of Pope is clear from *An Essay on Satire* (1730), and his *Essay on Reason* (1735) was much influenced by the latter's *Essay on Man*. Thereafter more worldly concerns took over. Harte was made a canon of Windsor 1750 and was given a lucrative crown living. *The Amaranth* (1767) contains his later religious verses.

Gilmore, Thomas B., introd., Walter Harte, *An Essay on Satire* (facsimile of 1730 ed.). Augustan Reprint Society, vol. 132 (William Andrews Clark Memorial Library, 1968).

McLaverty, James, *Pope, Print, and Meaning* (Oxford, 2001), pp. 107–41.

HILL, Aaron (1685–1750) Born in London, educated at Barnstaple Grammar School, Devon, and at Westminster. As a young man he travelled in the east and published his *Account of the Ottoman Empire* (1709). By this time he was back in London writing and producing for the theatre (he introduced Handel to the English stage in 1711 with *Rinaldo*). In 1710 he married Margaret Morris (d. 1731), by whom he had nine children, four of whom survived infancy. Hill drew round him a lively metropolitan circle of poetic friends who included Richard Savage and James Thomson. As a poet he published evocative descriptions of the first and last things, *The Creation* (1720) and *The Judgment-Day* (1721), and the satiric *Advice to the Poets* (1731). He corresponded extensively with Pope and Richardson. Hill moved in 1738 to Plaistow, Essex. His *Works* (4 vols, 1753) were published posthumously.

Belcher, William F., 'Aaron Hill's Earliest Poems', *Notes and Queries*, 29 (1982), 531–2.

Gerrard, Christine, *Aaron Hill: The Muses' Projector, 1685–1750* (Oxford, 2003).

Guest, Harriet, *A Form of Sound Words: The Religious Poetry of Christopher Smart* (Oxford, 1989), pp. 27–33.

Inglesfield, Robert, 'James Thomson, Aaron Hill and the Poetic Sublime', *British Journal for Eighteenth-Century Studies*, 13 (1990), 215–21.

HUGHES, John (1677–1720) Born at Marlborough, Wiltshire, son of a London clerk, Hughes was educated at a dissenting academy in London where he was a contemporary of Isaac Watts. Denied the possibility of a university place like all religious dissenters, he took up a civil service post and worked assiduously as a miscellaneous writer, translating, editing, and compiling two volumes of *A Complete History of England* (3 vols, 1706). He produced a valuable edition of Spenser's *Works* (6 vols, 1715) and wrote opera, masque, and tragedy for the stage. His separately published poems include *The Court of Neptune* (1700), *The House of Nassau* (1702, a tribute to the dissenters' hero, William III), and *The Ecstasy* (1720). Hughes's translation of the *Letters of Abelard and Heloise* (1713) was Pope's most important source. His *Poems* (2 vols, 1735) were edited by John Duncombe.

JAGO, Richard (1715–81) Son of a Warwickshire rector, he attended Solihull School with William Shenstone, his lifelong friend. Entered University College, Oxford, as a 'servitor' (poor scholar) 1732. After graduation he took orders and became curate of Snitterfield, near Stratford (1737), and in 1744 married Dorothea Fancourt (d. 1751) who bore seven children. Jago remarried 1758. Became Vicar of Snitterfield 1754 and spent much time improving the vicarage and grounds. His topographical poem *Edge-Hill* (1767) is a tribute to his south Warwickshire landscape. Jago's collected *Poems, Moral and Descriptive* were edited in 1784.

Bending, Stephen 'Prospects and Trifles: The Views of William Shenstone and Richard Jago', *Qwerty*, 10 (October 2000), 125–31.
Spate, O.H.K., 'The Muse of Mercantilism: Jago, Grainger and Dyer', in *Studies in the Eighteenth Century* (Canberra, 1968), pp. 119–31.

JOHNSON, Samuel (1709–84) Son of a bookseller in Lichfield, Staffordshire, Johnson was an omnivorous reader from childhood. Lack of funds forced him to leave Pembroke College, Oxford, in 1730 without taking a degree. In 1737 he set out for London with his pupil David Garrick, and endured the uncertainties of living by his pen. He gained critical praise for *London* (1738), a diatribe against modern corruption based on Juvenal's Third Satire, but was wary of cultivating patrons. During the 1740s the hardship continued while he contributed essays, poems, and parliamentary reviews to *The Gentleman's Magazine*. In 1749 Johnson published a second imitation of Juvenal, *The Vanity of Human Wishes*; and his verse tragedy *Irene* (staged by Garrick at Drury Lane) earned him much needed funds. In 1750 he started *The Rambler*, an outlet for his distinctive weighty 'Johnsonian' voice as a critic and moralist. After many years' labour his *Dictionary of the English Language* (1755) made his name. Now an honorary M.A. of Oxford, he began to emerge as a major literary landmark and critical authority, though his moral tale *Rasselas* (1759) had mixed reviews. In 1762 a royal pension of £300 from George III relieved his money worries. Johnson's remarkable command over literary reputations was confirmed with his edition of Shakespeare (1765) and *The Lives of the Poets* (1779–81). At the centre of the London cultural scene was 'The Club', founded by Johnson and Sir Joshua Reynolds, whose members included Boswell, Burke, Goldsmith, Garrick, the Wartons, Sheridan, Gibbon, Adam Smith, and Charles James Fox. Johnson's memorable conversation was recorded in detail by Boswell in his classic *Life* of his friend.

Bate, Walter Jackson, *Samuel Johnson* (London, 1978).
Budick, Sanford, *Poetry of Civilization: Mythopoeic Displacement in the Verse of Milton, Dryden, Pope, and Johnson* (New Haven and London, 1974), pp. 156–72.
DeMaria, Jr., Robert, *The Life of Samuel Johnson. A Critical Biography* (Oxford and Cambridge, Mass., 1993).
Fleeman, J.D., ed., *Samuel Johnson: The Complete English Poems* (London, 1974).
Griffin, Dustin, 'Johnson's Funeral Writings', *ELH*, 41 (1974), 192–211.
Hill, George Birkbeck, ed., revised by L.F. Powell, *Boswell's Life of Johnson*, 6 vols (Oxford, 1934–64).
Redford, Bruce, ed., *The Letters of Samuel Johnson*, The Hyde Edition, 5 vols (Princeton, 1992–4).
Rudd, Niall, ed., *Johnson's Juvenal* (Bristol, 1981).
Sitter, John, 'To the *Vanity of Human Wishes* through the 1740s', *Studies in Philology*, 74 (1977), 445–64.

Smith, David Nichol, and Edward L. McAdam, eds., *The Poems of Samuel Johnson*, 2nd ed. (Oxford, 1974).

Venturo, David F., *Johnson the Poet: The Poetic Career of Samuel Johnson* (Newark, 1999).

JONES, Mary (1707–78) Jones lived with her brother Oliver, Precentor of Christ Church, Oxford, and she was a valued member of the university's literary scene (Thomas Warton remembered her as 'a most sensible, agreeable, and amiable woman'). But she also paid long visits to Windsor Castle (where her friend Martha Lovelace was a maid of honour at court) and other aristocratic houses. Her friends encouraged her to bring out by subscription her *Miscellanies in Prose and Verse* (1750). It is clear from this that she was a lively and amusing letter-writer, and a sharp observer of courtly manners. Jones claimed that most of her poems were written 'at a very early age', and she appears to have written little after the 1730s. In spite of critical success with her *Miscellanies* she never published a second volume.

KING, Anthony (fl. 1770–84) As the eldest son of Anthony King of Dublin, he entered the Middle Temple, London, in 1770, and graduated barrister-at-law 1772. His anonymous *The Frequented Village. A Poem. By a Gentleman of the Middle Temple* (n.d.) was printed three times: (1) London: J. Godwin, n.d. [1771] (discouragingly reviewed in the *Monthly Review* and the *Critical Review*; (2) London: Printed for Obadiah Pirate, Black-Boy-Alley, n.d. [evidently a pirated edition]; the 490 lines were expanded to 522 for a further edition 'in Compliance with the Wishes of the Public' (Dublin, 1784). King dedicated the poem to Goldsmith ('in whose acquaintance he is personally honoured'). King contributed a poem to the *Miscellaneous Works* of Gorges Edmond Howard (3 vols, Dublin, 1782), and he seems to have been the author of *Thoughts on the Expediency of Adopting a System of Education, etc.* (Dublin, 1793). As yet, nothing more is known of him.

LEAPOR, Mary (1722–46) Her father was a gardener and nurseryman in Brackley, Northamptonshire. Having probably attended the local free school, she entered service at Weston Hall, where her employer, Susanna Jennens, wrote poems and may have encouraged her reading. Leapor then worked as a kitchen maid at Edgcote House, eight miles north-west of Brackley. Being dismissed, she returned to keep house for her father. In 1745 she gained the friendship of Bridget Fremantle (the 'Artemisia' of her poems) and developed a local reputation as a poetic phenomenon. Her library of 'about sixteen or seventeen books' included her favourite Pope. Leapor died from measles in 1746. Her *Poems upon Several Occasions* (1748) published for the benefit of her father drew six hundred subscribers, including her fellow-labourer Stephen Duck. A second subscription volume with Fremantle's biographical memoir appeared in 1751.

Chaden, Caryn, ' "Mentored from the Page": Mary Leapor's Relationship with Alexander Pope', in Mell, Donald C., ed., *Pope, Swift, and Women Writers* (Newark, 1996), pp. 31–47.

Dalporto, Jeannie, 'Landscape, Labor, and the Ideology of Improvement in Mary Leapor's "Crumble Hall" ', *The Eighteenth Century: Theory and Interpretation*, 42 (2001), 228–44.

Greene, Richard, *Mary Leapor: A Study in Eighteenth-Century Women's Poetry* (Oxford, 1993).

Greene, Richard, 'Mary Leapor: The Problem of Personal Identity', *The Eighteenth Century: Theory and Interpretation*, 42 (2001), 218–27.

Griffin, Dustin, *Literary Patronage in England 1650–1800* (Cambridge, 1996), pp. 189–203.

King, Kathryn R., 'Jane Barker, Mary Leapor and a Chain of Very Odd Contingencies', *English Language Notes*, 33 (1996), pp. 78–119, 14–27.

275

Landry, Donna, *The Muses of Resistance: Laboring-Class Women's Poetry in Britain, 1739–1796* (Cambridge, 1990), pp. 78–119.

Mandell, Laura, 'Demystifying (with) the Repugnant Female Body: Mary Leapor and Feminist Literary History', *Criticism*, 38 (1996), 551–82.

Rizzo, Betty, 'Molly Leapor: An Anxiety for Influence', *The Age of Johnson*, 4 (1991), 313–43.

Rumbold, Valerie, 'The Alienated Insider: Mary Leapor in "Crumble Hall,"' *British Journal for Eighteenth-Century Studies*, 19 (1996), 63–76.

LLOYD, Robert (1733–64) Lloyd had a classical education at Westminster School, where his father was second master, and he went on to Trinity College, Cambridge. Turning his back on a professional career, he plunged into the coffee-house scene with other schoolfriends, Churchill, Cowper, George Colman, and Bonnell Thornton, who formed the 'Nonsense Club'. He wrote regularly for Colman and Thornton's humorous periodical, *The Connoisseur* (1754–6). Lloyd's satire *The Actor* (1760) was a success with the public, and his lively *Poems* were published by subscription in 1762; but dissipation took its toll. Arrested for debt the following year, he died in the 'Fleet'. In 1774 William Kenrick edited his *Poems* in two volumes, with a biographical memoir.

Bertelsen, Lance, *The Nonsense Club: Literature and Popular Culture, 1749–1764* (Oxford, 1986).

Lockwood, Thomas, *Post-Augustan Satire: Charles Churchill and Satirical Poetry 1750–1800* (Seattle, 1979).

MACPHERSON, James (1736–96) He was born on the family's small farm at Ruthven, near Kingussie in the Highlands of Scotland, and studied at the University of Aberdeen. He returned to teach for a while at the local school. In 1759 his translation of a Gaelic heroic fragment, 'The Death of Oscur', caused great scholarly interest and he was sponsored to travel in search of more materials. These were published as *Fragments of Ancient Poetry* (1760). It seemed that the great national epic of Scotland was about to be discovered, and after a further journey gathering examples of oral poetry Macpherson produced two finished works 'translated' by himself: *Fingal* (six books, 1761) and *Temora* (eight books, 1763), published together as *The Works of Ossian* (1765). The texts were largely imaginative reconstructions, and without manuscript evidence they were easily dismissed as 'forgeries'. Dr Johnson was especially scathing about Macpherson's motives. But they caught the taste of the time, and 'Ossian', his third-century bard, achieved immediate and European-wide fame.

deGategno, Paul J., *James Macpherson* (Boston, 1989).

Fitzgerald, Robert, 'The Style of Ossian', *Studies in Romanticism*, 6 (1966), 22–33.

Gaskill, Howard, ed., *Ossian Revisited* (Edinburgh, 1991).

Gaskill, Howard, ed., *The Poems of Ossian and Related Works*, with an introduction by Fiona Stafford (Edinburgh, 1996).

Groom, Nick, 'Celts, Goths, and the Nature of the Literary Source', in Ribeiro, Alvaro, SJ, and James G. Basker, eds., *Tradition in Transition: Women Writers, Marginal Texts, and the Eighteenth-Century Canon* (Oxford, 1996), pp. 275–96.

Kersey, Mel, 'Politeness, Macpherson and Anglicisation', in Brown, Michael, and Stephen H. Harrison, eds., *The Medieval World and the Modern Mind* (Dublin and Portland, 2000), pp. 127–41.

Keymer, Thomas, 'Narratives of Loss: The *Poems of Ossian* and *Tristram Shandy*', in Stafford, Fiona, and Howard Gaskill, eds., *From Gaelic to Romantic: Ossianic Translations* (Amsterdam and Atlanta, 1998), pp. 79–96.

Moore, Dafydd, 'Heroic Incoherence in James Macpherson's *The Poems of Ossian*', *Eighteenth-Century Studies*, 34 (2000), 43–59.

Radcliffe, David Hill, 'Ossian and the Genres of Culture', *Studies in Romanticism*, 31 (1992), 213–32.

Stafford, Fiona, *The Sublime Savage: A Study of James Macpherson and the Poems of Ossian* (Edinburgh, 1988).

Stafford, Fiona, 'Primitivism and the "Primitive" Poet: A Cultural Context for Macpherson's Ossian', in *Celticism*, ed. Terence Brown (Amsterdam and Atlanta, 1996), pp. 79–87.

Thomson, Derick S., *The Gaelic Sources of Macpherson's 'Ossian'* (Edinburgh, 1952).

MADAN, Judith (1702–81) Niece of the 1st Earl Cowper and aunt of William Cowper, Judith Cowper spent her youth at the family estate in Hertfordshire. She became a correspondent of Pope 1722–3. In 1723 she married Martin Madan (1700–56), later equerry to the Prince of Wales and M.P., by whom she had nine children. She became a methodist and was a friend of John Wesley. Her poem 'Abelard to Eloisa' written in 1720 oddly appeared among the posthumous *Poetical Works* (1728) of William Pattison. Pieces by her were included in *Poems by Eminent Ladies* (1755), but there was no separate edition in her lifetime.

Rumbold, Valerie, 'The Poetic Career of Judith Cowper: An Exemplary Failure?', in Mell, Donald C., ed., *Pope, Swift, and Women Writers* (Newark and London, 1996), pp. 48–66.

MANDEVILLE, Bernard (1670–1733) Born in Holland, the son of a Dutch physician, Bernard de Mandeville studied medicine at the University of Leyden, and he took the degree of M.D. 1691. By 1699 he had settled as a physician in London, where he married Elizabeth Laurence, and at his death the couple had two surviving children. Mandeville seems not to have frequented the London literary scene, and little is known of his life and character, but Benjamin Franklin described him as 'a most facetious, entertaining companion'. His satiric verses, *The Grumbling Hive: or, Knaves Turn'd Honest* (1705) were reprinted in 1714 with a full commentary as *The Fable of the Bees: or, Private Vices, Publick Benefits*. A continuation appeared in 1729. He incorporated into the book various controversial treatises that included *An Essay on Charity and Charity Schools* and *An Enquiry into the Origin of Moral Virtue*. In these analyses of human motives Mandeville developed his Hobbesian picture of a human nature rooted in selfishness.

Cook, Richard I., *Bernard Mandeville* (Boston, 1974).

Farrell, William J., 'The Role of Mandeville's Bee Analogy in "The Grumbling Hive"', *Studies in English Literature*, 25 (1985), 511–27.

Kaye, F.B., ed., *The Fable of the Bees*, 2 vols (Oxford, 1924).

Price, Martin, *To the Palace of Wisdom: Studies in Order and Energy from Dryden to Blake* (Carbondale and Edwardsville, 1964), pp. 106–29.

Prior, Charles W.A., ed., *Mandeville and Augustan Ideas* (Victoria, B.C., 2000).

MASON, William (1724–97) Son of the Vicar of Holy Trinity, Hull, Mason was educated at St John's College, Cambridge, and took holy orders. In 1747 his elegy on Pope, *Musaeus*, was well received and he was elected a fellow of Pembroke College. His *Isis, An Elegy* (1749), attacking Oxford Jacobitism, brought Thomas Warton's reply, *The Triumph of Isis*. Mason turned to poetic drama with *Elfrida* (1752) and *Caractacus* (1759), both later developed for the stage. A close friend and correspondent of Gray, Mason became one of the King's chaplains 1757, and a residentiary canon of York Minster 1762. He had a fine voice and cultured tastes in music and painting. In 1764 he married Mary Sherman, who died three years later. Mason's *Poems* were collected in 1764 and 1774 (2 vols). As Gray's executor, he edited *The Poems of Mr. Gray* (1774) with a biography. At first a Whig in politics, he became a supporter of the Tory Pitt in the 1780s. His landscape poem *The English Garden* appeared in four books (1772–82), and he caused a stir with his anonymous satire, *An Heroic Epistle to Sir William Chambers* (1773). Mason's *Works* appeared in 1811.

Bending, Stephen, 'A Natural Revolution? Garden Politics in Eighteenth-Century England', in Sharpe, Kevin, and Steven Zwicker, eds., *Refiguring Revolutions: British Politics and Aesthetics, 1642–1789* (Berkeley and London, 1998), pp. 241–66.

Nabholz, John R., 'Wordsworth and William Mason', *Review of English Studies*, 15 (1964), 297–302.

Toynbee, Paget, ed., *Satirical Poems. Published Anonymously by William Mason with Notes by Horace Walpole* (Oxford, 1926).

Yost, George, 'The Celtic and Dramatic Background of Mason's *Caractacus*', *Restoration and Eighteenth-Century Theatre Research*, 13 (1974), 39–54.

MILLER, James (1706–44) Son of a Dorset rector, he was educated at Wadham College, Oxford, and went into holy orders. After his *Humours of Oxford* (1730) was a success at Drury Lane, stage comedy became his vein, although the Molière-like satiric portraits in plays such as *The Coffee-House* (1737) caused offence and made church preferment difficult. In his poem *Harlequin-Horace: or, The Art of Modern Poetry* (1731), an ironic rewriting of Horace's *Ars Poetica*, Miller took his cue from Pope's *Dunciad* and attacked the popular taste for farcical pantomimes (Pope thought the poem had 'a good deal of humour'). In 1743 Miller succeeded to his father's rectory, but died the following year in London.

Coleman, Antony, introd., James Miller, *Harlequin-Horace: Or, the Art of Modern Poetry* (facsimile of 1731 ed.). Augustan Reprint Society, vol. 178 (William Andrews Clark Memorial Library, 1976).

MONTAGU, Lady Mary Wortley (1689–1762) As the daughter of the first Duke of Kingston-upon-Hull, Lady Mary Pierrepont dazzled the court of Queen Anne and mixed easily in literary circles. Under the influence of Pope and Gay she combined her sharp intelligence and poetic skills in what became *Six Town Eclogues*. Written 1714–16, they were published as a group by Horace Walpole in 1747, although three were pirated by Edmund Curll as *Court Poems* (1716). Against her father's wishes Lady Mary married the ambitious Edward Wortley Montagu, M.P., and in 1716 on his appointment as Ambassador to Turkey she accompanied him to Constantinople. In her 'Embassy Letters' (published after her death) she gave a fascinating account of Turkish life, and on her return to Britain in 1718 she popularised their custom of smallpox inoculation (having lost her own beauty to the disease in December 1715). At the Hanoverian court she became distanced politically and socially from her former 'Scriblerian' friends, writing a short-lived paper, *The Nonsense of Common-Sense* (1737–8) in support of Walpole's government. By the 1730s she was Pope's inveterate enemy, and with the connivance of her intimate friend Lord Hervey (Pope's 'Sporus') she attacked him in the anonymous *Verses to the Imitator of Horace* (1733). Lady Mary did not publish under her own name, and two of her best poems of the 1720s ('Epistle from Arthur Gray' and 'An Epistle to Lord Bathurst') appeared together in Dodsley's *Collection of Poems* (1748). In 1739 she left her husband in pursuit of an elusive young Italian lover, and until the end of her life she lived abroad in Venice, Avignon, Brescia, and Padua, a popular port-of-call for Englishmen on the Grand Tour. She returned to England only in 1762.

Gardner, Kevin J., 'The Aesthetics of Intimacy: Lady Mary Wortley Montagu and her Readers', *Papers on Language and Literature*, 34 (1998), 113–33.

Grundy, Isobel, 'The Politics of Female Authorship: Lady Mary Wortley Montagu's Reaction to the Printing of Her Poems', *The Book Collector*, 31 (1982), 19–37.

Grundy, Isobel, *Lady Mary Wortley Montagu: Comet of the Enlightenment* (Oxford, 1999).

Halsband, Robert, and Isobel Grundy, eds., *Essays and Poems and Simplicity, a Comedy* (Oxford, 1977).

Halsband, Robert, ed., *The Complete Letters of Lady Mary Wortley Montagu*, 3 vols (Oxford, 1965–7).

Halsband, Robert, *The Life of Lady Mary Wortley Montagu* (Oxford, 1956).

Landry, Donna, 'Alexander Pope, Lady Mary Wortley Montagu, and the Literature of Social Comment', in Zwicker, Steven N., ed., *English Literature 1650–1740* (Cambridge, 1998), pp. 307–29.

McLaverty, James, ' "Of Which Being Publick the Publick Judge": Pope and the Publication of "Verses Address'd to the Imitator of Horace" ', *Studies in Bibliography*, 51 (1998), 183–204.

Snyder, Elizabeth, 'Female Heroism and Legal Discourse in Lady Mary Wortley Montagu's "Epistle from Mrs. Y(onge) to Her Husband" ', *English Language Notes*, 34 (1997), 10–22.

Spacks, Patricia Meyer, 'Imaginations Warm and Tender: Pope and Lady Mary', *South Atlantic Quarterly*, 83 (1984), 207–15.

MORE, Hannah (1745–1833) The precocious daughter of a schoolmaster at Stapleton, near Bristol, she attended her sisters' school in the city. By the 1770s she was part of the London circle of Garrick, Johnson, and Reynolds, and became close friends with Elizabeth Montagu and the 'bluestockings'. In her poems *Sensibility* (1782) and *The Bas Bleu* (1786) she dealt with some of the lively literary and social topics of the day. Like Cowper, More fell under the evangelical influence of John Newton and became an admirer of William Wilberforce, leader of the anti-slavery campaign, and in her poem *Slavery* (1788) she made an eloquent contribution to the debate. A enthusiastic moral and educational reformer, More established Sunday schools and during the 1790s wrote popular tracts to counter the influence of the French Revolution.

The Works of Hannah More, II vols. (London, 1854).

Demers, Patricia, ' "For Mine's a Stubborn and a Savage Will": "Lactilla" (Ann Yearsley) and "Stella" (Hannah More) Reconsidered', *Huntington Library Quarterly*, 56 (1993), 135–50.

Demers, Patricia, *The World of Hannah More* (Lexington, 1996).

Johnson, R. Brimley, ed., *Letters of Hannah More* (London, 1925).

Jones, M.G., *Hannah More* (Cambridge, 1968).

Richardson, Alan, 'Darkness Visible: Race and Representation in Bristol Abolitionist Poetry, 1770–1810', *Wordsworth Circle*, 27 (1996), 67–72.

NORRIS, John (1657–1711) Son of a Wiltshire clergyman, he was educated at Winchester and Exeter College, Oxford, and was elected a fellow of All Souls. In 1689 he married and became Rector of Bemerton, near Salisbury (the church of George Herbert). Norris's Platonism was influenced both by Henry More of Cambridge (with whom he corresponded) and the theories of Malebranche, and his *Christian Blessedness* (1690) was the earliest critique of Locke's *Essay*. Norris's poems, which develop his platonic ideas, were printed in his *Collection of Miscellanies* (1687; revised 5th ed. 1710).

Hoyles, John, *The Waning of the Renaissance, 1640–1740: Studies in the Thought and Poetry of Henry More, John Norris and Isaac Watts* (La Haye, 1971).

White, Peter D.E., ed., *Where's my Memorial?: The Religious, Philosophical and Metaphysical Poetry of John Norris of Bemerton* (Sidmouth [1991]).

PARNELL, Thomas (1679–1718) Born at Dublin of a parliamentarian family long prominent in Congleton, Cheshire, Parnell graduated M.A. in 1700 from Trinity College,

Dublin (D.D. 1712). He was appointed Archdeacon of Clogher 1706. While in England during 1711–14 he associated with Addison and Steele (for whom he wrote two *Spectator* papers), but he soon became drawn to the Scriblerian circle of Pope and Swift. Parnell's classical scholarship was of value to Pope, and his essay on Homer was printed in the first volume of Pope's *Iliad* (1715). His lively *Essay on the Different Stiles of Poetry* (1713) was an important contribution to the tradition of the critical verse epistle. The diffident Parnell published only a handful of poems during his lifetime, and it was with the posthumous *Poems on Several Occasions* (1722), edited by his literary executor Pope, that his reputation was secured. Much remained in manuscript, however, and in their important 1989 edition Rawson and Lock were able to double the size of Parnell's published output.

Gerrard, Christine, 'Parnell, Pope, and Pastoral', in Ribeiro, Alvaro, SJ, and James G. Basker, eds., *Tradition in Transition: Women Writers, Marginal Texts, and the Eighteenth-Century Canon* (Oxford, 1996), pp. 221–40.
Rawson, Claude, and F.P. Lock, eds., *Collected Poems of Thomas Parnell* (Newark, London and Toronto, 1989).
Woodman, Thomas, 'Parnell, Politeness and "Pre-Romanticism"', *Essays in Criticism*, 33 (1983), 205–19.
Woodman, Thomas M., *Thomas Parnell* (Boston, 1985).

PATTISON, William (1706–27) The son of a Sussex tenant farmer, he went to study at Appleby free school, Westmorland. In 1724 he entered Sidney Sussex College, Cambridge, but left in 1726 to make his way in London. He associated with the wits at Button's Coffee-House, and was taken under the wing of the publisher Edmund Curll, who seems not to have discouraged his young author's interest in erotic subjects. Pattison died at Curll's house of smallpox at the age of twenty. Curll published his *Poetical Works* the following year with a distinguished list of subscribers, and a second volume, *Cupid's Metamorphoses* (1728), included several Ovidian epistles.

PHILIPS, Ambrose (1674–1749) Philips was the son of a Shrewsbury draper, and was educated at Shrewsbury School and St John's College, Cambridge, of which he became a fellow 1699–1708. In 1705 he took a commission as a lieutenant and fought in Spain. In 1709 he went as secretary to the British envoy in Copenhagen, where he wrote 'A Winter-Piece', his most admired poem. Back in London, Philips's Whig sympathies drew him into Addison's circle, and his *Pastorals* appeared, along with Pope's, in Tonson's *Miscellany* (1709), but in 1713 he was drawn into an unfortunate 'Pastoral War' with Pope fuelled by Richard Steele in *The Guardian*. Among Philips's theatrical ventures were *The Distressed Mother* (1712), an adaptation of Racine's *Andromaque* popular throughout the century, and *The Briton* (1722), a play on early Celtic history. He successfully ran his own periodical, *The Freethinker* (1718–21). Much satirised in the literary world by Pope and his Tory friends, Philips was notable in public service. In 1724 he moved to Ireland as secretary to the Archbishop of Armagh, and there he became a member of the Irish parliament and a judge. In 1748 he returned to England and saw the publication of his *Pastorals, Epistles, Odes, and Other Original Poems* (1748).

Segar, M.G., ed., *The Poems of Ambrose Philips* (Oxford, 1937).

PHILIPS, John (1676–1709) Born into a Royalist family at Bampton, Oxfordshire, where his father was Vicar, Philips became a scholar of Winchester, from where he moved in 1697 to Christ Church, Oxford. An admirer of Milton, he was innovative in using Miltonic blank verse for his three major poems, each in a different character. His popular burlesque, *The Splendid Shilling*, was pirated in 1701, but revised for publication by Philips in 1705. His *Blenheim* (1705) was the Tory counterpart of Addison's

The Campaign; and in *Cyder* (1708) Philips established the tradition of eighteenth-century blank-verse georgic. His *Poems*, with a life by George Sewell, appeared in 1715.

Cope, Kevin L., 'When the Past Presses the Present: Shillings, Cyder, Malts, and Wine', in Kropf, Carl R., ed., *Reader Entrapment in Eighteenth-Century Literature* (New York, 1992), pp. 15–43.

Griffin, Dustin, 'The Bard of Cyder-Land: John Philips and Miltonic Imitation', *Studies in English Literature*, 24 (1984), 441–60.

Mounsey, Chris, 'Christopher Smart's *The Hop-Garden* and John Philips's *Cyder*: a Battle of the Georgics? Mid-Eighteenth-Century Poetic Discussions of Authority, Science and Experience', *British Journal for Eighteenth-Century Studies*, 22 (1999), 67–84.

Pellicer, J.C., 'The Politics of *Cyder*', in Goodridge, John, and J.C. Pellicer (eds.), *Cyder. A Poem in Two Books* (Cheltenham, 2001), pp. i–xvi.

Thomas, M.G. Lloyd, ed., *The Poems of John Philips* (Oxford, 1927).

POMFRET, John (1667–1702) Son of the Vicar of Luton, Bedfordshire, he attended Bedford Grammar School and Queens' College, Cambridge (M.A. 1688). In 1692 he married Elizabeth Wingate and the couple had one surviving son. Settled into an ecclesiastical career as Vicar of Maulden, Bedfordshire, 1695, Pomfret pursued an interest in poetry and gathered his *Poems on Several Occasions* (1699). But it was with *The Choice* (1700) that he won immediate fame, and the poem ran through many editions. It was included in his *Miscellany Poems* (1702). Pomfret died of smallpox in 1702.

Kallich, Martin, 'The Choice by John Pomfret: A Modern Criticism', *Enlightenment Essays*, 6 (1975), 12–18.

POPE, Alexander (1688–1744) Son of a London linen merchant, Pope moved with his parents to rural Binfield, Berkshire, in 1700. As a Roman Catholic he was denied a university education, but the precocious teenager read widely in the classics and in earlier English literature. He learned through imitation, and among his early poetic efforts were modernisations of Chaucer and verses in the manner of Spenser, Waller and Cowley, as well as translations from Homer, Statius and Ovid. With his beautifully polished *Pastorals* (1709) and his lively *Essay on Criticism* (1711) he mastered the measure and tonal range of the heroic couplet, the verse form he was to work in for the rest of his life. Pope's literary career falls naturally into three phases. His early works, which included the patriotic *Windsor-Forest* (1713), the mock-heroic *Rape of the Lock* (1712–14), and the Ovidian epistle *Eloisa to Abelard*, were gathered into *The Works of Mr Alexander Pope* (1717), a confident gesture for a young man in his twenties. The middle phase of his life was focused on translating and editing, with the enormously successful translations of Homer's *Iliad* (1715–20) and *Odyssey* (1725–6), and a six-volume edition of Shakespeare (1725). These subscription works made his fortune, and having rented a house on the Thames at Twickenham, he began to pursue an interest in landscape gardening. Pope's final chiefly satiric phase was announced by *The Dunciad* (1728), a work in three books issued the following year in 'scholarly' form as *The Dunciad Variorum* with mock notes and appendices. This epic assault on the literary culture of the age brought Pope into the very centre of satiric controversy. During the 1730s he used his series of *Imitations of Horace* to develop an authoritative, civilised and entertaining satiric voice, and in his 'Epistles to Several Persons' he addressed his friends on matters of taste and ethics, as part of a larger scheme for a comprehensive work on human morals, of which *An Essay on Man* (1734–5) was intended to be part. This *opus magnum* was never realised. In *The New Dunciad* Pope presented the fulfilment of the dark prophecies of his earlier poem, and this was incorporated as Book Four of a revised *Dunciad* in 1743.

Friendship and enmity were the twin driving forces of Pope's poetry, and he prided himself on the range of his friends and his political independence ('Tories call me Whig, and Whigs a Tory'). During Anne's Tory ministry of 1710–14 his admiration for Whig writers like Addison and Garth survived, but he grew closer to his Tory 'Scriblerian' friends, Swift, Gay, Parnell, Arbuthnot, and Harley (the Tory first minister). After Anne's death in 1714 Pope was out of sympathy with the Hanoverian court and Whig government and spent the rest of his life as an opposition voice. Queen Caroline, the courtier Lord Hervey, and Prime Minister Robert Walpole became choice subjects for his satire, and some of his closest friends were political 'exiles' (Swift, Bolingbroke, Atterbury). During the 1730s he was increasingly courted by the young 'Patriot' Whigs who had been driven into opposition. Having flirted with the idea of writing a national epic at the behest of his friends, Pope ended his life revising and preparing (with the help of his executor William Warburton) an authoritative 'deathbed' edition of his work.

Baines, Paul, *The Complete Critical Guide to Alexander Pope* (London and New York, 2000).

Brown, Laura, *Alexander Pope* (Oxford, 1985).

Brownell, Morris, *Alexander Pope and the Arts of Georgian England* (Oxford, 1978).

Butt, John, et al., eds., *The Twickenham Edition of the Poems of Alexander Pope*, 11 vols (London and New Haven, 1939–69).

Damrosch, Leopold, *The Imaginative World of Alexander Pope* (Berkeley and London, 1987).

Deutsch, Helen, *Resemblance and Disgrace: Alexander Pope and the Deformation of Culture* (Cambridge, Mass., 1996).

Dixon, Peter, *The World of Pope's Satires* (London, 1968).

Erskine-Hill, Howard, *The Social Milieu of Alexander Pope* (New Haven and London, 1975).

Erskine-Hill, Howard, and Anne Smith, eds., *The Art of Alexander Pope* (London, 1979).

Erskine-Hill, Howard, ed., *Alexander Pope: World and Word* (Oxford, 1998).

Fairer, David, *Pope's Imagination* (Manchester, 1984).

Fairer, David, *The Poetry of Alexander Pope* (Harmondsworth, 1989).

Fairer, David, ed., *Pope: New Contexts* (New York etc:, 1990).

Ferguson, Rebecca, *The Unbalanced Mind: Pope and the Rule of Passion* (Brighton, 1986).

Ferraro, Julian, 'The Satirist, the Text and "The World Beside": Pope's First Satire of the Second Book of Horace Imitated', *Translation and Literature*, 2 (1993), 37–63.

Guerinot, J.V., *Pamphlet Attacks on Alexander Pope, 1711–1744: A Descriptive Bibliography* (London, 1969).

Hammond, Brean, *Pope* (Brighton, 1986).

Hooker, Edward Niles, 'Pope on Wit: The *Essay on Criticism*', in *Eighteenth-Century Literature: Modern Essays in Criticism*, ed. James L. Clifford (1959), pp. 42–61.

Hunter, J. Paul, 'Satiric Apology as Satiric Instance: Pope's Arbuthnot', *Journal of English and Germanic Philology*, 68 (1969), 625–47.

Jones, Emrys, 'Pope and Dulness', *Proceedings of the British Academy*, 54 (1968), 231–63.

Knellwolf, Christa, *A Contradiction Still: Representations of Women in the Poetry of Alexander Pope* (Manchester, 1998).

Mack, Maynard, *The Garden and the City: Retirement and Politics in the Later Poetry of Pope 1731–1743* (Toronto, etc., 1969).

Mack, Maynard, *The Last and Greatest Art: Some Unpublished Poetical Manuscripts of Alexander Pope* (Newark, etc., 1984).

Mack, Maynard, *Alexander Pope. A Life* (New Haven, 1985).

McLaverty, James, *Pope, Print, and Meaning* (Oxford, 2001).

Morris, David B., *Alexander Pope: The Genius of Sense* (Cambridge, Mass., and London, 1984).

Rogers, Pat, *An Introduction to Pope* (London, 1975).

Rogers, Pat, ed., *Alexander Pope* (Oxford and New York, 1993).

Rousseau, G.S., and Pat Rogers, eds., *The Enduring Legacy: Alexander Pope Tercentenary Essays* (Cambridge, 1988).

Rumbold, Valerie, *Women's Place in Pope's World* (Cambridge, 1989).

Rumbold, Valerie, ed., *Alexander Pope: The Dunciad in Four Books (1743)* (Harlow, 1999).

Seidel, Michael, *Satiric Inheritance: Rabelais to Sterne* (Princeton, 1979), pp. 226–49.

Sherburn, George, ed., *The Correspondence of Alexander Pope*, 5 vols (Oxford, 1956).

Sitter, John, *The Poetry of Pope's 'Dunciad'* (Minneapolis, 1971).

Spacks, Patricia Meyer, *An Argument of Images: The Poetry of Alexander Pope* (Cambridge, Mass., 1971).

Thomas, Claudia, *Alexander Pope and his Eighteenth-Century Women Readers* (Carbondale, 1994).

Weinbrot, Howard D., *Alexander Pope and the Traditions of Formal Verse Satire* (Princeton, 1982).

Williams, Carolyn D., *Pope, Homer, and Manliness* (London and New York, 1993).

PRIOR, Matthew (1664–1721) Prior's father, a Westminster carpenter, was able to send his son to Westminster School, from where he won a scholarship to St John's College, Cambridge. In 1690 he began a distinguished diplomatic career with his appointment as secretary to Britain's minister at the Hague, and then as William III's travelling diplomatic agent. As a poet he celebrated William in his pindaric ode, *Carmen Seculare* (1700). Out of favour during the beginning of Anne's reign, Prior confirmed his poetic reputation with *Poems on Several Occasions* (1709). By this time his political allegiance was shifting and in 1710 he was collaborating with Swift on the *Examiner*, mouthpiece of the Tory ministry. Prior's experience as a skilled negotiator caused the Treaty of Utrecht (1713) to be known by some as 'Matt's Peace', and he became Britain's ambassador in Paris. His political fall in the Whig purge after 1714 was complete, but softened by the critical and financial success of his subscription edition of *Poems* (1718).

Eves, Charles Kenneth, *Matthew Prior, Poet and Diplomatist* (New York, 1939).

Gildenhuys, Faith, 'Convention and Consciousness in Prior's Love Lyrics', *Studies in English Literature*, 35 (1995), 437–55.

Sitter, John, 'About Wit: Locke, Addison, Prior, and the Order of Things', in Canfield, J. Douglas, and J. Paul Hunter, eds., *Rhetorics of Order/Ordering Rhetorics in English Neoclassical Literature* (Newark, 1989), pp. 137–57.

Wright, H. Bunker, and Monroe K. Spears, eds., *The Literary Works of Matthew Prior*, 2nd ed., 2 vols (Oxford, 1971).

PURNEY, Thomas (1695–1727?) Born in Kent of unknown parents, Purney spent a year at Merchant Taylors' School before entering Clare Hall, Cambridge, in 1711. Graduating in 1716 he produced two volumes of *Pastorals* 'after the Simple Manner of Theocritus' (1716–17) along with *A Full Enquiry into the True Nature of Pastoral* (1717), in which he theorised about his experiments with linguistic naivety, the poetic mode for which he is now known. Two lost works, a mock-heroic poem in six cantos and an epic on the Black Prince, would doubtless have extended his muse further. Purney was ordained priest in 1719 and became chaplain (or 'Ordinary') of Newgate prison, augmenting his meagre salary by publishing the supposed 'dying words' and 'true confessions' of convicted criminals. Nothing more is heard of Purney after his health broke down and he resigned his chaplaincy. His death is unrecorded.

Bergstrom, Carson, 'Purney, Pastoral, and the Polymorphous Perverse', *British Journal for Eighteenth-Century Studies*, 17 (1994), 149–63.

Wasserman, Earl, ed., Thomas Purney, *A Full Enquiry into the True Nature of Pastoral* (facsimile of 1717 ed.). Augustan Reprint Society, no. 11 (William Andrews Clark Memorial Library, 1948).

White, H.O., ed., *The Works of Thomas Purney* (Oxford, 1933).

PYE, Henry James (1745–1813) Son of Henry Pye, M.P. for Berkshire, he was educated at home before entering Magdalen College, Oxford, as a Gentleman-Commoner. He inherited the family estates and massive family debts in 1766. His ambitious and varied output as a writer included the topographical poem, *Faringdon Hill* (1774), a georgic on *Shooting* (1784), the amusing 'Aerophorion' (on the ballooning craze, 1787), and a poem on cultural history, *The Progress of Refinement* (1783). His *Poems on Various Subjects* appeared in two volumes, 1787. Pye himself became M.P. for Berkshire in 1784, and as a Pitt supporter he succeeded Thomas Warton as Poet Laureate in 1790, an appointment much derided by the Romantic poets. As the official metrical voice of the nation during the Napoleonic Wars Pye specialised in works of a patriotic and martial flavour, and also wrote several stage plays.

SAVAGE, Richard (c. 1697–1743) Savage's birth and parentage are unrecorded. When he emerged from obscurity in 1715 he claimed to be the illegitimate son of Earl Rivers and the Countess of Macclesfield, but he tested the allegiance of his patrons and supporters by a reckless and indigent style of living. He joined the literary circle of Aaron Hill, who organised a subscription volume, *Miscellaneous Poems and Translations* (1726) for his benefit. In 1727 Savage was sentenced to death after killing a man in a tavern brawl, but was eventually pardoned. There followed his best known pieces: an autobiographical poem, *The Bastard* (1728), and *The Wanderer* (1729), a visionary poem in five cantos. In the 1730s he became Queen Caroline's unofficial 'laureate'. But Savage also knew the miseries and indignities of 'Grub Street' at first hand and supplied material for Pope's *Dunciad*. From 1737 he had the friendship of the struggling young Samuel Johnson, who gave a moving account of their relationship in his *Life of Savage* (1744). Savage died in a debtor's prison.

Dussinger, John A., ' "The solemn magnificence of a stupendous ruin": Richard Savage, Poet Manqué', in Nath, Prem, ed., *Fresh Reflections on Samuel Johnson: Essays in Criticism* (Troy, 1987), 167–82.

Edwards, Gavin, 'The Illegitimation of Richard Savage', *Sydney Studies in English*, 17 (1991–2), 67–74.

Holmes, Richard, *Dr. Johnson and Mr. Savage* (London, 1993).

Tracy, Clarence, ed., Samuel Johnson, *An Account of the Life of Mr. Richard Savage* (Oxford, 1971).

Tracy, Clarence, ed., *The Poetical Works of Richard Savage* (Cambridge, 1962).

Tracy, Clarence, *The Artificial Bastard. A Bibliography of Richard Savage* (Toronto, 1953).

SHENSTONE, William (1714–63) A churchwarden's son, Shenstone was born at Halesowen, Worcestershire, and after being educated locally he entered Pembroke College, Oxford, in 1732. He remained on the college books for ten years but never graduated. In 1737 he had printed *Poems upon Various Occasions*, which contained the earliest version of his popular Spenserian poem, *The School-Mistress*, extended and published separately in 1742. He contributed extensively to Dodsley's *Collection of Poems* (1748–58), which included 'The Judgment of Hercules' (originally published 1741) and 'A Pastoral Ballad'. In 1745 Shenstone inherited a small estate at Halesowen, and transformed his farm into one of the most admired and influential landscape gardens of the age. It absorbed much of his creative energy. Dodsley included Shenstone's letters and writings on landscape and aesthetics in the poet's posthumous *Works in Verse and Prose* (3 vols, 1764–9).

Bending, Stephen 'Prospects and Trifles: The Views of William Shenstone and Richard Jago', *Qwerty*, 10 (October 2000), 125–31.

de Bolla, Peter, 'The Charm'd Eye', in Kelly, Veronica, and Dorothea Von Mücke, eds., *Body and Text in the Eighteenth Century* (Stanford, 1994), pp. 89–111.

Terry, Richard, 'Lamb, Shenstone and the Icon of Personality', *Charles Lamb Bulletin*, 76 (1991), 124–32.

Turner, James G., 'The Sexual Politics of Landscape: Images of Venus in Eighteenth-Century English Poetry and Landscape Gardening', *Studies in Eighteenth-Century Culture*, 11 (1982), 343–66.

Williams, Marjorie, ed., *The Letters of William Shenstone* (Oxford, 1939).

SMART, Christopher (1722–71) Son of Lord Vane's estate manager, Smart entered Pembroke College, Cambridge, in 1739 thanks to an annuity from the Vane family, and he distinguished himself in classical studies. A fellowship followed, but Smart was an unconventional don. In 1749 he moved to London to work as a miscellaneous writer, editing for the publisher Newbery *The Student* (1750–1) and *The Midwife* (1751–3), and performing in his own satiric stage entertainment, *Mother Midnight's Oratory*. In 1752 he married Newbery's step-daughter and thus had to give up his fellowship. Although he regularly won the university's Seatonian prize for religious poetry, his own *Poems on Several Occasions* (1752) made little mark and in 1757 after a breakdown he was admitted to a hospital for the insane. In 1759 he entered a private madhouse, where he dug the garden and worked steadily on *Jubilate Agno*, his 'Magnificat', or song of praise to God. Released in 1763, Smart found new scope for his religious enthusiasm. In that year he published *A Song to David* and two collections of *Poems*; in 1764 his oratorio *Hannah* was performed and another volume of poems appeared; in 1765 he issued both *A Translation of the Psalms of David* and *Hymns and Spiritual Songs*. 1767 saw a four-volume translation of Horace. Smart's finances nonetheless remained desperate, and the following year Frances Burney lamented that 'so ingenious a man should be reduced to such shocking circumstances', and she noted 'great wildness in his manner, looks & voice'. Smart died in a debtor's prison in 1771.

Dearnley, Moira, *The Poetry of Christopher Smart* (London, 1968).

Gedalof, Allan J., 'The Rise and Fall of Smart's David', *Philological Quarterly*, 60 (1981), 369–86.

Gedalof, Allan J., 'Smart's Poetics in *Jubilate Agno*', *English Studies in Canada*, 5 (1979), 262–74.

Greene, D.J., 'Smart, Berkeley, the Scientists and the Poets', *Journal of the History of Ideas*, 14 (1953), 327–52.

Guest, Harriet, *A Form of Sound Words: The Religious Poetry of Christopher Smart* (Oxford, 1989).

Hartman, Geoffrey H., 'Christopher Smart's *Magnificat*: Toward a Theory of Representation', *ELH*, 41 (1974), 429–54.

Hawes, Clement, ed., *Christopher Smart and the Enlightenment* (New York, 1999).

Kumbier, William, 'Sound and Signification in Christopher Smart's *Jubilate Agno*', *Texas Studies in Language and Literature*, 24 (1982), 293–312.

Mahony, Robert, and Betty W. Rizzo, *Christopher Smart. An Annotated Bibliography, 1743–1983* (New York and London, 1984).

Mounsey, Chris, *Christopher Smart, Clown of God* (Lewisburg, 2001).

Rizzo, Betty, and Robert Mahony, eds., *The Annotated Letters of Christopher Smart* (Carbondale and Edwardsville, 1991).

Sherbo, Arthur, *Christopher Smart, Scholar of the University* (East Lansing, 1967).

Walsh, Marcus, and Karina Williamson, eds., *The Poetical Works of Christopher Smart*, 6 vols (Oxford, 1980–96).

Williamson, Karina, 'Christopher Smart's Hymns and Spiritual Songs', *Philological Quarterly*, 38 (1959), 413–24.

Williamson, Karina, 'Smart's *Principia*: Science and Anti-Science in *Jubilate Agno*', *Review of English Studies*, 30 (1979), 409–22.

SMITH, Charlotte (1749–1806) She was the daughter of Nicholas Turner of Bignor Park, Sussex, but her mother died when she was three. On her father's remarriage in 1764 she was herself married off to Benjamin Smith, a feckless West Indies merchant. They had twelve children, of whom nine survived to maturity. Consistently in financial straits, the couple lived for a while in a debtor's prison and moved to Dieppe in France to escape his creditors. From 1776 she was enmeshed in legal disputes to release a family legacy for her children, and this unavailing struggle forms a background of fatalistic frustration to her poetry. Her *Elegiac Sonnets* (1784) were well received and a fifth (subscription) edition in 1789 was very successful. Further augmented editions followed. In 1788 Smith separated from her husband and moved with her children to Brighton. In the next decade she published ten novels, including the popular *Emmeline* (1788), and *Desmond* (1792) in which she showed her early enthusiasm for the French Revolution. This turned towards disillusionment in her poem *The Emigrants* (1793). Her meditative topographical poem, *Beachy Head*, was published posthumously in 1807.

Curran, Stuart, ed., *The Poems of Charlotte Smith* (New York and London, 1993).

Fletcher, Loraine, *Charlotte Smith: A Critical Biography* (Houndmills, 1998).

Hawley, Judith, 'Charlotte Smith's Elegiac Sonnets, Losses and Gains', in Armstrong, Isobel, and Virginia Blain, eds. *Women's Poetry in the Enlightenment: The Making of a Canon, 1730–1820* (London and New York, 1999), pp. 184–98.

Hunt, Bishop C., 'Wordsworth and Charlotte Smith', *Wordsworth Circle*, 1 (1970), 85–113.

Labbé, Jacqueline, ' "Transplanted into More Congenial Soil": Footnoting the Self in the Poetry of Charlotte Smith', in Bray, Joe, etc., eds., *Ma(r)king the Text: The Presentation of Meaning on the Literary Page* (Aldershot, 2000), pp. 71–86.

Kennedy, Deborah, 'Thorns and Roses: The Sonnets of Charlotte Smith', *Women's Writing*, 2 (1995); 43–54.

Pratt, Kathryn, 'Charlotte Smith's Melancholia on the Page and Stage', *Studies in English Literature 1500–1900*, 41 (2001), 563–81.

Stanton, Judith, ed., *The Collected Letters of Charlotte Smith* (Bloomington, 2002?).

White, Daniel E., 'Autobiography and Elegy: The Early Romantic Poetics of Thomas Gray and Charlotte Smith', in Woodman, Thomas, ed., *The Early Romantics: Perspectives in British Poetry from Pope to Wordsworth* (Houndmills, 1998), pp. 57–69.

SMITH, Edmund (1672–1710) Born Edmund Neale, he was the son of a London merchant, and after his father's death was brought up by a relative whose surname he took. Smith was educated at Westminster and Christ Church, Oxford, where he gained a high reputation as a classicist and poet. Nicknamed 'Rag' on account of his careless dress, he repeatedly tangled with the college authorities and was finally expelled in 1705. He moved to London and achieved critical success with a tragedy *Phaedra and Hippolitus* (1707). The prologue was by Addison and the epilogue by Prior. Smith's most notable poem was his elegy on the death of his Oxford friend, the poet John Philips, later praised by Johnson as 'among the best elegies which our language can shew'. His miscellaneous poems were collected into his posthumous *Works* (1714), of which an enlarged fourth edition was published in 1729.

SWIFT, Jonathan (1667–1745) Swift was born in Ireland, the posthumous son of an English lawyer. His earliest years were unsettled before he finally entered Kilkenny School at the age of six; and his student career at Trinity College, Dublin, was disrupted by the political unrest in Ireland during 1689–90. Swift spent most of the next decade in comparative peace at Moor Park, Surrey, as secretary to Sir William Temple (d. 1699), and there he wrote zealous pindaric odes and two of his finest prose satires, *A Tale of a Tub* and *The Battle of the Books*. He also began a lifelong friendship wih Esther Johnson ('Stella'), the daughter of Temple's housekeeper. After the death of his patron, Swift became Vicar of Laracor and a prebendary of St Patrick's Cathedral, Dublin; but on the accession of Queen Anne in 1702 he seized the opportunity to make a political career in England. His early allegiance was to Addison, Steele, and the Whigs, and he found a new poetic vein in the verse 'descriptions' printed in Steele's *Tatler*. But Swift was lured to the Tory side, becoming their media spokesman in 1710 as editor of *The Examiner*. During the Tory administration of 1710–14 Swift moved in the inner circle of the Scriblerus Club with his now close friends Pope, Gay, Parnell, Arbuthnot, and Harley. But his life changed radically with his appointment as Dean of St Patrick's – a consolation prize that got a troublesome figure out of the way. After the fall of the Tories in 1714 Swift returned to live in Ireland, where he campaigned for Irish economic freedom while growing exasperated during the 1720s over that nation's unwillingness to recognise and act on its best interests. The darkening trajectory of *Gulliver's Travels* (1726) was confirmed in the indignant despair of *A Modest Proposal* (1729), and Swift's increasing frustrations gave his poetry of the early 30s its cutting edge. 'The Lady's Dressing Room', 'Verses on the Death of Dr Swift', 'Strephon and Chloe', and 'A Beautiful Young Nymph Going to Bed' (all written 1730–1) are sceptical of optimistic ideals and confront disillusionment. Much of Swift's verse published during his lifetime emerged through pamphlets and miscellanies, and it was only with the second volume of the Faulkner edition of his *Works* (4 vols, Dublin, 1734–5) that Swift himself gathered together a corpus of his poetry.

Davies, Hugh Sykes, 'Irony and the English Tongue', in Vickers, Brian, ed., *The World of Jonathan Swift: Essays for the Tercentenary* (Oxford, 1968), pp. 129–53.

Davis, Herbert, ed., *Swift. Poetical Works* (London, 1967).

Doody, Margaret Anne, 'Swift among the Women', *Yearbook of English Studies*, 18 (1988), 68–92.

Ehrenpreis, Irvin, *Swift. The Man, His Works and the Age*, 3 vols (London, 1962–83).

England, A.B., *Energy and Order in the Poetry of Jonathan Swift* (Lewisburg, 1980).

Feingold, Richard, 'Swift in his Poems: The Range of his Positive Rhetoric', in Rawson, Claude, ed., *The Character of Swift's Satire: A Revised Focus* (Newark, 1983), pp. 166–202.

Fischer, John Irwin, and Donald C. Mell, eds. (assoc. ed. David M. Vieth), *Contemporary Studies of Swift's Poetry* (Newark, 1981).

Hill, Geoffrey, 'Jonathan Swift: The Poetry of Reaction', in Vickers, Brian, ed., *The World of Jonathan Swift: Essays for the Tercentenary* (Oxford, 1968), pp. 195–212.

Nokes, David, *Jonathan Swift: A Hypocrite Reversed. A Critical Biography* (Oxford, 1985).

Pollack, Ellen, *The Poetics of Sexual Myth: Gender and Ideology in the Verse of Swift and Pope* (Chicago, 1985).

Rogers, Pat, ed., *Jonathan Swift. The Complete Poems* (Harmondsworth, 1983).

Rogers, Pat, 'Swift and the Reanimation of Cliché', in Rawson, Claude, ed., *The Character of Swift's Satire: A Revised Focus* (Newark, 1983), pp. 203–26.

Savage, Roger, 'Swift's Fallen City: A Description of the Morning', in Vickers, Brian, ed., *The World of Jonathan Swift: Essays for the Tercentenary* (Oxford, 1968), pp. 171–94.

Scouten, Arthur H., and Robert D. Hume, 'Pope and Swift: Text and Interpretation of Swift's Verses on his Death', *Philological Quarterly*, 52 (1973), 204–31.

Williams, Harold, ed., *The Poems of Jonathan Swift*, 3 vols (Oxford, 1958).

Williams, Harold, ed., *The Correspondence of Jonathan Swift*, 5 vols (Oxford, 1963–5).

Woolley, David, ed., *The Correspondence of Jonathan Swift, D.D.*, 4 vols (Frankfurt, 1999–).

THOMPSON, Isaac (1703–76) A Quaker, he was born at Kendal, Westmorland, and received his education from several schoolmasters before becoming an accounts clerk in London. He soon returned north and settled in Newcastle, where he published *A Collection of Poems, Occasionally Writ on Several Subjects* (1731), and also *Poetic Essays, on Nature, Men, and Morals* (1750). By this time he had established a printing business, and in 1739 was co-founder and printer of *The Newcastle Journal*. Thompson gave lectures on Newtonian science, mathematics, and poetry, and he was also a skilled surveyor and draughtsman. His *Happiness: A Characteristic Poem* was published in 1773.

THOMPSON, William (?1712–66?) Son of the Vicar of Brough, Westmorland, he was educated at Appleby and from 1731 at Queen's College, Oxford, where he became a fellow, and subsequently Rector of Hampton Poyle with South Weston, Oxfordshire. He was a book-collector and had an interest in Italian literature. In *Sickness, a Poem* (Three books, 1745–6) Thompson paid tribute to the recently dead Swift and Pope in blank verse, and his *Hymn to May* (1746) is an early example of Spenserian descriptive writing. His *Poems on Several Occasions* was published in 1757.

THOMSON, James (1700–48) Thomson was born in Roxburghshire in the Scottish borders, son of a minister of the 'Kirk'. He was himself designed for the ministry, but had written poetry since his schooldays and the Muse was difficult to shake off. After ten years of study at the College of Edinburgh, his literary ambitions prevailed and he sailed for London in 1725. The following year his vivid blank-verse description, *Winter, a Poem*, was an immediate success and brought him into Aaron Hill's literary circle. Thomson saw the potential of his topic, and there followed *Summer* (1727), *Spring* (1728), and a full subscription edition of *The Seasons* (1730) which included a newly written 'Autumn'. *A Poem Sacred to the Memory of Sir Isaac Newton* (1727) was dedicated to Prime Minister Walpole. In 1730 Thomson made the Grand Tour to Italy, but the journey seemed only to confirm his sentiments as a British patriot, and on his return he was drawn to the opposition Whigs in the orbit of Frederick, Prince of Wales. Their leader, George Lyttelton, became his friend and patron. Thomson's ambitious five-book poem *Liberty* (1735–6), dedicated to Frederick, showed impeccable 'patriot' sentiments, but failed with the public. *Alfred, a Masque* (1740), written in collaboration with his friend David Mallet to celebrate Frederick's kingly virtues, gave the world Thomson's song 'Rule, Britannia'. In his last major poem, *The Castle of Indolence* (1748), he explored through Spenserian allegory some of the tensions between public duty and poetic vision that had marked his creative life.

Anderson, David R., 'Emotive Theodicy in *The Seasons*', *Studies in Eighteenth-Century Culture*, 12 (1983), 59–76.

Cohen, Michael, 'The Whig Sublime and James Thomson', *English Language Notes*, 24 (1986), 27–35.

Cohen, Ralph, *The Art of Discrimination: Thomson's 'The Seasons' and the Language of Criticism* (London, 1964).

Inglesfield, Robert, 'Shaftesbury's Influence on Thomson's *Seasons*', *British Journal for Eighteenth-Century Studies*, 9 (1986), 141–56.

McKillop, A.D., *The Background of Thomson's Seasons* (Minneapolis, 1942).

McKillop, A.D., ed., *James Thomson, 1700–1748. Letters and Documents* (Lawrence, 1958).

Sambrook, James, ed., James Thomson, *The Seasons* (Oxford, 1981).

Sambrook, James, ed., James Thomson, *Liberty, The Castle of Indolence, and Other Poems* (Oxford, 1986).

Sambrook, James, *James Thomson, 1700–1748. A Life* (Oxford, 1991).

Scott, Mary Jane W., *James Thomson, Anglo-Scot* (Athens and London, 1988).

Terry, Richard, ' "Through Nature shedding influence malign": Thomson's *The Seasons* as a Theodicy', *Durham University Journal*, 87 (1995), 257–68.

Terry, Richard, ed., *James Thomson: Essays for the Tercentenary* (Liverpool, 2000).

TICKELL, Thomas (1685–1740) Son of the Vicar of Bridekirk, Cumberland, Tickell entered Queen's College, Oxford, in 1701 and succeeded to a fellowship in 1710, which he held till his marriage in 1727. His *Oxford, a Poem* (1707) celebrated the history and architecture of the university ('Inspir'd like Athens, and adorn'd like Rome!'), and in *On the Prospect of Peace* (1712) he handled a tricky political topic to the admiration of both Pope and Addison. Soon Addison (an alumnus of his own college) became his patron and friend, and when appointed Secretary of State in 1717 he made Tickell under-secretary. Tickell's translation of Book One of the *Iliad* (1715) suffered by being published in the same week as the first volume of Pope's *Homer* (a design of Addison, Pope suspected, to undermine his own project). On his deathbed in 1719 Addison made Tickell his literary executor, and the latter's edition of Addison's *Works* (4 vols, 1721) was prefaced by his best known poem, 'To the Earl of Warwick, on the Death of Mr Addison'. Thereafter Tickell settled in Ireland as secretary to the lords justices and became quite friendly with Swift. Tickell's *Kensington Garden* (1722) is a fairy fable influenced by *The Rape of the Lock*.

Rogal, Samuel J., 'Thomas Tickell's Prospect of Peace', *Illinois Quarterly*, 35 (1973), 31–40.

Rosslyn, Felicity, 'Pope's Annotations to Tickell's Iliad Book One', *Review of English Studies*, 30 (1979), 49–59.

TOLLET, Elizabeth (1694–1754) Daughter of a Commissioner of the Navy, she spent her early years living in the Tower of London. The influence of this on her imagination is evident in her Ovidian epistle 'Anne Boleyn to King Henry VIII' which was printed in Tollet's anonymous collection, *Poems on Several Occasions* (1724). A posthumous volume with the same title (1755) included her later verse. She was well educated in history, languages and mathematics, and her poem on the death of Newton (a family friend) shows a grasp of technical detail lacking in Thomson's more famous poem.

WARTON, Joseph (1722–1800) Son of Thomas Warton the Elder (d. 1745), Professor of Poetry at Oxford, 1718–28, and from 1723 Vicar of Basingstoke, Hampshire. In 1736 Joseph was sent to Winchester, where he became friends with William Collins, and in 1739 the pair had some poems published together in *The Gentleman's Magazine*. While an undergraduate at Oriel College, Oxford, Warton published anonymously a heroic-couplet satire, *Fashion* (1742), and, in very different style, wrote *The Enthusiast: Or the Lover of Nature* published by Dodsley in 1744, the year he graduated. There followed *Odes on Various Subjects* (1746), which soon reached a second edition, and a collection of his father's verse, *Poems on Several Occasions* (1748). Joseph was a creative editor and silently incorporated a considerable number of poems by himself and his brother. In 1747 Warton became Rector of Winslade, Hampshire, and married Mary Daman. The couple had seven children. At this point the emphasis in Warton's literary life shifted towards criticism. His four-volume *Works of Virgil* (1753) included essays on pastoral, didactic poetry, and epic, and he contributed critical essays on Homer and Shakespeare to *The Adventurer* (1752–4). His best known critical work, *An Essay on the Writings and Genius of Pope* (1756) found much of Pope's work lacking in 'genuine poetry', but it is nonetheless the work of a fascinated reader. In 1755 Warton became second master at Winchester, and in 1766 the school's busy and devoted Headmaster. Under his benign rule the boys' literary talents flourished, but discipline was lax. Only in 1782 did the long-awaited second volume of his *Essay on Pope* appear, and his lifelong engagement with Pope's poetry reached its culmination in his edition of *The Works of Alexander Pope* (9 vols, 1797).

Fairer, David, 'The Poems of Thomas Warton the Elder?', *Review of English Studies*, 26 (1975), 287–300, 395–406; and 29 (1978), 61–5.

Hysham, Julia, 'Joseph Warton's Reputation as a Poet', *Studies in Romanticism*, 1 (1962), 220–9.

McKillop, Alan D., 'Shaftesbury in Joseph Warton's *Enthusiast*', *Modern Language Notes*, 70 (1955), 337–9.

Morris, David B., 'Joseph Warton's Figure of Virtue: Poetic Indirection in *The Enthusiast*', *Philological Quarterly*, 50 (1971), 678–83.

Pittock, Joan, *The Ascendancy of Taste: The Achievement of Joseph and Thomas Warton* (London, 1973).

Pittock, Joan, introd., Joseph Warton, *Odes on Various Subjects* (facsimile of 1st edn, 1746). Scholar's Facsimiles and Reprints (Delmar, NY, 1977).

Scouten, Arthur H., 'The Warton Forgeries and the Concept of Preromanticism in English Literature', *Etudes Anglaises*, 40 (1987), 434–47.

Vance, John A., *Joseph and Thomas Warton. An Annotated Bibliography* (New York and London, 1983).

Vance, John A., *Joseph and Thomas Warton* (Boston, 1983).

Wendorf, Richard, introd., Joseph Warton, *Odes on Various Subjects* (facsimile of 1st edn, 1746). Augustan Reprint Society, vol. 197 (William Andrews Clark Memorial Library, 1979).

Wooll, John, *Biographical Memoirs of the Late Revd. Joseph Warton, D.D.* (London, 1806).

WARTON, Thomas (1728–90) Younger brother of the above, he was educated by his father, and in 1744 entered Trinity College, Oxford, his home for the rest of his life. Warton was a poet from infancy, and by the time of his appointment to a college fellowship in 1752 he had published six volumes of verse, including *Five Pastoral Eclogues* (1745), *The Pleasures of Melancholy* (1747), and *The Triumph of Isis* (1750), his defence of Oxford against the attack of William Mason. He contributed verse to Dodsley's *Museum* (1746–7) and *The Student* (1750), two odes to his brother's 1746 collection, and at least four to the 1748 volume of their father's verse. But during these years Warton was also laying the foundations for a scholarly career with his historical researches into older poetry. Some of this fed into his *Observations on the Faerie Queene* (1754), a study of a poet who, along with the early Milton, exerted a deep influence on his own verse. Warton's later publications included *The History of English Poetry* (3 vols, 1774–81), left unfinished at his death, and an edition of Milton's early poems (1785). Unlike his brother, Warton continued to write poetry, and his *Poems* (1777) reached a third edition in 1779. His *Verses on Sir Joshua Reynolds's Painted Window* (1782) was addressed to the friend and patron who was to secure his appointment as the nation's Poet Laureate in 1785. By this time Warton had attracted a devoted following of young poets, many (like Bowles) from Winchester School.

Fairer, David, ed., *The Correspondence of Thomas Warton* (Athens and London, 1995).

Fairer, David, 'Thomas Warton, Thomas Gray, and the Recovery of the Past', in Hutchings, W.B., and William Ruddick, eds. *Thomas Gray: Contemporary Essays* (Liverpool, 1993), pp. 146–70.

Griffin, Robert J., 'The Eighteenth-Century Construction of Romanticism: Thomas Warton and the Pleasures of Melancholy', *ELH*, 59 (1992), 799–815.

Mant, Richard, ed., *The Poetical Works of the Late Thomas Warton, B.D.*, 2 vols (Oxford, 1802).

Martin, L.C., 'Thomas Warton and the Early Poems of Milton', *Proceedings of the British Academy*, 20 (1934), 25–43.

Pittock, Joan, 'Thomas Warton and the Oxford Chair of Poetry', *English Studies*, 62 (1981), 14–33.

Rinaker, Clarissa, *Thomas Warton: A Biographical and Critical Study*. Illinois Studies in Language and Literature, vol 2, no.1 (Urbana, 1916).

WATTS, Isaac (1674–1748) Son of a nonconformist tradesman and boarding-school keeper, Watts was educated at the local free school where he studied Latin, Greek, Hebrew, and French. Because he did not subscribe to the beliefs of the Church of England he was unable to enter university, and continued his education at Thomas Rowe's dissenting academy at Newington Green, the centre of London's thriving nonconformist community. An inspiring preacher, he became minister of Mark Lane Church in 1702 and attracted a large and devoted congregation. In this context, song was important to him, and he wrote some of the finest hymns in the language. His four verse collections are all lyric in emphasis: *Horae Lyricae* (1706; revised 2nd ed. 1709); *Hymns and Spiritual Songs* (1707), *Divine Songs for the Use of Children* (1715), and *The Psalms of David Imitated* (1719).

Bishop, Selma L., ed., *Isaac Watts, Hymns and Spiritual Songs, 1707–1748* (London, 1962).

Davis, Arthur P., *Isaac Watts: His Life and Works* (New York, 1943).

Hoyles, John, *The Waning of the Renaissance, 1640–1740: Studies in the Thought and Poetry of Henry More, John Norris and Isaac Watts* (La Haye, 1971).

Watson, J.R., *The English Hymn: A Critical and Historical Study* (Oxford, 1997), pp. 133–70.

WEST, Gilbert (1703–56) Son of a prebendary of Winchester, West was connected through his mother, Maria Temple, to the influential Temple family. He was educated at Eton and Christ Church, Oxford, from where he graduated in 1725. After a spell in the army and in government employment he married and settled at Wickham, Kent, supported from 1736 by a state pension of £250 a year. He became noted for his piety; but beyond his interest in religious ideas, West used his poetry in support of the opposition Whig 'patriots' led by his uncle Lord Cobham, and his cousin Lord Lyttelton. West's *A Canto of the Faerie Queene* (1739) is a Spenserian allegory with a political message, and his *Institution of the Order of the Garter* (1742) places the patriot agenda in a historical context. Both poems, along with another Spenserian imitation, *Education* (1751), were included in Dodsley's *Collection of Poems*. It was Dodsley who also published West's most popular work, a translation of the *Odes of Pindar* (1749).

WILSON, Anne (fl. 1778) As yet, nothing has been discovered of Anne Wilson, author of *Teisa: A Descriptive Poem of the River Tees, Its Towns and Antiquities* (1778). She may be the 'Ann Wilson' whose dramatic poem *Jephtha's Daughter* was published in London in 1783.

Keegan, Bridget, 'Writing against the Current: Anne Wilson's *Teisa* and the Tradition of British River Poetry', *Women's Studies*, 31 (Summer, 2002), 267–85.

WOODWARD, George (1708–90) He was born in London, son of Richard Woodward ('gentleman') and Rebecca London, whose father was George London, chief gardener to Queen Anne. He was educated at Eton and Lincoln College, Oxford; and after travelling to the West Indies he settled down in 1732 as a curate at Ticehurst, Sussex. He went on to become Rector of East Hendred, Berkshire (1744–90) and to marry the forty-year-old Albinia Courthope, whom he had known for sixteen years. The couple had two children. Woodward's letters to his uncle (George London junior) show a good humoured clergyman well settled into the routines of his rural parish. His one publication (not known to Gibson) was a subscription edition of his youthful *Poems on Several Occasions* (Oxford, 1730), in which poems like 'La Pensif', 'The Dream', and 'La Belle Romanesque' continue the romantic mode of 'An Evening Slumber'.

Gibson, Donald, ed., *A Parson in the Vale of White Horse: George Woodward's Letters from East Hendred, 1753–1761* (Gloucester, 1982).

YEARSLEY, Ann (1753–1806) Ann Cromartie was born into a poor family at Clifton, Bristol. In 1774 she married John Yearsley (1748–1803), owner of a modest property in the town. The couple had six children, and like her mother she sold milk from door to door. Her brother taught her to read, and by 1784 she knew *Paradise Lost*, some Shakespeare, Young's *Night Thoughts*, and Pope's *Eloisa to Abelard*. Yearsley came to the notice of Hannah More, who became her patron and instructor, and organised a successful subscription for the 'Milkwoman of Bristol's *Poems, on Several Occasions* (1785; 4th ed. 1786). More invested the proceeds (£350), but Yearsley demanded the cash, and the result was a bitter dispute between them. After securing her money Yearsley went on to develop an independent literary career with *Poems, on Various Subjects* (1787), a verse drama, *Earl Goodwin* (1791), a novel, *The Royal Captives* (1795), and another subscription volume, *The Rural Lyre* (1796). In 1793 she opened a circulating library in the colonnade at Hotwells, beneath Clifton Hill. After her husband's death in 1803 she retired to Melksham, Wiltshire.

Burke, Tim, 'Ann Yearsley and the Distribution of Genius in Early Romantic Culture', in *The Early Romantics: Perspectives in British Poetry from Pope to Wordsworth*, ed. Thomas Woodman (Houndmills, 1998), pp. 215–30.

Christmas, William J., *The Lab'ring Muses: Work, Writing and the Social Order in English Plebeian Poetry, 1730–1830* (Newark and London, 2001), pp. 235–66.

Demers, Patricia, ' "For Mine's a Stubborn and a Savage Will": "Lactilla" (Ann Yearsley) and "Stella" (Hannah More) Reconsidered', *Huntington Library Quarterly*, 56 (1993), 135–50.

Felsenstein, Frank, 'Ann Yearsley and the Politics of Patronage', *Tulsa Studies in Women's Literature*, 21:2 (Fall 2002) and 22:1 (Spring 2003).

Ferguson, Moira, 'Resistance and Power in the Life and Writings of Ann Yearsley', *The Eighteenth Century: Theory and Interpretation*, 27 (1986), 247–68.

Ferguson, Moira, 'The Unpublished Poems of Ann Yearsley', *Tulsa Studies in Women's Literature*, 12 (1993), 13–46.

Ferguson, Moira, *Eighteenth-Century Women Poets: Nation, Class, and Gender* (Albany, 1995), pp. 45–89.

Landry, Donna, *The Muses of Resistance: Laboring-Class Women's Poetry in Britain, 1739–1796* (Cambridge, 1990), pp. 120–85.

Waldron, Mary, *Lactilla, Milkwoman of Clifton. The Life and Writings of Ann Yearsley, 1753–1806* (Athens and London, 1996).

Zionkowski, Linda, 'Strategies of Containment: Stephen Duck, Ann Yearsley, and the Problem of Polite Culture', *Eighteenth-Century Life*, 13 (1989), 91–108.

YOUNG, Edward (1683–1765) His father was a fellow of Winchester College and later Dean of Salisbury. Young himself was educated at the school and in 1702 went on to New College, Oxford, then to Corpus Christi College as a gentleman-commoner. Parental influence smoothed his way, but Young's life was never to be free of a craving for patronage and preferment, and he specialised in poems with influential addressees or ambitious dedications. *A Poem on the Last Day* (1713) was dedicated to Queen Anne. A close friend of Thomas Tickell, Young was introduced to Addison's circle in London, and achieved some success with two plays, *Busiris* (1719) and *The Revenge* (1721). But it was with the 'laughing satire' of his *Love of Fame, the Universal Passion* (1728) that he made his reputation. In 1730 Young's expansive patriotism was expressed in *Imperium Pelagi: A Naval Lyrick: written in imitation of Pindar's spirit*, and in that year he was presented to the rectory of Welwyn, Hertfordshire. In 1731 he married Lady Elizabeth Lee, the Earl of Lichfield's daughter. Her death in 1741 was a stimulus to the writing of his influential blank verse poem, *The Complaint, Or, Night Thoughts on Life, Death, and Immortality* (nine books, 1742–5), a work of visionary devotion that won him fame in France and Germany as well as Britain. Young's short critical study, *Conjectures on Original Composition* (1759), was a celebration of original genius that showed an old man could write with laconic force and be in touch with the trends of his age.

Cornford, Stephen, ed., Edward Young, *Night Thoughts* (Cambridge, 1989).

Forster, Harold, *Edward Young: The Poet of the Night Thoughts, 1683–1765* (Aldeburgh, 1986).

Irlam, Shaun, *Elations: The Poetics of Enthusiasm in Eighteenth-Century Britain* (Stanford, 1999).

Odell, D.W., 'Young's *Night Thoughts* as an Answer to Pope's *Essay on Man*', *Studies in English Literature*, 12 (1972), 481–501.

Price, Martin, *To the Palace of Wisdom: Studies in Order and Energy from Dryden to Blake* (Carbondale and Edwardsville, 1964), pp. 345–51.

Sitter, John, 'Theodicy at Mid-Century: Young, Akenside, and Hume', *Eighteenth-Century Studies*, 12 (1978), 90–106.

Index

Longman Literature in English Series

General Editors:
David Carroll, formerly University of Lancaster
Chris Walsh, Chester College of Higher Education
Michael Wheeler, University of Southampton

Pre-Renaissance English Literature
English Literature before Chaucer *Michael Swanton*
English Literature in the Age of Chaucer *Dieter Mehl*
English Medieval Romance *W.R.J. Barron*

English Poetry
English Poetry of the Sixteenth Century *Gary Waller (Second Edition)*
English Poetry of the Seventeenth Century *George Parfitt (Second Edition)*
English Poetry of the Eighteenth Century, 1700–1789 *David Fairer*
English Poetry of the Romantic Period, 1789–1830 *J.R. Watson (Second Edition)*
English Poetry of the Victorian Period, 1830–1890 *Bernard Richards*
English Poetry since 1940 *Neil Corcoran*

English Drama
English Drama before Shakespeare *Peter Happé*
English Drama: Shakespeare to the Restoration, 1590–1660 *Alexander Leggatt*
English Drama: Restoration and Eighteenth Century, 1660–1789 *Richard W. Bevis*
English Drama of the Early Modern Period, 1890–1940 *Jean Chothia*
English Drama since 1940 *David Rabey*

English Fiction
English Fiction of the Eighteenth Century, 1700–1789 *Clive T. Probyn*
English Fiction of the Romantic Period, 1789–1830 *Gary Kelly*
English Fiction of the Victorian Period, 1830–1890 *Michael Wheeler (Second Edition)*
English Fiction of the Early Modern Period, 1890–1940 *Douglas Hewitt*

English Prose
English Prose of the Seventeenth Century, 1590–1700 *Roger Pooley*
English Prose of the Nineteenth Century *Hilary Fraser with Daniel Brown*

Criticism and Literary Theory
Criticism and Literary Theory, 1890 to the Present *Chris Baldick*

The Intellectual and Cultural Context
The Seventeenth Century, 1603–1700 *Graham Parry*
The Eighteenth Century, 1700–1789 *James Sambrook (Second Edition)*
The Victorian Period, 1830–1890 *Robin Gilmour*

American Literature
American Poetry of the Twentieth Century *Richard Gray*
American Drama of the Twentieth Century *Gerald M. Berkowitz*
American Fiction, 1865–1940 *Brian Lee*
American Fiction since 1940 *Tony Hilfer*
Twentieth-Century America *Douglas Tallack*

Other Literatures
Irish Literature since 1800 *Norman Vance*
Scottish Literature since 1707 *Marshall Walker*
Indian Literature in English *William Walsh*
African Literatures in English: East and West *Gareth Griffiths*
Southern African Literatures *Michael Chapman*
Caribbean Literature in English *Louis James*
Canadian Literature in English *W.J. Keith*

Future Titles
English Poetry of the Early Modern Period, 1890–1940
English Drama: Romantic and Victorian, 1789–1890
English Fiction since 1940
English Prose of the Eighteenth Century
Criticism and Literary Theory from Sidney to Johnson
Criticism and Literary Theory from Wordsworth to Arnold
The Sixteenth Century
The Romantic Period, 1789–1830
The Twentieth Century: 1890 to the Present
American Literature before 1880
Australian Literature